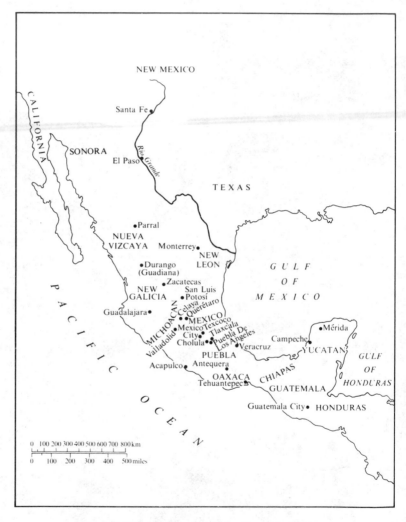

General Map of New Spain in the 17th Century

RACE, CLASS AND POLITICS IN COLONIAL MEXICO

1610-1670

BY

J. I. ISRAEL

OXFORD UNIVERSITY PRESS
1975

Oxford University Press, Ely House, London W. 1

GLASGOW NEW YORK TORONTO MELBOURNE WELLINGTON
CAPE TOWN IBADAN NAIROBI DAR ES SALAAM LUSAKA ADDIS ABABA
DELHI BOMBAY CALCUTTA MADRAS KARACHI LAHORE DACCA
KUALA LUMPUR SINGAPORE HONG KONG TOKYO

ISBN 0 19 821860 5

© Oxford University Press 1975

Printed in Great Britain
by The Pitman Press, Bath

ACKNOWLEDGEMENTS

This work owes a great deal to the help and encouragement of other scholars and I now gladly take the opportunity to record my debt to them. First and foremost I must thank Professor Hugh Trevor-Roper who supervised my research and writing from the outset until the work assumed the form of a D.Phil. thesis and who generously continued to give valuable advice after that stage until the work was completed. I am also much indebted to Professor J. H. Elliott who first aroused my interest in Mexican colonial history and who has on numerous occasions since freely given assistance and guidance. Other scholars for whose constructive criticisms and suggestions I am grateful are Professors J. L. Phelan, W. Borah, and Lewis Hanke, M. Jean-Pierre Berthe, and J. Ignacio Rubio Mañé. Finally, I wish to thank Raymond Carr and Theodore Zeldin, the Warden and Senior Tutor of St. Antony's College, Oxford, for their friendly support throughout and Jenny, José, Robert, Myron, Anthony, Lucette, and both Peters.

The greater part of the research for this study was undertaken in the Archivo General de Indias in Seville and the Archivo General de la Nación in Mexico City and I thank the staff of both of these archives, and also Gloria Grajales of the Biblioteca Nacional in Mexico City, for their constant co-operation and assistance. The later stages in the preparation of the work were completed at the University of Newcastle upon Tyne which admitted me among its staff for two years as a Sir James Knott Research Fellow and for this too I am glad to express my gratitude. Finally, I take the opportunity to thank his grace the Duke of Albuquerque for his permission for me to consult the letters of the eighth Duke of Albuquerque, and Viceroy Cadereita, in his private historical archive in Madrid, and his grace the Duke del Infantado for permission to use the Palafox papers in his private archive also in Madrid.

J.I.I.

CONTENTS

LIST OF ABBREVIATIONS   xi
LIST OF GOVERNORS AND VICEROYS   xii
INTRODUCTION
    i.   The setting   1
    ii.   The historical background   3

PART ONE
MEXICAN SOCIETY IN THE SEVENTEENTH CENTURY

I.   THE INDIANS
    i.   The dependence of the Mexican economy on Indian labour   25
    ii.   The population decline and the labour-shortage   26
    iii.   The Indians and the segregation policy   31
    iv.   Opposition to the segregation policy   33
    v.   The Indians and the *corregidores*   34
    vi.   Debt-labour   39
    vii.   Migration of Indians from the 'Indian' to the 'Spanish' sector   39
    viii.   Indian office-holders and local government   42
    ix.   The political alliance of Indian officers with the *corregidores* and friction between Indian officers and colonists   45
    x.   The Indians and the friars   47
    xi.   The political alliance of the friars with the *corregidores* and Indian officers   50
    xii.   Friction between friars and colonists over Indians   50
    xiii.   The Indians and the secular clergy   52
    xiv.   The Virgin of Guadalupe   53
    xv.   Ladino Indians   56

II.   MESTIZOS, NEGROES, AND MULATTOES
    i.   The Problem of the mestizo in seventeenth-century Mexico   60
    ii.   The late appearance of the mestizos as a separate social group   63
    iii.   The growth of the Negro and mulatto population   67
    iv.   Spanish fears of a black insurrection in Mexico   68
    v.   The waning of fears of a black insurrection   71
    vi.   The role of the Negro and mulatto in Mexican society   72
    vii.   The 'Chinese Indians'—Filipinos, Chinese and other Asiatics   75
    viii.   White vagrants   77

III. THE SPANIARDS
    i. The Creole nobility — 79
    ii. The importance of the quest for administrative and ecclesiastical offices — 82
    iii. The Gómez incident of 1618 — 84
    iv. The political alliance of the bishops with the Creoles — 86
    v. Peninsular Spanish prejudice against Creole Spaniards — 88
    vi. The Creoles' desire to show that they are 'true Spaniards' — 91
    vii. The relation of the tension between bureaucracy and colonists and between peninsulars and Creoles — 94
    viii. The Creole attitudes of the Mexico and Puebla City councils — 96
    ix. Opposition of the city councils to viceroy's officers, Indian officers, and friars — 97
    x. The significance of the controversy over the Peru trade — 100
    xi. Peninsular-Creole rivalry within the religious orders — 102
    xii. *Alternativa* and *ternativa* — 104

IV. BASQUES, PORTUGUESE, ITALIANS, AND JEWS
    i. The 'Spanish' nations — 110
    ii. The prominence of the Basques in Mexico — 111
    iii. The antipathy between Basques and Creoles — 116
    iv. Portuguese, Italian, and other foreign immigration — 117
    v. The role of the foreigners in Mexican commerce — 120
    vi. The administration and the foreigners — 122
    vii. The Jews — 124
    viii. Conclusion to part one — 130

PART TWO
MEXICAN POLITICS 1620–1670

V. GELVES AND THE INSURRECTION OF 1624
    i. Gelves and the reform movement in Spain — 135
    ii. Economic policies and the break between Gelves and the *Audiencia* of Mexico — 138
    iii. The Conflict between Gelves and Archbishop Pérez de la Serna — 140
    iv. The trial of Melchor de Varaez, *corregidor* of Metepec — 143
    v. Archbishop Pérez de la Serna excommunicates the viceroy — 145
    vi. The role of the Jesuits — 145
    vii. The viceroy expels the archbishop — 148
    viii. The insurrection in Mexico City of 15 January, 1624 — 150
    ix. Vergara Gabiria is proclaimed captain-general — 156
    x. The storming of the viceregal palace — 157
    xi. Order restored — 159
    xii. The return of Archbishop Pérez de la Serna — 159

VI. CERRALVO (1624–1635)

    i. The rule of the *Audiencia*, January-October, 1624   161
    ii. The attitude of the Basques   165
    iii. The arrival of Viceroy Cerralvo   167
    iv. The waning of Vergara Gabiria's influence   169
    v. The *visita* of Don Martín Carrillo, 1625–8   170
    vi. The conflict between Carrillo and Archbishop Manso   175
    vii. Archbishop Manso's pro-Creole stance on Indian labour, the *repartimiento*, and other issues   177
    viii. The conflict between Cerralvo and Archbishop Manso   178
    ix. The 'Union of Arms' in Mexico   178
    x. Political aspects of the inundation of Mexico City, 1629   180
    xi. The incident at Coyoacán   182
    xii. The Council of the Indies recommends that both Viceroy Cerralvo and Archbishop Manso be replaced   184
    xiii. The abolition of the agricultural *repartimiento*, 1632   186
    xiv. The later phase of the conflict between Cerralvo and Manso   186
    xv. Renewed friction between the secular and regular clergy   187

VII. CADEREITA. ESCALONA, AND PALAFOX (1635–1642)

    i. Cadereita's policies   190
    ii. The Armada of Barlovento and the response of the Mexico and Puebla city councils to Cadereita's proposals   193
    iii. Mounting opposition to Cadereita   198
    iv. The arrival of Viceroy Escalona and the visitor-general, Don Juan de Palafox y Mendoza   199
    v. Palafox's social and political ideas   201
    vi. The conflict between Palafox and Viceroy Escalona   206
    vii. Palafox's conflict with the Franciscans   207
    viii. The Portuguese scare of 1641–2   209
    ix. The removal of Viceroy Escalona   212
    x. Palafox's term as viceroy, June-October 1642   213
    xi. The uncovering of the 'complicidad grande'   214
    xii. Palafox and the Creoles   215

VIII. SALVATIERRA, TORRES DE RUEDA AND THE DISTURBANCES OF THE LATER 1640s

    i. The conflict between Palafox and the Jesuits   217
    ii. The conflict between Palafox and Viceroy Salvatierra, and its social and political implications   223
    iii. The truce between Palafox, and the Jesuits and Franciscans   227
    iv. The role of Archbishop Mañozca and the Inquisition   228
    v. Signs of widespread support for Palafox   230

vi. Renewed conflict between Palafox and the Jesuits   231
vii. Salvatierra and the bureaucratic party move against Palafox   233
viii. The flight of Palafox and the seizure of Puebla by the viceroy's officers   236
ix. The diocese of Puebla declared a *sede vacante*   239
x. The return of Palafox to Puebla   240
xi. The departure of Salvatierra and the advent of Torres y Rueda   241
xii. Further victories for the Palafoxistas   241
xiii. The intensification of the conflict between Palafox and the Jesuits   242
xiv. The *Auto General de la Fe*, 1649   245
xv. Palafox returns to Spain   247

IX. ALVA DE LISTE, ALBUQUERQUE, AND BAÑOS (1650–1665)
i. Further reverses for the Palafoxistas   248
ii. Alva de Liste and the *visitador*, Pedro de Gálvez   249
iii. Albuquerque's approach to government   252
iv. The conflict between Albuquerque and the bishops   257
v. The opposition to Viceroy Baños   260
vi. The role of Bishop Osorio de Escobar   263
vii. The removal of Baños   265
viii. Osorio de Escobar's term as viceroy, June-October 1664   265
ix. The coming of Viceroy Mancera   266

CONCLUSION   267

BIBLIOGRAPHY   274

INDEX   295

LIST OF ABBREVIATIONS

ACM   *Actas de cabildo de la ciudad de México* title varies (54 vols., Mexico, 1889–1916).

ACP   'Actas de cabildo de la ciudad de Puebla de los Angeles' on microfilm in the Instituto de Antropología e Historia, Mexico City.

ADA   Archivo de los duques de Albuquerque, Madrid.

ADI   Archivo de los duques del Infantado, Madrid.

AGI   Archivo General de Indias, Seville.

AGN   Archivo General de la Nación, Mexico City.

AHN   Archivo Histórico Nacional, Madrid.

BAGN   *Boletín del Archivo General de la Nación* (Mexico City, 1930-).

BL   Bancroft Library, Berkeley, California.

BM   British Museum.

BND   Biblioteca Nacional, Madrid.

BNX   Biblioteca Nacional, Mexico City.

Bodl.   Bodleian Library, Oxford.

BP   Biblioteca Palafoxiana, Puebla,

CDHE   *Colección de documentos inéditos para la historia de España* ed. M. Fernández Navarrete and others (112 vols., Madrid, 1864–84).

CDIIII   *Colección de documentos para la historia de la formación social de hispanoamérica, 1493–1810* (3 vols., Madrid, 1953–62).

DHM   *Documentos inéditos o muy raros para la historia de México* ed. Genaro García and Carlos Pereyra (35 vols., Mexico, 1905–11).

DRT   *Documentos relativos al tumulto de 1624* ed. M. Fernández de Echeverría y Veitia, in *Documentos para la Historia de México* second series, vols. ii and iii (Mexico, 1855).

FHT   *Fuentes para la historia del trabajo en Nueva España* ed. Silvio A. Zavala and Maria Castelo (8 vols., Mexico, 1939–46).

HAHR   Hispanic American Historical Review.

HSA   Manuscript and rare book collection of the Hispanic Society of America, New York.

IAH   Archivo Histórico of the Instituto de Antropología e Historia, Mexico City.

RLI   *Recopilación de leyes de los reynos de las Indias* (3 vols., Madrid 1791).

UTL   Latin American department of the University of Texas Library, Austin, Texas.

LIST OF THE GOVERNORS AND VICEROYS
OF MEXICO FROM THE CONQUEST TO 1696

1519–28	Hernán Cortés, leader of the Conquistadores and captain-general.
1528–30	The first ruling *Audiencia* headed by Beltrán Nuño de Guzmán.
1530–5	The second ruling *Audiencia* headed by Bishop Ramírez de Fuenleal.
1535–50	Don Antonio de Mendoza, 1st viceroy.
1550–64	Don Luis de Velasco, 2nd viceroy.
1564–6	the third ruling *Audiencia*.
1566–7	marqués de Falces, 3rd viceroy.
1567–8	the *visitadores* Alonso Muñoz and Luis Carrillo.
1568–80	Don Martín Enríquez de Almansa, 4th viceroy.
1580–3	conde de la Coruña, 5th viceroy.
1583–5	Archbishop Moya de Contreras, 6th viceroy and 1st prelate-viceroy.
1585–90	marqués de Villamanrique, 7th viceroy.
1590–5	Don Luis de Velasco II, 8th viceroy.
1595–1603	Don Gaspar de Zúñiga y Acevedo, conde de Monterrey, 9th viceroy
1603–7	marqués de Montesclaros, 10th viceroy.
1607–11	Luis de Velasco II, marqués de Salinas, second term, 8th viceroy.
1611–12	Archbishop Fray García Guerra, 11th viceroy and 2nd prelate-viceroy.
Feb. 1612–Oct. 1612	fourth ruling *Audiencia*.
28 Oct. 1612–14 Mar. 1621	marqués de Guadalcázar, 12th viceroy.
14 Mar. 1621–21 Sept. 1621	fifth ruling *Audiencia*, headed by Pedro de Vergara Gabiria.
21 Sept. 1621–15 Jan. 1624	Don Diego Carrillo Mendoza y Pimentel, marqués de Gelves.
15 Jan. 1624–31 Oct. 1624	sixth ruling *Audiencia*, headed by Pedro de Vergara Gabiria.
31 Oct. 1624–1 Nov. 1624	marqués de Gelves, second term (13th viceroy again).
1 Nov. 1624–16 Sept. 1635	Don Rodrigo Pacheco Osorio, marqués de Cerralvo, 14th viceroy.
16 Sept. 1635–28 Aug. 1640	Don Lope Diez de Armendariz, marqués de Cadereita, 15th viceroy.
28 Aug. 1640–9 June 1642	Don Diego López de Pacheco y Bobadilla, marqués de Villena, duque de Escalona, 16th viceroy.

9 June–23 Nov. 1642	Don Juan de Palafox y Mendoza, 17th viceroy and 3rd prelate-viceroy.
23 Nov. 1642–13 May 1648	Don García Sarmiento de Sotomayor, conde de Salvatierra, 18th viceroy.
13 May 1648–22 Apr. 1649	provisional government of Bishop Marcos de Torres y Rueda who held the title of bishop-governor.
22 Apr. 1649–28 June 1650	seventh ruling *Audiencia*, headed by Mathias de Peralta.
28 June 1650–15 Aug. 1653	Don Luis Enríquez de Guzmán, conde de Alva de Liste, 19th viceroy.
15 Aug. 1653–16 Sept. 1660	Don Francisco Fernández de la Cueva y Enríquez de Cabrera, eighth duque de Albuquerque, 20th viceroy.
16 Sept. 1660–29 June 1664	Don Juan Francisco de Leyva y de la Cerda, conde de Baños, 21st viceroy.
29 June 1664–15 Oct. 1664	Don Diego Osorio de Escobar y Llamas, bishop of Puebla, 22nd viceroy and 4th prelate-viceroy.
15 Oct. 1664–20 Nov. 1673	marqués de Mancera, 23rd viceroy.
20 Nov. 1673–13 Dec. 1673	Don Pedro Nuño Colón de Portugal y Castro, sixth duque de Veragua, 24th viceroy.
13 Dec. 1673– 7 Nov. 1680	Archbishop Fray Payo Enríquez de Rivera, 25th viceroy and 5th prelate-viceroy.
7 Nov. 1680–16 Nov. 1686	Don Tomas Antonio de la Cerda y Enríquez, third marqués de la Laguna, 26th viceroy.
16 Nov. 1686–20 Nov. 1688	Don Melchor Portocarrero y Lasso de la Vega, third conde de la Monclova, 27th viceroy.
20 Nov. 1688–27 Feb. 1696	Don Gaspar de Sandoval Cerda Silva y Mendoza, conde de Galve, 28th viceroy.

INTRODUCTION

This study consists of an investigation of the various stresses that troubled Mexican society in the mid-colonial period and of the ways in which these stresses influenced the course of Mexican colonial public life. It is undertaken in the belief that analysis of the politics of the viceroyalty in the light of the socio-economic pressures discernible in Mexican Society at the time affords a particularly valuable insight into the history of this as yet somewhat obscure but fascinating and undoubtedly formative period, in relation not only to Mexico itself, but also to the Spanish Indies generally. The division of the work into two—albeit two interconnected—parts doubtless has its drawbacks, but it is hoped that the arrangement does make it possible to relate the static picture of a socio-economic structure closely to the moving picture of personalities and specific political events without destroying the clarity of outline of either.

The viceroyalty of Mexico in the seventeenth century, even putting aside the Spanish West Indies and the captaincy-general of Guatemala which were only loosely connected with it, extended over an immense area somewhat larger than that of the modern Mexican republic. However, the distribution of population and resources in the seventeenth century was such as to make it possible, while not losing sight of the whole, to concentrate attention on certain parts of the viceroyalty at the expense of others. Indeed, the great bulk of the colony's inhabitants, Indian, Spanish, half-caste, and Negro, was to be found in a relatively small heartland contained within the four central provinces or dioceses of the viceroyalty, those of Mexico, Puebla de los Angeles, Oaxaca, and Michoacán, the provinces under the jurisdiction of the *Audiencia*, or regional court, of Mexico. The area of these four provinces amounted to less than one-third of that of the modern Mexican republic and at least half even of this was not part of the heartland, being barren sierra or torrid coastal strip. The heartland proper, composed of the inner sections of the four provinces, was the broad strip of country extending from the fertile Tlaxcala-Atlixco-Tecamachalco triangle in the south-east, north-westwards for about 300 miles, taking in the valleys of Mexico and Toluca, and the Bajío basin, and reaching to the sierra of Guanajuato. In this area were situated the two largest cities of the viceroyalty, Mexico City and Puebla de los Angeles, and numerous other towns, some ancient Indian centres such as Tlaxcala, Texcoco, Cholula, Tepeaca, and Huejotzingo, and others, such as Querétaro, Celaya, and Guanajuato, towns which had appeared since the Conquest. The rest of the viceroyalty, the immense periphery surrounding the four provinces, was made up of five remote and sparsely populated departments—New Galicia (the west), New Biscay (the north-west), New León (the north-east), New Mexico (the far north), and the Yucatán with Tabasco (the south-east). All of these were in some degree separate political entities: New Galicia, with its capital at Guadalajara, was administered by its own *Audiencia* while the other sections were administered by governors often only nominally responsible to the viceroys. Only the area under the jurisdiction of the *Audiencia* of Mexico, the four provinces, was governed directly by the latter, and thus the region which was New Spain's commercial, agricultural, and demographic hub was also its political centre.

Outside the heartland, in the vast expanse to its west, north, and south, there were, in the early and mid-seventeenth century, barely four or five towns with more than two or three hundred white householders. Of these the most important was Zacatecas, the richest of the silver-mining centres which, though very much smaller than Mexico City or Puebla, was the third largest town of the viceroyalty; situated some 370 miles by road north-west of the capital, its white population in the first decade of the century was in the region of 1,500 and its total population, white, black, Indian, and mixed blood, approximately 5,000.[1] The other main towns of outer Mexico were San Luis Potosí, lying 260 miles north-west of Mexico City in the northern part of the province of Mexico, the second most important silver-mining town, boasting a white population in 1620 of over 1,000;[2] Guadalajara, 360 miles west of Mexico City and nearly 200 south-west of Zacatecas, capital of New Galicia (which included Zacatecas) and an important commercial centre with, in 1621, nearly a quarter of its 200 white citizens being fairly substantial traders or storekeepers and a total white population of over 1,000;[3] Veracruz, some 270 miles east of Mexico City, Mexico's Atlantic port, but much smaller and poorer than it would have been had not its hot, unhealthy situation induced most of the big merchants to reside in Mexico City or Puebla;[4] and finally

---

[1] See P. J. Bakewell, *Silver Mining and Society in Colonial Mexico, Zacatecas 1546–1700* (Cambridge, 1971), p. 268.

[2] *Descripción de la Nueva España en el siglo xvii*, docs. ed. Mariano Cuevas (Mexico, 1944), pp. 142–3.

[3] Domingo Lázaro de Arregui, *Descripción de la Nueva Galicia* (1621), ed. François Chevalier (Seville, 1946), pp. 62, 66; see also Alonso de la Mota y Escobar, *Descripción geográfica de los reynos de Nueva Galicia, Nueva Vizcaya, y Nuevo León* (Guadalajara, Jalisco, 1966), pp. 24–5.

[4] Pierre Chaunu, 'Veracruz en la segunda mitad del siglo xvi y primera del xvii', *Historia Mexicana*, ix (1960), 520–57.

Oaxaca, then known as Antequera, some 280 mile⸱
Mexico City, a very pleasant city with some 3,000 inhab
where life at a modest level was easy but with little ⸱
Durango, capital of New Biscay, over 500 miles north-w⸱
City, though an important trading and mining centre, h⸱
little more than fifty Spanish families, a hundred or so l⸱
mulattoes, and a few hundred Indians.[5] Monterrey, some ⸱⸱ miles
north of Mexico City, capital of New León, a region that lacked silver
mines and was therefore much poorer than New Galicia or New Biscay
and very sparsely populated, and Santa Fe, capital of New Mexico,
located well over 1,000 miles north of Mexico City, were mere tiny
outposts.

Historically, the great division of Mexico was that between the zone
of sedentary Indians in the south and that of the nomadic tribes to the
north. The dividing line, up until the Spanish Conquest, had run
roughly east to west about a hundred miles above Tenochtitlan (Mexico
City), the Aztec capital. North of that line, neither the Aztecs, nor any
of the sedentary peoples of moist Mexico, had ever held sway. It was
only after the Conquest, and then only very slowly, that the various
appurtenances of settled societies—farming, towns, and elaborate forms
of political organization—had spread into the Bajío, and, very patchily,
further north into the arid country beyond. South of that line,
sedentary Indian civilization, thriving on a highly productive maize
economy, had flourished for many centuries, and, as will be seen, by
the time of the Spanish invasion a very dense population had
accumulated, especially in the southern half of the heartland around
Tenochtitlan, Texcoco, and Tlaxcala.

With the collapse of the Aztec empire in the years 1519–21, the
Mexican heartland, and soon the whole of southern Mexico, had fallen
into the hands of Cortés and his tiny Spanish army. This event marks
the great divide in Mexican history and the commencement of the
colonial era. The country was now officially known as New Spain and
formed part of the burgeoning empire of the monarchs of Castile.
Within Mexico the old framework of society, authority, and religion
was shattered.

The Spanish Conquistadores, though their brutality has in the past
often been exaggerated by Protestant propagandists and other foes of
Spain, were undoubtedly harsh and very greedy. Most of Cortés's army,
like Bernal Díaz del Castillo, the eloquent chronicler of their exploits,
had come to the Indies in search of fortune and had already been
disappointed once, in the Caribbean, having failed to find favour with
the governors of the newly subjugated islands, and were, consequently,

[5] Mota y Escobar, *Descripción geográfica*, pp. 83–6.

all the more determined not to be thwarted this time in obtaining what they considered their appropriate reward. Their original aim was to seize enough treasure from the Mexican Indians and their land to live at ease for the remainder of their lives, and thus they exhibited, on arrival in Mexico, a lust for treasure and valuables that perplexed and disgusted the Indians. However, since the amount of treasure taken in the Conquest was relatively small and most of that went to Cortés and his officers, and the Emperor Charles V, the great majority of the Conquistadores were soon compelled to look round for alternative forms of support.

Here the main possibility was the Indians themselves, for on the Caribbean islands the practice had arisen of sharing out the Indians so that those Spaniards who succeeded in obtaining *encomiendas*, as these Indian-grants were called, were able to live at ease off Indian labour.[6] In Mexico, when eventually *encomiendas* were allotted, beneficiaries received not only the right to exact labour service but pocketed the tribute which the Mexican Indians had formerly paid to Moctezuma and to their own aristocracy and priesthood, and which the Indians were now deemed to owe, by transference of rights, to the Emperor Charles V. The grants were conceived of in quasi-feudal terms, as rewards for military service, and, in theory, as well as assigning material benefits, involved recipients in military obligations to the crown and the duty to provide for the instruction of their Indians in Christianity.

However, at the very moment that the Aztec power collapsed, the institution of the Indian-grant was threatened. Charles V's government in Spain, worried by the havoc that Conquistador greed had already wrought on the Caribbean islands and by the excessive local power that the *encomienda* gave the Conquistadores, had resolved, with the encouragement of a group of Dominican friars led by the famous Bartolomé de las Casas, initiator of the Black Legend of Spanish cruelty, on its abolition.[7] But such was the pressure on Cortés in Mexico, such was the thirst of the Conquistadores for *encomiendas*, that the Emperor's wishes stood little chance of being obeyed. If the Conquistadores were agreed on anything, it was that they had not come to Mexico to eke out a humble existence, and that they insisted on being supported. 'I found myself practically forced to hand over the rulers and natives of these parts to the Spaniards,' wrote Cortés to the Emperor,[8] 'taking into consideration when doing so their estate and the services which they have rendered your Majesty in these parts, so that

[6] Charles Gibson, *Spain in America* (New York, 1966), pp. 49–51.
[7] Ibid., p. 54.
[8] *Five Letters of Cortés to the Emperor*, tr. and ed. J. B. Morris (New York, 1962), pp. 240–1.

until your Majesty shall make some fresh arrangement or confirm this one, the aforesaid rulers and natives will serve and provide the Spaniards, to whom they were respectively assigned, with whatever they need to sustain themselves.' Cortés, one should note, kept some of the choicest Indian-grants for himself, acquiring rights over vast tracts of southern Mexico, especially in Oaxaca.

The introduction of the *encomienda* into Mexico did not bring stability to the conquered territory. On the contrary, disorder and lawlessness were the rule in the 1520s. There were not enough *encomiendas* for all the Conquistadores and the adventurers who arrived after them; many were denied Indians, factions developed, and on several occasions the Spaniards came close to fighting among themselves. Moreover, the *encomienda* was a very crude instrument of exploitation, and the violence and misery to which it led outraged the early missionaries who were beginning to seep into the country in the 1520s, and, by way of their complaints, disturbed the government in Spain. To add to the confusion, Cortés himself, at first the unchallenged leader of the Spaniards in Mexico, was gradually weakened by a combination of groups headed by the Emperor's ministers in Spain, who were understandably suspicious of the vast claims that Cortés had staked out for himself in the new colony. In 1527 Cortés returned to Spain temporarily, in the hope of retrieving his position, which he failed to do, while in the following year, in Mexico City, the new capital which had arisen on the ruins of Tenochtitlan, a group of magistrates, appointed in Spain, assumed the government of the colony. This court, known as the first ruling *Audiencia* (1528–30), was headed by the corrupt, brutal, and sanctimonious Beltrán Nuño de Guzmán, a vehement foe of Cortés, and a man who has been remembered for his rapacity and total indifference to the policy of crown and Church. The Indians, evidently, suffered severely under his oppressive rule while the Cortés party, and indeed most of the Conquistadores, were bitterly resentful.[9]

However, intense though the opposition to Nuño de Guzmán was, there was no armed resistance. Eventually he was defeated by means of written complaint to Spain and by the co-operation of the Cortés party with the Franciscan missionaries. The growth of bureaucracy, which was astonishingly rapid in post-Conquest Mexico, was already putting an end to the chaotic freebooting phase which had begun with the Spanish invasion. It was no longer by the sword that disputes in New Spain were settled; from now until the end of the colonial era, for almost three centuries, the weapons of struggle were to be the various legal implements provided by Spanish state and Church and no others.

[9] L. B. Simpson, *Many Mexicos* (Berkeley and Los Angeles, 1959), pp. 34–8.

The rule of the second *Audiencia* (1530–5), the court sent out to replace Nuño de Guzmán and his underlings, proved to be a major landmark in Mexican colonial history, for not only did it press on with the work of bureaucratization which Nuño de Guzmán had begun, but it began the task of transforming the Mexican administration into a reasonably loyal instrument of the Spanish state, a goal towards which Nuño de Guzmán can hardly be said to have contributed. Moreover, by achieving this much, it ended what was probably the most miserable phase of the post-Conquest history of the Indians. For eleven years, the Indians had suffered appallingly from the consequences of the Conquest. It is true that many, possibly most, of the Indians of central and southern Mexico had resented the Aztecs, who by any reckoning made harsh and oppressive rulers, and had welcomed, or eventually welcomed, the Spanish invasion as a means of casting off the yoke of Moctezuma, but the Indians who had fought with Cortés in the campaigns of 1519–21, the Tlaxcaltecs, Texcocans, Totonacs, and the rest, can not have foreseen the widespread disruption which was to result from the Spanish invasion—the suppression of their priesthood and religion, the overthrow of their political and administrative system, economic exploitation by the Conquistadores, and the introduction of Old World diseases such as smallpox and measles which had previously been unknown in America and against which their bodies were defenceless. Under the impact of these disasters, the Indians reeled, and there were many signs that the elaborate order and very strict discipline which had characterized pre-Conquest Indian society was beginning to disintegrate.

The new *Audiencia*, headed by Sebastián Ramírez de Fuenleal, bishop of Santo Domingo, and including the saintly Erasmist Vasco de Quiroga, who fervently believed that the new order being set up by the Spaniards in America could and should be an improvement on pre-Conquest Indian society, were as remarkable and gifted a group as ever ruled New Spain. It was they who introduced the era of firm and orderly government which is one of the most distinctive features of mid-sixteenth-century Mexican history. It was they who first extended to the Indians a measure of protection and help, who first seriously tried to reduce Spanish lawlessness and freebooting in the countryside, and who enthusiastically encouraged the mendicant missionaries whose efforts to convert the Indians to Christianity were now gathering momentum. Above all, it was they who gave the first real impetus to the reconstruction of Indian society, that massive attempt by the Spanish government and Church to protect and rebuild the framework of Indian society preserving as much of the old orderliness and discipline as possible while replacing paganism and much of the old administrative and social structure with Catholicism and Castilian institutions.

The great Mexican reconstruction, as it might be called, which began under the aegis of the second *Audiencia* and retained its momentum for much of the rest of the century, is a truly remarkable historical phenomenon and impressive in its scope and degree of success. The essential impulse behind it was threefold: first, the desire of the Emperor, the *Audiencia*, and, after the *Audiencia*, of Mexico's first viceroy, Don Antonio de Mendoza (1535–50), to compel the Conquistadores to submit to the authority of the crown and make efficient administration possible in Mexico; second, the zeal of the mendicant missionaries and their determination not just to convert the Indians to Christianity but to build a genuinely Christian society; and third, the desire of those Indian caciques (chieftains or local leaders) and principals who had survived the war with the Spaniards and the chaos of the 1520s—and there were a considerable number—to retrieve what they could of their former authority and prestige, if only on a local basis.

Of the three groups involved, it was perhaps the friars who played the most creative and original role.[10] Their work had begun in earnest in 1524, when a batch of twelve Franciscans, hand-picked for their skill as missionaries, had established themselves in central Mexico. During the subsequent decade, as more Franciscans and groups of Dominican and Augustinian friars arrived, they had branched out all over southern and western Mexico. The Franciscans, being both the first and most numerous in the field, quickly established their spiritual hegemony in the chief Indian cities of central Mexico—Tenochtitlan, Texcoco, Tlaxcala, Cholula, Huejotzingo, and Cuernavaca—and took over the leadership of the conversion generally, except the south, in Oaxaca, where the Dominicans were supreme. The pagan priesthood, already undermined, quickly disintegrated. The Indian caciques and principals, seeing that the new faith offered their best chance of filling the breach opened by the overthrow of the old gods and building a new religious basis for their authority, positively welcomed the friars and hastened to have themselves and their people baptized and to put their children into the new mission schools. The destruction of ancient temples and idols proceeded at a brisk pace, and, in what soon became an orgy of pious vandalism, the Indian boys of the mission schools played a prominent rôle. Fray Juan de Zumárraga, a Franciscan and the first bishop of Mexico, avowed in a famous letter of June 1531 that already more than

---

[10]On this topic the classic work is Robert Ricard, *La 'Conquête Spirituelle' du Mexique, Essai sur l'apostolat et les méthodes missionnaires des ordres mendiants en Nouvelle-Espagne de 1523–4 à 1572* (Paris, 1933).

500 pagan temples had been levelled and more than 20,000 idols destroyed.

The friars, though amazed themselves at the extraordinary speed of their triumph, and though there were still only about a hundred of them in Mexico during the time of the second *Audiencia*, were by no means satisfied with the mere nominal allegiance of the Indians. They knew only too well from their own experience, and that of their colleagues in the morisco areas of Andalusia and Valencia, how great was the difference between a superficial and a real conversion. They were determined to extirpate paganism utterly and receive the Indians fully into the bosom of the Church, that is to Christianize Indian life profoundly. To achieve this they saw that they first needed to acquire a thorough knowledge of their new flock, familiarize themselves with its traditions and ways of thought, master its languages, and enter into the very fibre of its existence. Franciscans such as Fray Bernardino de Sahagún conducted exhaustive researches into the Aztec past and subsequently compiled some impressive works, Sahagún's *Historia general* being a towering landmark of early anthropology and Fray Toribio de Benavente Motolinía's *History of the Indians of New Spain* a eulogy of their morals and customs. Many of the missionaries became expert in Nahuatl, the principal Indian language, and in the other main languages, Tarascan, Otomi, Mixtec, and Zapotec, and at presenting their creed in them. Furthermore, using their new knowledge, the mendicants were quickly able to determine how to fuse what they considered best in Indian values with Christian precepts. And there was certainly a great deal in Mexican Indian society and tradition that the friars admired. Motolinía enthused over the severity of pre-Conquest discipline: Aztec children had not been permitted to speak at meals; boys and girls had been thoroughly and separately schooled; men did not eat with women; girls were chaste and austere to a degree which in his opinion left much to be learned by even the most secluded virgins of Spain. There had been harsh penalties for even the slightest infringements of the moral code, and as for murder, theft, adultery, and the consumption of alcoholic drinks by any other than the elderly, such offences had been rare, but when they had occurred had been punished with the heaviest punishments. Order and discipline had been prized above everything. And no less precious, in the view of the friars, was the age-old submissiveness of the Indian masses to authority and their readiness to acquiesce in whatever was demanded of them. Seeing in this meekness the essence of the Christian spirit, the mendicants believed that they had found a people uniquely fitted to receive the new faith. All the missionaries, however much they differed on other matters, were agreed on this; Indian meekness, not the ill-gotten plunder of the Conquistadores, was the true treasure of the Indies, the material from which a pure Apostolic Church might be formed again on earth. 'It may be asserted as an infallible truth,' wrote Fray Gerónimo de Mendieta, in the later sixteenth century, echoing the feelings of those early missionaries, 'that no nation or society has been discovered in the world that is better fitted or disposed to save its souls—being helped in this [by the friars]—than the Indians of this New Spain.'[11]

To protect the Indian moral heritage and adjust it in certain respects, the friars established new forms of education to replace those that were lost. If it was beyond their means to school the whole population as the Aztecs had done, they were successful in schooling the sons of the Indian leadership. The schools they founded for the instruction of sons of caciques and principals were effective not only in teaching those who subsequently became the leaders of the Indian community the rudiments of Catholic doctrine, but also in passing on some of the discipline of the past. Indian adults too quickly came, to a considerable extent, under the moral tutelage of the friars. Gradually, the mendicants were able to suppress polygamy and concubinage which the Aztecs had tolerated among the privileged, manifestations of homosexuality and other practices which the friars regarded as evil and abhorrent were hidden from the public view, Indian men were persuaded to abandon the age-old loin-cloth and cover their legs with the famous white trousers known as *zaragüelles* which by the end of the sixteenth century had become standard wear throughout central Mexico, and Indian women, who in some areas, particularly among the humbler classes, had been accustomed to leave their bosoms naked were induced to cover them with the *huipil*, the blouse of Indian womenfolk.

But it was not only the severity of Indian moral attitudes that the friars desired to perpetuate, they also wished to preserve, if not the whole elaborate class structure of traditional Indian society—for in the chaotic aftermath of the Conquest that was impossible—at least the general subordination of the mass of the Indian population to the caciques and principals. This was a matter of great concern to all three groups concerned in the reconstruction, for the collapse of the Aztec imperium and the disorder spread by the Conquistadores had severely shaken the traditional Indian hierarchy, allowing many commoners to usurp offices and functions and causing a crisis of local authority. The mendicants were appalled by the prospect of the disintegration of the old Indian ruling class for they regarded the process as the root cause of the deterioration in Indian discipline and morals. Moreover, seeing that neither the further Christianization of the Indians nor the maintenance

11 Jerónimo de Mendieta, *Historia Eclesiástica Indiana* (1596) (Mexico, 1870), p. 437.

of their own ascendancy over the religious and moral lives of the Indians would be possible without a stable and effective native leadership to preserve order and enforce Church attendance, the friars became firm supporters of the caciques and principals in their effort to develop new forms of local government and retrieve their old authority.

In addition, the mendicants quickly saw that magnificent ceremony and pomp and constant mass participation had been fundamental to Aztec religion, and the religion of all central and southern Mexico, and that if the Indians were to embrace the new faith wholeheartedly, the gap left by the lapsing of the old rituals had to be filled by the same basic material no matter how new the containers in which it came. And so one of the most characteristic and lasting features of the attempted reconstruction of Indian society was the creation by the friars, working with the Indians, of a highly elaborate Indian-Christian religious culture with its own distinctive styles in church building, church music, sculpture, ornaments, dances, celebrations, and services, an achievement which was largely successful, in the short run at any rate, in involving the Indian masses intimately with the new religion. Such was the yearning of the Indians to lift themselves from the spiritual void in which the Conquest had plunged them, such was their receptiveness to the spiritual and emotional succour which the friars offered them, that they seized upon the new religious rituals and art with passionate enthusiasm.

The goals of the second *Audiencia* and the first viceroy in the restructuring of Mexican society were the usual goals of governments—to impose order and mould a society that may be readily administered and taxed. But to achieve these ends, the administration in Mexico City had first to reduce drastically the local power of the Conquistadores and *encomienda*-holders (*encomenderos*), check Spanish lawlessness and vagrancy, and revive Indian local government. All this amounted to a task of immense difficulty, and, especially as regards the weakening of the *encomenderos*, of considerable danger. Even one ill-considered move might have been enough to drive the Conquistadores to rebellion and plunge Mexico into the kind of bloody chaos that engulfed Peru in the 1540s. However, both the *Audiencia* and viceroy were prudent and cautious as well as resolute. The second *Audiencia* suppressed a number of Indian-grants, especially those created by Nuño de Guzmán, but was careful to restore Cortés and his supporters to most of the privileges of which they had been stripped by the first *Audiencia*. Mendoza refrained from implementing the so-called New Laws of 1542, an outright attack on the *encomienda* prepared by Charles V's ministers partly under Dominican influence, but at the same time gradually whittled away Conquistador power, ensuring that Indian-grants that reverted to the crown, owing to the demise of *encomenderos* without heirs, were not reassigned, but left to lapse. The second *Audiencia* introduced the system of district governors or *corregidores* which was so potent an instrument of royal power in Castile, and which was destined to become potent in Mexico, but introduced it in a very rudimentary and conciliatory form, so that *corregidores'* jurisdictions did not yet encroach on the *encomiendas*.[12] Viceroy Mendoza slowly extended this fledgling bureaucracy and, little by little, increased its powers, encouraging his officers, where the system was working well, to act as a check to the *encomenderos*. Meanwhile the latter, feeling power slipping slowly but inexorably from their grasp, became increasingly exasperated and in 1540, Cortés, now a cantankerous and disappointed man, again left Mexico for Spain, this time for good.

In the field of Indian local government, considerable advances were made though we shall say little about the new system here, for the subject is entered into in some detail in chapter one. The chief point is that there was a strengthening and stabilization of the Indian ruling class in the period 1530–60, and that Indian local government was successfully remodelled on the pattern of the Spanish municipal council or *cabildo*. As a result, the caciques and principals became again a dependable instrument in the management and administration of the Indian masses and an integral part of the new order.

As regards settling the Spanish immigrants, little progress was made. By the 1530s, the presence of numerous white vagabonds who styled themselves hidalgos, who had no *encomiendas* or other legitimate means of support, and who refused to work, living by plundering the Indians, had become a very serious problem;[13] but it was a problem which the government had no means of solving. The situation was eased at times by the setting-out of fresh expeditions of exploration and conquest, especially Pedro de Alvarado's expedition to northern Peru, but such temporary improvements were soon cancelled out by fresh immigration. Nevertheless, the second *Audiencia* and Viceroy Mendoza took what positive action they could. One famous experiment by the second *Audiencia* was the founding of the new 'Spanish' city of Puebla de los Angeles, seventy miles south-east of Mexico City, a carefully planned community[14] complete with incentives, including the provision of Indian labour, designed to induce Spaniards to settle down

[12] C. Gibson, *The Aztecs under Spanish Rule. A History of the Indians of the Valley of Mexico 1519–1810* (Stanford, Calif., and Oxford, 1964), pp. 82, 488.

[13] N. F. Martin, *Los Vagabundos en la Nueva España, siglo xvi* (Mexico, 1957), pp. 13–38.

[14] François Chevalier, 'La Signification sociale de la fondation de la Puebla de los Angeles', *Revista de historia de América*, xxiii (1947), 105–30.

to farming. But Puebla, like the 'Spanish' centre of Mexico City, and the other new town, Guadalajara, founded in 1531 in the west by Nuño de Guzmán and named after his home town in Castile, grew only very slowly. In the 1530s and 1540s, before the big silver strikes had been made, the necessary economic basis for effective urbanization of Spaniards in Mexico simply did not exist.

The various evil effects of vagabondage in Mexico made both the administration in Mexico City and the government in Spain highly sensible of the political advantages of matrimony and the human family. The vast majority of the Spaniards in Mexico had left their womenfolk and families behind in Spain and this, the government soon realized, was not only a major cause of unruliness in the Spaniards who were free to wander where they pleased stealing from the wretched Indians and debauching their women, but, since the Spaniards were predatory and disruptive as well as vagrant and rootless, seriously impeded the administration of those who were married and settled, namely the Indians. Accordingly, the second *Audiencia* and Viceroy Mendoza,[15] with the encouragement of the clergy, made strenuous efforts to drive the Spaniards into matrimony, and, in the case of those who were already married, to induce them to bring over their wives from Spain. Lands and other concessions in and around the Spanish new towns were assigned only to married men of fixed residence, as also were *corregimientos* and other bureaucratic posts; with regard to *encomiendas*, it had already been established that only heirs born within wedlock were legally entitled to inherit. However, such measures, in this early period, had only a limited effect.

The projected reconstruction of Mexican society by the viceregal administration, the friars, and the Indian principals was very seriously damaged, after a decade and a half of steady progress, by the great catastrophe of 1545—8. This was a fearful pestilence called by the Indians *cocoliztli*, which caused one of the most terrible population disasters known in history. We have noted already that the Mexican Indians were defenceless against Old World viruses, but though there occurred two or three epidemics between 1519 and 1545, the earliest being that of 1520—1 in Tenochtitlán which carried off thousands of Aztecs including Cuitlahuac the penultimate Aztec ruler, sixteen years of contact between Indians and Europeans passed before the outbreak of a general and utterly devastating epidemic. The extent of the disaster when finally it came, was so great that it overwhelms the imagination.

[15] A. S. Aiton, *Antonio de Mendoza, First Viceroy of New Spain* (Durham, N. Carolina, 1927), p. 86; according to a document of 1549, there were then more than 700 Spaniards in Mexico whose wives were in Spain, see Martin, *Los Vagabundos*, pp. 29—30.

The friars calculated that the death toll during 1545—8 was so heavy that some three-quarters, even five-sixths, of the Indian population of central Mexico was wiped out.[16] Nor was this so gross an exaggeration as it might appear, for according to the calculations of demographic historians, the 20 million inhabitants of central Mexico of 1520, a population greater than that of contemporary France, had, by 1548, been reduced to little more than 6 million,[17] and undeniably a very considerable proportion of this loss of nearly 14 million occurred between 1545 and 1548.

The effect of so fearful a disaster was to plunge the whole viceroyalty into depression and despondency. If there had been much that was wrong before, at least the Indians' zest for the new faith, the optimism of the friars, and the competence of the government had given solid grounds for hope, but now the great *cocoliztli*, combined with the continuing growth of Spanish vagrancy, the restlessness of the Negro slaves who had been imported into the colony, and a definite slackening in the zeal of the Indians for the new faith, gave rise to a mood of deepening pessimism. Despite the silver strike at Zacatecas in 1546 and the beginnings of silver-mining in the north-west, the general economic prospect in Mexico in the 1550s was grim, and the second viceroy, Don Luis de Velasco (1550—64), advised the Emperor's ministers in Spain that the poverty, discontent, and idleness of Spaniards in Mexico was such that unless some of the vagrants were drawn off by organizing a new conquest, or emigration from Spain was stopped, the stability of the viceroyalty would be gravely endangered.[18] He also advised that there should be no further importation of Negroes into the colony as they were unreliable and added to the danger. The friars, appalled by the *cocoliztli* and embittered by the increasing apathy of the Indians, shared in the general disillusionment. In despair, they strove to comprehend how the Almighty could have struck the Indians down in their millions at the very moment that they had glimpsed the light and embraced His holy doctrine. The Almighty, they concluded, had wished to punish the Conquistadores for their brutal rapacity by taking from them the blessed and meek whom they had exploited, and to reward the Indians by taking them to heaven before they became less deserving

---

[16] Juan de Grijalva, *Crónica de la orden de N. P. S. Augustín en las provincias de la Nueva España* (1924) (Mexico, 1924), pp. 214—15; *The Conquistadors, First person Accounts of the Conquest of Mexico* (chronicle of Fray Francisco de Aguilar), ed. and tr. Patricia de Fuentes (New York), p.163.

[17] S. F. Cook and W. Borah, *The Indian population of central Mexico, 1531—1610* (Berkeley and Los Angeles, 1960), p. 48.

[18] Luis de Velasco to the Council of the Indies, 4 May 1553 in *Cartas de Indias* (Madrid, 1877), pp. 263—9, 264f.

of that reward and sank back into unchristian ways.[19] The drift of the Indians into lukewarm Christianity was certainly gathering momentum by the 1540s and 1550s. 'Now that [the Indians] are Christians,' wrote Fray Francisco de Aguilar dejectedly in 1549, 'and as though in retribution for our sins, most of them come to church by force and with very little fear and reverence, they gossip and talk and walk out during the principal part of the mass and sermon; in their time then [under Aztec rule] great strictness was observed in the ceremonies to their gods, but now they feel neither fear nor shame.'[20] Their distress and demoralization became the more evident as their zeal for the new faith waned.[21] Alcoholism, that age-old fearful menace to the Indians against which the Aztecs had taken such harsh precautions and against which the friars had fought unremittingly, having become a problem in the immediate aftermath of the Conquest, now assumed the proportions of a major catastrophe. Drinking *pulque*, the pungent beverage they drew from the maguey cactus, and, when they could get it, Spanish wine, the Indians lapsed into a morbid condition in which, to the consternation of the friars, the formidable moral controls which they had inherited from their forebears were gradually undermined.

Yet despite the general disillusionment of the 1550s, the process of reconstruction and building a new social order in Mexico continued. If anything, the second viceroy, Don Luis de Velasco, an austere, uncompromising man, was even more determined to safeguard the existence of Indian society (and make the best of the flagging level of Indian tribute payments to the crown) and to discipline the Spaniards than his predecessors had been. He developed the system of *corregidores* so that these officers were now posted in areas where Indians were held in *encomienda* as well as elsewhere; and they were assigned jurisdiction over the Spaniards and the Negroes as well as over the Indians.[22] He also developed the segregation policy which the crown was groping towards and which the friars were fervently advocating, a policy which led him to try to expel non-Indian vagrants from Indian communities and remove Spanish ranches and other establishments from Indian lands.[23] Although his segregation policy was exceedingly difficult to implement, Viceroy Velasco nevertheless achieved a considerable measure of success, being helped in this by the depopulation which, by having left huge tracts of cultivable land

[19]Mendieta, *Historia Eclesiástica Indiana*, pp. 518–19; Grijalva, *Crónica* p. 215.
[20]*The Conquistadors*, p. 164.   [21]Gibson, *The Aztecs*, pp. 111–12, 150.
[22]Gibson, *The Aztecs*, p. 82.
[23]Magnus Mörner and Charles Gibson, 'Diego Muñoz Carmargo and the Segregation Policy of the Spanish Crown', *HAHR* xliii (1963), 559–60; Charles Gibson, *Tlaxcala in the Sixteenth Century* (New Haven, Conn., 1952), pp. 81–5.

vacant, made it possible to divert Spanish energies into newly designated 'Spanish' areas and relieve the pressure on Indian agriculture. And Indian agriculture, as historians have recently began to take note, in central and even more in southern Mexico was showing, and was to continue to show throughout the colonial era, far more vitality and resilience than was at one time supposed.[24]

During the same period the friars developed their theoretical justification of segregation. The Franciscan Fray Gerónimo de Mendieta was prominent in this endeavour.[25] According to him, it was the duty of King Philip to see to it that there was as little contact as possible between the Indians and the non-Indian population, for unimpeded contact would mean the ruin of Indian society and the destruction of all that the mendicants had worked for. The chance to create a model Christian community under royal protection was still there, he asserted, the Indians being 'soft wax' which would be readily moulded into a perfectly ordered utopia. 'Their temperament is so good for this purpose', he pleaded, 'that I, a poor useless good-for-nothing . . . could rule, with little help from others, a province of fifty thousand Indians organized and arranged with such excellent Christianity, that it would appear as if the whole province were a monastery.'[26] But should the Spanish colonists and their Negroes be allowed to infiltrate the Indian communities, he warned, then the wretched Indians would soon become utterly corrupted and depraved and everything would be lost.

Despite the continued progress of the reconstruction under Viceroy Velasco, however, and the progress of segregation, his work, during the last two years of his term, was seriously threatened by the arrival in Mexico of Don Martín Cortés, son of the Conqueror and heir not only to his wealth, name, and prestige, but also to his influence with the Spanish settlers. The sons of the Conquistadores, or Creoles as the locally born Spaniards came to be known, joyfully received the new arrival, seeing that his presence would greatly strengthen their hand against the viceroy and his officers. In 1564 Viceroy Velasco died in the midst of a difficult and somewhat tense situation which was rapidly made worse by the circulation of rumours that Philip II now intended to do away with the *encomienda* once and for all. The *Audiençia*,

---

24 See W. B. Taylor, *Landlord and Peasant in Colonial Oaxaca* (Stanford, Calif., 1972), pp. 108, 163, 195; W. S. Osborn, 'Indian Land Retention in Colonial Metztitlán', *HAHR* liii (1973), 217–38.

25 *Cartas de Religiosos, 1539–94*, ed. J. G. Icazbalceta (Mexico, 1941), esp. pp. 31–45, 101–15; J. L. Phelan, *The Millennial Kingdom of the Franciscans in the New World. A Study of the Writings of Gerónimo de Mendieta* (Berkeley and Los Angeles, 1956), pp. 58–66, 82; see also Mendieta's later work, the *Historia Eclesiástica Indiana* esp. pp. 500–5.

26 Mendieta, *Historia Eclesiástica Indiana*, pp. 448–9.

which assumed the conduct of government on the viceroy's death, did little or nothing to allay these fears and soon a group of Creole *encomenderos*, headed by the brothers Alonso and Gil González de Avila, became involved in a conspiracy designed to wrest power from the *Audiencia*, sever the links between Mexico and Spain, and crown Martín Cortés king of an independent Mexico. The rather inept plot was betrayed to the *Audiencia* magistrates by one of the conspirators, and in July 1566 the *Audiencia* working with Luis de Velasco, son of the late viceroy, arrested the Avila brothers, Martín Cortés, Luis Cortés, and a number of other conspirators and clergy. An emergency was declared in Mexico City and troops and cannon served as a warning to the white population. These steps were followed by a series of trials and then the sentencing and beheading of Alonso and Gil González de Avila. Luis Cortés, also sentenced to death, survived owing to the timely arrival of Mexico's third viceroy, Don Gaston de Peralta, marqués de Falces. However, the marquis was unable to do much more than dispatch Martín and Luis Cortés to Spain before the *Audiencia* with which he was sharply at odds, managed to undermine his position in Spain by insinuating, in a report to King Philip, that he was in sympathy with the traitors. This led the king to remove Falces and place Mexico under a special commission which proceeded to terrorize the Creole leadership with investigations, torturings, more trials, and more beheadings, under pretext of extirpating every trace of treason. The repression only finally ended in 1568 when the fourth viceroy, the formidable Don Martín Enríquez de Almansa (1568–80) took up his post. By that time, the *encomenderos* were well and truly cowed and the conspiracy with which they had hoped to halt the progress of bureaucracy in Mexico had led to exactly the opposite result and smoothed its path.

Enríquez's rule marked an important new phase in the development of the colony. Under his direction the *encomienda* was pushed still further into the background, the powers of the *corregidores* were increased, and the system of forced labour known as the *repartimiento*, or Indian share-out, a system which had been introduced under Viceroy Velasco, was developed as the main legal means of exploiting Indian labour.[27] The *repartimiento* was a very different institution from the *encomienda*, though it too weighed heavily on the Indians, the chief difference being that it was operated not by the colonists but by the viceroy's officers. Entrepreneurs who needed Indians had to apply to specially appointed *repartimiento* supervisors for them and abide by strict rules, receiving workmen in weekly relays or shifts, paying them a

[27]Gibson, *Spain in America*, pp. 143–4; Gibson, *The Aztecs*, pp. 224–36; C. H. Haring, *The Spanish Empire in America* (New York, 1963), pp. 59–63.

stipulated wage, and sending them back, at the end of each stipulated stint, to their communities. Though an unsavoury contrivance in many respects, the *repartimiento* was an integral part of the reconstruction of Indian society both because it denied the colonists direct access to the labour supply and because, by placing Indian labour under Spanish officers who relied on the Indian leadership for actually drafting and dispatching the workmen, it employed methods of organizing forced labour not unlike those used under the Aztecs.

Viceroy Enríquez was also a strong believer in keeping non-Indians away from Indians, but less for the moral reasons that had had weight with Viceroy Velasco than for political and administrative ones. In his view, anything that did not contribute to the greater efficiency of the royal administration was secondary, and this made him much less sympathetic to the friars than Viceroy Velasco had been. 'Because the friars wish to control both the spiritual and the temporal affairs of the Indian communities,' he wrote in his report to his successor, the conde de la Coruña, in 1580, 'and because they allow neither Indians nor Spaniards to think that there are any supervisors other than themselves, they are generally on bad terms both with officers and with other Spaniards.'[28] Enríquez was particularly annoyed by mendicant complaints respecting the *repartimiento* and the methods used by his *corregidores*. He was in no doubt that the mendicant influence in the Indian communities should be reduced, and in his time there began a friction between *corregidores* and friars, which if not altogether new was certainly new in its intensity.

Three further aspects of Enríquez's Mexico require comment: the continuing decline of the Indian population; the economic advance of the colony; and the extension of the forms of the new central Mexican civilization northwards. The population decline continued throughout Enríquez's term and indeed after it, but was particularly steep during the second great *cocoliztli* of 1576—80, after which the Indian population of central Mexico had sunk to a wretched 2½ million or so. Again the friars and Indians were plunged in despair. But despite this fresh disaster, the steady economic growth which had begun with the stepping up of silver production, particularly at Zacatecas, following the introduction of the mercury amalgamation method of processing silver ore in the mid 1550s and the discovery of new mines, was not only sustained but quickened, and was further stimulated by the rising demand for food and supplies in the mining camps, nearly all of which were situated in the arid country. This in turn caused the movement of central Mexican society across the line between sedentary and nomadic Mexico to accelerate. Already in the 1550s the process had begun with

[28]*CDHE* xvi. 379.

the founding of Querétaro, Guanajuato, and San Miguel in the north of the Mexican heartland, and Enríquez, determined to secure his lines of communication with Zacatecas which were threatened by the increasingly daring raids of the nomads, founded a line of towns of which Celaya, Silao, León, Aguascalientes, and Jerez were the most notable, extending from the Bajío basin north-westwards towards the great silver-mining centre. These towns and Zacatecas, Querétaro, and Guanajuato were populated with colonies of sedentary Indians, mainly Aztecs, Tarascans, and Otomis, as well as groups of Spaniards and pacified former nomads, and placed under the secular administration of *corregidores* and the ecclesiastical administration of the friars.[29] Meanwhile, in the 1560s and 1570s, the Basque Conquistador, Francisco de Ibarra, had penetrated far to the north of Zacatecas, and established the realm of New Biscay with its capital at Durango which he founded in 1563, while in the mid-1560s another Basque Conquistador, Miguel López de Legazpi, using Mexico as his base, conquered the Philippines, on the far side of the Pacific.

The penetration of sedentary society into the Bajío, and beyond the Bajío towards Zacatecas, brought the war between the Spaniards and the wild Chichimec Indians of the region to its climax. As in Cortés's campaigns and in the conquest of New Galicia in the early 1530s, the great bulk of the Spaniards' fighting force in the Chichimec war was made up of sedentary Indian auxiliaries, again mainly Aztec, Tarascan, and Otomi. But although, under Enríquez, increasing numbers of men and increasingly large sums of money were devoted to the cause of subduing the Chichimecs, the task proved extremely difficult since the nomads had readily taken to riding horseback, and, unlike the sedentary Indians of Cortés's time, preferred hit-and-run tactics to set-piece battles. The long-haired nomads were greatly feared for their swiftness in attack, the savagery with which they tortured and mutilated those whom they captured and killed, and their general reputation for barbarousness. They were also reputed to be sexually licentious. The friars, who regarded the Chichimecs as the antithesis to everything that they valued in the Indian, were bitterly hostile to them and advocated vigorous war to drive them back. However, when groups of Chichimecs were pacified and settled in the new towns, they were swiftly Christianized, transformed into sedentary Indians, and made by

[29]P. W. Powell, *Soldiers, Indians, and Silver. The Northward Advance of New Spain, 1550–1600* (Berkeley and Los Angeles, 1952), pp. 159–71; François Chevalier, *Land and Society in Colonial Mexico. The Great Hacienda*, tr. A. Eustis, ed. L. B. Simpson (Berkeley and Los Angeles, 1963), p. 64; Wigberto Jiménez Moreno, *Estudios de Historia Colonial* (Mexico, 1958), pp. 83, 93, 97; R. Ricard (ed.), 'Documents pour l'histoire des franciscains au Mexique', *Revue d'histoire Franciscaine*, i (1924), 232–3.

the friars to cut their hair short, as the Aztecs had been in the years after the Conquest; indeed, once settled, the Chichimecs soon lost their separate identity.

Mexico's fifth viceroy, the undistinguished conde de la Coruña, ruled only briefly (1580–3), dying before the end of his term. In this contingency, the executive power was assumed by the *Audiencia*, which at this juncture appears to have been a somewhat corrupt body. King Philip, at any rate, disturbed by reports of a deterioration in standards of bureaucratic honesty in Mexico, soon appointed the puritanical Pedro Moya de Contreras, archbishop and chief inquisitor of Mexico, as visitor-general of New Spain with very wide powers to delve into the conduct of administration and root out corruption. Moya de Contreras went to work with a zeal which earned prompt recognition from his monarch: by 1584, he was not only archbishop, chief inquisitor, and visitor-general, but temporary viceroy as well; with this the purge of officers intensified, several of the most guilty being hanged, and the whole Mexican administration was thoroughly and rigorously disciplined.[30] It was shown beyond any doubt that even in remote Mexico the system of inspecting, used to check abuse in the administration in Spain, might, under certain circumstances at least, be effective.

The seventh viceroy of Mexico, the marqués de Villamanrique (1585–90), though prudent and cautious, according to the great Franciscan chronicler Fray Juan de Torquemada,[31] and though, or perhaps because, he was very effective at enforcing segregation of Indians from non-Indians,[32] in the end failed badly. He became embroiled with the bishops, especially Archbishop Moya de Contreras and Bishop Romano of Tlaxcala (who, being at odds with the Franciscans, actually resided among the colonists in Puebla) both of whom bitterly opposed mendicant possession of the Indian parishes and vehemently criticized the orders. Indeed, Villamanrique suffered severely in his *residencia*, the judicial inquiry which followed the rule of all the viceroys of Mexico but which did not usually prove a useful

[30] *Cartas de Indias*, pp. 225–30; H. H. Bancroft, *History of Mexico* (6 vols., San Francisco, 1883–8), ii. 739–41.

[31] Juan de Torquemada, *Los Veynte y un libros rituales y Monarchia Yndiana* (henceforward *Monarchia Yndiana*) (3 vols., Seville, 1615), i. 712–13; Torquemada was the leading Franciscan writer in Mexico in the early seventeenth century and in many respects the heir of Mendieta; he believed that the conversion of the Indians to Christian doctrine was the only good that came out of the Spanish Conquest of Mexico, 'all the rest being just greed, disease, and misery'; see the passage quoted by Alejandra Moreno Toscano in *Fray Juan de Torquemada y su Monarchía Indiana* (Mexico, 1963), p. 78.

[32] Mörner and Gibson, 'Diego Muñoz Camargo and the Segregation Policy of the Spanish Crown', *HAHR* xlii. 561–2.

instrument to their opponents, and returned to Spain with his reputation and career in tatters. This episode foreshadowed in several ways the pattern of Mexican politics of the seventeenth century, in particular demonstrating the capacity of the bishops, under certain circumstances, to give teeth to the colonists' opposition to the viceroys, opposition which otherwise was virtually impotent.

In one respect, however, Villamanrique was successful: under him the backbone of the Chichimec resistance was finally broken and the path made clearer for the great Mexican boom, the period of particularly rapid growth and expansion that began in the 1590s under the second Luis de Velasco (1590–5), son of the first. San Luis Potosí was founded in 1592 on a site where silver ores had been found a decade earlier,[33] at the height of the war, and within a few years was producing silver in quantities exceeded only by Zacatecas, while additional valuable mines were established in the period 1592–4 at Sierra de Pinos and elsewhere in the Chichimeca. More new towns were founded, and a fresh trek of sedentary Indians from central Mexico to the north, under *corregidor* and Franciscan (and in some cases now, Jesuit) supervision, began, this time with the Tlaxcaltecs playing a notable role.[34] Meanwhile cereal production and stock-raising in the Bajío advanced in line with the rising demand for supplies in the north; indigo, cochineal, sugar, and cacao, the valuable products of tropical lowland Mexico, surged forward; and Pacific trade between the Philippines and Mexico and Mexico and Peru (both routes being in the hands of Mexican merchants) grew luxuriantly with huge quantities of oriental silks passing from China to Peru via Manila and Mexico and Peruvian silver passing to Mexico and China.[35] Mexican textile manufacture, which like the tropical lowland products had gathered momentum in the time of Viceroy Enríquez, now entered its heyday. By 1604 there were 25 textile mills (*obrajes*) in Mexico City producing quality or coarse cloths and ten more producing hats; Puebla contained 35 of the largest *obrajes* in the viceroyalty, and there were 11 mills at Tlaxcala, 8 at Texcoco, 5 at Tepeaca, 4 each at Celaya and Xochimilco, and others at Querétaro, Valladolid, Atlixco, Cuernavaca, Cholula, and Tecamachalco; the average work-force in these factories was 50 to 70, with one of the largest, in Mexico City, employing 120, a remarkable number for a manufacturing enterprise at that time.[36]

Under Viceroy Velasco's successors, the conde de Monterrey

[33] Bakewell, *Silver Mining and Society*, p. 38.

[34] Gibson, *Tlaxcala in the sixteenth century*, pp. 184–9.

[35] J. H. Parry, *The Spanish Seaborne Empire* (London, 1966), pp. 131–3; see also BND 3636, fols. 194–5: Velasco II to council (of the Indies), 10 March 1592.

[36] AGI México 26: Montesclaros to council, 20 May 1604 (*obrajes*).

(1595–1603), the marqués de Montesclaros (1603–7), and during Velasco's second term (1607–11), the boom entered its best years; it was to continue until about 1620. Silver production mounted steadily, especially at Zacatecas and San Luis, increasing almost every year.[37] Agricultural production in the Puebla district (the Tlaxcala-Atlixco-Tecamachalco triangle) and the Bajío basin reached the peak to which it had been climbing for more than half a century.[38] The period 1596–1620, which in many respects marks the zenith of Spanish influence in Europe, the Orient, and America, also marks the zenith of Mexico in the Spanish Atlantic system: in some years more than 50 per cent of the shipping plying between Spain and the New World was bound for Mexico. Territorially, the triumphant progress northwards which led to the opening up of New León and the founding of Monterrey during the term of the viceroy of that name culminated, in the first decade of the new century, in the conquest of New Mexico and the founding of Santa Fe.[39]

But though the economy was booming as never before at the outset of the seventeenth century, the viceroys were well aware that the colony was facing some very serious problems. The Indian population of central Mexico had now sunk below the 2 million mark, which naturally caused widespread concern, while in New Galicia, where there were only about 40,000 Indians in 1610,[40] the population was declining even faster. Meanwhile, the white population and the Negro and half-caste communities were expanding more rapidly than the economy, so that idleness and vagrancy were again causing grave concern.[41] The great boom had caused a special emphasis on Mexico in Spanish emigration to the New World so that by the mid-seventeenth century New Spain was to have, it is thought, some 150,000 white inhabitants,[42] or roughly a quarter of all the white population in Spanish and Portuguese America, and it is estimated that the Negro and mulatto population was almost as large, standing at about 130,000.[43]

[37] Bakewell, *Silver Mining and Society*, pp. 241–2; according to Basalenque, silver production at San Luis reached its peak in the years around 1612, Fray Diego Basalenque, *Historia de la provincia de San Nicolás de Tolentino de Michoacán del orden de N. P. S. Agustin* (Mexico, 1963), p. 225.

[38] Ibid., pp. 296, 314–15, 364.

[39] Bakewell, *Silver Mining and Society*, pp. 38–9.

[40] Mota y Escobar, *Descripción geográfica*, pp. 92–4; Lázaro de Arregui, *Descripción de la Nueva Galicia*, p. 29.

[41] BND 3636, 'Cartas del virrey don Luis de Velasco II', fols. 80v–81, 116v–117, 124v–126, 128v, 154v, 167.

[42] W. Borah, 'Latin America, 1610–1660', in *The New Cambridge Modern History*, iv (Cambridge, 1970), p. 715.

[43] Gonzalo Aguirre Beltrán, *La Población negra de México, 1519–1810* (Mexico, 1946), pp. 213–21; D. M. Davidson, 'Negro slave control and resistance in colonial Mexico, 1519–1650', *HAHR* xlvi (1966), 236–7.

Furthermore, though it is impossible to estimate the size of the mestizo (part Indian, part white) population, it can hardly have numbered less than 150,000, so that there was now, very roughly, one non-Indian for every four Indians in the viceroyalty. All this naturally created innumerable difficulties regarding settlement, the maintaining of order, and employment, and introduced a whole range of new pressures into the Mexican body politic.

Such, then, was the position of Mexico at the end of the sixteenth century and at the threshold of the seventeenth: prosperous but faced with a declining Indian labour force; ruled by a strong and confident administration but plagued by unemployment and vagabondage; uniform, or almost uniform, in religion but divided in religious administration between opposing clerical factions; and racially one of the most diverse and complicated societies the world had yet seen. The mass of the Indian population remained, to a considerable extent, a distinct community regulated by a local government system, morality, and religion compounded of mixed Indian and Spanish ingredients; but the other community, consisting of Spaniards and espanolized Indians, Negroes, and mixed bloods, which in theory, and to a large extent in practice, was separated from it, was rapidly growing in numbers and importance and posing a host of new problems for the viceregal government, not least by reason of its complex relations with the Indian community.

PART ONE
MEXICAN SOCIETY IN THE
SEVENTEENTH CENTURY

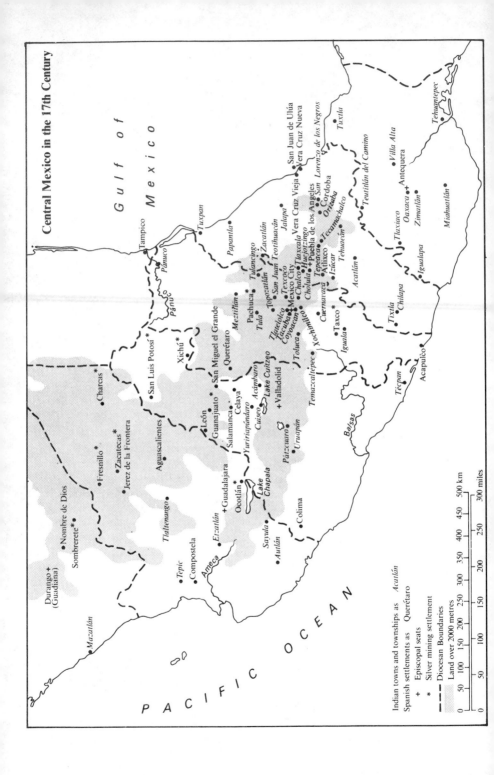

I

THE INDIANS

The sedentary Indians of seventeenth-century Mexico—for after the pacification of the Chichimecs there were still various nomadic and hostile tribes to the north in New Biscay and New León—at the same time as they remained in their traditional communities occupied with their traditional occupations, also supplied the great bulk of the labour force working in the non-Indian sector. Indeed Spanish enterprise in Mexico was dependent on Indian labour.

That this is true is unlikely to be disputed notwithstanding the rise of a sizeable Negro, mulatto, and mestizo population and the increasingly prominent role of these new elements in the life of the viceroyalty. There were of course certain sectors such as the docks at Veracruz and Acapulco—the coastal strips were by this time virtually denuded of Indians[1]—and some of the sugar plantations and refineries in the hot lowlands to the south and east of the Mexican heartland where the work force was predominantly black; but, generally speaking, employment of non-Indians remained selective and limited. One reason for this was the cheapness of Indian labour in relation to non-Indian labour. Negro slaves, for instance, were very costly, selling at 300 pesos or more apiece, and were rarely expended on mere unskilled manual labour; they were reserved for more specialized tasks and for supervising Indian work-gangs. Also ill-adapted from the entrepreneurial point of view were the free blacks, free mulattoes, and mestizos (those of mixed Spanish and Indian blood) who, though much more numerous than the slaves, were usually somewhat unruly and could command a comparatively high wage. Only the Indians of central and southern Mexico and the settled Indian colonies in the north, moulded by centuries of sedentary existence, could be relied on for cheap, easily disciplined work-gangs that would submit to virtually any conditions or drudgery. Viceroy Velasco, in a report to the Council of the Indies of 1610, affirmed that very few non-Indian workers were to be found in the silver mines; for while mulattoes and mestizos disdained them, slaves

---

[1] Veracruz in the 1640s apparently had a population of roughly 6,000 of which about 5,000 were Negroes and mulattoes; Juan Diez de la Calle, *Memorial y noticias sacras y reales del imperio de las Indias Occidentales* (Madrid, 1646), fol. 68; Francesco Gamelli Careri, *Voyage du tour du monde* (6 vols., Paris, 1727), vi (*De la Nouvelle Espagne*, 1697), p. 10.

were unsuitable and in any case too expensive.[2] Moreover, the blacks, though generally stronger and hardier than the Indians, were nevertheless more vulnerable to the cold and damp underground.[3] Accordingly, the non-Indian section of the work force at the silver-mining centres was never more than a fairly small fraction of the total.[4] And as with the mines, so with Spanish agriculture. It is clear from dozens of the documents collected by Silvio Zavala and Maria Castelo, relating to labour conditions in colonial Mexico, that although non-Indian labourers and especially foremen were widely employed on Spanish haciendas in the seventeenth century, they made up only a small part of the labour force; Spanish landowners, and particularly the cereal producers of the lush Atlixco-Tlaxcala-Tecamachalco triangle, of the valleys of Mexico, Toluca, and Valladolid, and of the Bajío basin were heavily dependent on large numbers of Indian labourers.[5] The position with respect to public works is clearer still. Efforts were made, to take a notable example, to recruit mulattoes and mestizos for work on the ditches and dikes needed to protect Mexico City from the waters of Lake Texcoco, but almost totally without success. It was the Indians who had to bear the brunt of the burden.

The fact of the reliance of Spanish entrepreneurs on Indian labour in seventeenth-century Mexico has given rise to an important hypothesis regarding the great recession in Atlantic trade that set in in the 1620s with dire effects for Spain and, it has been presumed, for Mexico. Twenty years ago Professor Borah put forward the argument that Mexico was economically depressed from about 1580 onwards for roughly a century, owing to the collapse of the Indian population and the consequent drastic reduction in the amount of labour available. Though proven untenable in certain respects, and particularly in that it sets the start of the depression back far too early to a time when New Spain was in fact entering a long boom, this argument has been made use of in a modified form by Pierre and Huguette Chaunu.[6] The Chaunus used Professor Borah's theory as part of a complicated

[2] AGI México 2, r 3: Velasco to council, 4 April 1610.

[3] Mota y Escobar, *Descripción geográfica*, p. 68.

[4] R. C. West, *The Mining Community in Northern New Spain: the Parral Mining Districts*, Ibero-Americana xxx (Berkeley and Los Angeles, 1949), p. 53; Bakewell, *Silver Mining and Society*, p. 124.

[5] See the *Fuentes para la historia del trabajo en Nueva España* ed. S. A. Zavala and M. Castelo (8 vols., Mexico, 1939–46) (henceforward *FHT*), vols. vi, vii, and viii.

[6] See W. W. Borah, *New Spain's Century of Depression*, Ibero-Americana xxxv (Berkeley and Los Angeles, 1951), pp. 20–5; Pierre and Huguette Chaunu, *Séville et l'Atlantique, 1504–1650* (8 vols., Paris, 1955–60), viii. 2 (bis), pp. 1523–60; Pierre Chaunu, 'Pour un tableau triste du Mexique au milieu du xviie siècle', *Annales. Economies, Sociétés, Civilisations*, x (1955), 79–85.

argument intended to explain the decline of trade between Spain and Mexico, a decline which they themselves had shown to have begun in 1620 and which they identified as the root cause of the Atlantic depression. They argue that the falling-off in Spanish-Mexican trade (which was not only a prime cause of the Atlantic depression but coincided with the general 'decay of trade' which set in in Europe in 1620)[7] was to be explained in terms of a major recession in Mexico which in turn, they held, following Borah, was to be explained by the dwindling of the labour supply, that is to say the supply of Indians. At this point, however, the Chaunus' argument became purely hypothetical and speculative:[8] there was, they conjectured, such a thing as a certain minimum population level, of somewhat less than 2 million Indians for central Mexico, after which further depopulation so depleted the labour reserve that it became impossible to sustain economic activity at its previous level. This floor, they suggested, was reached during the decade 1620–30.

In support of this argument, it must be said that the Indian population of central Mexico, having fallen to a level of between 1½ and 2 million in 1607,[9] continued to decline at least until the middle of the century. The decline was very gradual, except during the two epidemics of 1629–34, but constant, reducing the figure for 1607 by perhaps three or four hundred thousand by 1650.[10] It was not until 1671 in fact that the administration in Mexico discovered, from the slight but unmistakable lengthening of their tribute lists for the first time since the Conquest, that the Indian population of the four provinces had at

[7] E. J. Hobsbawm, 'The Crisis of the Seventeenth Century', and H. R. Trevor-Roper, 'The General Crisis of the Seventeenth Century', in *Crisis in Europe, 1560–1660*, ed. T. Aston (London, 1965), pp. 9–11, 95.

[8] 'le drame se situe', wrote Chaunu, 'entre 1620 et 1630. Sans que rien d'exceptionnel et d'exterieur n'intervienne, la masse globale de la population indienne du plateau du Mexique central, reservoir de l'économie coloniale nouvelle espagnole, a dû, dans son evolution décroissante, crever un seuil de sécurité et provoquer une mutation dans l'économie coloniale. Ce seuil decisif se situerait autant qu'on en puisse juger d'après les travaux des historiens démographes de Berkeley un peu en dessous de deux millions d'habitants. Entre 1620 et 1630, la population indienne de l'Anahuac, support de l'économie mexicaine, passerait de 1·9 a 1·7 millions environ. La seuil de deux millions franchi, la chute de la population indienne entraîne toute l'économie coloniale mexicaine dans une zone de freinage intense', Chaunu, op. cit., viii–ii–ii, 1559.

[9] AGI Indiferente de Nueva España 77: Landeras de Velasco to council, 10 Jan. 1607 (estimates 344,000 adult male tributaries); Borah, *New Spain's Century of Depression*, p. 3.

[10] ADA a15c17 (1654), no. 27: Albuquerque to council, 17 March 1654; Borah, *New Spain's Century of Depression*, pp. 3, 43; Miranda believes that the lowest point occurred between 1620 and 1630, which seems unlikely owing to the epidemics of 1629–31 and 1634–5, José Miranda, 'La población indígena de México en el siglo xvii', *Historia Mexicana*, xii (1962–3), 182–9, 185 f.

last ceased to stagnate and had begun to increase again.[11] Furthermore, it is clear that the continued dwindling of the Indians did lead to a labour shortage. Employers everywhere in seventeenth-century Mexico complained of the lack of workers even, at times, at Zacatecas which exercised a stronger pull on workers than almost any other centre in the country.[12]

But did the continued decline of the Indian population in the half-century 1600–50, together with the consequent labour shortage, cause a long and severe economic depression? Recently this argument, both in its original form put forward by Professor Borah and the modified version of Pierre and Huguette Chaunu, has been subjected to some searching and fruitful criticism, which has led to a new if rather complex view of Mexican economic development in the seventeenth century. It has been pointed out that the decline in trade between Spain and Mexico starting in 1620, which itself seems beyond doubt, does not necessarily indicate a serious slump in Mexico; the Atlantic trade depression from 1620 onwards might be explained, or largely explained, in terms of a New Spain becoming more self-sufficient with regard to many commodities, notably textiles and foodstuffs, a development which would have harmed Spain but constituted a gain for Mexico.[13] There are strong indications of economic buoyancy in the crucial decades in New Spain which in Professor Lynch's words are 'not easy to reconcile with the hypothesis of absolute depression'.[14] The *alcabala*, the tax on sales, for example, a most valuable indication of the state of internal trade, increased until 1638 and then suffered only a slight decline. Some sectors of overseas commerce, especially trade between Mexico and Central America and Mexico and Venezuela, expanded dramatically and it is difficult to know to what extent this expansion offset the loss of ground in depressed sectors such as trade with Spain. Venezuela's principal export, cacao, was, as the English visitor Thomas Gage noted enthusiastically, in tremendous demand in Mexico where chocolate was the favourite non-alcoholic beverage, and beginning in the 1620s, a vigorous commerce development which by 1640 had drawn Venezuela firmly into the economic orbit of Mexico.[15] There are also certain imponderables such as the question of how far the mounting restrictions imposed by Madrid on Mexico's Peru trade

[11] AGI México 45, r i: Mancera to council, 5 April 1671.
[12] AGI México 27, r 2: Velasco to council, 23 June 1608; *FHT* vi. 299–300, vii. 425–6; Gibson, *The Aztecs*, pp. 242, 533; Bakewell, *Silver Mining and Society*, pp. 128–9, 199–200, 219–20; Chevalier, *Land and Society*, pp. 280, 284.
[13] Bakewell, op. cit., pp. 226–30.
[14] J. Lynch, *Spain Under the Habsburgs* (2 vols., Oxford, 1965–9), ii. 212.
[15] Eduardo Arcila Farías, *Comercio entre Venezuela y México en los siglos XVII y XVIII* (Mexico, 1950), pp. 51–61, 72–3.

culminating in the total prohibition of 1634 were effective in suppressing trade, imponderables which make accurate analysis extremely difficult. Nevertheless, it is clear that in the half-century 1620—70 New Spain entered a period of economic crisis in which the structure of the Mexican economy was greatly altered, certain sectors were depressed whilst others expanded, and in which there was a good deal of economic dislocation and readjustment. The old belief of historians that the Mexican silver-mining industry went into decline in the seventeenth century has been confirmed, but it has been shown that this decline was less severe, less uniform, and more complex than was once supposed. If San Luis Potosí, the second most important silver-mining centre, went into decline in the 1620s at the time of the onset of the Atlantic recession and was apparently severely hit,[16] Zacatecas, the leading centre, continued to expand production until 1635 when it too entered a period of depression which was to last some three decades.[17] While some important mining areas of New Biscay such as that of the capital Durango were hit by depression in the 1630s,[18] others, notably Parral away to the north, experienced a boom.[19] On balance however, it is clear that there was a severe depression in Mexican silver mining. The same is probably true of Mexico's highly lucrative Pacific commerce—importing Chinese silks and other high-quality cloths from Manila and exporting finished silks and cloths to Peru. The matter is difficult to judge because it is known that there was widespread evasion of the restrictions imposed by Madrid and much movement of contraband between the two American viceroyalties, especially through Central American ports such as Realejo; however, it does seem likely, in view of the intensity of complaints from the *cabildos* of Mexico City and Puebla in the 1630s and 1640s, that the prohibition did have at least some adverse effect not only on the silk merchants but also on the textile manufacturers of Puebla.[20] Indeed yet another victim of the economic crisis was the formerly flourishing textile industry, for although without further research it is impossible to know to what extent, it is clear that after

16 Basalenque, *Historia de la provincia de San Nicolás* (Mexico 1693), p. 225; Primo F. Velázquez, *Historia de San Luis Potosí* (2 vols., Mexico, 1947), ii. 166.
17 Bakewell, *Silver Mining and Society*, pp. 197, 242—3, 246.
18 AGI México 34, fols. 81—2: Cadereita to council, 12 July 1638 (Hacienda); for the decline of the Chichicapa mines of Oaxaca in this period, see Taylor, *Landlord and Peasant in Colonial Oaxaca*, 144—5; Zacatecas, it should be remembered, accounted for only about 40% of Mexican silver production during this period, probably slightly less, see Bakewell, *Silver Mining and Society*, p. 222.
20 See the *Relazion de los fundamentos, informes, y pareceres . . .* (Madrid, 1644), and also pp. 196—7.

1620, and perhaps even from a few years before, the cloth manufacturers of Mexico's three leading textile centres—Puebla, Mexico City, and Tlaxcala—were hit by recession.[21] Among other effects, this development proved the death-blow to the once great city of Tlaxcala whose population dwindled in the middle decades of the century from roughly 11,000 to under 4,000.[22] Meanwhile, Mexico City, the economic hub of the viceroyalty, suffered considerably from misfortunes such as the seizure of the Mexican treasure fleet by the Dutch in 1628 and the disastrous floods of 1629–34, the worst in the history of the capital, which severely disrupted life in the city and caused a marked loss of population, especially white population, to other centres such as Puebla, Querétaro, and Antequera (Oaxaca). It may well be that the white population of the capital in 1654 was still some 25 per cent less than it had been before 1629.[23] Finally, to complete the picture of economic dislocation, there is evidence that the silver slump caused a severe depression in the fertile Bajío where many grain producers, especially in the districts of Celaya and Salamanca, were impoverished or ruined, for they were the chief food suppliers to Zacatecas and San Luis Potosí.[24] There was also considerable distress among cattle ranchers in parts of the north, notably around Durango.[25] This is not enough to justify speaking of a general agricultural recession, for the rich Puebla area and the key valleys of Mexico, Toluca, and Oaxaca were quite possibly unaffected by the crisis of overproduction further north, but it does unmistakably point to a loss of economic momentum in much of north-central Mexico.

But given that there was a painful period of structural change in the Mexican economy in the period 1620–70, is it likely that the continued decline of the Indian population and hence of the labour supply was a major factor behind the changes? Actually there is little reason, despite the arguments of Professor Borah and Pierre and Huguette Chaunu, to link the Mexican economic crisis with an absolute labour shortage. Research has shown that the mounting costs of mining were rendering the industry fundamentally unprofitable,[26] and that the consequent decision of Madrid in 1634 to end the era of easy credit for the mercury supplies needed to process the silver ore and, more generally, the highly changeable and uncertain outlook for Mexican

[21] Jan Bazant, 'Evolución de la industria textil poblana, 1544–1845' *Historia Mexicana*, xiii (1963–4), 473–516, 488 f.

[22] BNX 1066, fols. I^v, 53^v–54.

[23] AGI México 3, r 4: Archbishop Manso to council, 8 Nov. 1629. IAH 101 ant.: 'Itinerario del distrito de la Inquisición de México', p. 14.

[24] Basalenque, *Historia de la provincia de San Nicolás*, pp. 296, 314–15.

[25] Ibid., p. 364.

[26] Bakewell, *Silver Mining and Society*, pp. 208–12, 234.

commerce and finance were more important causes of the crisis than labour shortage. Diego Basalenque when speaking of the severe agricultural depression in the Bajío specifically ascribes the misfortunes of the farmers to the decline of the silver towns, the disruption of the farmers' markets, and a consequent glut of supplies. Labour shortage as such had little to do with it. Besides, it seems inherently unlikely that the dwindling of the central Mexican Indians from roughly 1⅔ million by some three or four hundred thousand could in itself seriously hamper Mexican mining, industry, or agriculture, for the labour needs of Spanish enterprise in seventeenth-century Mexico were really quite modest. The Indian labour force at Zacatecas amounted to only between 2,000 and 5,000[27] and at all the other mining centres it was, presumably, less. Even the most optimistic estimate of the total number of textile workers in the mills of central Mexico in the early seventeenth century (not all of whom were Indians) was 14,000, and the real figure, as near as one can judge, was probably less than 7,000, though admittedly this was a large figure by the industrial standards of the time.[28] The labour needs of the hacienda owners doubtless were greater and there are signs that the labour shortage was more serious further south than in the Bajío which had tended to attract Indian migration from other areas, but there is no real reason to suppose that labour was so short as to prevent expansion and harm production substantially. Indeed, Professor Borah came close to pulling the mat from under his own theory when he admitted that 'probably even at the low point of the [Indian] population, approximately 1,500,000 about 1650, there were enough Indians available to man all essential services and even to provide a considerable margin of labour if a fairly large proportion of the Indians' working-time could have been secured for the white population.'[29]

The latter part of Professor Borah's observation leads to a line of inquiry which may well replace the old notion of absolute labour shortage with the notion of restricted availability of Indian labour. For if the economic crisis was not caused primarily by shortage of Indian labour but by other factors, it remains true that Spanish enterprise was dependent on Indian labour and that Indian labour, chiefly because of the social system created by the Spanish administration in Mexico

[27] Ibid., pp. 127–8.
[28] *Relazion de los fundamentos, informes, y pareceres*, fol. 2ᵛ; this seems a reasonable conclusion given that there were roughly 120 textile *obrajes* in central Mexico in 1604 and that one can assume on the basis of Viceroy Montesclaros's remarks in AGI Mexico 26, Montesclaros to council, 20 May 1604 (*obrajes*), that the average work-force per *obraje* was about 50 to 60.
[29] Borah, *New Spain's Century of Depression*, p. 43.

during the sixteenth century, in combination with the population catastrophe, was in short supply. In the later sixteenth century, the viceroys had, with a considerable degree of success, imposed a system of segregation intended to preserve, however imperfectly, the traditional Indian communities and Indian agriculture, a system which continued to operate in the seventeenth century. Not only had towns designated as 'Indian', such as Tlaxcala, Cholula, Texcoco, and the Tlatelolco division of Mexico City, been enveloped in protective institutions of various kinds, but Mexico City proper and all the new towns had been fairly rigorously divided with the non-Indian quarters, under the parochial administration of the secular clergy, at the centre, and the Indian quarters, under the ecclesiastical sway of the friars, forming the suburbs.[30] In many cases, Indian and non-Indian quarters were separated by stretches of open ground, and in the case of the new towns there had been a distinct tendency for each of the main colonizing Indian nations—Aztec, Tarascan, Otomi, and Tlaxcaltec—to have its own quarter. Of course, a large proportion of the Indians living in 'Indian' areas or 'Indian' quarters were, by the early and mid seventeenth century, employed directly by Spanish employers, outside the *repartimiento* context, in 'Spanish' urban districts, in mines, and on haciendas. Indeed in some places, such as Texcoco[31] (particularly after 1630), Querétaro,[32] and Zacatecas, they were clearly the majority. Nevertheless, except in a few areas such as Tepeaca,[33] Tecamachalco, and Atlixco, where Spanish settlement was so heavy that traditional Indian communities were disrupted and the majority of the Indians moved into Spanish residences and on to haciendas, only a restricted portion of the labour force was fully at the settlers' disposal. Indian agriculture and continued Indian possession of much of the land, Indian community obligations and *repartimiento* service all syphoned off valuable working time; many Indians preferred their own activities or idleness and avoided working for the Spaniards; and whole Indian communities remained in places too distant from Spanish enterprises to

---

[30] Mörner and Gibson, 'Diego Muñoz Camargo and the Segregation Policy of the Spanish Crown', *HAHR* xliii. 558 f.; for segregation in Mexico City, see AGN Historia 413, fols. 4, 6, 8, 10, 12, and *passim*; Edmundo O'Gorman, *Reflexiones sobre la distribución urbana colonial de la ciudad de México* (Mexico, 1951); Gibson, *The Aztecs*, pp. 370–7; on the Indian outskirts of Zacatecas, see Bakewell, *Silver Mining and Society*, pp. 37, 56; for Guadalajara, see Mota y Escobar, *Descripción geográfica*, p. 26.

[31] AGN Indios x, fols. 228[v] 275.

[32] AGN Indios xii, fols. 195[v]–197; *FHT* vii. 425–6.

[33] See the passage from Mota y Escobar's *memoriales* quoted by Alejandra Morena Toscano in 'Tres problemas de la geografía del Maíz, 1600–1624', *Historia Mexicana*, xiv (1964–5), 649.

be convenient, or in some cases any use at all, to Spanish employers, a factor important everywhere but particularly in Oaxaca and Michoacán.

The Spaniards' response to this situation, naturally, was to aspire to disrupt traditional Indian communities more extensively. Indeed, the real significance of the labour shortage in the seventeenth century, it may be argued, is not that it caused the economic depression—that was caused mainly by other factors—but that it led to an intensification of the friction between Spanish enterprise, which was determined to secure a higher proportion of the Indians' working-time and a greater measure of control over the Indians, and those groups in whose interest it was to deny the colonists that greater measure of control. The Mexican labour shortage, in other words, instilled new life into the old battle between Mexican enterprise and bureaucracy.

The typical seventeenth-century Creole approach to the subject of the Indians is already evident in the work of Gonzalo Gómez de Cervantes, a Creole noble writing in 1599;[34] he demanded less segregation and more Creole contact with the Indians, but he was not yet so preoccupied with bureaucratic control of the labour supply and the *repartimiento* as his successors in the seventeenth century. The next stage in the colonists' critique of the established system in Mexico was reached in 1625 when Cristobal de Molina, a member of the Mexico City council (*cabildo*) published, probably in Spain, with the approval of both the Mexico City council and that of Puebla, a tract complaining of the damage done to both the Spanish settlers and the Indians specifically by the *repartimiento* and bureaucratic interference in labour relations;[35] he called for a drastic overhaul of the system and a reduction in the powers of the *corregidores*. Soon after this, Hernán Carrillo Altamirano, a Creole nobleman of Mexico City, published a tract in Madrid similarly complaining of the *repartimiento*; attributed a great part of the suffering and misery of the Mexican Indians to the *repartimiento* and suggested that it be abolished and what he called a free wage-labour system—free that is from compulsion and official intervention be put in its place.[36] In 1632, the Mexico City council, repeating its arguments of former years, again condemned

---

[34] Gonzalo Gómez de Cervantes, *La Vida económica y social de Nueva España al finalizar el siglo xvi*, ed. Alberto María Carreño (Mexico, 1944), pp. 77, 82, 91.

[35] *Informe que presenta a Felipe IV Christoval de Molina* . . . (AHN), fols. 3ᵛ–7ᵛ.

[36] *El doctor Hernan Carrillo Altamirano vezino y natural de Mexico* . . . *y protector general de los indios* . . . *dize* (Madrid, c. 1626), esp. fol. 4; shortly afterwards there was published in Mexico by Viceroy Cerralvo's associate Fernando Carrillo, a tract sharply criticizing the Creole view, see Fernando Carrillo, *Origen y causa de los repartimientos de indios, daños que resultaràn de quitarlos a las labores de panes, y el medio de que se podrà Vsar* . ·. (Mexico, 1632) (BM).

the *repartimiento*.[37] After 1633, when it became clear, as we shall see in chapter six, that the *repartimiento* itself was merely a symptom not the source of the trouble, Creole demands became more radical and Creoles such as Luis García de Najera, a powerful hacendado of the Tlaxcala region, and the famous Bishop Alonso de Cuevas Dávalos went the whole way in calling for the abolition of *corregidores* and the assignment of local government to the Spanish town councils.[38]

But disagreement over labour exploitation was by no means the only aspect of the argument between enterprise and bureaucracy in seventeenth-century Mexico over who was to exploit the Indians. Apart from the matter of Indian tribute which was taken very seriously by viceroys, *Audiencia*, and *corregidores* alike and which could only be effectively collected, as experience showed, while the Indians remained in their traditional communities, there was also the very important question of who was to reap the benefit of the Indians as a market and source of food and supplies. The *corregidores*, despite the laws forbidding them to engage in such activities and despite the *residencia* to which, in theory at any rate, all *corregidores* were subjected at the end of their terms of office,[39] used their political and administrative power in the Indian localities to ensure that it was they who did most of the exploiting, at least in areas away from the main concentrations of Spanish population, that is to say in most areas.[40] It was quite usual for *corregidores* to sell quantities of wholly unnecessary and unwanted goods to their Indians forcibly and at grossly inflated prices. It was also common for *corregidores* to buy up the crops of the Indians of their districts at brutally low prices and then to sell, at certain times after an astute period of hoarding, in Mexico City and Puebla, or the silver-mining towns, at great profit. Moreover, when collecting the king's tribute, which was very difficult, as has been said, in the case of

[37] AGI México 31, r 4, i: 'Copia de parezer de la ciudad de Mexico sobre el repartimiento de yndios'.

[38] ADI Palafox papers liv, fols. 521–4: Cuevas y Dávalos to council, 26 Nov. 1663, quoted in full in Mariano Cuevas, *Historia de la Iglesia en México* (5 vols., Mexico, 1946), iii. 458–63.

[39] The *residencia* with respect to *corregidores* was largely ineffective, for the *residencia* of each officer was conducted by his successor who in most cases was disinclined to find fault with conduct which he himself proposed to emulate, ADI Palafox papers lxxx, fols. 35–8: Palafox to council, 10 July 1641.

[40] See the 'Discurso de Juan Fernández de Vivero, natural y vezino de la ciudad y provincia de Tlaxcala del reino de Nueva España, de dos puntos en las materias mas principales y necessarias que necessitan de remedio en el dicho reino . . .', BM Add. MS 13, 974, doc. 33, fols. 157–160ᵛ, esp. 160: Cuevas y Dávalos to council, 26 Nov. 1663; Gibson, *The Aztecs*, pp. 93–4; the fact was acknowledged by several of the viceroys, see BND 3636, fol. 53: Velasco II to crown, 2 Dec. 1590; *CDHE* xxvi. 168–9.

Indians living on haciendas or in 'Spanish' districts but much easier where the Indians remained under the authority of their own community officers, *corregidores* and their deputies often extorted and pocketed additional sums. When administering the *repartimiento*, they were considerate towards those settlers who made it worth their while, and ignored the interests of those who did not. To supplement their gains from these activities, the *corregidores* took fees for signatures, favours, and 'righting of wrongs', and exacted fines for civil and criminal transgressions.

Some of these activities of course counted as acceptable in the viceroy's eyes and those of the royal council of the Indies in Madrid; they were the recognized perquisites of office. In providing such opportunities, the Mexican *corregidor*'s post was similar to those of whole classes of officers in seventeenth-century Spain, or France or England, where the state, unable to pay its officers realistic salaries, sold offices together with the opportunities that attached to them. Nor was any other method of maintaining bureaucracy possible under the circumstances. For as long as the *corregidores*, as Viceroy Cerralvo observed,[41] were paid only trifling salaries of two or three hundred pesos a year, no one could expect them to do otherwise than take advantage of their position. But there was also an accepted if somewhat vague distinction between honest and dishonest conduct, certain practices being officially frowned upon, and in this respect, the *corregidores* were, even by seventeenth-century standards, notably corrupt.[42] For unlike officers serving in centres of Spanish population, the *corregidores* of Indian jurisdictions were notoriously free of constraints, being unimpeded by the presence of other officers, remote from centres of authority, and confronted by an exceptionally docile population.

Moreover, the general deterioration in standards of bureaucratic honesty in Spain and Spanish America following the death of the austere King Philip II and the accession of the weak-willed, pleasure-loving, and irresponsible Philip III, may well have encouraged the *corregidores* of the early seventeenth century to be even worse than their predecessors. At any rate, Landeras de Velasco, Philip III's visitor-general to Mexico in the years 1607–9, a notably upright and zealous man in Torquemada's view, was appalled by the extent of corruption both in Mexico City and the other towns and in the

[41] *Descripción de la Nueva España*, pp. 231–2; the *corregidores* of important towns, however, were paid rather more; there were roughly 105 *corregidores* in the three provinces of Mexico, Puebla, and Michoacán.

[42] See particularly ADI Palafox papers lxxx, fols. 35–8: Palafox to council, 10 July 1641, and Cuevas Dávalos to council, 26 Nov. 1663.

countryside.[43] He described the viceroy's officers as little despots intent only on power and gain. 'I am no prophet,' he wrote, 'but I am convinced that this land will soon be ruined unless there is some improvement in government and administration; and when I hear it said that the present scheme to drain Lake Texcoco is designed to save Mexico City, I reply that no drainage scheme in the world is adequate, unless it be of avarice, extortion, and immoral government, to preserve this city. . .'[44]

Madrid was aware of the drawbacks inherent in the system of *corregidores* as it existed in Mexico, but was unable or unwilling to take effective steps to overcome them. These drawbacks were political and administrative as well as financial and moral. The *corregidores* tended to be tied, with respect to their political allegiances, not to Madrid but to Mexico City. It was not the king who pulled the strings of administrative patronage in Mexico, but the viceroy; excepting only a handful of *corregidores* appointed in Spain—such as those of Mexico City itself, Zacatecas, Tlaxcala, Veracruz, and Acapulco[45]—the *corregidores* were the viceroy's nominees and therefore the viceroy's men. There was talk of increasing Madrid's share in appointments during the reign of Philip IV, but in the event no action was taken. It was felt by the Council of the Indies that since control of the *corregidores*, or rather provision of the *corregidores*, was the basis of viceregal authority in Mexico, tampering with the viceroy's powers of patronage might undermine the whole edifice of the colonial administration.[46]

The viceroys, naturally, made the most of their opportunity, selecting for their *corregidores* such men as would be wholly or chiefly dependent on the viceregal favour for their position and power. Occasionally, they chose prominent Creoles, especially for the post of *corregidor* of Puebla, for they had no wish to exclude the Creole nobility from the establishment entirely; but normally they chose persons unconnected with the Mexican-Spanish population and its interests, whose only actual link with New Spain was with the viceroy himself. Consequently, the *corregidores*, nearly always, were not of Mexican-Spanish extraction but were European Spanish newcomers,

[43] Torquemada, *Monarchia Yndiana* i. 808, 833.

[44] AGI Indiferente de Nueva España 77, fols. 5v–6: Landeras de Velasco to council, 24 June 1608.

[45] Indeed, the total number of secular appointments in Mexico filled by Madrid was remarkably small; for a list of them see Juan Diez de la Calle. *Memorial Informatorio al Rey nuestro señor en su real y supremo Conseio de las Indias* (Madrid, 1645) (BM).

[46] See for instance the Council's deliberations on the *corregimiento* of San Luis Potosí, AGI México 4, r 2, exp. 53.

that is men of the sort known in Mexico as *gachupines*.[47] Often they belonged to a class of professional officers that circulated from post to post in the Indies. Frequently also, they were members of the retinues of gentlemen that accompanied the viceroys to Mexico from Spain. In some cases, they were family relatives or friends of the viceroy or vicereine.

As well as being *gachupines*, the *corregidores* were of course usually gentlemen and in some cases members of the Spanish military orders. This added at least a tinge of class jealousy to the friction between officers and the bulk of the Creoles, a tinge which is clearly discernible in the following extract from the memoirs of the Dominican missionary, Fray Domingo Fernández de Navarrete, who was in Mexico during the period 1646–8

Some governours, magistrates, commanders, officers, and others monopolize in their provinces and circuits the wine, oyl, vinegar, Indian wheat [maize], and all the other mean commodities; and by so doing, besides the breach of the king's orders, they taint and vilify their blood, which they so much glory in and do boast of; taking upon them without any scruple all the mischiefs they bring upon the poor people. It happen'd at Mexico, before I came to that city, that some gentlemen and merchants meeting in connection with a religious brotherhood, one of the gentlemen stept forth and very proudly said, it was not proper that the gentry should walk indiscriminately mingled with the merchants in that procession; but that each rank should go by itself distinct from the rest. One of the merchants stood up and said: 'I like what Mr N— has proposed, for it is not proper that we merchants who deal in velvet, rich silks, cloth of gold, etc. should have to mix with the gentlemen who trade in Indian wheat, tomatoes, peppers and such like things!'[48]

The *corregidores*, being the lieutenants of the king, were in a position to pick and choose when it came to implementing crown decisions; some they acted upon, others they simply disregarded. This circumstance was particularly irritating to the Creoles, for as they saw it, the viceroy's officers were very lax with whatever did not suit their interests and very strict with whatever did, especially anything connected with the segregation policy. Juan Fernández de Vivero, a Creole citizen of Tlaxcala who composed a tract in 1634, addressed to

[47]Juan de Palafox, *Cartas Reservadas al Rey, BAGN* 1st series, ii (1931), 814–19; *CDHE* xxvi. 171; the term *gachupín* or *cachupín* is defined by Juan de Cárdenas, a Creole author, as meaning 'newcomer', see Cárdenas, *Problemas y Secretas Maravillosos de las Indias* (1591; Madrid, 1945), pp. 170–7, and this is the sense in which it was used in contemporary documents.
[48]See *The Travels and Controversies of Friar Domingo Navarrete, 1618–1686*, ed. J. S. Cummins, Hakluyt Society publications, 2nd series, cxviii (2 vols., Cambridge, 1962), i. 36–7.

the king, calling for an end to segregation and the merging of the 'Indian' and 'Spanish' communities, was particularly irate in this respect. He denounced the viceroy's officers not only as extortioners but hypocrites who wrapped their actions in the wording of the king's enactments, while in reality caring nothing for the king's justice. The very same people who were the chief oppressors of the Indians, he declared, tied the hands of the Spaniards and restricted them to certain areas saying that they did this to protect the Indians from them! One readily understands, reading Fernández de Vivero's comments on the *corregidores'* style of protecting of the Indians, Viceroy Mancera's observation: 'human malice so perverts everything that it changes the very shields designed to protect these poor people into weapons for attacking them.'[49]

Of course the Spanish population in Mexico was not wholly confined to the areas of the Spanish republic, but the point that Fernández de Vivero and his fellow Creoles were making was that the colonists were concentrated in certain districts owing to the efforts of the administration, to such an extent that the smattering of Spaniards resident in such 'Indian' centres as his own home town of Tlaxcala was too small to be able to evade the economic grip of the *corregidores* over those areas. Consequently trade and other economic relations between Spaniards and Indians was subject to all kinds of interference, so much so that such intercourse was impossible unless with the *corregidor*'s consent. Any Spaniard, asserted Fernández de Vivero, who had not cleared himself with the right officer and was caught trading with the Indians of that officer's district would be stripped of all he had with him and be lucky to be left with the wherewithal to make his way home.[50]

The habit of the viceroys and of their officers of defending the existing system and the segregation policy in social and moral terms provoked a great controversy in seventeenth-century Mexico over the real situation of the Indians in Mexican society. While the administration was content to reiterate the traditional view of the crown that the Indians, or what was left of them, could be saved only by shielding them as far as possible from contact with the Spaniards, Negroes, and *mestizos*, the Creoles vigorously rejected such thinking. They held that the Indians could scarcely suffer worse oppression than that from which they suffered already in the 'Indian' republic, and that they would in fact benefit from being merged with the elements of the

[49]Quoted by François Chevalier, *Land and Society*, p. 207.
[50]Fernández de Vivero, op. cit., BM Add. MS. 13, 974, fol. 160; see also Cristobal de Molina, *Informe*, fol. 4, and Cuevas Dávalos's letter to council.

'Spanish' republic.[51] They supported this contention with the argument that the Indians who lived and worked in the Spanish zones enjoyed a higher standard of living than did their brethren who remained in the Indian communities, and tended to become stronger and more resistant to disease by imitating the life-style of the Spaniards and mestizos, and by eating more and better food.

It is difficult to know how much weight to ascribe to this Creole assertion. In their tracts, the colonists spoke of the labour system prevailing in the 'Spanish' republic as a free-bargaining wage system which left the Indian worker at liberty to work where he pleased and which put money in his pocket. In reality the Indian in Spanish employ, weak and gullible, was pitilessly exploited, and in many cases, in the mines as well as on the haciendas, subjected to the system of service known as debt-labour.[52] He would be given an advance of wages or goods, and then be put to work to pay off this debt; meanwhile, the debt was perpetuated by fresh advances in such a way that it was never paid off. Debt-labour in the textile mills differed from debt-peonage on the haciendas only in being even more squalid. The Carmelite friar Antonio Vázquez de Espinosa observes that the factory owners of Puebla, the textile capital of New Spain, though 'persons correct in their Christianity', were accustomed to hire special bullies to ensnare and trick the Indians and get them into their *obrajes*, from which, once they were enclosed, they had about as much chance of escaping as from prison.[53] In some cases, *obraje* owners locked their Indians up at night in guarded dormitories.

Yet however deplorable in many respects were conditions on the haciendas and in the mines and mills, they may well have been better than conditions under the Indian hierarchy and the *corregidores*. One has to admit, at least, that there was a continual seepage of Indians, despite the efforts of both Spanish and Indian officers to arrest it, away from the traditional Indian towns and congregations and villages, to the centres of Spanish population. Indeed, Indian migration in the seventeenth as in the sixteenth century, little discussed though it is, was one of the major factors shaping the development of the viceroyalty. In general, the ancient Indian cities and towns, especially those where few Spaniards had settled, lost population faster than the over-all rate of

[51] Gómez de Cervantes *La Vida económica*, p. 138; *El Doctor Hernan Carrillo Altamirano...* fol. 4; Fernández de Vivero, op. cit. BM Add. 13, 974, fol. 160[v]; Domingo Lázaro de Arregui, *Descripción de la Nueva Galicia* (1621), ed. F. Chevalier (Seville, 1946), p. 27; Cuevas Dávalos to council, 26 Nov. 1663, in M. Cueras, *Historia de la Iglesia en México* (5 vols., Mexico, 1946), iii. 458–63.
[52] Gibson, *The Aztecs*, pp. 252–4; Bakewell, *Silver Mining and Society*, p. 126.
[53] *Descripción de la Nueva España*, p. 89.

depopulation and continued to lose inhabitants until very late in the seventeenth century, while the Spanish new towns steadily gained Indians. The Indian population of Texcoco fell from roughly 77,000 in 1570 to a miserable 8,000 or so (2,074 adult male tributaries) in 1644,[54] a level almost certainly less than one-fifteenth of the Texcocan population of 1519. Tlaxcala, as we have seen, had fallen by 1669 to a level far less than one-fifteenth of the population it had boasted in 1519. Cholula, whose deserted suburbs in 1630 seemed more extensive to Bernabé Cobo than those of contemporary Seville, had only some 12,000 Indians in 1644 (2,873 tributaries),[55] and only 9,000 by 1669.[56] Huejotzingo, by 1644, had dwindled to about 9,000.[57] The Tlatelolco division of Mexico City had shrunk to about 12,000 Indians in 1623 (2,896 tributaries),[58] to 6,000 (1,480 tributaries) in 1634,[59] to under 6,000 (1,251 tributaries) at its low point in 1646,[60] and had only registered a very slight recovery (1,510 tributaries) by 1658.[61] The Indian population of Mexico City minus Tlatelolco had fallen, by the mid-seventeenth century, to approximately 20,000.[62] Puebla de los Angeles, on the other hand, which had had no Indian population in 1519, had 10,000–12,000 Indians in the 1640s,[63] in its 'Indian' or outer wards, besides another 5,000 or so living in the large 'Spanish' city centre; the Indians were mainly Tlaxcaltec and Cholultec by extraction but with Mixtec, Zapotec, and many other elements mixed

[54] Miranda, 'La población indígena', *Historia Mexicana*, xii. 188.
[55] Ibid.
[56] BNX 1066, fol. 56.
[57] Miranda, 'La población indígena'.
[58] *Moderación de doctrinas de la real corona administrados por las ordenes mendicantes*, 1623, in *Documentos Para la Historia del México Colonial* ed. F. V. Scholes and E. B. Adams (Mexico, 1959), vi. 49.
[59] Gibson, *The Aztecs*, p. 461, citing AGN Indios.
[60] ADI Palafox papers liv, fol. 160.
[61] Miranda, 'La población indígena'; Viceroy Albuquerque gives 1,476 tributaries for 1654, ADA A15c17 exp. 27: Albuquerque to Méndez de Haro, 17 Mar. 1654.
[62] Gibson, *The Aztecs*, p. 462, gives 4,940 tributaries for 1659 citing AGI contaduría; Albuquerque gives 4,624 tributaries for 1654, ADA a15c17, exp. 27; Palafox gives 4,814 for 1646, ADI Palafox papers liv, fol. 154v. One must remember, in the case of Mexico City particularly, that a certain number of espanolized or mestizoized Indians living in the Spanish city centre were not registered on the tribute lists.
[63] Palafox gives 2,238 tributaries for the wards of San Pablo, San Sebastian, San Francisco, and Santiago in 1646, ADI Palafox papers liv, fol. 154v; Miranda gives 3,143 tributaries for all of 'Indian' or outer Puebla, Miranda, 'La población indígena'; Albuquerque, however gives 3,943 tributaries for the whole of Puebla, ADA a15c17 exp. 27 indicating a total Indian population for Puebla in 1654 of about 16,000.

in. Valladolid, capital of Michoacán, another new town, had in the 1620s approximately 3,000 Indians, chiefly Tarascans.[64] The Querétaro-Xilotepec district, again newly developed, had some 10,000 sedentary Indians (2,500 tributaries) in 1644, Aztec, Chichimec, Otomi, and Tarascan.[65] The Celaya-Acámbaro region had some 8,000 sedentary Indians, again of very mixed origin.[66] Zacatecas had several thousand Indians, Aztecs, Tlaxcaltecs, Otomies, and especially Tarascans; though some of these Indians were not really settled, being part of that sizeable floating population characteristic of all the mining towns, at least in times of prosperity.[67]

Admittedly, one might object that much of this Indian migration, being migration into the outer wards of the new towns, is not necessarily evidence of seepage from the 'Indian' republic into the 'Spanish'. Indeed, the new towns, Puebla and Valladolid particularly, tended to keep their 'Indian' wards at some distance from the inner city. But it is also true that flight into the non-Indian zones was, for at least some Indians, an attractive prospect. Many Indians, it is clear, were quite willing to move on to the haciendas.[68] Many others showed an unmistakable preference for the city centres. The flight of Texcocan Indians to the 'Spanish' sector of Mexico City in the 1620s and 1630s, for example, was a source of considerable concern to the Spanish authorities; Viceroy Cerralvo actually ordered his officers in the capital to help the Indian officers of Texcoco retrieve fugitives working in Spanish workshops, residences, and other establishments and take them back to their home town.[69] Some of these Texcocans, we are told, had abandoned womenfolk, children, and plots of land in expectation of better things under the Spaniards.

But the truth or falsity of the conflicting claims of viceroys' officers and colonists is less important with respect to our present purpose, than the fact that they were conflicting. Having established that there was this clash of interests between officers and settlers over the Indians, it is important to ascertain whether the conflict was of an essentially

[64]*Documentos para la historia de la ciudad de Valladolid, hoy Morelia, 1541–1624*, sobretiro del *BAGN*, 2nd series, iii. 2 (Mexico, 1962), docs. xxiv and xxv.

[65]Miranda, 'La población indígena', p. 188.

[66]Ibid.

[67]Mota y Escobar says that for this reason it is not possible to be exact concerning the number of Indians in the city, *Descripción geográfica*, p. 66.

[68]See Mota y Escobar's remarks quoted by Alejandra Moreno Toscano in 'Tres problemas en la geografía del maíz, 1600–1624', *Historia Mexicana*, xiv (1965), 649, where he speaks of ordinary Indians 'fleeing' from their communities to the haciendas.

[69]AGN Indios x, fol. 19.

marginal or short-term character, barely scraping the surface of Indian life, or whether, on the other hand, it was a major social tension affecting the situation and development of the Indian community in a much more fundamental way. To this end it is necessary to examine Indian community structure more closely.

The Conquest, the overthrow of the Aztecs, and the elimination of the pagan priesthood had dealt a severe blow to the Indian ruling class. Although many Indian nobles retained power and wealth, much, if not most, of the old hierarchy of offices and dignities was swept away. However, this disruption, as was indicated in the Introduction, was quickly compensated for in the sixteenth century by the formation of a new Indian ruling class partly out of elements of the old and partly out of new elements. On the one hand, some of the old caciques and principals and their heirs remained, while in other cases ambitious *maceguales* (commoners) who had succeeded in thrusting themselves forward during the immediate post-Conquest disorders managed to establish themselves as principals. Once the reconstruction of Indian society had made some progress, the class distinction became more rigid and there ceased to be much real possibility of advancement from macegual to principal status. Almost from the first, the principals consciously sought to widen the gap between themselves and the Indian mass by adopting Spanish culture, or at least certain strands of it, and seeking to conform to the Spanish image of the gentleman and hidalgo. They built residences for themselves in the Spanish manner which stood out in stark contrast to the humble adobe dwellings of those beneath them, sought permission of the viceroys to wear Spanish costume, bear arms, and ride horseback with saddle and spurs, permission that was fairly freely given, and usually adopted Spanish names sometimes with quite comic results.[70] Those Indian principals who could trace their lineage back to pre-Conquest aristocratic, or better still princely, clans indulged in a taste for genealogy comparable with that of any Spanish hidalgo, as the *Crónica Mexicoyotl* of Alvarado Tezozomoc amply demonstrates.[71] In some cases, Indian principals became considerable landowners or took to trading on a large scale; sometimes they owned Negro slaves and employed mulatto servants. Juan Hernández, for example, cacique of San Sebastian near Tehuacán in the 1620s, owned among other things a train of fifty mules with which he traded in fruit,

---

[70] Fray Domingo Navarrete mentions a cacique whom he met in a village on the road to Acapulco whose son was named Don Francisco de Aragón y Portugal y Mendoza y Guzmán y Manrique y Campuzano, *The Travels and Controversies of Friar Domingo Navarrete*, i. 36.

[71] Hernando Alvarado Tezozomoc, *Crónica Mexicoyotl*, tr. and ed. A. León (Mexico, 1949).

herbs, and other foodstuffs, and had Negroes and mulattoes in his service as well as Indians.[72]

The political activity of the Indian ruling class, in form at least, changed considerably with the reconstruction.[73] In the mid-sixteenth century, there arose what the Nahuatl-speaking Indians called *gobernadoryotl*, the system of electing community leaders, or governors, who served as the heads of the Indian community councils which were also new. The governor of a community was elected for a term of one year from among the principals of the community,[74] as also were the rest of the council, the *alcaldes* and *regidores*. The system was closely derived from Spanish *cabildo* practice though with a number of specifically Indian adjustments. Re-election, though theoretically illegal, was fairly widespread and some governors and councillors held office for years on end. In general, it was quite usual for offices to rotate among a small clique. Also some principals, such as the seventeenth-century Indian historian Fernando de Alva Ixtlilxochitl, who served at different times as governor of Tlalmanalco and Texcoco,[75] tended to become professional officers circulating from one position to another. The total number of councillors in an Indian *cabildo* varied from place to place, but was usually between five and ten, depending normally on the size of the town. The Indian *cabildo* of Mexico City, which was the largest of all, had more than a dozen members.

The Indian governors and councillors were responsible for the internal management of the 'Indian' republic and in theory represented the interests of the Indian community as a whole. Their main functions in practice were to maintain order, to supervise communal lands, food and water stocks, and the local market, to organize the *repartimiento* and collect the tribute on behalf of the *corregidor*, and to enforce church attendance. They handled the mass of the Indian population by means of an intermediate class who, for want of a better term, might be called the Indian lesser officers. These consisted of major-domos responsible for communal properties, *mandones* or constables whose job was to carry out the *cabildo*'s instructions, inflict floggings and other punishments on wrongdoers, and compel church-going, and various sorts of ecclesiastical officers. All of these officials were paid salaries from the communal chest and were marked off from the rest of

[72] AGN Indios x, fol. 11.

[73] Gibson, *The Aztecs*, pp. 166–93; see also François Chevalier, 'Les Municipalités indiennes en Nouvelle Espagne, 1520–1620', *Anuario de historia de derecho español*, xv (1944), 352–86.

[74] Gibson, *The Aztecs*, p. 176.

[75] Ibid., p. 172.

the Indians by the privilege of exemption from the Indian share-out. Altogether principals and lesser officers in the early seventeenth century seem to have amounted to about 5 to 10 per cent of the Indian population; in Cuernavaca in 1629, for instance, there were 3,000 tributaries of whom 200, or one-fifteenth, were exempt from forced labour, being either principals or office-holders, secular or ecclesiastical or both.[76]

There is little sign that these privileged Indians were held in any particular esteem or affection by ordinary Indians, and some considerable evidence to suggest that they were generally harsh, domineering, and corrupt.[77] The meekness and docility for which the sedentary Indian was renowned seemed to undergo, the moment an Indian was promoted over his fellows, an immediate change into arrogance. This distasteful trait in Indian society, still conspicuous in the time of Baron von Humboldt,[78] added considerably to the burden borne by the mass of Indians. If the Indians were oppressed by those who were not Indians, they were additionally oppressed by their own hierarchy. The flight of Indians from Texcoco to Mexico City, we are told, was motivated as much by desire to evade the tyranny of the *mandones* as by any other factor. In some cases, Indian principals were guilty of appalling callousness; they would even, on occasion, consign Indians, for trifling offences, to years, even a life-time, of drudgery in the textile mills in return for money from the owners.[79]

However, there were grave weaknesses in the position of the Indian principals, and in the seventeenth century they were losing ground. The heyday of Indian local government under the reconstruction (1550–80) was now long passed.[80] Losses from disease among privileged Indians, combined with the passing of the bulk of the labour force in some 'Indian' areas into Spanish employ, rendered it increasingly difficult, in those areas at least, to maintain the hierarchy

[76]AGN Indios x, fol. 85.

[77]See, for instance, Martín Enríques, *Instrución*, *CDHE*, xvi. 377; *Parecer del doctor Alonso Zorita* (1584) in *Documentos Inéditos del Siglo xvi* doc. lxiii, p. 338; Mendieta, *Historia eclesiástica Indiana*, p. 448; BND 3636, fols. 116ᵛ–117: Velasco II to council, 10 Mar. 1592. Viceroy Velasco affirmed that the Indian principals treated their own people even more harshly than did the Spaniards and Negroes.

[78]'Les villages indiens sont gouvernés', remarked von Humboldt, 'par des magistrats de la race cuivrée: un alcalde indien exerce son pouvoir avec un dureté d'autant plus grande, qu'il est sûr d'être soutenu ou par le curé ou par le subdelegué espagnol. L'oppression a partout les mêmes effets, partout elle corrompt la morale.' Alexander von Humboldt, *Essai politique sur le royaume de la Nouvelle Espagne* (4 vols., Paris, 1811), i. 412–13.

[79]*FHT* vii. 137–8.

[80]Gibson, *The Aztecs*, pp. 190–1.

at all. The *cabildo* of Texcoco, for example, a city which suffered particularly severely from the plague of 1629–34,[81] informed the viceroy in the early 1630s that owing to the pestilence there were hardly any Indians left from whom to elect *regidores* and *mandones* apart from those who were working as debt-labourers on haciendas or in *obrajes*, and that it was impossible to elect the latter since their employers refused to let them go, claiming that they were in debt and had to work off that debt.[82] The hierarchy at Tepeaca and Tecamachalco, according to Bishop Mota y Escobar, had been gravely weakened even by the beginning of the century.[83] Undoubtedly, the rewards of service and the value of privilege in Indian communities located in areas of heavy Spanish settlement were steadily withering away.

Nevertheless, where Indian principals still had something left to defend apart from their trade and haciendas, they became involved in the conflict between Spanish bureaucracy and enterprise. This was quite natural, for the colonists generally aspired to promote the dissolution of the segregation policy and to subject the whole Indian population to the mechanism of their own economic needs, and this inevitably meant the disintegration of the Indian hierarchy and an end to community obligations and traditional community life. Accordingly, in general, the Indian principals opposed the interests of the colonists and joined forces with the *corregidores* in forming a united bureaucratic front. In particular, they intervened in the tug-of-war for Indian workers and tried to halt the inexorable drift on to the haciendas and into the mines and *obrajes* while at the same time striving to preserve at least a minimum of control over those Indians who did migrate into the 'Spanish' sector. This effort on the part of the Indian officer class is not difficult to document. The collection of Zavala and Castelo gives various instances in the seventeenth century in which Indian officers, usually encouraged by Spanish officers, acted to remove labourers from Spanish haciendas and more or less forcibly resettled them in their native towns and villages.[84] The officers of the town council of Chalco, for instance, urged on by the local *corregidor*, took workers from the fields of Francisco Pérez, owner of three haciendas in the region. The officers of Huejotzingo deprived Diego de Zumoza, owner of two haciendas, of part of his work force. The wheat producers of the Atlixco valley were frequently at loggerheads with the governor and

81 Especially in 1631, see AGN Indios x, fols. 229, 275.
82 AGN Indios x, fol. 228V.
83 See once again Alejandra Moreno Toscano, 'Tres problemas en la geografía del maíz, 1600–1624', *Historia Mexicana*, xiv. 649.
84 *FHT* vi. 547–86; and also vii. 4–10, 471–8.

cabildo of Cholula again over workers whom Indian officers were trying to retrieve from Spanish fields.

As in the countryside, so in the city centres. In Mexico City, for instance, in the 1620s and 1630s Indian officers became entangled in a whole variety of squabbles with spanish employers as is illustrated by the following extract from an ordinance of Viceroy Cerralvo:

... the governor and *Regidores* of the Indians of San Juan ... inform me that in the bakeries, meat-stores, and residences of the Spaniards of this city, there work many Indian tributaries. But when the *mandones* come to collect the tribute from the said Indians ... the Spaniards who employ them do not let the officers collect the money ... rather they insult and hit them. Consequently, the *cabildo* finds itself unable to submit its tribute on time and asks me that I should remedy the situation. Wherefore I empower the Indian officers of the *cabildo* to enter any establishment or house where Indians work, both to collect tribute, and to remove any carpenters, masons, and other skilled workmen who are listed for labour service on the viceregal palace, or the city drainage works, and neither shall Spaniards in whose employ such workmen may be attempt to prevent this ...[85]

Mexico City was an exception among the cities with a large Spanish citizenry, regarding the effectiveness of Indian institutions; for here the authority of the *corregidor* was reinforced by the proximity of the viceroy. Elsewhere, in towns with many Spaniards, the position of the Indian authorities was generally very weak. In Querétaro, the Indian *cabildo* was, for everything other than maintaining discipline in the suburbs, virtually powerless, as can be seen from the extreme difficulty that it experienced in drafting labour. The Indians of Querétaro were under obligation to supply *repartimiento* labour to the ailing mines of Xichu, fifty miles to the north, but the native officers of Querétaro were quite unable to provide the amount of labour due, for by the early seventeenth century nearly all the Indians of Querétaro were employees on haciendas or in Spanish establishments in the town, and therefore effectively beyond the reach of the *mandones*. In this exigency, the *cabildo* was reduced to snatching workers from a hacienda belonging to the nuns of Querétaro's convent of Santa Clara though it only created further difficulties for itself by so doing.[86] In Zacatecas, though little is known of the role of the Indian officers in the suburbs, it seems clear once again that their role was mainly confined to the maintaining of order in the Indian districts.[87]

The Indian principals and lesser officers, then, in many areas, joined

[85] AGN Indios xii, fol. 23.
[86] AGN Indios xii, fols. 195^V–197; *FHT* vii. 425–6.
[87] Bakewell, *Silver Mining and Society*, pp. 110–11.

in the contest between Spanish officers and colonists on the side of the former, thus forming a broad bureaucratic front. This fact leads on to the question of what other element or elements had a stake in the 'Indian' republic and therefore in the segregation policy, and were therefore likely to respond, in the political sphere, in the same way. Certainly there was at least one other such group, the friars.

The record of the mendicant clergy in post-Conquest Mexico, and particularly of the Franciscans, is, as we have seen, one full of distinction and interest. The friars had played a leading role in the reconstruction of Indian society, had interpreted Christianity for the Indians, and become their religious and moral tutors, taking control of the bulk of the Indian parishes in the process. Moreover, despite the *cocoliztli* of 1545–8 and the subsequent alienation of many ordinary Indians from the friars and the corresponding mendicant disillusionment with the Indians, relations between the religious orders and the Indian communities had remained very close. However, from as early as the 1530s[88] the friars had been on bad terms with the bishops and the secular clergy, and by the 1560s and 1570s, with the growth of the secular clergy, friction between the two clerical factions had become acute. The secular clergy considered that the Indian parishes, especially in Mexico City and Puebla and other areas where there were large concentrations of Spanish population, should be administered by themselves, while the friars ensconced in the Indian communities, with their buildings and property and rights to food and labour service from the Indians, were naturally disinclined to surrender them. There were cases of violence, notably in 1559 in Puebla, when the diocesan clergy invaded the Dominican friary and broke the teeth of the prior, and in 1569 in Mexico City, when an attempt by the diocesans backed by Creoles to stop a procession of Franciscans and Indians was repulsed by volleys of stones from the Indians. Then, in 1583, partly under pressure from Archbishop Moya de Contreras, a harsh critic of the mendicants whom he accounted a heavy burden on the Indians, vain parasites who used Indian labour not just for chores and providing food but to build an excessive number of excessively well-adorned ecclesiastical buildings,[89] Madrid empowered the bishops to 'secularize' Indian parishes under certain circumstances. The ruling was soon withdrawn when the strength of mendicant resistance to the policy was felt,[90] but the friars remained, and were to remain throughout the seventeenth century, hard pressed and on the defensive. And yet, though the secular

[88] Ricard, *La 'Conquête Spirituelle'*, 292.
[89] *Cartas de Indias*, pp. 222–3.
[90] *Un desconocido cedulario del siglo xvi*, ed. A. M. Carreño (Mexico, 1944), pp. 358–60.

clergy advanced rapidly in both numbers and education, during the period of the economic boom, 1580—1620, regarding numbers because of the great increase of the white population during the period and regarding education because of the highly effective activities of the newly arrived Jesuits, the mendicants proved able to hold most of what they had. Although the bishops' showing in the race to expand clerical resources and numbers was strong, the friars more than matched their effort, building up from 800 friars in New Spain in 1559[91] to 1,500 by the 1580s,[92] and roughly 3,000 by 1650,[93] with about 1,000 friars in Mexico City alone.[94] This compared with diocesan forces of about 1,500 in the three provinces of Mexico, Puebla, and Michoacán, and probably less than 2,000 all told.[95]

[91] Ricard, La 'Conquête Spirituelle', p. 35

[92] Cartas de religiosos, p. 176.

[93] In the 1650s, there were somewhat over 2,000 regular clergy in the mendicant province of Mexico (which included the diocese of Puebla), excluding about 300 Jesuits, made up of some 650 Franciscans, 490 Augustinians, 264 Mercenarians, 238 Carmelites, 54 discalced Franciscans, and approximately 500 Dominicans and other sorts of friars, ADA a15c17 no. 25: Albuquerque to council, 12 Mar. 1654; ACM xxiii. 35; in addition there were 140 friars in the Franciscan province of Zacatecas, AHN documentos de Indias 356: 'Noticias sobre el orden de los franciscanos', fol. 5; roughly 250 Franciscans and Augustinians in the mendicant province of Michoacán, Isidro Felix de Espinosa, Crónica de la provincia franciscana de los apóstoles San Pedro y San Pablo de Michoacán (1731) (Mexico, 1945) pp. 459—62; about 110 Franciscans in the Yucatan, Descripción de la Nueva España, p. 77; perhaps 300 Dominicans in Oaxaca, and another 100 to 200 friars, possibly, in Guadalajara, New Biscay, and New León.

[94] The total number of ecclesiastical personnel in Mexico City in the mid-seventeenth century, including about 1,000 nuns, was more than 2,500, a not inconsiderable proportion of the white population; in Puebla, apparently, there were some 1,400, including some 600 nuns; in Valladolid, capital of Michoacán, there were in 1654, according to the Inquisition, more ecclesiastical personnel than white laity; see Fray Balthasar de Medina, Chronica de la santa provincia de San Diego de Mexico, de religiosos descalcos de N.S.P.S. Francisco en la Nueva España (Mexico, 1682), pp. 238, 244; La Puebla de los Angeles en el siglo xvii, doc. ed. Mariano Cuevas (Mexico, 1945), pp. 80—96; IAH 101 ant., p. 130.

[95] In 1635 there were 700 secular clergy in the diocese of Puebla, rising to well over 1,000 by the 1690s, Alegaciones del clero, fols. 3, 5ᵛ; La Puebla de los Angeles, p. 53; in the diocese of Mexico somewhat less, in the region of 500, Cedulario de los siglos, p. 275; and in Michoacán by the 1640s, some 300, ADI Palafox papers liv, fol. 366; when one includes the Jesuits, of whom there were between 350 and 400 in the mid-seventeenth century, the figure of 6,000 for the total number of ordained priests in New Spain in the 1640s, the figure accepted at the time, appears to be only a slight exaggeration, see Diez de la Calle, Memorial y noticias, fol. 45, and Gil González Dávila, Teatro eclesiastico de la primitiva iglesia de las Indias occidentales, vidas de sus arzobispos, obispos, y cosas memorables de sus sedes (Madrid, 1649), pp. 16—17; Viceroy Mancera calculated that there were 2,000 altogether in the province of Puebla alone, Instrucciones que los virreyes dejaron, pp. 268—9.

Obviously, so large a mendicant establishment required considerable support, and despite the growth of the white population and the increase in donations that may be supposed to have gone with it, much of this sustenance had to be found by the friars themselves, and found where they were strong, in the 'Indian' republic. The Dominican and Augustinian friars began to acquire landed property on a large scale, in emulation perhaps of the Jesuits, but the Franciscans, worried perhaps by the implications of property in regard to their vows, tended to avoid this recourse and seek more discreet means.[96] Traditionally, as Mendieta avowed enthusiastically, the main burden of supporting the Franciscan establishment in Mexico had rested with the Indians who had always given liberally, and now the Franciscans met their expanded needs by doubling and trebling the support they received from their flock, despite the fact that that flock was now sadly reduced in size. The friars drew their support in various forms; for the provisioning of their friaries they made full use of their old privilege of receiving their food free or at only a nominal price, for building and doing general chores they received *repartimiento* labour in considerable quantities, and in some cases they charged fees, sometimes exorbitant fees,[97] for the sacraments.

But there was also another reason for the comparative strength of the friars in the seventeenth century, a reason which pertains closely to the argument that the clash of interests between Creoles and administration was a major, possibly overriding, factor in the development of the viceroyalty in this period: for the friars joined hands in alliance with the viceroy's officers. This undoubtedly is a remarkable development, for, as we have seen, although the friars were on good terms with various sixteenth-century viceroys, notably Velasco I, Villamanrique, and Monterrey,[98] there was also a strong tendency to conflict with the *corregidores*, a tendency motivated partly by outrage at the rapacity of those officials, especially in the case of Mendieta,[99] but also unhappily by less moral considerations regarding influence and power in the Indian communities.[100] Moreover, mendicants and administration were still very much at loggerheads in the time of Viceroy Montesclaros (1603–7) who reveals in his report to his successor a sordid picture of friars and officers contending for control of an unresisting and pitilessly exploited Indian population; 'the pretext that is given,' wrote the marquis, 'for everything that the friars propose regarding the Indians in

[96] Chevalier, *Land and Society*, pp. 237–9.
[97] AGN Indios x, fols. 2, 9, AGN Indios xii, fol. 101ᵛ, AGN Indios xvi, fol. 22; IAH col. P. T. xxxi–i, fol. 28.
[98] Mendieta, *Historia eclesiástica Indiana*, p. 517
[99] Ibid., p. 511.
[100] Ricard, *La 'Conquête Spirituelle'*, p. 183.

these provinces is the defence and betterment of the Indians, however the truth is . . . that the heaviest oppression that the Indians suffer, as regards labour service, payments, and contributions, is that of the friars.'[101] But, from Montesclaros's time onwards, the picture changes rapidly. The friars, perceiving that the rising tide of Creole dissatisfaction and the anger of the secular clergy now posed a much greater threat to their position than the viceroy's officers, cease to complain of the *corregidores'* methods and accept that they must share dominance of the Indians, while the *corregidores*, coming under pressure themselves from the same forces, cease to regard the friars as rivals and begin to look on them instead as welcome allies in the fight against the colonists; thus was a united bureaucratic front of viceroy's officers, Indian officers, and mendicants formed. From Viceroy Guadalcázar's time onwards, as we shall see repeatedly, friars and administration, as far as politics were concerned, worked always together.

As a result of the change, it ceased to be the viceroys and their officers who accused the friars of hypocrisy and corruption, and was increasingly the colonists themselves who performed this role. Moreover, they had every reason to extend their anger to the friars, for the alliance of the mendicants with the *corregidores* was in practice far more than a mere tacit understanding. The collection of Zavala and Castelo provides instances not only of friars encouraging Spanish and Indian officers to remove Indian workers from Spanish estates, but of their actually intervening and whisking off Indians from haciendas themselves, to take them back to their communities and restore them to the control of principals and *mandones*.[102] Fernández de Vivero, in fact, piles even more blame at the door of the mendicants for New Spain's ills, and for the rigours of segregation, than he does at the door of the *corregidores* and speaks of mendicant motivation as Montesclaros had done, accusing them of pretending to protect the Indians while in fact only indulging their own repulsive greed.[103] For their part, the friars showed their feelings for the colonists in various ways, removing labourers from their estates being only one of them. There was also a tendency, in 'Indian' areas, for the friars to obstruct the religious life of Spaniards and on occasion to withhold the sacraments from them.[104]

However, it would be unjust to say that the regulars joined with the Spanish and Indian officers against Creole economic, social, and political interests, solely to protect their influence and holdings. There was another side to the question, for undoubtedly there were some

[101] *CDHE* xxvi. 163–4.
[102] See, for instance, *FHT* vii. 4–5, and 137–8.
[103] Fernández de Vivero, op. cit., BM Add. MS. 13, 974, fols. 158–9.
[104] AGN Indios x, fols. 35, 213^v.

friars in Mexico, despite the moral deterioration of the orders in the seventeenth century, who were deeply worried concerning the spiritual situation of the Indians, and convinced, on moral and religious grounds, that it would be wrong of the regulars to relinquish their hold on the Indian Church.

The seriousness of the Indian question from the moral and religious point of view cannot be doubted. As we have seen, the Indians, or many of them, had turned from faith to despair. 'Even in Mexico City,' wrote Torquemada, 'if we were not to show the perseverance that we do in collecting [the Indians] on Sundays and in making them hear mass, I can not doubt that in a short time they would not only forget the Christian prayers that they have been taught, but would even neglect to attend mass and sermon.'[105] Indian alcoholism, though already a fearful problem by the middle of the sixteenth century, continued to wreak havoc among the Indians throughout the seventeenth as well. The Indians showed no sign of developing any resistance to the demoralizing effects of drinking to excess, but rather were becoming more and more demoralized.[106]

The remedy, in the view of conscientious friars, the only way to relieve the suffering of the Indians and to restore some meaning to their lives was to revive and strengthen that particular Indian Catholicism that had sprung up in the wake of the conversion. Torquemada, like Mendieta before him, was forever harking back to the achievements of Peter of Ghent and the first missionaries and praising their work. The path to be followed now, declared Torquemada, was the same as that which had led to such spectacular successes eight decades before—the presenting of a glittering and magnificent Catholicism, a Catholicism of elaborate ceremony, music, dance, flowers, and song. 'No one can deny', insisted Torquemada, 'that highly decorative churches and splendid services are essential if we are to redeem these Indians and infuse them with a deeper love for the faith.' For this reason, he explained

...such care is taken by the friars to conduct services with so many musicians, singers, and instrumentalists, with deacons assisting the officiating friar, with long coloured cassocks and white surplices, with the altar bedecked with candelabra and incensories ... (so that) at the moment of raising the host and sacred body of Christ our Lord, the

---

[105]Juan de Torquemada, *Razones informativas que las tres ordenes mendicantes ... dan por donde no les conviene subjectar sus religiosos al examen de los obispos* (1622) in the *Nueva Colección de documentos para la historia de México* ed. Joaquín García Icazbalceta (5 vols., Mexico, 1886–92), v. 130.

[106]See particularly Agustín de Vetancurt, *Teatro Mexicano*, part 1 (Mexico, 1698), pp. 95–100.

scene with its magnificence, hierarchy, and ringing of bells, seems like heaven enacted here upon earth.[107]

This indeed was the crux of the mendicant defence of their refusal to relinquish control of the Indian parishes. For what, as Torquemada enquired, could one or two secular priests do to compare with the glittering manifestations of faith of which the friars were capable? Undoubtedly, the answer was very little. Should the bishops have their way, ran the mendicant argument, everything would be put at risk; the Indians would lose what little reverence they still had, and might even abandon the church entirely.

Such then was the position of the friars in seventeenth-century Mexico: they joined hands with the viceroy's officers and the Indian hierarchy. The diocesan clergy, as we have already suggested and as one would expect, took the other side and joined with the colonists. This was quite natural, for the secular clergy in colonial Mexico, like the secular clergy in most Catholic societies, enjoyed much closer links with the (white) laity than did the regulars. Moreover, as we have said, the friars, preoccupied with the Indians, had always been content to leave the spiritual administration of the Spaniards, and indeed the Negroes, mulattoes, and mestizos, to the seculars. Futhermore, the secular clergy were closely tied to the Mexican-Spanish population by blood, and the lower secular clergy in particular were strongly Creole in character. They were not only priests to the colonists, but also relatives, and this, in an age when bonds of kinship loomed large in economic and political life, was an extremely significant connection. The mendicants placed considerable emphasis on it in their criticisms of the seculars.[108] Would not the secular clergy, if ever they took over the Indian parishes, use their ecclesiastical power as a lever with which to subject the Indian population more effectively to the desires of their lay cousins and friends? The suggestion had much logic to it. Certainly Creole laymen, knowing the effects of the ecclesiastical ascendancy of the secular clergy over Indians from their experience of it in the 'Spanish' zones, vigorously advocated extending that ascendancy to the Indian church as a whole. Nor can Creole enthusiasm for the idea be explained simply in terms of the colonists' concern to find more livings and situations for the secular clergy. It was clear to everyone that the victory of the diocesans would inevitably involve a great strengthening in the economic position of the settlers. Indeed Fernández de Vivero valued

---

[107]Torquemada, *Razones Informativas, Nueva Colección*, v. 173.

[108]*Cartas de Religiosos*, p. 175; *Documentos inéditos del siglo xvi para la historia de México*, ed. Mariano Cuevas (Mexico, 1914), pp. 298–300; see also AGI México 43, r 2: 'Memorial puntado a su ex. por el procurador de indios', fol. 4.

the secular clergy so highly as a prop to Creole interests that he seems to have thought that the 'secularization' of the Indian parishes alone would create a sufficient shift in the balance of social power to destroy the system defended by the *corregidores*, friars, and Indian Principals.

The seculars for their part made no secret of their Creole affiliations. They argued that a Creole background, far from being a disqualification regarding guardianship of Indians, was a positive merit, because it meant that the priest was familiar with the Indians from childhood and therefore much more likely than any European Spaniard to know their ways and to speak one or more of their languages. What, they asked, could a *gachupín* possibly know of the Indian mind, of Indian traditions, and of Indian problems? [109] They backed up this point with the assertion that ordinary Indians, mercilessly exploited by the friars, had come to prefer the secular clergy. In any case, they said, the Indians would benefit, in the event of secularization of their parishes from having far fewer clergy to provide for, if from nothing else. Here then, in the arguments of the diocesan clergy, we find a neat parallel to the claims of the Creole laity: a shift in their favour, they contended, would also be beneficial to the Indians.

Secular priests ministered to the Indians in various localities besides the 'Spanish' centres of the main cities. In the valley of Mexico, for instance, they held nine or ten parishes outside Mexico City, the most important of them being the famous township of Guadalupe. They had therefore some experience with Indian Catholicism and with Indian religious and emotional needs, and fully appreciated the necessity for powerful imagery if they were to achieve their aim of extending their grasp over the Indian population generally. This, arguably, was the particular significance of the cult of the Virgin of Guadalupe, a cult which made considerable headway during the seventeenth century and which in the eighteenth was to sweep all Mexico, finally becoming the nationalist emblem of the Mexican insurgents under Hidalgo and Morelos. There has in the past perhaps been some confusion concerning the role of the Virgin of Guadalupe in the sixteenth and seventeenth centuries owing to the widespread conviction that she was essentially an Indian phenomenon which became very important at an early stage and facilitated the progress of the conversion. It is therefore important to note that although the appearance of the Virgin to the humble Indian Juan Diego on the hill of Tepeacac in 1531, took place at the time of

---

[109] *Alegaciones en favor del clero, estado eclesiastico i secular, espanoles e indios del obispado de la Puebla de los Angeles en el pleyto con las sagradas religiones de S. Domingo, S. Francisco, i S. Agustin* ... (? Puebla, ? *c.*1650) (BNX), fols. 3, 6, 28, 51, and *passim*; Juan Bueno de Roxas, *Por la clerecia de la provincia de Yucatan* ... (n.p., ? *c.* 1650), fol. 9.

the conversion, the cult played only a very restricted role in the conversion and was disapproved of in the sixteenth century and during most of the seventeenth century by the friars.[110] Sahagún identified the cult as a survival and adaptation of the Aztec cult of the mother goddess Tonantzin whose temple had been situated at Tepeacac, and the Franciscans generally condemned it as a piece of thinly disguised idolatry. Furthermore, for a century or so after 1531 María of Guadalupe seems to have attained no general significance and to have remained strictly a local phenomenon tied to the actual shrine and site of Guadalupe, as Tepeacac was renamed. However, the cult was promoted by the sixteenth-century archbishops of Mexico, especially Zumárraga and Montúfar who saw in it a means of helping the diocesan clergy in the Mexico City area,[111] and it did gain a certain popularity among the Creoles of Mexico City,[112] this attachment of the Creoles being a particularly important point. In the early seventeenth century, though the cult was still of comparatively small importance—scarcely any writers of the first half of the seventeenth century even so much as mention it—the dark-faced Indian Virgin began to gain ground. She was promoted apparently exclusively by the secular clergy who recognized in her a subtle and effective means of forging a Mexican Catholicism that appealed to both Creoles and Indians and would help undermine segregation in religion. Archbishop Pérez de la Serna (1613–24) in particular deliberately and systematically advanced the cult as a means of unifying or rather merging the Creole and Indian populations under the influence of the secular clergy.[113] The viceroys, on the other hand, apparently rarely made gestures on behalf of this particular Virgin and the friars continued to resist her advance. Only in 1648, with the publication of Miguel Sánchez's book,[114] arguably the most important single publication of colonial Mexico, did the cult begin to gain real

110 Ricard, *La 'Conquête Spirituelle'*, pp. 227–31; *CDHE* lvii. 107; the mendicant chroniclers of the sixteenth century and of the early and mid seventeenth century scarcely ever even give a hint of the existence of the cult. In 1570 there was only one priest at the site of the shrine of Guadalupe, which was scarcely yet a township and had barely any people; see the memorandum of the priest Antonio Freyre quoted in Antonio Pompa y Pompa, *El Gran Acontecimiento Guadalupano* (Mexico, 1967), pp. 15–17.
111 Ricard, *La 'Conquête Spirituelle'*, p. 231; Pompa y Pompa, op. cit., p. 126.
112 Enríquez to crown, 25 Sept. 1575, in *Cartas de Indias*, p. 310.
113 Diego Cisneros, *Sitio, naturaleza, y propiedades de la ciudad de Mexico* (Mexico, 1618), fols. 113ᵛ–115ᵛ; Francisco de Florencia, *La Estrella de el norte de Mexico* (Mexico, 1741); see also Pompa y Pompa, op. cit., p. 19.
114 Miguel Sánchez, *Imagen de la Virgen Maria madre de Dios de Guadalupe milagrosamente aparecida en la ciudad de Mexico* (Mexico, 1648); Robles remarked in his diary, at the time of Sánchez's death in 1674, that María of Guadalupe was 'forgotten even by the citizens of Mexico City until this venerable

momentum and acquire general acceptance. Sánchez's work was followed by a stream of other publications on the Virgin of Guadalupe as well as by paintings and carvings, and within two or three decades Nuestra Señora de Guadalupe was entrenched at last as the most widely venerated Virgin of the viceroyalty.

The question arises in relation to the controversy between secular clergy and friars, as in that between Creoles and *corregidores*, as to how much truth there was in the Creole assertion that the Indians too wanted desegregation and would benefit from it. A possible test of the question might be the religious development of the batch of thirty-six Indian parishes in the diocese of Puebla which were forcibly transferred by Bishop Palafox from mendicant to diocesan hands in 1641.[115] In the years after the transfers, a dispute continued for several decades between Franciscans and secular clergy as to whether the parishes should be left in the hands of the seculars or not; both sides vying for the support of the crown. The ecclesiastical administration of some very important towns, including Tlaxcala, Cholula, Tepeaca, and Tecamachalco, and two to three hundred clerical livings were at stake. Madrid, anxious to ascertain exactly which clerical faction was the better loved and respected by the Indians, authorized a special investigation into the matter which was carried out in 1669.[116] Nearly all the Indian officers questioned in the course of the inquiry asserted, despite the fact that they had by then been compromising with the secular clergy for twenty-eight years, that the seculars were generally lazy and corrupt and often hopelessly ignorant of Nahuatl. Some of the Indian officers claimed that the mass of the Indians regretted the passing of the friars and still preferred them to the diocesans; most, however, admitted that the mass of Indians scarcely cared who administered their parishes. Certainly there was no particular anxiety to have the friars back and the general mood was one of apathy and indifference. Only the Indian officers positively favoured the friars.

The mixing of Indians with non-Indians, the inevitable consequence and to a large extent the aim of Creole and diocesan policies, had more than merely jurisdictional, economic, and clerical implications. There was also a whole cultural and moral dimension to the problem of which contemporaries were intensely aware. The steady erosion of the 'Indian'

priest made her known, for there was not a single image of this sovereign lady in the whole of Mexico City apart from that in the Dominican friary, whereas today there is no friary or church where she is not worshipped', Antonio de Robles, *Diario de sucesos notables, 1665–1703* (3 vols., Mexico, 1946), i. 144–5.

---

115 See pp. 206–9.
116 BNX 1066 fols. 2–5, 18–26ᵛ, 54ᵛ–60; AGN Indios xvi, fol. 22; see also AGI México 43, r 2: 'Memorial puntado a su ex. por el procurador de jndios'.

republic and drift of Indians on to the haciendas and into the city centres was creating a new Mexico of colourful and vigorous but somewhat disorderly and squalid countenance. There was coming into being, all over the viceroyalty, a new type of Mexican—the Spanish-speaking or ladino Indian who aped the ways of the Spaniard and the mestizo.

The friars regarded the Indian of the 'Spanish' republic not only as a fugitive from his proper sphere, a sphere blessed with discipline, hierarchy, and spiritual order, but as a lost soul, a perverse and degraded wretch. 'In Spanish towns', wrote Torquemada,

there are Indians known as those of the Indian quarters [de barrios] and those who are workers [in the 'Spanish' sector]. The former live under the supervision of the regulars, as can be seen in Mexico City, Puebla de los Angeles, and Atlixco, while the workers are ministered to by secular priests. Of these two sorts of Indians, those who live in the native quarters are fetched and looked after every Sunday and holiday in order that they should revere those days and attend mass, be preached to, and spiritually cared for. With the workers, however, one can scarcely contend that the same care is taken. Never have I seen workers being preached to or fetched on a holiday ... And so these latter Indians are among the basest people of the world, being compulsive thieves and alcoholics, slovenly in dress, unwashed and filthy, so filthy indeed that unless one is used to it, one is scarcely able to look at them. And if their bodies are in this state, what condition must their souls be in? [117]

Torquemada's picture is of course biased and exaggerated. Drunkenness was certainly a fearful plague upon Indian society, but it afflicted the city suburbs and Indian townships as well as the city centres. The Indians of the 'Spanish' republic undoubtedly received less clerical attention than the Indians under the friars, but they received more attention from the seculars (and Jesuits) than Torquemada allowed. Nevertheless, Torquemada's assertion is surely securely anchored in fact. Ladino Indians dwelt in a social milieu so distinct from that of the traditional Indian communities that they constituted a separate social grouping, different not only in economic and religious life but in speech, conduct, and dress. What were the traits of the new Indians? Essentially, they were the traits of natives who went the whole way in discarding traditional Indian habits, completing a process which, for the bulk of the Indian population after the Conquest, had not gone beyond a certain point. The Indians of the 'Indian' republic had been stripped of their ancient religion and their warlike and polygamous customs, but had been moulded into a way of life that remained unmistakably Indian. The mass of Indian men had had their hair cut short as this,

117Torquemada, *Razones informativas, Nueva Colección*, v. 178–9.

both to Indians and friars, signified resignation and submission,[118] and the warrior tradition had lapsed; but this merely reduced the mass of Indians to the position that the defeated, captured, and enslaved had always had under the Aztecs. The ladino Indian, however, marked a real break with tradition and with the Indian community. 'When an Indian takes to wearing mestizo clothes and grows his hair long, wrote the Franciscan curate of the Mexico City suburb of Santa María in 1692, 'he becomes a mestizo, and in a short time will be a Spaniard, rid of having to pay tribute, and an enemy of God, of the Church, and of the king.'[119] 'With the communication that [Indians in the city centre] constantly have', wrote an Augustinian curate of the San Pablo suburb of Mexico City, 'with such vile people as the mulattoes, Negroes, and mestizos, they learn Spanish and become ladinos—which is always the first step toward effrontery, for while they speak their own language they are more humble—and they are forever conspiring vile acts and learning new vices and evil skills; and they defer to no officer and no minister of God.'[120]

The assertion of the friars that the new Indian tendency towards crime was due to the rise of the ladino Indians and confined to them was in the main well founded. Spanish concern with Indian crime is very much a seventeenth-century phenomenon—in the sixteenth century Indian society had been remarkably free of crime—and was mainly directed towards conditions in the city centres. Even a secular clergyman, Bishop Palafox, accepted that 'if there are thieves among the Indians they are the ones who have been brought up and dwell among those who are not Indians.'[121] Signs of the increase in Indian criminal activity in seventeenth-century Mexico are fairly numerous. In the early 1620s, for example, there was such a wave of break-ins by Indians into Spanish properties in Mexico City that Viceroy Gelves imposed a dusk-to-dawn curfew on Indians in the 'Spanish' sector of the city, a curfew reimposed by Viceroy Cerralvo in 1626.[122] In 1638 the *Audiencia* of Mexico reported to the Council of the Indies that the number of robberies committed by Indians in Mexico City was increasing alarmingly,[123] as was their general unruliness and depravity.

The mingling of Spanish-speaking Indians with the Negroes,

[118]*The Broken Spears, the Aztec account of the Conquest of Mexico*, ed. M. León-Portilla (Boston, Mass., 1966), p. 134.
[119]AGN Historia 413, fol. 63ᵛ. Report of Fray Joseph de la Barrera, 16 July 1692.
[120]AGN Historia 413, fol. 10: Fray Bernabé Núñez de Paez, 4 July 1692.
[121]Juan de Palafox, *De la naturaleza del Indio* in *Ideas Políticas*, a selection of Palafox's writings, ed. José Rojas Garcidueñas (Mexico, 1946), p. 121.
[122]AGN ordenanzas iv, fols. 65, 81.
[123]AGI México 75, r 4: *Audiencia* to council, 8 July 1638.

mulattoes, and mestizos was undeniably disturbing to the Spaniards, even to the Creole citizen class who had an economic interest, as a Franciscan curate of Tlatelolco observed,[124] in the rise of the ladino Indian. Several officials and Creoles of the early seventeenth century speak of their fears that there might one day be a combination of Negroes and half-castes perhaps with Indians so strong that the Spaniards would be overpowered and slaughtered and the churches and convents sacked.[125] In 1663 the *Audiencia* of Mexico warned Madrid that whereas formerly Indians and Negroes had hated each other and never fraternized, now in certain areas they fraternized constantly, joining in each other's drinking, gambling, and crimes.[126]

Fears that the Spaniards and clergy might be massacred turned out to be groundless, but there did occur, towards the end of the seventeenth century, one great eruption of violence and looting by Indians, Negroes, and mestizos combined.[127] The year 1692 was one of the most tense of the colonial era in Mexico owing to the destruction of the maize and wheat crops by excessively heavy rainfall and mildew, or at least to the effects of a bad harvest made worse by racketeering. In the spring, food prices in Mexico City soared, despite energetic measures taken by the viceroy and the commandeering of grain stocks in the Bajío. On Sunday 8 June 1692, a riot started at the Mexico City corn exchange which developed swiftly, if not exactly into a rising, into a frenzied rampage by a mob that was very mixed but predominantly Indian. In a few hours, the viceregal palace was burned down as also were the city hall and the offices of the *Audiencia* and the treasury; 280 shops and stalls were ransacked and burned and large stocks of food and clothing looted. The tumult was certainly not an attack on the Spaniards as such, though apparently some of the rabble cried 'Death to the Spaniards and *gachupines*!';[128] most of the whites that the mob encountered were merely disarmed and insulted. The clergy, churches, convents, and ecclesiastical property, were all unharmed. The majority of those killed during those few frantic hours were Indians and half-castes shot by the viceroy's soldiers. But clearly the Spaniards were

[124] AGN Historia 413, fol. 17.
[125] See for instance BNX 890, letters of Leonardo de Saldaña to an unnamed correspondent, fol. 6ᵛ.
[126] AGI México 77: *Audiencia* to council, 8 June 1663.
[127] AGN Historia 413: the report of Don Carlos de Sigüenza y Góngora of 5 July 1692; I. A. Leonard, *Alboroto y Motín de los Indios de México del 8 de Junio de 1692* (Mexico, 1932), which contains the whole of Sigüenza y Góngora's account of the outbreak; Robles, *Diario de Sucesos Notables*, ii. 250–8; R. Feijóo, 'El Tumulto de 1692', *Historia Mexicana*, xiv. 4 (April–June 1965), 656–79.
[128] Feijóo, op. cit., p. 661, citing Sigüenza y Góngora.

shocked and stunned.[129] Most of the Spanish functionaries and officers in the city, like the rest of the white population, kept within doors or sought refuge in the priories and convents, such was their lack of preparedness for such an occurrence. Carlos de Sigüenza y Góngora, the noted Creole scholar, who distinguished himself on that day by saving some of the *cabildo*'s records from the burning city hall, and a man greatly interested in the history and customs of the Indians, was amazed and appalled by what he saw. For days afterwards the white citizenry of the capital were subject to periodic attacks of jitters occasioned by rumours that the Indians were intending fresh violence,[130] fears which the sight of the blackened shell of the palace and of the widespread destruction of property did nothing to allay. In fact, though there was no further disturbance in Mexico City, there was a violent commotion in the vicinity of Tlaxcala soon afterwards, in which, according to Robles, the *corregidor*, two Spaniards, a priest, and 100 Indians were killed.[131]

But though the *tumultos* of June 1692 were a clear indication of what might occur in times of chronic food shortage, they were nevertheless isolated incidents, without either precedent or sequel. The months following June 1692 were the only occasion in the seventeenth century when the prospect and implications of major Indian unrest in central Mexico, as opposed to northern and southern Mexico, were seriously considered by the viceroy and his advisors. The disturbances showed conclusively that constant Indian passivity could no longer be taken for granted, that the espanolized Indians especially, sullen, unruly, and potentially rebellious, were a force to be reckoned with. But they also showed by their limited and, as far as Spanish lives were concerned, relatively harmless character, that if Spanish rule was now more vulnerable than it had been, it was only very slightly so.

[129]Robles, *Diario de Sucesos Notables*, ii. 252, 255.
[130]Ibid., pp. 258–61.
[131]Ibid., pp. 260–1.

II

MESTIZOS, NEGROES, AND MULATTOES

After the Indians, the mestizos constituted the second most numerous element in the colony. The rise of the mestizo, undeniably, is one of the most baffling aspects of Mexican history. Clearly, he is of fundamental importance. He was destined to become the main part, the central block of the Mexican nation, for in the last two centuries most Mexicans have been mestizo. And yet, in the seventeenth century, though he was undoubtedly the fastest-growing element in Mexican society, he receives so little mention that one almost forgets his existence. By comparison with the Indian, Negro, or Spaniard, he is almost nothing; where he does appear, it is usually only as a tag on the end of the much bandied phrase 'Negroes, mulattoes, and mestizos'. Thus it may be said that the problem of the seventeenth-century mestizo is, in the first place, the problem of explaining his obscurity.

It is plain that there was from the first a high rate of miscegenation in Mexico between Indian and Spaniard. This was due much less to the willingness of a few Conquistadores to marry Indian women than to the vigour of those who did not marry them, and also to a marked readiness on the part of Indian women to enter into casual unions with Spaniards. Mixed marriages, despite the fact that there were hardly any Spanish women in Mexico in the early years after the Conquest, occurred less often than has sometimes been supposed.[1] Even in Puebla in 1534, the most ordered, disciplined, and settled Spanish community in New Spain, where in theory there were no unmarried citizens, Spaniards with 'Spanish' wives outnumbered those with Indian wives by two to one.[2] Most of the Conquistadores and early settlers either remained unmarried or separated from wives whom they had left behind in Spain, or were married later on to the mestiza daughters of other Spaniards who had been raised as 'Spanish' girls. Provision of mestiza girls indeed was so effective that by the middle of the sixteenth

[1] For details on individual Conquistadores, see Francisco de Icaza, *Conquistadores y Pobladores de Nueva España, diccionario autobiográfico* (2 vols., Madrid, 1923).

[2] C. E. Marshall, 'The Birth of the Mestizo in New Spain', *HAHR* xix (1939), 167.

century, despite the fact that in the two decades 1520–40 only some 6 per cent of the immigrants from Spain had been women,[3] 'Spanish' girls, far from being in short supply, were actually in surfeit and this depressed the rate of mixed marriages almost to zero;[4] for, in general, it was not thought fitting or honourable that Spaniards should marry Indian women. In this matter as in so much else, Cortés himself set the precedent: he passed over the opportunity to marry into the royal house of Moctezuma and Cuauhtemoc, and took instead, as his second wife, Doña Juana de Zúñiga, daughter of the conde de Aguilar. When Conquistadores did take Indian spouses, they usually aimed for the highest stratum of native society. Thus Juan Cano married the princess Isabel Moctezuma, daughter of the luckless ruler, while Juan Jamarillo espoused (though it was rumoured that Cortés made him drunk for the purpose) Doña Marina (Malinche), Cortés's Indian interpreter and mistress, and a cacica.

Casual liaisons then gave rise to most of the prolific half-caste population that began to appear even before the fall of Tenochtitlan. Apart from the rapaciousness of the conquerors, it does appear that one has to take account, in explaining this, of a marked readiness on the part of Indian women to cohabit with Spaniards when their menfolk were defeated. Also the Tlaxcaltecs and other allies of the Spaniards seem to have deliberately encouraged such unions, according to Muñoz Camargo, who was himself a mestizo, in the hope of gaining nephews and grandsons of valour and strength equal to that of the Spaniards.[5] Possibly, in the years after the Conquest, Indian women were reacting, in the midst of the general disruption, to the repressiveness of the past, in the same way as their menfolk reacted to the collapse of the ancient controls against alcohol; at any rate, Indian women were attracted by the superior bearing and strength of the Spaniards, and were eager to have children by them.[6] In this respect, Doña Marina, though usually depicted by modern Mexicans as an infamous traitress, was in fact merely sharing the common attitude of her sisters.

Although it was not long before mestizo children abounded, mestizos did not at first form part of any third community or element distinguishable from Indian society and Spanish society. Mixed bloods

[3] Peter Boyd-Bowman, 'La Emigración Peninsular a América, 1520–39', *Historia Mexicana*, xiii (1958–9), 176.

[4] Richard Konetzke, 'La Emigración de las Mujeres españoles a América durante la época colonial', *Revista Internacional de la Sociología*, i (1949), 441–80.

[5] Muñoz Camargo, *Historia de Tlaxcala*, pp. 190–2.

[6] Richard Konetzke, 'El Mestizaje y su importancia en el desarrollo de la población hispanoamericana durante la época colonial', *Revista de Indias*, xxiii (1946), 7–44 and xxiv (1947), 215–37, esp. xxiii. 25–7.

though they were, they lived either as 'Spaniards' or else as 'Indians'.[7] Those mestizos born within wedlock, or born without of aristocratic mothers, or who were adopted for some other reason by their fathers, were absorbed into the first generation of Creoles who were therefore often really mestizos. Gonzalo Cano Moctezuma, son of Juan Cano and Isabel Moctezuma, established himself as one of the leaders of the Creole nobility. Martín Cortés, the illegitimate mestizo son of Cortés, by Doña Marina and half-brother to the other Martín Cortés, Cortés's legitimate son and heir, was also a prominent Creole noble. Doña Leonor de Alvarado Xicotencatl, the legitimized mestiza daughter of Pedro de Alvarado by a sister of the Tlaxcaltec cacique Xictencatl, rose so high as to be married to a cousin of the Duke of Albuquerque, one of the greatest nobles of Castile. A considerable number of other mestizos, legitimate and illegitimate, were raised as Spanish gentlemen and ladies. The crown approved of this process, for it was thought expedient that the tiny Spanish presence in Mexico should be thus strengthened. The mestizos of the other category, the fruit of more casual liaisons, were raised in the Indian townships and villages by their mothers as 'Indians'. These mestizos learned no Spanish, knew nothing of their fathers, and tended to become a barely distinguishable part of the Indian community. This phenomenon caused some disquiet in Spanish official circles, for it was considered wrong and impolitic that 'sons of Spaniards by Indian women' should be thus 'lost among the Indians'. Instructions were issued that mestizo boys whose fathers were not known should be retrieved from among the Indians by the viceregal administration and raised as 'Spaniards'.[8] In the later sixteenth century, and still more in the seventeenth century, there were many mestizo Indian principals, and numerous mestizos were elected governors and principals of Indian communities.[9] It is true that a large number of mestizos, as well as of Spaniards and Negroes, were expelled from the Indian communities, particularly under viceroys Velasco, Enríquez, Villamanrique, and Monterrey, but generally these were either free-booting outsiders or else insiders, such as Muñoz Camargo, expelled

---

[7]That is from the strictly social point of view; psychologically speaking, espanolized mestizos were often strongly aware of their strange position between Spanish and Indian society, hence perhaps that remarkable flowering of mestizo historians in the sixteenth and seventeenth centuries. From Pedro Gutiérrez de Santa Clara, a Mexican mestizo who went to Peru, we have the *Quinquenarios o Historia de las Guerras Civiles del Peru*, from Muñoz Camargo the *Historia de Tlaxcala*, and from Fernandoda Alva Ixtlilxochitl the *Historia de la nacion chichimeca*. One might add that there is also the *Royal Commentaries of the Incas* by the Peruvian mestizo historian, Garcilaso de la Vega. Muñoz Camargo evinced a curious mixture of disdain and affection for the Indians which was, one may presume, typical of the espanolized mestizo.

[8]*CDHH* i, 147, 315.   [9]Gibson, *The Aztecs*, pp. 160, 176.

from Tlaxcala in 1589, who were political victims of local Indian officer factions.[10] Many Nahuatl-speaking mestizos remained, and the Indian office-holding class in the seventeenth century, and indeed to a certain extent the Indian population as a whole, was, strictly speaking, Indian-mestizo.

The early mestizos then, even when bilingual and in spite of their complex psychology, were generally classified socially as either 'Spaniards' or 'Indians'. Marriages between mestizos and mestiza women and the existence of mestizo families as such were comparatively rare. Very few mestizos were classified as belonging to a third grouping in society. Now this, one may presume, is the key to the paradox of the seventeenth-century mestizo—the paradox that the mestizos were many and important while apparently few and unimportant: the bulk of the mestizo population was disguised socially as something else. The actual 'mestizo' population, that element labelled as 'mestizo' in sixteenth-century Mexican society, grew up slowly around the fringe of the 'Spanish' republic and in the shadow of the black community. It may seem strange that that element which makes up the majority of the Mexican people today was categorized in the seventeenth century as a mere sub-section of the Negro population, but such evidently is the case. A late-sixteenth-century census of the non-Indian population of Central Mexico placed the total black community, Negro and mulatto, of the provinces of Mexico, Puebla, and Michoacán as slightly larger than the total white, castizo, and mestizo population labelled as 'Spanish' and no less than seven times as great as the number labelled as 'mestizo'! [11] The document gives over 16,000 for the black population, 12,000 for the 'Spanish', and only 2,300 for the 'mestizo'.

This style of classifying racial types in colonial Mexico helps to explain certain seventeenth-century statements which might otherwise be inexplicable. Vázquez de Espinosa, for instance, when listing the elements of population in Mexico City, includes Spaniards, Indians, Negroes, and mulattoes but says nothing about the mestizos;[12] one might regard this as a mere slip of the pen, but probably the omission is significant especially in view of the fact that Samuel de Champlain[13] and the Italian, Gemelli Carreri, writing in 1697,[14] do the same.

[10] Mörner and Gibson, 'Diego Muñoz Camargo and the Segregation Policy of the Spanish Crown', *HAHR* xliii (1963), 562–8.
[11] See the 'Relación de todos los pueblos de castellanos de la Nueva España' in Alfonso Toro, 'La Influencia de la Raza negra en la formación del pueblo mexicano', *Ethnos*, i (Mexico, 1920–2), 215–18.
[12] *Descripción de la Nueva España*, p. 118.
[13] Champlain, *Oeuvres*, i. 23.
[14] Francisco Gemelli Carreri, *Voyage du Tour du Monde*, vi. 36.

Viceroy Mancera, writing in 1673, explicitly states that the Negroes and mulattoes in Central Mexico outnumbered the mestizos.[15] It seems clear that when officials and secretaries in seventeenth-century New Spain spoke of 'negroes, mulattoes, and mestizos', and this was their stock formula for the third community, it was no idle quirk which moved them to place the mestizos last. For if one sets aside the realities of race and psychology and approaches the matter from the purely social standpoint, the phrase reflected the reality.

The rise of the 'mestizo' as a sub-section of the third community, distinct from Spaniards and Indians, did not improve the mestizo's position in Mexican society or enhance his reputation. The epithet 'sons of Spaniards' is used progressively less while the association of mestizos with Negroes in the Spaniard's eyes becomes closer. Although in theory still rated as *gente de razon* (rational folk), equivalent in potential intellect to white people, the mestizo was identified increasingly in the Spanish mind with the *gente vil* (base folk), the categorization reserved for those non-Indians, mainly blacks, who were not permitted to wear European costume or hold royal, municipal, or ecclesiastical office.[16] Moreover, as the mestizo grouping in Mexican society came to be defined more and more by the new mestizos, mestizos marrying and reproducing among themselves, the old mestizos, and especially mestizo Creole gentlemen and mestizo Indian principals, took care to dissociate themselves as far as possible from the new community. They regarded themselves, and were regarded, as Spaniards or Indian principals and were well to the fore in disparaging the 'mestizos'. Reminders of mixed descent were suppressed except where such illustrious names as Moctezuma, Tezozomoc, or Ixtlilxochitl still added lustre.

The Spanish view of the mestizo in the seventeenth century was essentially ambivalent and shifting, turning on the question of whether to label him *gente de razón* or *gente vil*. The verdict was apparently most favourable in New Galicia and the frontier regions of the north where the Negro was relatively rare and where the image of the mestizos as 'sons of Spaniards' remained unimpaired. Lázaro de Arregui, writing in 1621 in reference to New Galicia, characterized the mestizo as 'talented, energetic, and honourable, owing to the repression of the Indian blood in him'.[17] In Central Mexico, however, views were not so clear-cut and never so favourable. Viceroy Mancera considered that

The mestizos, sons and descendants of the Spaniards, are no less presumptuous than the [Negroes and mulattoes]. . . but in a somewhat more elevated manner. Their presumption is better controlled and more

[15]*Instrucciones que los Virreyes de Nueva España dejaron*, p. 259.
[16]Haring, *The Spanish Empire*, pp. 201–2.
[17]Lázaro de Arregui, *Descripción de la Nueva Galicia*, p. 39.

subject to reason. They are proud that they have our blood in them and on various occasions have shown that they know how to carry out their responsibilities.[18]

Thus Mancera, while accepting that there was an element of perversity in the mestizo, nevertheless regarded him as a valuable supplement to the white population. Juan de Solórzano however, the noted early-seventeenth-century authority on Spanish American questions, despite conceding that the mestizos were 'sons of Spaniards' and therefore arguably eligible for posts in state, Church, and municipality, held that this consideration was overruled by another: the mestizos, generally speaking, were of illegitimate birth and this in his view constituted an insurmountable obstacle to their admission to the citizen class.[19] Mestizos, he asserted, being the fruit of profligacy, were a tainted nation unfitted for any honourable living or office.

Solórzano's view was essentially a summing up of the attitude inherent in royal policy toward the mestizo. Already by the 1540s, when the first generation of mestizos was reaching manhood, the crown had issued instructions barring mestizos of illegitimate birth from public office;[20] in one sense this ruling was no different from the bar that applied in the case of Spaniards, for Spaniards born out of wedlock were not eligible for office either, but whereas this bar applied only to a minority of Spaniards, in the case of the mestizos it applied to the great majority. Despite this ruling, however, considerable confusion and doubt concerning the mestizo remained, especially with regard to the ordaining of mestizos as priests. In the later sixteenth century, the Mexican bishops were inclined to adopt a liberal stance on the reception of mestizos into the clergy, or at least into the secular clergy, probably for political reasons; by their flexibility on this issue, the bishops hoped to swell the ranks of the diocesan priesthood faster than the friars could swell their priestly ranks. Madrid cautioned the Mexican bishops several times about their willingness to receive almost anyone into the secular priesthood while observing the ban on the ordination of mestizos as mendicant priests.[21] However, the government had no objection to the ordaining of *castizos*, the offspring of Spaniards by mestizas. Indeed, it is clear that the secular clergy in New Spain, which we have classified as Creole, had in its veins a strain of Indian blood also and was really Creole-castizo-mestizo.

[18]*Instrucciones que los Virreyes de Nueva España dejaron*, p. 259; López de Velasco, writing in the 1570s, similarly linked the mestizos with the Negroes, and then qualified his assertion saying that they were not quite so bad, *Geografía y Descripción*, p. 43.
[19]Juan de Solórzano y Pereira, *Política Indiana* (Madrid, 1647), pp. 246–8.
[20]*CDHH* i. 256.
[21]*CDHH* i. 377–8, 409, 436.

The Jesuits, as regards the question of whether mestizos should be admitted into their own ranks, took a hard line. They admitted no mestizos into their order as a rule, and in general favoured the levelling of the mestizos to roughly the same status as that of the Negroes and mulattoes. Not that they viewed the mestizo with distaste. They regarded the middle area of Mexican society as a hopeful field for themselves, since neither friars nor secular clergy had accomplished much there. In the eyes of the Jesuits, the mestizos were not so much 'sons of Spaniards' as a new and as yet unformed race that stood in particular need of moral and social guidance.[22] Like the Negroes and mulattoes, the mestizos were, in the Jesuit view, neophytes of the Church, a precious but delicate spiritual acquisition.

The uncertainty of the Spaniards as to where to place the mestizo between the white apex and Afro-Indian base of the social hierarchy was mirrored by the variations in the constitutions of the Mexico City craft guilds.[23] In some trades the mestizo was accorded a status clearly superior to that of the rest of the non-white population; but in others he was not. The glove-makers, porcelain-makers, cotton dealers, and milliners went the whole way in favouring the mestizo and permitted him to become master craftsman. The guild of the pressers, manglers, and calenderers stipulated in 1605 that although mestizos were not eligible to become master craftsmen, they might ascend to the second rank and set up their own workshops, while free Negroes and mulattoes could not pass beyond the grade of journeyman. Some of the humbler guilds, such as those of the candle-makers and cobblers, allowed Negroes and mulattoes as well as mestizos to rise to the upper ranks. On the other hand, such relatively prestigious trades as those of the armourers, swordmakers, needlemakers, and most varieties of metalsmiths professed, at least, to depress the mestizo to the same humble status as the Negro and mulatto.

Such then was the variety to be found in the position of the seventeenth-century Mexican mestizo. He was of great importance, being present in every social category and group in the colony, but he does not emerge as a distinct and identifiable element in the pattern of social strains and stresses to which Mexican society was subject. There was no guise which he did not assume; he could be a 'Creole', 'Indian', cacique, friar, secular priest, 'mestizo', even a 'mulatto', and it is difficult or impossible to say that it was more usual or typical for him to be one rather than another.

[22] BNX 645: Francisco Calderón S. J., 'Cuestion moral en que se trata si los negros son comprehendidos en este nombre, neophitos y si gozan los privilegios de los indios', pp. 14. 28–30; see also Solorzano, *Política Indiana*, p. 247.

[23] See the *Ordenanzas de Gremios de la Nueva España*, ed. Francisco del Barrio Lorenzot (Mexico, 1920).

Having said this much of the mestizo, we may proceed to the Negro, that element which, though barely perceptible in the Mexican people today, outside certain localities along the coasts of the states of Veracruz and Guerrero, was, as has been suggested, of great importance in the Mexico of the seventeenth century.

The Negro slave was, as is well known, in considerable demand with the Conquistadores. In addition to being attractive as domestic servants unconnected by language or any other ties with the defeated Indian mass, Negroes had, for several generations, accorded social prestige to those who owned them, in southern Spain and Portugal, and more recently in Santo Domingo, Cuba, and Jamaica. Furthermore, it was swiftly seen that the Negro, who tended to be bigger, stronger, and more vigorous than the Indian, readily and almost inevitably made Indians fear and obey him and would therefore serve as a most useful tool in the management of the defeated mass. It was also seen that there need be no fear of fraternization between blacks and Indians, for the two were so different and the blacks were so contemptuous of the weaker Indians, that there was clearly no risk of it. And so, with the encouragement of the friars who tended to dislike the Negro and hoped that, with the presence of the black man, some of the burden of work in Mexico would be shifted from the shoulders of the Indians, the slave trade flourished.

It was not long, however, before Spaniards in Mexico began to become nervous regarding the black immigration. Mexico experienced its first black scare as early as 1537.[24] In 1553, Viceroy Velasco asserted that there were 'more than 20,000' Negroes and mulattoes in the colony or considerably more than the number of Spaniards, that they were fast becoming a serious threat to the stability of the viceroyalty, and the Emperor should prohibit the entry of any more of them. But despite this growing fear, importation of slaves continued at a high rate and indeed accelerated,[25] the high-point coming in the period 1580–1640, during the six decades in which the crowns of Portugal and Castile were joined and in which Portuguese slave-traders handled the transport of Negroes to Mexico. The effects of this increased rate of slave importation were offset, as far as the relative proportions of the white and black races in Mexico were concerned, by the even greater influx of white immigrants during those years; but fear of the Negro remained intense. The Spaniards were caught in a dilemma with economic needs and snobbery clashing with considerations of

[24] D. M. Davidson, 'Negro Slave Control and Resistance in Colonial Mexico, 1519–1650', *HAHR* xlvi (1966), 243.

[25] See Gonzalo Aguirre Beltrán, 'The Slave Trade in Mexico', *HAHR* xxiv (1944), 415.

security. Gómez de Cervantes, writing in 1599, spoke of the Negroes and mulattoes as 'those who are well known to be our enemies'.[26] Mota y Escobar, discussing the blacks of Zacatecas in 1604, wrote that 'there are here some 800 Negro and mulatto slaves, men and women, and also some free Negroes who pass in and out of the city taking jobs on ranches and farms, and in the mines, and, generally speaking, they are vicious and unruly, both slaves and freemen; but then, as is said here, though things are bad with them, they would be worse without them.'[27]

Indeed the degree of friction between Spaniard and Negro at the turn of the seventeenth century was such that one must judge that the contemporary observer, had he been informed that some difficulties and tension would beset the viceroyalty during that century, would certainly have supposed that the form of it would be racial conflict between black and white. Negroes born and raised in Mexico, known as Creole Negroes, were usually much less submissive than those who had been transported from Africa, known as bozals, and by 1600 a large proportion of the black population in Mexico was Creole. Also, by this time there were something like three times as many mulattoes as Negroes—it has been estimated that in the early seventeenth century the total number of Negroes and mulattoes in Mexico was about 140,000[28]—and many of these mulattoes were descendants of Conquistadores and therefore often proud and haughty.[29] Furthermore, the fact that by this time a large proportion of the black population was free tended to make the part that was still enslaved all the more restless. Bands of runaway slaves, or maroons, became active along the highway between Puebla and Veracruz, particularly in the sierra, and these took to terrorizing Spaniard and Indian alike. And then, towards the beginning of the second viceregal term of Luis de Velasco II (1607–11), the maroon movement assumed the proportions of a serious revolt headed by Yanga, an old runaway slave who had once been a chieftain in Africa.[30] At the same time, other maroon bands became active along the Pacific coast in the vicinity of Acapulco.

The danger in the countryside provoked a severe attack of jitters in the capital.[31] Rumours circulated of a fearful conspiracy by the

[26]Gómez de Cervantes, *La Vida Económica*, p. 100.
[27]Mota y Escobar, *Descripción geográfica*, p. 66.
[28]Gonzalo Aguirre Beltrán, *La Población Negra de México, 1519–1810* (Mexico, 1946), pp. 213–21; Davidson, op. cit., pp. 236–7.
[29]Montesclaros, *Advertimientos*, *CDHE* xxvi. 170–1.
[30]AGI México 27, r 3: Velasco to council, 13 Feb. 1609, and r 2: Velasco to council, 24 May 1609.
[31]Ibid.; Torquemada, *Monarchia Yndiana*, i. 833; and the *Relacion del alcamiento que los negros y mulattos . . . de la ciudad de Mexico . . . pretendieron*

Negroes of Mexico City to choose and anoint a black king, appoint black dukes and lords, and to bring to pass a black St. Bartholomew's day upon which the entire white population of the capital would be butchered and New Spain would fall into the hands of the Negroes. The viceroy was sufficiently alarmed to order a special investigation. A number of Negroes and mulattoes were seized and tortured and it was found that the election of a black king had indeed occurred, but that the event had been more in the nature of a drunken revel than a sinister plot.

To subdue Yanga and the maroons of the sierra, Don Luis had a force of 200 Spanish soldiers and adventurers, 200 Tlaxcaltec archers, and 200 armed mestizos and mulattoes made ready in Puebla and sent out into the mountains. The fight was long and arduous. The Spaniards were relieved to find that Yanga made no attempt to stir up the Indians, but were dismayed to find how skilful at hit-and-run tactics his men were. Spanish casualties were light as the maroons lacked arms, but of the two Jesuits who had accompanied the expedition in the hope of pacifying the Negroes by priestly intercession, one was struck in the face by a stone while the other received an arrow in the leg.[32] At length, the Spaniards, having exhausted their supplies of food and ammunition, decided that the best thing to do was to accept a stalemate.[33] In the subsequent talks, it was agreed that Yanga and his men should go free and keep their mountain settlement, but also that their raiding should cease and that they should return all future runaway slaves to the Spanish authorities.

Peace with Yanga relieved the tension in New Spain only temporarily. The maroons were on the rampage again the next year, this time along the two coasts. The viceroy, echoing the advice that his father had given in 1553, urged Madrid to stop the Portuguese bringing any more slaves into the colony lest the situation deteriorate further.[34] In 1611 the burial of a Negress who was said to have been flogged to death by her master caused a riot in Mexico City with some 1,500 blacks out in the streets, stoning the house of the deceased Negress's owner and shouting protests outside the viceregal palace and the

hacer (1612) in *Anales de la Universidad de Valencia*, xii (1935), 28. This anonymous account of the commotions of 1608–12 may well be the lost narrative by Antonio Morga mentioned in *ACM* xviii. 379; Morga was a prominent *Audiencia* official who had, in 1609, published a history of the Philippines.

---

[32] Though it should be noted that Yanga's movement did not reject Christianity; see Francisco Javier Alegre, *Historia de la Compañía de Jesús en Nueva España*, ed. Carlos María Bustamente (3 vols., Mexico, 1841–2), ii. 10–12.

[33] AGI México 29, r 1b: Velasco to council, 30 May 1610.

[34] AGI México 2, r 3: Velasco to council, 4 Apr. 1610.

Inquisition. According to the *Relacion del Alcamiento*, the Negroes afterwards let out their frustration by selecting a new king, and this time a queen as well, Pablo and María, an Angolan couple, and planning an uprising, this time in earnest, for Holy Thursday 1612.

The plot, if there was one, collapsed when two Portuguese slave-traders who knew the 'Angola language' overheard some Negroes discussing it in a Mexico City market-place. The slave-traders informed Antonio Morga who promptly took charge of the business and went into it with notable zeal. While he was at work, Viceroy Velasco II's successor, the ailing Viceroy-Archbishop García Guerra, died, and it was in the midst of the general gloom that followed this occurrence that Morga announced the details of the conspiracy, a truly blood-curdling plot intended to achieve the slaughter of every white man, woman, and child in the city. Immediately the authorities sprang into action with Morga well to the fore. The heads of all the Negro *confradías*, or religious sodalities, the principal organs of Negro expression and organization in New Spain, were seized and tortured. Torture produced 'confessions' and abundant details of the conspiracy, and armed with this knowledge the *Audiencia*, which had taken over the government of the viceroyalty following the archbishop's decease, declared an emergency, mobilized the Mexico City militia, suspended all religious processions and services arranged for Holy Week, closed the churches, and admonished the Puebla city council to take the same measures in Puebla.[35]

At the same time, Morga pressed ahead with his investigations and arrested more Negroes and subjected them to torture, and the *Audiencia* came out with a package of laws of draconian severity designed to strip the black population of all means of resistance.[36] Every restriction that had been imposed on the Negro during the last century and which had been allowed to lapse was reimposed: arms, offensive and defensive, were forbidden to slaves and freemen alike; a dusk-to-dawn curfew was ordered again applying to both slaves and freemen; meetings, of whatever sort, of more than three blacks were prohibited; all the black sodalities were dissolved and the Jesuits, Mercenarian friars, and other clergy who had interested themselves in the black community were admonished to make sure that the sodalities went out of existence; while the decrees forbidding Negresses and mulattas to adorn themselves with silks, jewellery, and low-cut dresses were reissued.

At length, Morga announced that the emergency was over and that all

[35] Torquemada, *Monarchia Yndiana*, i. 843; ACP xiv, fol. 222ᵛ; I. A. Leonard, *Baroque Times in Old Mexico* (Ann Arbor, Michigan, 1966), p. 19.
[36] AGN ordenanzas 1, fols. 146–9: *Audiencia* decrees of Apr. 1612.

the culprits were in chains. The Spaniards recovered from their fright and began to look forward to taking revenge on those whom they held responsible for it. On 2 May 1612, in the Plaza Mayor of Mexico City, on a line of nine gallows and watched by a great multitude of the populace of the capital, twenty-nine Negroes and seven Negresses were hanged. Their heads were then severed and displayed on pikes.

The year 1612 marked the high-point of racial tension in Colonial Mexico. After 1612, the friction between Spaniard and Negro quickly receded from being the foremost peril confronting the viceroyalty to being a question of no immediate urgency whatever.[37] Why this was the case is not easy to explain. One might argue that the April laws and the executions of 2 May succeeded in their object of cowing the black population, and that the dissolution of the black religious sodalities and the disarming of the Negroes extinguished all hope of a successful rising. Perhaps, but such an explanation is unlikely to satisfy. It is difficult to believe that the tension would have been eased in the long run had not the factors making for acute friction in the period 1590—1612 ceased to operate with the same force after 1612. Certainly the Spaniards quickly saw that their fears had been exaggerated and this in itself did a great deal to reduce tension; the small scale and ineffectuality of the Negro movements of 1608—12 showed that black discontent was less intense than had been supposed. Also reassuring were the marked disinclination of the maroons to ally with Indians and the notable failure of the Dutch invaders under van Spillbergen, who occupied Acapulco bay in 1614, to elicit any anti-Spanish response from the Pacific coast Negroes.

There was another maroon rising in 1617—18, but the alarums that it caused were much less than those of 1609;[38] a number of haciendas were pillaged and burned, some Indian women and girls raped, and a Spaniard killed, but a small force was quickly able to put the insurgents down. The Spanish authorities captured the Negro leader and thirty-five of his men and struck a bargain with them like that which had been struck with Yanga in 1609. The marauding was to stop and future fugitives were to be returned to the Spaniards, but they were granted their freedom and their own town in the sierra near Córdoba, complete with *cabildo*, known as San Lorenzo of the Negroes.[39]

---

[37]Viceroy Cerralvo, in his viceregal report of 1636, devotes only five lines to the negro question out of twenty-six pages, just mentioning that the problem was over, and claiming credit for finally putting down the maroons, see the *Descripción de la Nueva España*, p. 230.

[38]AGI México 29, r 1: Guadalcázar to council, 25 May 1618(g).

[39]Alegre, *Historia de la Compañía*, ii. 16; it is sad to think that in the 1630s and 1640s the Negroes of San Lorenzo earned their bread chiefly by obtaining reward money for returning fugitive slaves to the Spaniards, AGN cédulas duplicadas xlix, fols. 14—15ᵛ.

The rising of 1617—18 was the last significant incident of white-black friction for almost three decades until 1646 when there was violence between soldiers of the mulatto garrison at Veracruz (the Spaniards employed some Negro and mulatto troops at Veracruz as they did in Cuba, Santo Domingo, and elsewhere) and white soldiers of the garrison which resulted in the death of two of the latter.[40] There were then another nineteen years of quiet until, in 1665, there occurred the only other scare in seventeenth-century Mexico which came near to rivalling that of the 1608—12 period. For several months there was tension in Mexico City, rumours of a mulatto conspiracy, and constant heavy patrols by Spanish infantry and militia, and during this period the viceroy was more concerned with this matter than with any other.[41] Moreover, there is fairly solid evidence that at least some mulattoes were in a defiant mood, in their speech and songs at any rate, and some mulattoes spoke and sang of what they would do when the Spaniards were overpowered and they had the power. The Inquisition, which was an important instrument of social surveillance, picked up a number of signs of unusual excitement among the black population of the capital and was in close touch with the viceroy throughout this time. In the end, however, the tension eased without any serious outbreak.

But although 1665 shows that a heightening of tension between white and black was always possible, in general, white-black relations after 1612 were relatively good. The reader will already have seen that the position of the Mexican Negro was rather different from that of the Negro in some other parts of the New World in the early modern era, and indeed it has long been acknowledged that the Spaniards treated their slaves somewhat better than did the French, English, and Dutch.[42] Moreover, in the Spanish colonies there was always a large body of free blacks owing to the practice of freeing, under certain circumstances, the offspring of Negresses and mulattas by Spaniards; also, slaves could buy their freedom and that of their wives and children at the market price, a right of which, in Mexico, they were often able to avail themselves.[43] Furthermore, local conditions in Mexico added to

---

[40] AGI México 76, r 1: Pedro Melián to council, 3 Sept. 1646.

[41] AGI México 40, r 2: ordenanza de Mancera, 2 Mar. 1665; r 3: Mancera to council, 15 Nov. 1665, and Mexican Inquisition to Mancera, 3 Oct. 1665; one night in August there was a minor commotion with some fifty Negroes, mulattoes, and mestizos shouting and brandishing weapons. However, Antonio de Robles, in the entries to his diary for 1665, says nothing about the mulatto scare of that year.

[42] See, for instance, William Robertson, *The History of America* (1788) (4 vols., London, 1817), iv. 35 and the Abbé Raynal, *A Philosophical and Political History of the Settlements and Trade of the Europeans in the East and West Indies* (5 vols., London 1776), ii. 401—2.

[43] *CDHH* i, doc. 346.

the comparatively favoured position of the Negro. He was not, as we have seen, usually used for mere manual labour; his uses were of a more specialized sort. Entrepreneurs valued him as a tool in the exploitation of Indian workers, as an overseer, foreman, and work boss, for it was a standard joke in Mexico that one Negro could twist a dozen Indians round his finger. *Corregidores* found Negroes to be excellent intermediaries in the forcing of sales and purchases on Indians and in others of their operations; a *corregidor* of Puebla in the 1630s employed his mulattoes to ensure that no Indian sold pulque in the city without having bought permission to do so; a *corregidor* of Toluca posted Negroes in the market-place of that town to ensure that movements of prices were to his liking. Spanish dignitaries of all sorts prized the Negro for the social prestige that he reflected on them. No Spaniard of pretensions to prominence or rank could do without black servants. All *Audiencia* and treasury officials in Mexico City had Negroes, though, as one of them wrote, they served no purpose other than to inflate their masters' vanity. The more select female convents of Mexico City and Puebla had more black girls to do the chores than they had nuns. Furthermore, as an additional sign of the confidence they placed in Negroes, many Spaniards, especially crown officials, inquisitors, and the like, evaded or sought exemption from the prohibition on the arming of Negroes, and employed slaves as body-guards.

The relatively favoured position of the Mexican Negroes was shared by their womenfolk. The Spaniards in Mexico, like the Portuguese in Brazil, emphatically preferred Negresses, and especially mulattas, to Indian women, and it was common in seventeenth-century Mexico City and Puebla for good-looking black girls to earn a great deal as courtesans and mistresses of merchants and officials. As the law denied the Negress both the *huipil* of her Indian sisters and the dress of Spanish women, she developed a somewhat brassy fashion of her own and was accustomed to wear an amount of silk and jewellery that quite astonished the English traveller Thomas Gage.[44]

The immorality of the Negro population, in the eyes of Spanish puritans, church and lay, constituted a serious threat to the viceroyalty. The black community was seen as not only sexually vicious and naturally turbulent and defiant, but as cruel and malevolent. This malevolence, it was said, with a degree of justification, was particularly

---

[44] 'A blackamoor or tawny young maid and slave', wrote Gage, 'will make hard shift, but she will be in fashion with her neck-chain and bracelets of pearls and her ear-bobs of some considerable jewels. The attire of this baser sort of people of blackamoors and mulattoes ... is so light, and their carriage so enticing, that many Spaniards even of the better sort (who are too prone to venery) disdain their wives for them, *Thomas Gage's Travels*, p. 69.

well illustrated by the Negro's treatment of the Indian. Daily, the Negro intimidated the Indian for his master, and so it was natural that he should also do so on his own account. One particularly common practice was for Negroes and mulattoes to wait around the outskirts of Mexico City and Puebla for Indian women and boys bringing fruit and vegetables to market and then to steal their produce and sell it themselves.[45] This behaviour was paralleled by all sorts of other similarly unbecoming practices. There was, consequently, in seventeenth-century Mexico, a great deal of condemnation of the Negro. The *Audiencia* judge, Montemayor y Cuenca, wrote in 1664 that the Negroes were accustomed 'to treat the Indians as their slaves, while they themselves enjoy more leisure and comfort than anyone else'.[46] Morga, who was harshly hostile to the Negro, took a similar view[47] and so did Viceroy Gelves, an uncompromising puritan who considered the negroes 'licentious people and badly inclined, having little virtue or Christianity'.[48] Gelves indeed, with the possible exception of Morga, was the fiercest critic—it is not too much to say adversary—of the Negro in seventeenth-century Mexico. As he saw it, the social role of the Negro and his turbulent style of life were elements of corruption high on the list of factors responsible for the moral decay of the viceroyalty. The ordinances issued by Gelves in 1622–3, designed to tighten the restrictions on the Negro, are certainly the severest of the century, equalled only by the April laws of 1612.[49] Gelves tried to stop the proliferation of black servants and lackeys in the retinues of dignitaries, decreeing that those black employees who did no useful work should register with the authorities so that they might be reassigned to useful work, and threatening that those who failed to comply would be despatched for service in the Philippines, Mexico's Siberia. Also, believing that the homes of free Negroes and mulattoes who were not fully engaged in 'useful' work were dens of vice and crime, he decreed that Negroes were no longer to live on their own or with other blacks, unless they were registered members of craft guilds, and from then on might live only in workshops, and other establishments owned by Spaniards.

The Mexican Negroes and mulattoes, then, though they were on both sides in the conflict between bureaucracy and enterprise, in the sense that it was in their best interest to serve their masters whether these

---

[45] Gibson, *The Aztecs*, pp. 147, 502: *ACM* xxx. 138.

[46] AGI México 77: 'Consulta al real acuerdo sobre tributos de negros y mulatos', fol. 1^v.

[47] *Relacion del alcamiento*, p. 27.

[48] AGN ordenanzas iv, fol. 57^v.

[49] AGN ordenanzas ii, fols. 36^v–37; iv, fols. 34^v–35, 40^v–42, 50^v–51, 57^v–58, 60–2, 68^v.

were *corregidores* or entrepreneurs, caciques or secular clergy, did have a place in Mexican politics in the sense that they were among those who profited from easy-going government and disorderly conditions and were the enemies of those who wanted tighter discipline and stringent application of the regulations. The relationship of the friction between bureaucracy and enterprise with the friction between the advocates of strict and lax government will become clearer, it is hoped, as the argument proceeds.

From the Negroes, we may turn briefly to the Filipinos and other Asiatics; for the Mexican people, though primarily a compound of red, white, and black, admits also to a strain of yellow. The migration from the Far East to Mexico never vied with that from Europe or Africa, but it was far from negligible. The route from Manila to Acapulco was, like all trading routes, more than merely a commercial link; the connection was also cultural and demographic.[50] Every year the Manila galleons, on the return run to Mexico, bore Asian as well as Spanish passengers. Most of these Asians were Filipinos,[51] others were of Chinese extraction, or mixed Chinese and Filipino, or of mixed Spanish and Chinese or Spanish and Filipino. There was also, in the 1640s, at least one native of Portuguese India residing in Mexico City, a man who earned his bread peddling cloth in the Indian suburbs.[52]

A proportion of these orientals were brought to New Spain as the slaves of Spaniards. At a time of chronic labour shortage, Filipino slaves were a welcome addition to the work force. They were not prized for social reasons in the way that Negroes were, but they were valued for their quickness and aptitude in the crafts and humble professions. Some inkling of the number of Filipino slaves imported into Mexico can perhaps be gleaned from a royal order directed to Viceroy Cerralvo in 1626.[53] In that year, the crown estimated that it was losing 15,000 pesos yearly in unpaid import duties on Filipino slaves, with the impost standing at 50 pesos a head; this suggests that something like 300 Asians were smuggled into the colony annually on top of a possibly

[50] For the influence of Mexico on the Philippines, see Rafael Bernal, 'México en Filipinas', and Luis González, 'Expansión de Nueva España en el Lejano Oriente', *Historia Mexicana*, xiv (1964), 187–205, 206–26.

[51] The Filipinos in Mexico were commonly called *Chinos* or *Indios Chinos*. The classification *Chino* in Nicolas León's list of Mexican racial types, signifying the offspring of an Indian woman by a quadroon, does not apply for the seventeenth century; N. León, *Las Castas del Mexico Colonial o Nueva España* (Mexico, 1924), p. 9; when *Chinos* are referred to in seventeenth-century viceregal or Inquisition papers, they are invariably natives of the Philippines or some other part of Asia.

[52] AGN Indios xvi, fol. 29.

[53] *CDHH*, ii. 1, pp. 291–2.

similar number imported legally. If this is so, then it is possible that some 6,000 orientals were entering the colony each decade.

The free Asiatics in Mexico were divided between the 'Indian' republic and the 'Spanish' republic in much the same way as the Indians were, a situation arising from the Spanish conception or definition of Asians as 'Chinese Indians'.[54] Thus Filipino and Chinese peddlers—and it is clear that petty trading was the chief activity of the free Asians—were freely permitted to dwell among the Indians and to pass from one Indian community to another.[55] They paid tribute in the same way as the Indians and were exempt, like the Indians, from paying the *alcabala* or sales tax on what they sold.[56] Sometimes, we find Filipinos married to Indian women. However, in cases where Filipinos or Chinese in Indian communities behaved badly, as in the case of the Chinese baker who in 1638 was forcing the Indians of Atlacomulco to buy his bread against their will,[57] they were expelled. In the 'Spanish' republic, orientals peddled cloth, candles, aguardiente, herbs, and medicines, much as they did in the 'Indian'. They were also prominent as barbers, especially in Mexico City, and their skill in this field brought them into collision with the Spanish barbers. Indeed, in 1635 the Spanish barbers of the capital went so far as to ask the Mexico City council to ask the viceroy to drive the oriental barbers out of the Plaza Mayor and fashionable districts and to confine them to more plebeian areas,[58] though not apparently with much success, for there were certainly still Filipino barbers in the Plaza Mayor in the 1640s.[59]

Although in law the orientals were 'Indians', in practice, especially in the cities, they were generally linked with the Negroes, mulattoes, and mestizos. Asians were often involved in the underworld of vice and crime in Mexico City and Puebla, and one often finds Filipinos and Chinese mentioned alongside Negroes and mulattoes in reports of robberies and the like. Several of the ordinances forbidding arms to the middle community, like that of Viceroy Mancera in 1665,[60] included the *Chinos* with the Negroes and mulattoes, and some other restrictive measures link the Asiatics with the blacks rather than with the Indians.[61] However, the constitutions of the craft guilds, even those of

[54] N. F. Martin also gives the phrase 'indianos de Filipinas', *Los Vagabundos*, p. 105.

[55] AGN Indios x, fol. 115^v; xi, fol. 137; *Chinos* were not included in seventeenth-century segregation orders applying to Negroes, mulattoes, and mestizos, AGN Indios xii, fol. 148.

[56] AGN Indios xi, fol. 363; xiii, fols. 116, 135^v.

[57] AGN Indios x, fol. 155.

[58] ACM xxx, fol. 24.

[59] AGN Indios xv, fols. 20^v–21.

[60] AGI México 40, r 2: Mancera, 2 Mar. 1665.

[61] Gregorio Martín de Guijo, *Diario, 1648–1664* (2 vols., Mexico, 1953), i. 229.

seventeenth-century as opposed to sixteenth-century origin, do not treat the *Chinos* as a specific category in the hierarchy of labour or make any reference to them. Like the ladino Indians, and indeed like the Negroes, mulattoes, and mestizos, Filipinos and Chinese in seventeenth-century Mexico usually bore simple Spanish names.

Finally, to conclude this chapter, it might be appropriate to glance at the bottom rung of the white community in Mexico, those whom Bishop Palafox called the 'base and factious Spaniards' and who were generally classed together with the Negroes, mulattoes, and mestizos— the white vagabonds, rogues, and drifters. White vagrancy, as we have seen, had long been a serious problem in Colonial Mexico. It had been at its worst in the mid-sixteenth century, but despite the subsequent improvement due to the economic progress of the viceroyalty, Spanish vagabondage remained a problem of some seriousness throughout the seventeenth century. The problem was aggravated by the decay of agriculture and industry in Spain itself during the early seventeenth century and the appearance, or rather growth, in Spain of a vagabond or *pícaro* class which was dauntingly large even by the standards of contemporary France and England. The *pícaros*, whose style of life inspired a whole tradition of novel-writing in Spain, were famous for their skill at getting along without recourse to work, and for their knavery and aptitude for the art of deception. Naturally, hordes of those vagrants gathered in Seville, the largest city in Spain in the early seventeenth century, and the seat of the Indies trade, and in Cadiz and San Lucar de Barrameda, the other Indies ports, and despite repeated orders from the crown that they should be prevented, many of them, male and female, managed to board ship for the New World. It is difficult to see how so many of these don Pablos were able to stow or bribe their way, but it is clear that they succeeded in crossing the Atlantic in considerable numbers. Powerless to prevent the seepage at Seville and Cadiz, Madrid instructed the viceroys to intercept the *pícaros* as they came off the ships at Veracruz and pack them off to the Philippines,[62] but it is evident that many or most of these ragged immigrants and prostitutes slipped the net, if there was a net, at least in most years.[63]

These vagrants were regarded with marked distaste by 'respectable' society in Mexico. They tended to mix with the mulattoes and mestizos, and in many cases were the leaders of tavern and low life. They were consequently, often depicted as outcasts, renegades, and enemies of their own race and kind.[64] One can say therefore that there

[62] AGN reales cédulas 1, fols. 39–40.

[63] BND 3636, fols. 167: Velasco II to council, 6 Apr. 1594; AGI México 29, r 4: Gelves to council, 14 Nov. 1621.

[64] As for instance in Gómez de Cervantes, *La Vida Económica*, p. 124.

was a certain tension between them and the rest of white society, the *pícaros* being regarded as a threat to the established order, though one could not say that it amounted to anything more than similar tensions between vagabonds and society in much of contemporary Europe. The one major drive against the vagrants in Mexico in the seventeenth century was launched by the reforming Viceroy Gelves, the same as had clamped down on the Negroes. Gelves's officers arrested so many vagabonds that even after the dispatch of a large number to Manila, the prisons of Mexico City were filled literally to overflowing,[65] with the result that some of these imprisoned vagrants were able to escape and rejoin their Negro and mestizo friends, taking their grudge against Gelves with them. But even in the context of Gelves's term (1621–4), the role of the white vagabond in building up tension in society was undoubtedly a subsidiary one: they were quick to join in the insurrection against the viceroy when it came, but they were not strong enough to do more than participate in what was essentially the work of other groups; but of the rising of January 1624, more later. Beyond the context of Gelves's term, one can say that the vagabond question was one of importance, but not that it was a really pressing one. Neither Viceroy Cerralvo nor Bishop Palafox in their long and detailed viceregal reports, nor any of the other viceroys of the seventeenth century depicted the vagrants as a major threat to government or society. And so we may fairly keep the vagabond question in mind as a minor piece in the framework of strains and stresses while denying it a position of any special significance.

[65] AGI México 29, r 4: Gelves to council, 14 Nov. 1621; and Gelves to council, 26 Feb. 1622, in *Descripción de la Nueva España*, p. 216.

III

THE SPANIARDS

So far in this study one complex of stresses has been singled out as a major source of tension in seventeenth-century Mexican society, that is the conflict of interests between the Spanish, Indian, and mendicant bureaucracies on the one hand, and the colonists (Creoles) and the diocesan (secular) clergy on the other. Another less important but still significant source of friction has also been identified, that between those elements in administration and society who preferred and benefited from weak government emanating from Madrid, and Mexico City, and those elements desirous of a greater measure of centralized control. Both of these stresses, and the relationship between them, will receive more attention as the study progresses, and as the first step in this direction it is now proposed to examine the position of the white population more closely than has been done hitherto, beginning with the Creole nobility.

In seventeenth-century Europe, and perhaps especially in France and Spain, the aristocracy played a major role in fomenting and leading opposition to central government. Thus one might fairly approach the Creole nobility of New Spain in the expectation of finding that it was a notable source of disturbance in the viceroyalty were it not for what has been said already of the events of 1565–6, of the great Creole conspiracy and of the defeat and crushing of the *encomenderos*. Unquestionably, the defeat of the Creole leadership had been complete and final. *Encomendero* morale was all but broken and the *encomienda* declined even faster after 1566 than it had done in the three decades before. Indian-grants escheated to the crown at such a rate that as against 480 *encomienda*-holders in 1560, there were apparently only 140 remaining by 1642.[1] Furthermore, the Conquistador lineages proved to be singularly unfortunate. Many *encomenderos* died without leaving heirs and those who did produce legitimate or legitimized Spanish or 'Spanish' sons did not produce many. Dorantes de Carranza, scion of one of the prominent Creole families, recorded sadly in 1604 that the living descendants of the 1,326 acknowledged Conquistadores of Mexico amounted only to 109 sons, 65 sons-in-law, 479 grandsons,

---

1 Chevalier, *Land and Society*, pp. 118–19.

and 85 great-grandsons—in all 934.[2] Moreover, the Creole aristocracy was extremely weak militarily, having little military knowledge or experience and hardly any arms. Gómez de Cervantes, like others of his class, bitterly resented the lack of firearms and other weapons other than the gentleman's sword in New Spain,[3] for he knew that neither the Creole, nor any nobility, can advance its fortunes far unarmed.

Yet despite its defeat and lack of military capability, the Mexican aristocracy did survive as a distinct and major element in Mexican society. Dorantes de Carranza and Gómez de Cervantes both lay great stress on the distinction between nobles—that is descendants of Conquistadores and relatives of Spanish nobles—and ordinary Creoles who made up the bulk of the colonists. At the head of this rather feeble élite, in the early seventeenth century, stood a tiny group of titled lords. The most eminent of these was, of course, the reigning Cortés, the fourth marqués del Valle, Don Pedro Cortés, head of the Cortés family from 1602 to 1629, (and a notable acquirer of land). However, with Don Pedro's death, the Creoles lost their first lord, for he, like so many of his class, died without male issue. The Cortés title and estates passed to the Duchess of Terranova and later to the Duchess of Monteleone, both of whom resided with their spouses in Italy. The second Mexican magnate and second biggest landowner of the viceroyalty was Don Fernando de Altamirano y Velasco (1597–1657), first conde de Santiago Calimaya, a relative through his mother of Viceroy Velasco II and owner of an immense territory in the Bajío; in the years 1651–2, the conde was *corregidor* of Mexico City and for the last two years of his life governor of Guatemala. His son, Juan de Altamirano y Velasco, second conde de Santiago Calimaya, was a member of the Mexico City council for some years and, in 1661, *corregidor* of Puebla. The third Creole magnate, also a great hacienda-owner of the Bajío, was Don Francisco Pacheco de Córdoba y Bocanegra, first marqués de Villamayor de las Ibiernas, a title conceded in 1617. His son, Carlos Pacheco de Córdoba y Bocanegra, the second marquis, moved in 1625 to Spain where, presumably, he preferred to live; however, other members of the Córdoba y Bocanegra clan remained prominent in Mexican life, particularly in the Puebla city council, through much of the rest of the century. The fourth lordly line stemmed from Don Rodrigo de Vivero, an important figure who had held high office in the Philippines, New Granada, and New Biscay and who, at the beginning of the seventeenth century, had visited Japan; in

[2] Balthasar Dorantes de Carranza, *Sumaria Relación de las Cosas de la Nueva España con noticia individual de los descendientes legítimos de los Conquistadores y primeros pobladores españoles* (1604) (Mexico, 1902), p. 234.
[3] Gómez de Cervantes, *La Vida económica*, pp. 96–8.

Mexico, he held the *encomienda* of Tecamachalco, an immense sugar plantation, as well as the largest sugar refinery in the viceroyalty, in the Orizaba district, and several vast haciendas. In recognition of his services, he and his descendants were granted the title of condes del Valle de Orizaba; however, the second marquis, Luis de Vivero y Velasco, appears to have been much less active than his father. The three or four other titles in Mexico in the seventeenth century were all sold to wealthy landowners very late on in the century and had not the same significance as far as the seventeenth century was concerned as these four.

Among untitled aristocratic Creole families[4] one of the most noteworthy were the Gómez de Cervantes Casaus descended from Juan de Cervantes Casaus, son of a *corregidor* of Jerez de la Frontera, knight of Santiago, a Sevillean hidalgo who had distinguished himself in the suppression of the Castilian *comuneros* and who had migrated to Mexico in 1524, and become governor of Pánuco in 1529 in succession to Nuño de Guzmán. His heir was the author Gonzalo Gómez de Cervantes and his grandson was Juan de Cervantes Casaus de Carvajal, knight of Santiago, *corregidor* of Zacatecas in 1621,[5] and head of the Mexico City militia in 1624. Don Juan's heir, Don Gonzalo Gómez de Cervantes y López, knight of Santiago, was captain of the viceroy's guard in 1640–2, *alcalde mayor* of Puebla in 1644, and captain-general of New Biscay in 1645. His first son, Gonzalo Gómez de Cervantes Mújica y Carvajal, was an undistinguished member of the Puebla city council in the 1670s. Other prominent Creole lineages were the La Mota, descended from the Conquistador Jerónimo de la Mota, son of a *Regidor* of Burgos, which included the author and famous churchman, Alonson de la Mota y Escobar, first Creole bishop of Puebla (1608–20), and Antonio de la Mota, knight of Santiago and *corregidor* of Puebla in 1617; the Cano Moctezuma, descended from Gonzalo Cano Moctezuma, the mestizo son of the Aztec princess Isabel Moctezuma, and including, in the early seventeenth century, the notable gentleman of Mexico City, Diego de Cano Moctezuma y Contreras, knight of Santiago and captain in the militia; the Sámano y Turcios, *encomienda*-holders, who were important in both the Mexico

---

4 AGI Patronato Real 223, r 4, fols. 22ᵛ–23, gives a list of 37 of the most eminent gentlemen of Mexico City; see also Leopoldo Martínez Cosio, *Los Caballeros de las órdenes militares en México* (Mexico 1946), Guillermo Lohmann Villena, *Los Americanos en las Ordenes Nobiliarias, 1529–1900* (2 vols., Madrid, 1947), and, for a list of all the *alcaldes mayores* and *alcaldes ordinarios* of Puebla in the seventeenth century, *La Puebla de los Angeles en el siglo XVII*, ed. Mariano Cuevas (Mexico, 1945), pp. 64–74.

5 Juan de Cervantes was the only Creole among seven *corregidores* of Zacatecas nominated between 1605 and 1632, Bakewell, *Silver Mining and Society*, p. 90.

and Puebla city councils and included the Felipe de Sámano who was one of the militia officers in Mexico City in 1624 and *corregidor* of Puebla in 1637; and the Solís y Barrasa, *encomenderos* of Alcolmán, who included Francisco de Solís Barrasa y Quiñones Ulloa Orduña y Vázquez de Ulloa, knight of Calatrava and for many years representative of the Mexico City council in Madrid.

The Mexican nobility, as is evident from its writings, was truly Creole in character. Admittedly there were some points at which the interests of Creole nobility and commonalty collided, as Gómez de Cervantes makes clear with his assertion that birth, not money, should determine the membership of the Mexico City council. 'Those who secure these positions', he says, 'are those who have most cash and not those who are the most honourable and the best fitted to serve the republic.'[6] He proposes that a dozen seats on the *cabildo* be permanently reserved for noblemen, a suggestion unlikely to have met with the approval of the non-noble. In general however, the writings of Gómez de Cervantes, like those of Dorantes de Carranza, Carrillo Altamirano, and other aristocratic writers, show that the interests of the Creole élite and of the main body of the colonists coincided: both groups vociferously demanded the intermingling of Indians with Spaniards; both called for drastic reductions in the powers of the *corregidores* and friars; both wanted to see more administrative and clerical offices assigned to Creoles with fewer strings attached. 'It is a great affront', declared Gómez de Cervantes,' that requests for honours by descendants of Conquistadores are hopeless unless they are aided and preferred by a member of the viceroy's entourage.'[7]

The question of offices was crucial, for, apart from individual considerations, it was only by the acquisition of numerous important positions that the colonists could hope to extend their control over New Spain's labour force and economy. The Creoles did not expect to be given the very top posts. Virtually no viceroys or archbishops of Mexico in the seventeenth century were of Mexican birth, but no one complained of this.[8] The Creoles acquiesced in that fundamental rule of the royal appointments system whereby no high officer of the crown could ordinarily be appointed to a province in which he had extensive personal ties. Three viceroys were technically Creoles, Velasco II, Cadereita, and Montezuma, but even of these Cadereita was born outside Mexico in the South American province of Quito. Of the archbishops of Mexico, only two were American-born, Feliciano de la

6 Gómez de Cervantes, *La Vida económica*, pp. 93–4.
7 Ibid., p. 124.
8 Parry, *The Spanish Seaborne Empire*, p. 335.

Vega (1639–40) a Peruvian Creole, and the rather feeble Alonso de Cuevas y Dávalos (1664–5) a native of Mexico City. As a rule, the heads of state and Church in New Spain were not of New Spanish origin and this was accepted.

The point at which Madrid and the Creoles failed to see eye to eye was over all the rest of the administrative and ecclesiastical hierarchy from immediately below the highest authorities down to intermediate levels. The third institution of New Spain, following the viceroy and archbishop in precedence, and the highest therefore to which the Creoles aspired, was the *Audiencia* of Mexico. But because the *Audiencia* was of such obvious political importance, Madrid desired that this bench, which usually numbered six to eight justices in the seventeenth century, should have as few ties with interests and personages within its area of jurisdiction as possible. The judges were enveloped in an elaborate protocol designed to set them apart from Creole society, and, like the viceroys, *Audiencia* justices could not, in law at any rate, marry whilst holding office without special royal permission.[9] The Creoles, however, resentfully aware that in Castile it was sufficient for an *Audiencia* justice to move to another province than his own so that for instance Sevilleans could serve on the *Audiencia* of Granada, demanded at least some of the seats on the bench.[10] In 1637 the Mexico City council asked that half the places on the *Audiencia* of Mexico, as well as half of those on the three lesser *Audiencias* of the viceroyalty, those of New Galicia, Guatemala, and the Philippines, should be reserved for Mexican Creoles.[11] But though they wanted these positions, Mexican Spaniards cannot have been surprised that they failed to get them. Madrid consistently appointed only *gachupines* to the *Audiencia* of Mexico, and when a Mexican jurist was nominated *Audiencia* judge, it was to one of the three lesser benches that he went.

What Mexican Spaniards not only wanted but expected and demanded was possession of a much larger share of the intermediate

---

[9] Haring, *The Spanish Empire*, p. 126.

[10] Positions on *Audiencias* were not kept in largely Castilian hands as a matter of policy in all parts of the Spanish Monarchy; the *Audiencia* of Catalonia, for instance, was staffed mainly by Catalans, so on this point the Creoles could very convincingly claim discrimination; J. H. Elliott, *The Revolt of the Catalans* (Cambridge, 1963), p. 86.

[11] ACM xxxi. 70; the Peruvian Creoles, at this time, made the same claim much more emphatically; see Alonso de Solórzano y Velasco, *Discurso legal e informacion en derecho en favor de los nacidos en los reynos del Piru y Conveniencias para que en el . . . puedan obtener placas de oydor . . .* (n.p., n.d.).

positions in bureaucracy and Church.[12] They did receive a certain number, but these made up only a small, some said insultingly small, proportion. Legally speaking, the only limitation or rule regarding appointment of *corregidores* was that they could not serve in their native districts, but in practice, as we have seen, Creoles obtained only a tiny fraction of these places. Creoles spoke of discrimination and there is no doubt that they were to some extent justified; in Castile, as Mexican Spaniards pointed out, non-Castilian and American Spaniards were actually barred from the office by law; the only stipulation in Castile was that *corregidores* had to serve away from their place of origin.[13] Some viceroys, notably the marqués de Montesclaros and Bishop Palafox, were in favour of conceding or at least selling more of these posts to Mexican Spaniards, arguing that this would strengthen the Monarchy by binding the Creole population more closely to it;[14] but most viceroys held to the opposite view. They regarded their own power, the viceregal authority, as the primary instrument of the Monarchy in Mexico and acted on the principle, which in itself was perfectly logical, that Creole subordinates were far less dependent on that authority than non-Creoles.

The suitability of Mexican Spaniards for positions of responsibility was hotly debated not only in legal and clerical tracts but in the streets, in the university, and from the pulpit. One climax in this controversy was the furious Gómez incident of 1618. Father Gómez was a leading Jesuit of Mexico City and like most of his order in seventeenth-century Mexico was peninsular in both origin and outlook.[15] Being one of the most eloquent preachers of his day in Mexico, he was widely known;[16] but he was also widely resented owing to his utter lack of tact. On 13 August 1618 he delivered a sermon in the chapel of the hospital of San Hipólito in Mexico City, one the largest and most richly endowed in the Indies, with particular *gachupín* associations and specializing in passengers who arrived sick from Spain. In this sermon he referred to the recent controversial sale by Viceroy Guadalcázar of a number of

12ACM xxxi. 70–1; ACP xviii, fol. 252; Juan Ortiz de Cervantes, *Informacion en favor del derecho que tienen los nacidos en las Indias a ser preferidos en las prelacias, dignidades, canongias, y otros beneficios eclesiasticos y oficios seculares* (Madrid, 1619).

13Ortiz de Cervantes, *Informacion en favor*, fol. 4ỹ.

14Though Montesclaros, at least, was probably just defending himself against the complaints of angry Creoles, *CDHE* xxvi. 170–1.

15Gerard Décorme, *La Obra de los Jesuitas Mexicanos durante la Epoca Colonial, 1572–1767* (3 vols., Mexico, 1941), i. 385–96.

16BL M–M149–50: 'México y sus disturbios, documentos para servir a la historia de los disturbios y tumultos acaecidos en México durante el siglo XVII', copiado and edited by José F. Ramírez in 2 vols., i. 121, 129.

prestigious positions to Creoles, and criticized the action bitterly. In the course of his remarks, he ventured to denigrate the Creoles in no uncertain terms and declared that they were incompetent to run anything, even a hen-pen, let alone a district governorship or municipality. At these words, not surprisingly, his congregation fell into uproar, swords were drawn, and the service ended in chaos.[17]

The storm that Gómez provoked lasted for some months. The archbishop, Juan Pérez de la Serna, was placed in a difficult position, for certain of the lower secular clergy in the capital had been demanding the chastisement of Gómez for some time and now this demand had become irresistible. A rupture between secular clergy and Jesuits, despite the closeness of the links between the two, seemed certain. Gómez was treated to a stern archiepiscopal rebuke and had his preaching licence withdrawn. At this, the Jesuits, feeling insulted, threw their customary caution to the winds, and entered the lists on Gómez's behalf, challenging the legality of the archbishop's action. As a result, the popularity and standing of the Jesuits with the Creoles slumped, though only temporarily, and donations to the Society fell off sharply.[18]

The quarrel continued through the autumn, enabling the archbishop to make considerable political capital out of the situation. On 20 September, for instance, sermons were delivered all over Mexico City in praise of the Creoles and of their abilities and intellect, one of these sermons being attended by the Mexico City council, the *Audiencia*, and the viceroy, as well as by the archbishop. For their part, the Jesuits persisted in Gómez's defence and brought in Antonio de Brámbila y Arriaga, the absentee *maestrescuela* of the cathedral of Oaxaca, a noted enemy of bishops and critic of Creoles, as his counsel. Brámbila had hardly begun his task however, when Pérez de la Serna had him incarcerated in the archiepiscopal gaol. The Jesuit reply to this was to appeal to *Audiencia* and viceroy, which led to their obtaining an order for Brámbila's release.[19] As the archbishop refused to release him, a mixed commission of *Audiencia* officials and Jesuits forcibly released him.

Soon after this, a compromise was reached between archbishop and Jesuits, for which the viceroy claimed the credit.[20] It was agreed that Gómez should deliver the official Jesuit New Year sermon for 1619 in Mexico City, thus showing that neither Gómez nor the Jesuits had incurred dishonour, but that from 2 January Gómez was to reside

17 'México y sus disturbios', i. 218.
18 'México y sus disturbios', i. 187, 219.
19 Alegre, *Historia de la Compañía*, ii. 109.
20 AGI México 29, r 2: Guadalcázar to council, 31 Jan. 1619.

outside Mexico City for at least some months, in order to soothe Creole pride. This compromise marked the beginning of an important resumption in Jesuit policy: the Society recognized that it had blundered badly in wounding Creole feelings and jeopardized its own vital interests and influence over a point of no intrinsic importance, and now sought to repair the damage as speedily as possible. By means of a resolute volte-face, it reverted to its traditional pro-Creole stance,[21] and restored good relations with Archbishop Pérez de la Serna.[22] Thus in the years 1621–4, as we shall see, under the rule of Viceroy Gelves, archbishop and Jesuits co-operated in what was perhaps the most notable instance of pro-Creole policy by *gachupines* in Mexico in the whole of the seventeenth century.

Archbishop Pérez de la Serna's policy, in the Gómez as in other cases, was typical of the tendency of the bishops in seventeenth-century Mexico to identify, or at least strongly sympathize, with the Creole cause. Many other outstanding leaders of the secular clergy in the mid-Colonial period, especially Archbishop Manso (1628–35) and Juan de Palafox, bishop of Puebla (1640–9), the one Castilian and the other Aragonese, followed closely in Pérez de la Serna's footsteps. Each of these three, and others like them, were keenly aware that their power, and their chances of extending their power, depended on what they could do to strengthen the secular clergy as a whole, and this in turn involved pursuing Creole goals, for, as we have seen, the rank and file of the diocesan clergy were overwhelmingly Creole. This tendency on the part of peninsular Spanish bishops, like the policy of the Jesuits, suggests that Creole-*gachupín* friction was often less a matter of social and cultural distinctions and prejudice, though undoubtedly it was a matter of those things too, than of policy and political convenience. After all the friction between the settlers in New Spain and a bureaucracy emanating from Castile had existed even before the appearance of the first generation of Creoles, having begun as soon as the Conquest was over. Moreover, the attitude of the bishops and the Jesuits indicates that the political rift continued to be the most important cleavage throughout. It was the political rift which did most to exacerbate the differences between Creole and *gachupín*, while it

21 As Sánchez Bacquero explains, the Jesuits, having arrived in Mexico too late to help in the conversion of any other than the nomadic tribes of the north, had established themselves in the viceroyalty by concentrating on colleges for the education of the Creoles; Juan Sánchez Baquero, *Relación breve* (Mexico 1945), pp. 148–50; see also BND 3636, fols. 80ᵛ–81.

22 See p. 146; the rapprochement between Serna and the Society was completed by 1621 and in that year Serna delivered the sermon in the main Jesuit church in Mexico City on the anniversary of the canonization of St Francis Xavier; the sermon was published (Andrade no. 94).

also sometimes cut across Creole-*gachupín* lines. Just as there were peninsulars who sided with the colonists in the political battle, so there were a number of individual Creoles, as we shall see, who threw in their lot with the bureaucratic party.

As a rule, it was easier for Creoles to rise into the ranks of the upper secular clergy than to obtain high office in the secular administration.[23] One reason for this was that most of the arguments used to justify the exclusion of Mexican Spaniards from magistracies, governorships, and military command, arguments to the effect that they were too partial to local interests, were barely applicable in the ecclesiastical sphere. Another was the tendency of *gachupín* bishops to favour the Creole cause, for although it was for Madrid to make the appointments—Madrid's monopoly of ecclesiastical patronage in the Indies stands in sharp contrast to the very limited patronage that it wielded, or chose to wield, in the secular sphere—the bishops of the Indies had a say in the matter and this tended to facilitate preferment of Creoles. And so Mexican Spaniards rose in the hierarchy in New Spain and aspired to the rank of bishop. It is true that the majority of the bishops in seventeenth-century Mexico were peninsulars, but Creoles made up a substantial minority. The four highest positions, the sees of Mexico, Puebla, Michoacán, and Guadalajara, were the ones which went least often to Creoles. We have already pointed out that only two of the fourteen archbishops of Mexico in the seventeenth century were of American birth. Of six bishops of Puebla in the century, two were Creoles, the eloquent Mota y Escobar, whom we have mentioned, and the fanatical Don Juan Sáenz de Mañozca (1674–5), a sadistic Basque-Creole inquisitor. Of ten bishops of Michoacán, again only two were Creoles and one of these Peruvian. Among the bishops of Guadalajara, or New Galicia, there were three Creoles out of ten. In the remaining dioceses, Mexican-Spaniards fared better. In one, that of Oaxaca, they were the majority, supplying no fewer than eight bishops out of eleven. In the dioceses of Chiapas, the Yucatán, and New Biscay Creoles made up a third to half of the bishops. In addition, various Mexican ecclesiastics secured preferment to important sees elsewhere in the Indies. Diego de Guevara, a native of Mexico City, became archbishop of Santo Domingo in 1640; Nicolás de la Torre, who for many years was rector of the University of Mexico, became bishop of Cuba in 1646.

Mexican Spaniards disliked the fact that the majority of the bishops of New Spain were *gachupines*.[24] It appeared to them to be a grave

[23] Cuevas, *Historia de la Iglesia en México*, iii. 139–40; see also Gil González Dávila, *Teatro Eclesiastico*.

[24] ACP xviii, fol. 257; Luis de Betancurt, *Memorial i informacion por las Iglesias*

injustice that most of the bishops in their country should be taken not from Mexican cathedral chapters, but from among the clergy in Spain. It angered Creoles to think that the pick of the ecclesiastical positions of Mexico went to Castilians, while there was not an instance of a Creole obtaining equivalent preferment in Castile. Yet this very real grievance did not reflect itself in the seventeenth century in a split between upper and lower secular clergy of the sort that disturbed the cathedral chapters of Catalonia at this time.[25] In the eighteenth century in Mexico the situation was to be different, for it appears that under the Bourbons the two levels of secular clergy became seriously estranged, with the bishops identifying themselves with the bureaucratic and *gachupín* party.[26] In the seventeenth century the grievance remained beneath the surface, a tension that found no political outlet, for under the circumstances of the time, in the midst of the fight with the mendicant orders and the bureaucratic party, each level was dependent on the support of the other.

Having conveyed something of the position of the Creole nobility, of the chances and grievances of Creoles who sought high office in state and Church, and of the leverage which the Creoles had with the bishops, we might now proceed to consider the position, in the eyes of European Spaniards, of the Creole population as a whole. We have already suggested that there was a social, cultural, and even ethnic dimension to the estrangement between bureaucracy and colonists in that the former was staffed mainly by peninsulars while the latter were predominantly Creole; it is appropriate now to examine this question further and assess its effects on the friction between bureaucracy and colonists.

It is clear that we may not say, even in a guarded manner, that tension between peninsulars and Creoles as such became more acute after 1600 or after 1620 when the economic slump began. Indeed peninsular prejudice against Creoles and the tendency of peninsulars to regard American Spaniards as an alien and inferior breed seem to have been most marked in a much earlier period, in the second half of the sixteenth century. It was while the Creoles were still a novelty and while peninsular distrust was added to by peninsular ignorance that European Spaniards harboured their more fantastic notions concerning

Metropolitanas i Catedrales de las Indias sobre que sean proveidas sus prelacias en los naturales i capitulares dellas (Madrid, 1634).

---

25 See Elliott, *The Revolt of the Catalans*, pp. 251–2.

26 See K. M. Schmitt, 'The Clergy and the Independence of New Spain', *HAHR* xxxiv (1954), 289–312.

them. López de Velasco, for instance, writing in 1570,[27] declared that Spanish Americans were distinctly darker in skin colour than Europeans and that they would eventually become indistinguishable from the Indians, even if they were to avoid mixing their blood with theirs; he also thought that the brain and mind would degenerate under the physical and climatic conditions of the New World, and that the unfortunate Creoles would therefore become progressively more barbarous and stupid. This process of degeneration, in López de Velasco's view, would be hastened by the socially base character and vileness of the majority of the settlers.[28] Scarcely less unkind to the Creoles was the Franciscan leadership in Mexico in the 1580s, at the time when the friction between regular and secular clergy was becoming more intense. One of the reasons why secular clergy should be excluded from Indian parishes in Mexico, argued the Franciscan leadership of that period, was that the lower secular clergy in Mexico were mostly Creole and that the Creoles were unfitted to be the moral and religious guardians of anyone, being by nature lazy, incompetent, and untrustworthy.[29]

By the early seventeenth century, peninsular authors were markedly more cautious in their utterances regarding the Creoles and, in many cases, were inclined to speak in favour of them. Circumstances had changed and it was no longer respectable or politic to disparage Creoles openly, as Gómez discovered, nor was it feasible any longer to insist on the natural inferiority of the Creole, citing in support theories about climate and environment, for the Mexican Spanish population, far larger and richer than it had been before, was now a reality to be reckoned with. Creoles were obviously not degenerating, changing colour, or taking to wearing loincloths, nor could they any more be dismissed as a homespun people hopelessly ignorant and illiterate. As we have seen, the Jesuits were fast providing the Creoles with the reading, writing, and Latin that they had lacked, raising the level of their hopes and encouraging them to regard themselves as the intellectual, physical, and moral equals of the peninsulars.[30] The improvement was reflected at the University in Mexico City which

[27]Juan López de Velasco, *Geografía y descripción universal de las Indias* (Madrid, 1894), pp. 37–8.

[28]The social background of the settlers was denigrated with some vehemence by several peninsulars in sixteenth-century Mexico, notably Motolinía and Mendieta.

[29]*Cartas de Religiosos*, pp. 173–4.

[30]Viceroy Velasco II, himself a Creole, was particularly enthusiastic over the moral improvement of Creole youth resulting from Jesuit educational activity; see BND 3636, fols. 80ᵛ–81: Velasco II to council, 30 May 1591.

attained academic standards in this period which impressed a number of European Spanish scholars. Vázquez de Espinosa, writing in the second decade of the century, asserted that the accomplishments of the university students were of a high order and cited this as proof that the Mexican climate was not in fact unconducive to intellectual develop-ment.[31] The one and only reason in his opinion for the difficulties met with by Creole graduates in their search for positions was that they were so remote from the eyes of the king. Juan de Solórzano, in his great treatise, the *Política Indiana*, held that American Spaniards should be classed as genuine and authentic Spaniards and that, being such, they should have exactly the same opportunities and privileges as penin-sulars.[32] Emphasizing that the Spanish American communities were true offshoots of the Spanish stem, he compared them to the colonies of the ancient Romans established around the Mediterranean. He scornfully dismissed the idea that Creoles were in any way inferior or that the climate of the New World caused degeneration, pointing out that every kind of climate and environment, including the Castilian, was to be met with in the Indies. In support of his assertion that Creoles were capable of attaining the same degree of intellectual excellence as their peninsular cousins he cited the case of that most prodigious of seventeenth-century Mexican academics, the Dominican friar Francisco Naranjo, who not only knew by heart the whole output of Saint Thomas Aquinas but could reel off relevant passages from it at devastating speed for or against any point whatever.[33]

The Creoles bided by the scientific principles of the age no less than did European Spaniards and adopted similar premises to those of their detractors. Even their conclusions were not always wholly different. Escobar y Mota, for instance, considered that

Spaniards born and raised [in Zacatecas] are, experience has shown, stronger, more vigorous, and harder-working than those from other parts [of Mexico] and thus they distinguished themselves in their professions and occupations and those who are of an academic bent study longer and harder and with less damage to their health than those from [central] New Spain and so it is the common opinion here that people born and raised in Zacatecas are very similar to Castilian people both in their sharpness of mind and strength of body . . .; also experience has shown that Castilian wines mature better in this city than elsewhere [in Mexico].[34]

[31]*Descripción de la Nueva España*, p. 127; see also Sánchez Baquero, *Relacion breve*, p. 43.

[32]Solórzano, *Política Indiana*, pp. 244–6.

[33]Ibid., 246; Alonso Franco y Ortega, *Segunda parte de la historia de la Provincia de Santiago de México, orden de predicadores de la Nueva España* (Mexico, 1900), p. 481; Leonard, *Baroque Times in Old Mexico*, p. 26.

[34]Mota y Escobar, *Descripción geográfica*, p. 67.

Other Creoles, however, still using arguments relating to climate and environment, showed greater determination to stand by Central Mexico. In 1618, at the time of the Gómez affair, a time also of exceptional bitterness between peninsular and Creole Franciscans in New Spain, an eminent Creole physician, Diego Cisneros, in response to popular pressure for a learned defence of the intellectual and bodily qualities of the white inhabitants of Mexico City, published a treatise on the medical implications of the climate and environment of the capital.[35] In it, he subjected the winds, waters, temperatures, soil properties, and products of the valley of Mexico to rigorous scrutiny in terms of the medical criteria laid down by Hippocrates and Galen and endeavoured to set the minds of his countrymen at rest. The effects of the environment of Mexico City, he declared, were very similar to those of some of the choicest parts of Old Castile. The diet of the Mexican Spaniards, too, he pronounced wholesome and like the Castilian. Thus he was able to conclude that the differences between peninsular and Creole were really very slight and afforded no grounds whatever for discrimination.

Cisneros's anxiety to demonstrate the similarity and resemblance of *gachupín* and Creole was typical of the attitude of seventeenth-century Mexican Spanish authors. Lázaro de Arregui, for instance, referring to the Creoles of New Galicia, declared that even 'on the ranches and in the remotest places, the Spanish language is spoken as faultlessly and eloquently as at Court or in Toledo'.[36] Alonso Franco, a Creole Dominican friar, contended that peninsular-Creole bad feeling would have made some sense had the two sets of Spaniards been, in any real sense, different, but that as they were essentially the same in blood, speech and traditions, it made no sense whatever.[37] Probably this is what one would expect. After all, the Creoles in their political aspirations were not seeking more independence from Spain or anything resembling autonomy; what they wanted was more effective integration into the Monarchy as a whole. Mexican Creoles wanted to expand their opportunities within the existing framework of the empire and it was therefore logical that they should stress their Spanishness and stress also their loyalty to the crown. Esteban García, the Creole Augustinian chronicler, was even more anxious to prove that the Mexican climate inspired obedience and respect for Spanish institutions than he was to show that it favoured development of the intellect.[38]

[35] Diego Cisneros, *Sitio, naturaleza, y propriedades de la ciudad de Mexico* (Mexico, 1618), esp. fols. 113ᵛ–115ᵛ.
[36] Lázaro de Arregui, *Descripción de la Nueva Galicia*, p. 38.
[37] Franco y Ortega, *Segunda parte*, pp. 420, 535.
[38] Esteban García, *Crónica de la provincia Augustiniana del santisimo nombre de Jesús de México, libro quinto* (Madrid, 1918), pp. 222–3; *ACM* xxvi. 350–2.

The suggestion made by some peninsulars that the tumult of 1624 in Mexico City showed that the Creoles were of questionable loyalty moved him to ask whether it was any reflection on the Spaniards of Granada that the moriscos had risen in rebellion in King Philip II's time; of course not, he contended, and neither were the Creoles to blame if the vile plebeian mass of Indians, Negroes, and half-castes had plunged Mexico City into turmoil. 'The Mexican climate,' he declared, 'whatever prejudiced persons may say, fosters love, veneration, and obedience not only for the king, but also for his viceroys and ministers.'

Although Creole writers, with the exception of Mota y Escobar, were reluctant to admit that Creoles were lethargic and lacking in drive by comparison with European Spaniards, they readily admitted that Mexican Spaniards suffered from idleness.[39] This they blamed on their distance from Madrid and the consequent difficulty they experienced in finding positions in the bureaucracy and Church. No one considered it pertinent that the majority of Creoles disdained manual labour and the crafts and had come to Mexico, as Viceroy Velasco II put it, 'to eat and spend but never to work'. On the contrary, it was considered an important mark of Creole quality that even those of the most humble ancestry had turned their backs on the callings of their immigrant fathers and grandfathers.[40] Also, Creole authors avoided discussing the military ability, or rather lack of military ability, of their people. One is very struck that although descent from the Conquistadores is vehemently insisted upon, the military tradition and ethic which one might suppose to have been integral to the Conquistador legend are never mentioned; this of course amounts to a tacit avowal that the Creoles were essentially a demilitarized élite, a community totally without experience or taste for war, which indeed they were.[41] One is frequently informed of Creole skill with horses, but of Creole skill with arms, never.

The Creoles may have regarded themselves as an essentially noble people, claiming descent from the Conquistadores and avoiding work, but peninsulars and indeed other Europeans, including the English Catholic later turned Protestant, Thomas Gage, found Creole pride preposterous. Even those, and they were a tiny minority, who really were descended from the Conquistadores failed to impress peninsulars, for it was an open secret that the Conquistadores themselves had been a very mixed bunch. There were hidalgos, even a few relatives of great

[39] *ACM* xxx. 213; ACP xviii, fol. 252^v; Sánchez Baquero, *Relación breve*, p. 42; Vetancurt, *Theatro Mexicano*, part i, p. 12.

[40] Vetancurt, *Theatro Mexicano*, part ii, p. 3.

[41] The military feebleness of the American Spaniards in general is commented on by R. D. Hussey, 'Spanish Reaction to Foreign Aggression in the Caribbean to about 1680', *HAHR* ix (1929).

aristocrats, among the conquerors, but the majority were mere commoner adventurers, and by the seventeenth century the two strands were inextricable. Furthermore, although Creole nobles sometimes spoke as if nobles and non-nobles engaged in different economic activities,[42] peninsulars were very unfavourably struck by the closeness between the Mexican nobility and the commercial element. 'In these provinces', wrote Viceroy Mancera, exaggerating somewhat and with a hint of contempt, 'the gentleman is usually a merchant, and the merchant a gentleman.'[43]

Moreover, quite apart from questions of class origin and economic conduct, Creoles, including the Creole nobility, were suspect in peninsular eyes for another reason: there was grave doubt regarding the purity of their blood. In Spain, the purity of blood controversy had assumed a new form in the mid-sixteenth century, following the acceptance of the purity of blood statute by the cathedral chapter of Toledo, seat of the primate of the Spanish church, in 1547.[44] From that time on, and increasingly, candidates for offices, both secular and clerical, had had to present legal certificates to show that their lineage was free from the taint of either Moorish or Jewish blood. A mania for purity of blood and purity of blood certificates swept Spain and, soon after, the Indies too. The many hundreds of purity of blood certificates preserved in the Mexican Inquisition files testify to their great importance in seventeenth-century Mexican society and politics. Unfortunately, however, for Mexican Spaniards, it was often far more difficult for third- and fourth-generation Creoles to meet the conditions for the granting of such certificates than for peninsular newcomers. The Conquest of Mexico had preceded the main purity of blood movement by more than three decades, and so many seventeenth-century Creoles, having no means of contact with the places of origin of their grandfathers and great-grandfathers, or with persons able to give legally valid testimony that they were pure in blood, could not prove that they were of unsullied 'Old Christian' ancestry; and indeed, in many cases, they were not.[45] Although strictly speaking it was illegal for Christians

---

[42]'There are few nobles who are rich,' says Mota y Escobar, speaking of Zacatecas, 'and they are mine-owners; among middle-class people (*gente intermedia*) however, there are many who are wealthy with twenty thirty, and forty thousand pesos and three or four with a hundred thousand, and these are all retail merchants;' see Mota y Escobar, *Descripción geográfica*, p. 66.

[43]*Instrucciones que los virreyes de la Nueva España dejaron*, p. 258; see also Durand, *La Transformación del Conquistador*, ii. 64.

[44]Elliott, *Imperial Spain* (London, 1963), pp. 212–17.

[45]José Durand, *La Transformación social del Conquistador* (2 vols., Mexico, 1953), i. 35–9; Lucia García de Proodian. *Los Judíos en América. Sus Actividades en los virreinatos de Nueva Castilla y Nueva Granada, siglo xvii* (Madrid, 1966), pp. 27–31.

of Moorish or Jewish blood, that is to say 'New Christians', to cross the Atlantic, as it was also for gypsies, it is certain that unlicensed New Christian passengers experienced no more difficulty in reaching the New World than did unlicensed vagabonds and misfits. Generally speaking, those New Christians who crossed the Atlantic and were of Moorish descent were few, for most moriscos, as they were called, were poor peasants, but those of Jewish origin, being much more prominent in the Spanish middle class, were quite numerous, and there was no way of knowing where they had infiltrated and where they had not.

Thus, to sum up on Creole-peninsular relations in seventeenth-century Mexico, it may be said that the differences between the two groups of Spaniards were a major cause of friction, always likely to give rise to incidents such as the Gómez affair of 1618, despite the efforts of some European Spanish authors to combat anti-Creole prejudice among their countrymen; indeed the very fact that such efforts were made indicates the extent of the fault. Much of the prejudice sprang from social snobbery, from a growing awareness of the cultural differences between the two communities, and from the idea that the Creoles were racially impure; there was also an element of moral snobbery rooted in the belief that Creoles conducted their lives less strictly than peninsulars and permitted their women too much freedom. (Europeans were particularly shocked to see that even 'respectable' women, or relatively 'respectable' women, were permitted, in America, to play cards and dice in mixed company.) However, this cleavage between Creole and peninsular was nothing new in the seventeenth century and was subsidiary, in certain respects, to what we have accounted the overriding tension in the colony in the seventeenth century—the conflict between bureaucracy and colonists.

To throw further light on this key point, the interaction of the tensions between peninsulars and Creoles and bureaucrats and colonists, let us turn next to examine the principal political and representative institution of the colonists—the city councils (cabildos).

From the time of the Conquest onwards, the principal organ of expression at the disposal of the settlers in America had been the cabildo. One of Cortés's very first actions after his landing at San Juan de Ulúa had been to found the city of Veracruz complete with city council, and by so doing he had acted in the true Castilian tradition of colonization, for in the later Middle Ages the cabildo had played a prominent role in the recovery of southern Spain from Islam. Instinctively the Conquistadores had adopted the cabildo as their mouthpiece.

The routine functions of the Mexican Spanish city council were similar to those of municipal councils everywhere. Councillors assembled twice weekly to discuss municipal business, came to their decisions by vote, and kept records of their meetings. The composition of the Mexican Spanish *cabildo* varied from town to town, but usually it consisted of one or two senior councillors known as *alcaldes ordinarios* and six or more ordinary councillors or *regidores*. Mexico City and Puebla, as the first and second city of the viceroyalty, each had two senior aldermen; Mexico City had a varying number, usually ten, of ordinary aldermen in the seventeenth century, and Puebla, which had the largest number of councillors of any city in the Indies, a score;[46] Zacatecas, the third city of the viceroyalty, had two *alcaldes ordinarios* and six or seven *regidores*. The *corregidor* was not, strictly speaking, a member of the *cabildo*, but he could sit in on *cabildo* meetings and vote when he chose; essentially, his task was to mediate between viceroy and municipality and represent the crown in the municipality. Beneath the *cabildo* itself, there was a staff of lesser functionaries attached to it, secretaries and constables whose job was to carry out the council's instructions.

At first the Mexican *cabildos* had been truly representative of the towns. By an ordinance of Charles V of 1523, the municipal councils of the Indies were to be elected democratically by the white citizenry in annual elections.[47] In privileges and functions the Mexican municipalities were authentic offspring of the powerful city councils of late medieval Castile and in politics they were an important force working for the colonists. Thus in the years 1528—30 the Mexico City council was one of the chief focuses of opposition to Nuño de Guzmán. However, the 'democratic complexion' as Haring called it, fruit of an era when the cities had experienced a golden age throughout Europe, an era which came to its definitive end with the crushing of the revolt of the Castilian towns by Charles V in 1521, was gradually altered during the course of the sixteenth century by the crown and by city councillors who wished to perpetuate their privileges and become a closed oligarchy. The same considerations which led the Spanish government to seek to weaken and restrict the Conquistadores led it also to seek the weakening of the *cabildo*. Apart from the *corregidores*, who speedily became the most important single check to the councils, various changes were introduced.[48] Council elections were turned into closed elections with only former members of the council entitled to

---

[46]See the lists of new *cabildo* members in January of each year in the ACM and ACP; also Constantino Bayle, *Los Cabildos seculares en la América Española* (Madrid, 1952), p. 101.

[47]Haring, *The Spanish Empire*, p. 152.

[48]Bayle, *Los Cabildos seculares*, p. 102.

vote. Some council positions were sold[49] and became proprietary for varying periods, sometimes for life. In short, city government became, with the encouragement of Madrid, the preserve of a narrow self-perpetuating clique that was highly vulnerable to viceregal interference. The perquisites of *cabildo* office were great, for the councillors had certain price-fixing and many other lucrative powers; in the period 1606–40, positions on the Mexico City council commanded up to 10,000 pesos apiece. Also it became usual for one or two *gachupines* to find their way into the councils; Felipe de Sámano y Turcios, the Creole nobleman and *corregidor* of Puebla in 1637, observed that it had become customary for one of the two *alcaldes ordinarios* elected each year in that city to be a peninsular and the other Creole.[50]

These developments certainly reduced the representativeness of the Mexican *cabildos*, but it would be wrong to conclude that they rendered the councils completely, or even largely, unrepresentative. J. H. Parry has written that *'regidores* were not necessarily representative of local interests. It is unlikely that they felt, in general, any strong sense of responsibility toward the mass of the townspeople. If they were responsible to anyone, it was to the authority which appointed them.'[51] This view requires at least some qualification. It is true that the *cabildos* had become the preserve of a narrow oligarchy, but this oligarchy included commoner hacienda-owners, merchants, and manufacturers, as well as nobles who, in any case, as we have seen, had many basic interests in common with the mass of the colonists. Local interests were precisely what the *cabildos* did represent; the *cabildos* represented the Mexican entrepreneurial class together with such elements as the secular clergy which stood to gain by the triumph of that class. Of course, there were many Creoles, ranging from Gómez de Cervantes who thought them insufficiently aristocratic to ordinary colonists who considered them too narrow and enclosed, who looked forward to changes in the working of the *cabildos*. There were even some Creoles, principally artisans and vagabonds who did not stand to gain by the triumph of the proprietors, who loathed the *cabildos*; Bishop Palafox received an unsigned letter from a 'poor citizen' of Mexico City in 1641, written in the name of the poor, which denounced *cabildo* government as a wicked contrivance whose only

[49]J. H. Parry, *The Sale of Public Office in the Spanish Indies under the Habsburgs*, Ibero-Americana, xxxvii (Berkeley and Los Angeles, 1953), pp. 32–45.

[50]ADA 7b–cn–3: Felipe de Sámano to Viceroy Cadereita, 3 Jan. 1637.

[51]Parry, op. cit., p. 33; there has in fact been a general tendency to suggest that by the seventeenth century Spanish American *cabildos* had been 'deprived of whatever initiative and independence they may have possessed in the beginning' (Haring, *The Spanish Empire*, p. 163).

prupose was to inflate food prices on behalf of the producers at the expense of the needy.[52] But none of this alters the basic fact that for a broad combination of groups in Creole society, the city councils, principally the city councils of Mexico and Puebla, did provide positive political leadership.

City councillors, unable to claim benefit of clergy, were out of necessity less outspoken than Creole diocesan priests, but they were not afraid to identify openly with the Creole cause and to assume leadership of it. The records of both the Mexico and Puebla city councils make this clear. Indeed, Mexico City claimed a special pre-eminence among the Mexican *cabildos*, considering itself supreme spokesman and guardian of all Mexican Creoles, a claim hotly contested by Puebla which considered its own efforts for the Creole cause to be of comparable worth.[53] The *cabildos* of Mexico City and Puebla took the Creole line on all the major political issues of the early and mid seventeenth century, even where this brought them directly into collision with viceregal policy. Where the viceroys sought to maintain segregation, the *cabildos* sought to put an end to it; they wanted the *repartimiento* discontinued;[54] they wanted to see the viceroy's grip over the *corregidores* loosened and the length of *corregidores'* terms of office reduced;[55] and they wanted the Indian Church to pass from the friars to the secular clergy.[56] Where the viceroys wanted to keep as many posts as possible in the hands of their own men, the municipal councils pressed again and again in favour of Creole candidates.[57] Where the viceroys acted in the peninsular Spanish interest in the commercial sphere, in line with Madrid's commercial policies, the Mexican city councils sought to defend the Mexican interest, siding with the Mexico City merchant guild (*consulado*).[58] In moments of serious political crisis such as the great dissension of 1647 when the triple alliance of *corregidores*, friars, and Indian officers, united under the viceroy, were at loggerheads with the opponents of the 'Indian' republic, the Mexico and Puebla city councils definitely if somewhat timidly sided with the latter.[59]

[52] ADI Palafox papers xlix, fols. 345–6.

[53] *ACM* xxx. 172–6; ACP xviii, fol. 256[v].

[54] Molina, *Informe*, fol. 7[v]; AGI Mexico 31, r 1: 'Copia de parezer de la ciudad de Mexico sobre el repartimiento de yndios', 15 Nov. 1632.

[55] *ACM* xxi. 70; xxv. 58, xxxi. 70.

[56] *ACM* xxiv. 296, xxv. 58; ACP xix, fol. 224.

[57] See, for instance, ACP xvii, fol. 56[v], and ACP xviii, fol. 257.

[58] See pp. 196–7.

[59] See the Creole attack on Viceroy Salvatierra, *Copia de las Cartas que las Civdades de Mexico y la Pvebla escrivieron a la real persona y a sus consejos de estado y de las Indias, informando la verdad de lo qve svcedio en la Nueva España* (not in Toribio de Medina or Andrade) (BNX) (Mexico, 1648).

The viceroys, for their part, acknowledged the political importance of the city councils, and at the same time partially neutralized them by their interference in *cabildo* elections. In theory, viceroys were forbidden by the crown to put pressure on voters to make them elect 'satisfactory' candidates,[60] but in practice it was quite usual for viceroys to manipulate, or try to manipulate, the vote so as to exclude 'inconvenient' persons and seat those whom they favoured. Viceroy Cadereita, for instance, late in 1636, dispatched instructions to the *corregidores* of various towns where there were Spanish councils, listing those whom the *corregidores* were to press for, and whom against, in the pending New Year elections.[61] In 1629 the 'friends' of the marqués de Cerralvo in the Mexico City council managed to shut out virtually all the opponents of the viceroy.[62] Thus when the viceroys were fully in control of the political situation, the *cabildos* were, to a considerable extent, gagged. However, in the seventeenth century, the viceroys frequently had less than complete control and it was in those moments especially that the city councils showed their true colours. In December 1648, to take just one example, and in the second part of this work we shall consider several in detail, the interim bishop-governor of Mexico, Marcos de Torres y Rueda, found himself in a difficult situation with the Mexico City council. He had sent his instructions regarding the election of the following January to the *corregidor* of Mexico who was then the Creole nobleman Jerónimo de Bañuelos Carrillo y Peñaloza, knight of Alcántara; but, to his consternation, the *corregidor* and *cabildo* had banded together (the *corregidor* of Mexico was one of the few administrative staff in the viceroyalty appointed by Madrid and not by the viceroy) and declared that the bishop-governor's action was illegal. They demanded that the *cabildo* election be free of viceregal interference. Don Marcos retorted by having the *corregidor* and two or three *regidores* arrested, a drastic move which caused a large and angry crowd to gather in Mexico City's Plaza Mayor and almost caused a riot.[63]

The Mexico and Puebla city councils, as the chief representative organs of New Spain, were represented at court in Madrid. This connection, although somewhat tenuous, was important in times of friction between the municipalities and the viceroy as it enabled the municipalities to appeal to the crown over the viceroy's head. In some cases, the status of procurator of the capital of New Spain was

60 Haring, *The Spanish Empire*, p. 157.
61 ADA 7b–cn–3: *Corregidor* of Oaxaca to Cadereyta, 27 Dec. 1636, and 1 Jan. 1637 and *corregidor* of Puebla to Cadereita, 3 Jan. 1637.
62 AGI México 3, r 4. Archbishop Manso to council, 7 Nov. 1629.
63 AGI México 76, r 3: *Audiencia* to council, 8 Jan. 1649.

conferred on Creole noblemen of Mexico City who were resident for private reasons in Madrid. Prominent examples are Francisco de Solís, knight of Calatrava and *encomendero* of Alcolmán, who represented Mexico City in Madrid for some years in the second decade of the seventeenth century, and Melchor de Barrassa, also a member of the Solís family, who was appointed representative in 1641. In other cases special delegates were sent from Mexico, though only with the viceroy's permission, on a particular mission to court. Perhaps the pre-eminent example of this procedure was the sending of the delegation of 1636–9 to Madrid in an attempt to win concessions from the crown in return for the consent of Mexico City to the raising of new taxes needed for the war against the Dutch.[64]

The most important cause taken up by the Mexican city councils in the middle decades of the century, apart from the drive against the 'Indian' republic and the drive to obtain more posts for Creoles, was undoubtedly that of the big Mexico City merchants. Overseas commerce, asserted the *cabildos*,[65] had been the basis of the great Mexican prosperity, and although it had been in a state of decline since the 1620s, commerce offered the best hope of achieving a measure of recovery. It is remarkable that Mexico and Puebla city councils were consistently louder in their demands for concessions to Mexican trade than they were in calling for more mercury and other relief for mine-owners, a tendency which was the opposite to that of the viceroys who were, understandably, much more concerned to increase silver production than improve trade.

It has in the past been suggested that the merchant guild or *consulado* of Mexico City was an association of importers and exporters whose interests coincided in the main with those of the merchant oligarchy of Seville and Cadiz.[66] Now this is not borne out by the evidence for the period of the great depression, 1620–70: rather, the contrary appears to be true, that there was a clash of interests. Mexican trade, as we have seen, had gained a new dimension in the later sixteenth century with the development of the new Pacific commerce. Mexican traders, linking up at Manila with Portuguese merchants based on Macao, had started to buy huge quantities of Chinese silk and brocades, paying with silver, in order to import the fabrics thus purchased into Mexico for finishing and manufacture into outfits and

---

[64]*ACM* xxx. 219; xxxi. 387; xxxiii. 351–2.

[65]The assertion is made in numerous *cabildo* petitions and tracts, one of the most important being the *Consulta de la ciudad de Mexico al excelentisimo señor virrey marques de Cadereyta sobre que se abra la contratacion del Piru, se comersie libremente con este reyno por las causas expressas* (Mexico, 1636).

[66]Haring, *The Spanish Empire*, p. 300.

hats, and then to re-export the end-products with great profit to centres all over Spanish America and particularly to Peru. The Peruvians paid for their Mexican textile imports with silver, so that a great stream of silver had begun to flow from Peru to Mexico to the Philippines and on to bullion-thirsty China. The annual export of silver from Acapulco to Manila had come to exceed 3,000,000 pesos in value, and in the peak year, 1597, specie despatched to the Far East in payment for silk reached the enormous sum of 12,000,000 pesos or considerably more than the value of the official Atlantic trade.[67]

Mexican Pacific trade came to be regarded, in Seville and Madrid, as a serious menace to the Spanish economy for two main reasons. First and foremost, it cornered much of the South American textile market thereby dealing a severe blow, so it seemed, to the textile manufacturers of Spain, and particularly the silk producers of Toledo and Granada.[68] Secondly, the diversion of Peruvian silver to China was regarded as a loss of silver which would otherwise have been imported into Spain. The Spanish attack on Mexican Pacific trade began in 1604 when Madrid, under pressure from Seville, stipulated that no more than three ships, of a maximum weight of 400 tons each, might sail between Mexico and Peru yearly; moreover, they were forbidden to carry Oriental fabrics on the outward run or bullion on the homeward. In 1609 the rules were altered so that now only two vessels of no more than 200 tons each might ply the Acapulco-Callao run but that 200,000 pesos of silver might be exported from Peru to Mexico annually to compensate for the meagreness of other Peruvian commodities; the ban on the movement of Chinese cloths remained. Then in 1620, in response to indications and complaints from Sevillean merchants[69] that Mexican traders were engaging in fraud on a huge scale, pouring contraband silk into Peru and smuggling out bullion far in excess of the permitted amount, Madrid ordered the American viceroys to overhaul their customs machinery thoroughly and make sure that the rules were

---

[67]Parry, *The Spanish Seaborne Empire*, pp. 132–3.

[68] However, it has not been established that there was any direct connection between the decay of the Spanish textile industry and the florescence of the Mexican; at Toledo, for instance, the silk industry only showed a serious falling off after 1616, by which time the Mexican industry was also past its prime; see the *Memoriales que presento Juan Belluga de Moncada sobre la decadencia de Toledo* ... (1621) in Antonio Domínguez Ortiz, *La Sociedad española en el siglo XVII* (Madrid, 1963), pp. 349–52.

[69]Some of these complaints were very angry; Pedro de Avendaño Villela, for instance, asked Philip III to swop the Philippines with Portugal for Brazil so as to make it possible to stop all intercourse between Asia and America; see Avendaño's tract on the decline of the Spanish Atlantic trade printed in Madrid without title in 1608 (BM), fols. 3v–4.

enforced,[70] the crown also clapped a ban on the export of Peruvian wines to Mexico in response to the decline in Andalusian wine exports. In 1634, however, a great stir was caused in Spanish commercial circles when Francisco de Vitoria Baraona, a merchant of Puebla and of Jewish descent though that was not then known, revealed, or claimed to reveal, that three or four million pesos were being exported from Mexico to the Far East yearly instead of the permitted 400,000[71] and that vast quantities of oriental fabrics were still entering Peru.[72] This time Madrid went the whole way, and on 23 November 1634 the King signed a decree prohibiting all trade of whatever category for five years between Mexico and Peru. When these five years elapsed, the ban was renewed, this time indefinitely.

The closure of the sea lane to Peru and the strict limitation of trade with the Far East were of course resented bitterly by the Creoles. It is true that Madrid's regulations were only partially effective and that smuggling flourished; nevertheless, Mexican enterprise was badly hit. For one thing, the official Mexico City merchant oligarchy operating in the Pacific through Acapulco lost the initiative to contrabandists infiltrating Chinese silks into Peru through Realejo and other small ports in Nicaragua and Guatemala.[73] For another, the viceroys, though often markedly less hostile to Pacific trade than the authorities[74] in Spain and usually willing to allow contraband on official passenger and communications vessels still sailing between Mexico and Peru, manipulated this fraud for their own profit and that of their friends. As far as the city councils, *consulado*, and merchants of New Spain were concerned, Pacific commerce was severely depressed and urgently required reflating, and the textile manufacturers of Puebla, of course, were emphatically of the same opinion.[75] Undoubtedly there were some merchants of Mexico City and Puebla, such as Vitoria Baraona, who were opposed to the reopening of the Pacific trade and wanted the

---

70 *Relacion de los fundamentos, informes, y pareceres que por una y otra parte se han deduzido y visto en el consejo real de las Indias sobre si se ha de abrir el comercio que solia aver entre el Peru, i Nueva España o continuarse la suspension o prohibicion que del corre* (Madrid, 1644) (BM), fol. 1ᵛ.

71 After 1593, only two galleons could sail between Acapulco and Manila yearly carrying bullion with an upper limit fixed, at different stages, between 300,000 and 500,000 pesos; Lynch, *Spain Under the Habsburgs*, ii. 226.

72 *Relacion de los fundamentos*, fol. 1ᵛ. Vitoria Baraona seems to have been involved in Atlantic trade and to have blamed its decline on Pacific commerce; see his tract in 6 fols. printed without title in Madrid in 1639 (BM).

73 Josephe Ferriol, *En nombre del prior y consules, consulado, y comercio de la ciudad de Mexico y de toda la Nueva España* (Madrid, 1646) (BM), fols. 5ᵛ–7.

74 Viceroys Escalona and Salvatierra were both in favour of reopening the trade, *Relacion de los fundamentos*, fol. 2ᵛ.

75 ACP xviii, fol. 257.

whole stress of Mexican commerce to be on Atlantic trade, but, as far as one can tell from the tracts that have survived, they were an isolated minority, regarded almost as enemies, being allies of the detested *consulado* of Seville. The feud between Mexico City and Seville, which is very evident in the *Consulta de la ciudad de Mexico* cited above, was certainly a key aspect of the whole question; the dispute conducted before the Council of the Indies in Madrid in the 1640s, took the form of a contest between Mexico City and Seville, with Manila supporting Mexico City, as one would expect, and Lima remaining neutral.[76]

The Pacific trade question, in one respect, gives a new twist to the alignment of political forces in Mexico as we have described it so far. The Creole city councils on most issues, and especially over the 'Indian' republic and bureaucratic and clerical patronage, found themselves primarily at odds with the viceroys and not with the crown, and in their efforts to strengthen their hand sought the support of the visitors general and other officials appointed by Madrid, against the viceroys. With the Peru trade, however, the position was different. Here it was the crown itself that the city councils were principally at odds with, and the viceroys, not the crown, who were most likely to treat their grievance sympathetically, at least in cases where the viceroy and his officers placed their own economic interest before that of the state; which, it must be confessed, was most of the time. Thus in the commercial sphere one must be prepared to encounter shifts in the alignment of forces, and instead of finding colonists at loggerheads with officers, to find colonists and officers together at loggerheads with the state.

It is appropriate in the concluding part of this chapter to turn back to the question of the peninsular leanings of the bureaucratic party, for there is one aspect of that question about which, as yet, nothing has been said. No one could deny that the viceroy's officers in seventeenth-century Mexico were chiefly peninsulars, but one can hardly say the same for the mendicant clergy who were another important element in the bureaucratic party and who were, it is clear, predominantly Creole. However, despite the clear numerical ascendancy of the Creoles in all three of the main mendicant orders, there are grounds for believing that *gachupín* friars wielded at least as much and probably more power than their American-born brethren.

Dissension among the regular clergy on peninsular-Creole lines was certainly nothing new in the early seventeenth century. Such friction had, by that time, had a history of at least three or four decades. 'It is the unanimous judgement of old and experienced friars who know this country', wrote Mendieta in 1574, 'that when the Franciscan order in

76*Relacion de los fundamentos*, fol. 2.

the Indies ceases to be staffed predominantly by friars from Spain, it will suffer ruin.'[77] The reason given by Mendieta for this ruin was that Creole friars did not possess the same sense of vocation and discipline as that displayed by *gachupín* mendicants; instead of pursuing the lofty goals set by the early missionaries, and particularly the goal of sealing off the Indian population and transforming it into a model Christian society, they would put the interests of their relatives and friends and their own economic interests first, thus sacrificing the Indians to the greed of the colonists. But already by Mendieta's time peninsular supremacy in the orders was beginning to be challenged. Well before 1610 the Creoles had taken control of the Augustinian province of Mexico[78] and almost full control of the Dominican;[79] even among the Franciscans, the most important order and the order in which *gachupín* resistance was most formidable, the Creoles were making notable advances. However, the power struggle among the friars was to drag on for much longer than seemed likely in 1610, and indeed the peninsulars were able to rally and deny the Creoles half, and in some cases more than half, of the spoils of victory.

This struggle among the friars was intense and very bitter.[80] It was fed by peninsular-Creole jealousy and rivalry, and made possible by the highly elaborate, medieval constitutions of the mendicant orders. The Jesuits, having a quite different constitution and much tighter discipline, and being more rigorously subordinated to their superior general in Rome, for the most part managed to avoid internal disruption. It is true that the Jesuits, unlike the mendicants, were mainly peninsular, but a substantial number of the 350 to 400 Jesuits in Mexico were Creole, and the Society was much troubled by peninsular-Creole bickering;[81] nevertheless, the dissension found no political outlet. The main reason why the mendicant constitutions favoured the institutional expression of *gachupín*-Creole rivalry was that each mendicant province elected its Provincial, priors, and other office-holders, every three years in the case of the Franciscans and Augustinians, and every four in that of the Dominicans.

---

[77] *Documentos inéditos del siglo XVI para la historia de México*, ed. Mariano Cuevas (Mexico, 1914), p. 298.

[78] Esteban García, *Crónica Augustiniana*, p. 261.

[79] Franco y Ortega, *Segunda parte*, pp. 557–61.

[80] Thomas Gage's reference to the 'inveterate spite and hatred which [Creole friars] bare to such as come from Spain', including, it is worth adding, Gage and sundry Irish, Italian, and Portuguese friars who went to Mexico, has been supposed to have been exaggerated; however, the Mexican sources demonstrate that it was not; *Thomas Gage's Travels*, p. 105.

[81] See esp. Antonio Astrain, *Historia de la Compañía de Jesús en la asistencia de España* (7 vols., Madrid, 1902–25), v. 318–25.

The Dominicans were the first order in Mexico to make provision for the peninsular-Creole split and were also the most successful in damping down the strife.[82] The system of *alternativa* or the alternation of the provincial government between peninsulars and Creoles every triennium or, in the Dominican case, quadrennium, was established in the 1590s and accorded papal sanction by Gregory XV in 1623.[83] By the *alternativa*, control of the province and of the Indian parishes administered by the order within its area was shared evenly between the two parties despite the fact that the Creoles made up the vast majority of the friars of the province.[84] The relative smoothness with which the Dominican *alternativa* functioned probably owed something to the fact that it had been introduced so early. The Augustinian *alternativa* was a much more turbulent affair because it was introduced at a considerably later stage, and as the result of a blatant attempt by the *gachupín* minority of the order in Mexico to overthrow the supremacy which the Creole Augustinians had enjoyed for several decades.[85] This piece of *gachupín* manoeuvring occurred in 1626–7. Pope Urban VIII bowed to *gachupín* pressure with a brief establishing the Augustinian *alternativa* in Mexico, but then, after second thoughts, withdrew permission; in 1629, however, upon renewed *gachupín* pressure, powerfully supported this time from Madrid, the Pope reissued the brief.[86] All this was done in the face of loud protests not only from Creole Augustinian friars but from the Creole city councils and nobility as well. It was utterly unfair, claimed the Creoles, that the provincial government should be shared equally between the two parties when the peninsular friars of the province of Mexico numbered only 45 as against 400 Creoles.[87] These protests were of course ignored, and from 1630 onwards *alternativa* prevailed in both the Augustinian provinces of New Spain.

[82] As the Mexico City council remarked, *ACM* xxiii. 36.

[83] IAH col. GO, no. 21: Balthasar de Thobar, 'Compendio indico de las bullas y breves que por los sumos pontifices se han concedido ... pertenecientes al gobierno espiritual de las Indias Occidentales', fol. 269.

[84] I have no figures, but it seems clear that the Creoles were the majority from the fact that the *alternativa* was introduced so early.

[85] That is in the province of Mexico; in the separate Augustinian province of Michoacán, the Creoles were also dominant, but a temporary *alternativa* of four triennia had already been established in 1614. On that occasion Viceroy Guadalcázar, having received word from the Augustinian General in Rome and supporting material from Madrid, quashed the chapter election which was about to be held at Yuririapúndaro and forced the Augustinians of Michoacán to convene in his presence in Mexico City and choose a *gachupín* Provincial, which they would not otherwise have done; Basalenque, *Historia de la Provincia de San Nicolás*, p. 371.

[86] Thobar, 'Compendio', fol. 292.

[87] Esteban García, *Crónica Augustiniana*, p. 261.

The chief object of Creole discontent as regards mendicant government, however, was not the *alternativa* of the Dominicans and Augustinians but that remarkable contrivance, the *ternativa* of the Franciscans. Possibly it was inevitable that *gachupín* resistance should be most effective within the order of Saint Francis, for there the stakes were highest. The Franciscans possessed the lion's share of the Indian parishes administered by the regular clergy in central Mexico and they were the largest and most influential of the orders; the tendencies of their government were therefore of particular consequence in the general political conjuncture.

The early years of the seventeenth century saw the peninsular Franciscans still in command of a precarious numerical majority and therefore still able to dominate provincial chapter elections, without the aid of any special contrivance, by outvoting their rivals. The discriminatory regulations designed to restrict intake of Creoles to the novitiate of the Franciscan province of Mexico, though quashed by the Franciscan Superior General at Valladolid in Spain in 1602, in practice remained in force for some years after that date.[88] The Mexico City council, acting on behalf of the Creole friars, found itself appealing again in 1611, as it had already done in 1603 and 1605, to the Franciscan Provincial in Mexico City, urging him to comply with the Superior General's orders and end the discrimination.[89] There is nothing to suggest that he did so, but it is likely that in the second decade of the century the *gachupín* Franciscans, though still the majority in the province of Mexico, were the majority by an increasingly narrow margin. At any rate, the peninsulars decided that their ascendancy, if it was to last, had to be placed on a new basis. There was discussion of *alternativa*,[90] notably at the chapter of Xochimilco, and in 1615 the Pope both imposed *alternativa* on the province and laid down that from then on admissions to the Franciscan novitiate should be exactly balanced, half Mexican and half Spanish. However, the Franciscan leadership in Mexico refused to settle for merely 50 per cent control and proposed a different arrangement—the *ternativa*. By this scheme, the friars of the Franciscan province of Mexico were divided not into two parties but into three: friars born in Spain who took the habit in Spain, labelled 'Spaniards'; friars born in

[88]There were various restrictions including one of age; whereas *gachupín* youths could become novices at fifteen, Creole youths could enter only at twenty-two; *ACM* xviii. 42.

[89]*ACM* xvi. 66, 188–90; xviii. 42–3, 48.

[90]Whereas the Mexico City council was against *alternativa* for the Augustinians because it would lessen Creole influence within the order, it was very much in favour of it for the Franciscans, for there it would have constituted a great gain; see *ACM* xvi. 66 and xxiii. 35–6.

Spain who took the habit in Mexico, labelled 'mestizos'; and friars born in Mexico who took the habit in Mexico, labelled Creoles.[91] The three parties were to administer the province in turn by triennia, so that, in effect, peninsulars had control of the province for six years out of every nine. The *ternativa* was accepted by the friar commissaries-general of Mexico and of Castile, and ratified by the general chapter of the Franciscan order at Salamanca in Castile in 1618.[92] The Pope, one presumes, then acquiesced. In 1618, one should note, the number of *gachupín* friars of the Franciscan province of Mexico who had taken the habit in Spain was only 50, the number of *gachupines* who had entered the order in Mexico was 300, while the party of the *patria*, the Creoles, amounted to slightly less than 300.[93] Once established, the *ternativa* endured, with only occasional lapses, throughout the seventeenth century and on into the late colonial period.[94]

In their province of Michoacán, the Franciscans followed a slightly different course, but once again peninsular supremacy was maintained. The province debated the peninsular-Creole issue at great length at the provincial chapter at Acámbaro in 1626. By that time, a large number of the Franciscan priests of the province were Creole, but the *gachupines* still had enough of an upper hand to impose their own solution. The division into three parties employed in the province of Mexico was adopted and a rigorous admissions policy worked out on the basis of it. It was planned to have 120 priests in the province—50 peninsulars, 35 'mestizos', and only 35 Creoles.[95] However, the *ternativa* was not yet applied to chapter elections; for some two decades, the government of the Franciscans of Michoacán remained entirely in peninsular hands, alternating between *gachupines* who entered in Spain and *gachupines* entered in Mexico. The first Mexican-born Provincial of the Franciscans of Michoacán, Fray Alonso de la Rea, author of one of the most important chronicles of Michoacán, was not elected until 1649.

The Creoles were, naturally enough, extremely offended by the *ternativa*.[96] Peninsular Franciscans already had an important initial advantage in the politics of their order in Mexico in that the office of friar commissary-general, which was filled by the Superior General in

91*Instrucciones que los virreyes dejaron*, p. 273; Solórzano, *Política Indiana*, p. 735.
92Pedro Joseph Parras, *Gobierno de los regulares de la América* (2 vols., Madrid, 1783), ii. 258.
93*ACM* xxiii. 35; the figures are of ordained priests only.
94Parras, op. cit. ii. 258; Vetancurt, *Teatro Mexicano*, v. 150–1.
95Isidro Felix de Espinosa, *Crónica de la provincia Franciscana de los apóstoles San Pedro y San Pablo de Michoacán* (1731) (Mexico, 1945), pp. 459–62.
96*ACM* xxiii. 35–6, 42, 68, 150.

Rome, was generally conferred on a *gachupín*.[97] The commissary-general was entrusted with supervising the administration of the whole family of the Franciscan provinces of New Spain—Mexico, Michoacán, New Galicia, New Vizcaya, the Yucatán, Guatemala, and the Philippines. Now in addition, peninsulars were securing two-thirds control in all those provinces where they were unable to retain total control. The implication of this was that the Franciscan leadership could be sure of being able to keep the greater part of the Indian parishes entrusted to it in the hands of *gachupín* friar curates. That the mendicant priors always passed over Creole friars no matter how well qualified, and always promoted peninsulars even if they knew nothing of the relevant Indian language, if they possibly could, was a stock Creole complaint.[98]

In view of the fact that *gachupín* friars could be trusted to hold the line against the colonists in the Indian villages, while Creole friars could not, at least not to the same extent, it can cause little surprise that the viceroys in the seventeenth century tended to back the *gachupín* party in the mendicant orders against the Creoles; it was the viceroys who ensured that the *alternativa* was followed in such cases as that of the Agustinian province of Michoacán where the *gachupín* party had become very weak. However, it is less easy to see why Madrid and Rome also supported the *alternativa* and *ternativa* and why Madrid helped to make them workable by paying the passage from Spain to Mexico of considerable numbers of friars at a time when the crown was desperately short of funds and when it was widely thought that the number of mendicants in Mexico was too many; and when, one might add, Madrid was often annoyed to find that peninsular Provincials in southern and central Mexico were accustomed to tempt friars in transit to the newer missionary areas such as the Philippines, China, Japan, New Biscay, and New Mexico, to desert their mission parties and join the ranks of *gachupín* friars in the old-established provinces.[99] The answer is probably not political so much as moral, for the suspicion of the *gachupín* officer class that Creole mendicant curates would be softer on the colonists than peninsular curates was paralleled by the

97 The Creoles were very anxious to secure this office, which was one of the most important in New Spain, but were frustrated again and again; see Cuevas, *Historia de la Iglesia*, iii. 247 and Vetancurt, *Teatro Mexicano*, v. 151.

98 *Alegaciones en favor del clero*, pp. 50–60.

99 There are numerous seventeenth-century royal *cédulas* admonishing the viceroys to put a stop to this practice, but it is likely that at least some viceroys turned a blind eye, as it was in their interest to do; see, for instance, AGN, 'reales cédulas duplicadas', viii, fol. 325 and *ACM* xxii. 180. Thomas Gage himself was one of these deserters as he originally came to Mexico as a member of a Dominican mission on its way, at the expense of the crown, to Manila. He

conviction of the authorities in Spain, secular and ecclesiastical, that Creole friars, or at any rate friars raised in Mexico, were of greatly inferior moral calibre to peninsular friars. Allow the Creoles to take control of the mendicant organization in Mexico, believed the Council of the Indies, and discipline would quickly disintegrate.[100]

Such then was the struggle between Creole and peninsular in the three principal mendicant orders in seventeenth-century Mexico. These three were quite possibly not the most disturbed orders in the viceroyalty; in the early part of the century at least, the Mercenarian friars were divided even more bitterly, though this is scarcely hinted at in the official chronicle of the Mercenarian province of Mexico.[101] Viceroy Gelves reported to the council of the Indies that the Mercenarians were in an appalling state and that the affairs of their order were the most scandalous thing happening in the country';[102] on the fleet that bore Thomas Gage to Mexico in 1624, we are told there 'went four and twenty Mercenarian friars bound for Mexico, part of those that afterwards drew their knives to slash and cut the Creoles of their profession'.[103] But the commotions of the Franciscans, Dominicans, and Augustinians are the ones that relate most particularly to the general political situation in seventeenth-century Mexico, for they were the orders with interests and influence in the 'Indian' republic. Consequently, they are the orders to which reference will be made at several points in the second part of this work.

At this juncture, it is as well to pause to recapitulate. As we now see it, the conflict between bureaucracy and colonists is still the main piece in our pattern of strains and stresses, but one that has been rendered more complicated by being shown to have in it elements of peninsular-Creole rivalry. To a considerable extent, we have suggested, it is possible to equate the Creoles with the party of the colonists and of enterprise; but the equation is not exact, for some important *gachupín* elements, including the bishops and Jesuits and also, it is worth noting, the discalced Carmelites, tended to support the colonist/Creole cause.

deserted in the company of an Irish friar and three Spaniards and made his way with them to Chiapas. There, he reports, 'we were joyfully entertained by those friars who looked upon us as members of their province, and assured us that the Provincial and chief superior would be very glad of our coming, for they wanted Spanish friars to oppose the Creoles and natives who strived to get ahead as they had done in Mexico and Oaxaca', *Thomas Gage's Travels*, p. 125.

---

[100] AGI México 3, r 2, doc. 71.

[101] Francisco de Pareja, *Crónica de la provincia de la visitación de Nuestra Señora de la Merced* (1688) (Mexico, 1882).

[102] AGI México 29, r 4, Gelves to council, 14 Nov. 1621, and r 5, 16 June 1622.

[103] *Thomas Gage's Travels*, pp. 17, 71.

One may therefore also expect to find Creoles who, by virtue of holding office in the administration or mendicant orders, or for some other reason, sided with the bureaucratic party. At the same time, however, we have also seen that this whole alignment of groups was likely to be modified when and where the political debate centred on trade questions; under certain circumstances then, it was in the interest of the colonists, and at least some of the officers, to combine against the policy of Madrid.

IV

BASQUES, PORTUGUESE, ITALIANS, AND JEWS

We come now to the last part of this first stage of our study and turn to those elements in the white population of seventeenth-century Mexico which were not either Castilian, Andalusian, or Extremenian, or Creole of Castilian, Andalusian, or Extremenian descent. Part of this extraneous white population was of Iberian origin, primarily Basque, Portuguese, and Jewish; the rest was mainly Italian with a sprinkling of French, Flemish, German, and Scottish.

The Spaniards of the seventeenth century, as is well known, were much influenced by local patriotism and were wont to think of themselves as belonging to a dozen or so 'Spanish nations'—Castilians, Asturians, Galicians, Aragonese, Catalans, and so forth. In the main, these nations were related closely enough in language and culture to prevent any very serious development of particularism or alienation from the other nations. There were many isolated instances of friction and rivalry between groups of Castilians and Aragonese, or Galicians and Asturians, in the Spanish armies of Italy and Flanders, at the universities of Salamanca, Sigüenza, and Alcalá, and in the colonization of America, but for the most part there were no difficulties between the Spanish nations of a more serious and lasting character. However, there were two exceptions, or partial exceptions, to this rule which were both of considerable importance—the relationship between the Castilians and the Catalans, and that between the Castilians (and indeed most of the other Spanish nations) and the Basques. Of these two problem relationships, the most serious for Spain itself was certainly that involving the Catalans. During the reigns of Philip III and Philip IV, as Professor Elliott has shown, the Catalans were becoming increasingly estranged from Castile, the hub and dominant section of the Spanish empire, until finally, in that *annus terribilis* of Spanish history, 1640, they rose under their leader Pau Claris in revolt and threw themselves on the protection of France. This revolution was followed by French intervention and a terrible war which ended only with the fall of a starved and decimated Barcelona to Castilian arms in 1652. But in America the Catalan question had none of the prominence that it had in metropolitan Spain. The Catalans, because they were largely cut off from the great Indies ports of Seville and Cadiz, and because, like the other inhabitants of the territories of the crown of Aragon, they were not legally entitled to settle or trade in the Indies, played only a very minor part in the colonization of the New World. It was otherwise with the Basques. The Basques, though they were in many ways the most distinct of the peoples of Spain and though they enjoyed considerable political autonomy and many special privileges in their provinces of Vizcaya (Biscay), Guipúzcoa, Alava, and Navarre, were subjects of the crown of Castile and fully entitled to avail themselves of the New World.

Although the proportion of the Spanish emigrants to Mexico in the first decades after the Conquest who were Basque, or who were of the related nations of Navarre and Santander, was evidently very small,[1] these northerners were astoundingly successful. Three of the four founders and early leaders of Zacatecas—Cristobal de Oñate, Juan de Tolosa, and Diego de Ibarra—were Basques.[2] Cristobal de Zaldívar and numerous other Basques took a leading part in the Chichimec campaigns of the later sixteenth century. The whole vast territory to the north and west of Zacatecas was dubbed New Biscay and opened up by the Basque Conquistadores Francisco de Ibarra[3] and Francisco de Urdiñola, both of whom had many Basques among their followers. Another Biscayan, Martín de Zavala, and after him his descendants played a leading role in New León. The Philippines were conquered by an expedition that set out from Mexico under López de Legazpi y Gurruchategui, a Basque, leading a force which included many other Basques.[4] In 1609 the Oñate and Zaldívar brothers, continuing the Basque drive to the north, founded the settlement of Santa Fe in New Mexico, while at the same time Sebastián Vizcaino (a surname which means Biscayan) was making his name as an explorer of the Californian coasts and of the Pacific. Moreover, as in the military and entrepreneurial spheres, so in the ecclesiastical. Juan de Zumárraga, the first

[1] See Peter Boyd-Bowman, 'La Procedencia de los españoles de América, 1540–59', *Historia Mexicana*, xvii (1967–8), 37–71; according to this study, almost half of the immigrants to Mexico in the two middle decades of the sixteenth century were Andalusians, mostly from the region of Seville. This was a higher proportion of Andalusians than for any other part of the Indies. Most of the rest of the immigration into Mexico was Castilian, particularly New (southern) Castilian and Extremenian. Basques, Navarrese, Catalans, Asturians, Galicians, and Aragonese supplied together, according to Boyd-Bowman, less than 4 per cent of the total.

[2] Bakewell, *Silver Mining and Society*, pp. 9–13.

[3] J. Lloyd Mecham, *Francisco de Ibarra and Nueva Vizcaya* (Durham, North Carolina, 1927), p. 113.

[4] J. de Aralar, 'Miguel López de Legazpi y Gurrutzategui', *Boletín del Instituto de Estudios Vascos*, vii (Buenos Aires, 1956), 32–40; see also Vicente Lascurain, 'Los Primeros vascos pobladores de la Nueva España' *Boletín del Instituto Americano de Estudios Vascos*, v (1954).

bishop and archbishop of Mexico was a native of Durango, one of the chief towns of Vizcaya, and brought over many Basques in his entourage. The first bishop of Oaxaca was also a Basque, as was Fray Gerónimo de Mendieta, a native of Vitoria in Alava, and numerous other churchmen prominent in sixteenth-century Mexico.

This record of Basque success continued in Mexico as in the rest of Spanish America, into and right through the seventeenth century. Furthermore, as they continued to be successful, the signs are that the Basques began to settle in America, from about the beginning of the seventeenth century, in much greater numbers than they had done previously.[5] In some places where they had earlier had only very slight importance—Potosí, the great silver-mining centre of upper Peru, being the classic example[6]—the Basques now rapidly achieved a position of economic and even political pre-eminence. At no place in Mexico did the phenomenon take so extreme a form as at Potosí, and later at Laicacota and Puno and other districts of Spanish South America, but in the big cities of central Mexico the Basques undoubtedly did become one of the most important and powerful sections of the substantial citizenry. In Puebla in 1612, for example, 113 Basque merchants and substantial citizens made an independent 'Basque' offer of military aid to the *Audiencia* in Mexico City which was then in the midst of the emergency occasioned by the supposed threat of a Negro insurrection.[7] The Basques of Mexico City were similarly rich and prominent and had their own Basque detachment in the city militia.[8] Zacatecas also was accounted a major Basque centre.[9]

To understand the nature of the relationship between the Basques and the other Spaniards in seventeenth-century Mexico, one must take into consideration several features of the historical development of the Basques in Spain. Perhaps the most remarkable characteristic of Basque society was the possession by every Basque of noble status. In theory at least, anyone, wherever he lived, who could prove that he was descended directly and without admixture of impure blood from one of the familial lineages of Vizcaya or Guipúzcoa was recognized in Castilian law, and in the law of all the dependencies of Castile, as a

[5]W. Borah, 'Latin America, 1610–60', *The New Cambridge Modern History*, iv (Cambridge, 1970), 715.

[6]Bartolomé Arzáns de Orsúa, *Historia de la Villa Imperial de Potosí* (3 vols., Providence, Rhode Island, 1965), i. 321–402.

[7]AGI Patronato real 221, r 12: 'Carta scrita al rl. acuerdo de Mexico por los Vascongados de la Puebla de los Angeles, año de mill seicientos y doce quando el rumor del motin de los negros. . .'

[8]AGI Patronato real 221, r 14: 'Relacion de los subcesos de Mexico . . ., fols. 4–5.

[9]Cuevas, *Historia de la Iglesia en México*, iii. 282.

noble. Furthermore, this unique birthright was acknowledged afresh with every accession to the Spanish throne and every new publication of the *fueros* or privileges of the Basque provinces.[10] Of course, in the economic sphere the Basques, like most peoples, were divided into landowning, bourgeois, artisan, and peasant sections; but the right to noble status in law was nevertheless extremely important, especially to the Basque middle class. In the Middle Ages the Basque provinces had been one of the few parts of Spain from which the Jews had been totally excluded, and so there the commercial element had traditionally been solidly Basque. Consequently, the bourgeoisie of the Basque provinces was noble, was exempt from numerous taxes that the non-noble middle classes of Spain had to pay, and had the advantage of ready access to high position in Church and state. Also, being both bourgeois and noble, the Basque middle class was inclined to take a pride in itself, and in hard work and the pursuit of profit, in a way that no other bourgeois or noble class of Spain did;[11] while conversely, the Basque landowning class felt not the slightest reluctance to engage in trade and industry. Indeed, zest for economic enterprise combined with noble pride was one of the chief traits of the Basques in America, and perhaps also one of the most irritating to Castilian and Creole sensibilities.

If the nobility of the Basque entrepreneur was a great advantage to him, so also was his varied economic experience.[12] The Basque country in the seventeenth century, as indeed in the eighteenth century and after, was the centre of the Spanish metal industry and mining. It was dotted with mines and foundries, a circumstance almost certainly related to the prominence of the Biscayans in American silver-mining and smelting. Vizcaya was also Spain's chief centre of ship-building and chief source of seamen. Moreover, on account of this, the Basque homeland had the closest connections with Seville, Cadiz, and San Lucar de Barrameda. From the beginning of the sixteenth century, and indeed even earlier, there had been prosperous and active colonies of

10 See *El Fvero privilegios franqvezas, y libertads de los caballeros hijos dalgo del señorío de Vizcaya, confirmados por el rey don Felippe IIII* (Bilbao, 1643), fols. 10ᵛ−12ᵛ; and the *Nueva recopilacion de los fueros, privilegios, leyes, ordenanzas, buenos usos, y costumbres de la muy noble y muy leal provincia de Guipuzcoa, confirmados y aprobados por el rey N. Senor Don Phelipe Quinto* (Tolosa, 1696), pp. 9−10.

11 Alberto Crespo Rodas, *La Guerra entre vicuñas y vascongados, Potosí 1622−5* (Lima, Peru, 1956 and La Paz, Bolivia, 1960), p. 42; *Memorial y Relacion qve el antiqvissimo reyno de Navarra y las nobilissimas prouincias de Gvipvzcoa, Vizcaya, y Alaua, presentan a la reyna nvestra senora en sv real consejo de Indias . . .* (n.p., n.d. [Madrid?, 1669?]), fols. 17−18.

12 Lynch, *Spain Under the Habsburgs*, ii. 149−50.

Basques in the Andalusian ports,[13] and by the seventeenth century the bulk of the ships and a high proportion of the officers, crews, merchants, and goods on the Atlantic run were Basque.

The good fortune of the Basques was further increased by their penetration of the Spanish legal profession, the administration, and the Church. The Basques had long been accepted as the most talented of the Iberian people as bureaucrats, and the kings of Castile had long been accustomed to make use of Basque intelligence, punctiliousness, and assiduity. It was no accident that Basques were generally very keen on university education and that no people was better represented than they, after the Castilians, at the Castilian universities. In Mexico in the seventeenth century, as will emerge several times in this study, a very significant proportion of administrative officers and senior ecclesiastics were Basque.

But however much one emphasizes the good fortune of the Basques and the ease with which they made good in America, this alone can not entirely account for the suspicion and dislike felt for the Basques by the rest of the Spanish population. When the Basques of Potosí in Peru complained to the assembly of Vizcaya in Spain that their enemies hate them 'out of envy of the skilful management and astuteness with which they [the Basques] acquire offices and riches, and because they are and have been zealous in the king's service . . . and in the maintenance of justice against the idle and against vagabonds', they spoke of themselves as a separate community in a way that was very typical of the Basques.[14] We have already noted how in Mexico the Basques were the only white minority to have their own separate contingents in the militia. The same phenomenon can be seen in other places outside the Basque homeland. In Cadiz in 1596 the Basque detachment was the only part of the defence that put up any serious resistance to the English assault force under the Earl of Essex.[15]

The separateness of the Basques is perhaps best explained in terms of cultural and ethnic factors. The Basques are not a Latin, Germanic, or Celtic people, but are descended from an obscure pre-Indo-European stock. The Basque idiom has no connection with any other known language. Admittedly, the linguistic aspect was probably not of major

13 For the Basques in Cadiz see Hipólito Sánchez de Sopranis, 'Las Naciones Extranjeras en Cadiz durante el siglo xvii', in *Estudios de Historia Social de España*, ed. Carmelo Viñas y Mey, iv. 2 (Madrid, 1960), pp. 701–33.

14 Quoted by Estanislao de Labayru y Goicoechea in his *Historia general del Señorío de Bizcaya* (6 vols., Bilbao and Madrid, 1895–1903), v. 144; see also Gabriel Gómez de Sanabria, 'Relacion de las Inquietudes y alborotos de la Villa Imperial de Potosí . . .'. BM MS. Sloan 3055, no. 7, fol. 134ᵛ where he refers to the unity and conformity with which the Basque nation always conducts itself wherever it may be found.

15 Sánchez de Sopranis, op. cit., p. 703.

significance. By the seventeenth century, the Basque upper classes were becoming increasingly proficient with Castilian, and in Alava and Navarre at least, so were the peasantry. In Mexico, as was greatly deplored by the Mexican Basque enthusiast Balthasar de Echave in 1607,[16] Castilian had largely replaced the Basque tongue among the Basques. However, other cultural and ethnic factors appear to have retained a very considerable significance. One encounters in seventeenth-century Basque writings not only an obtrusive pride in Basque national solidarity but also a marked insistence that the Basques are racially purer than other Spaniards. The Basques alone of the Iberian peoples, we are told, except for the Galicians and Asturians, had never succumbed to domination by another people nor had their blood been infiltrated by Roman, Visigoth, Moor, or Jew.[17] This *limpieza de sangre* was closely linked in the Basque mind with the nobility of the Basque nation, and helps to explain perhaps that peculiar preference of the Basques for their own sort, marrying among themselves and keeping to their own religious sodalities and fraternities.[18] This exclusive attitude was naturally extremely irritating to other Spaniards, especially to southern Spaniards, who, though darker-skinned and very much infiltrated by alien blood, and particularly Latin and Semitic blood, were only too conscious of the desirability of 'pure' blood and of the nobility it was taken to confer. Indeed, in the friction between Basques and southern Spaniards—and the Basques were always on worse terms with southern than with northern Spaniards—there was a marked tinge of what can only be described as racial prejudice. In the period before the outbreaks of violence between Basques and Andalusians at the silver-mining camps of Laicacota and Puno, there were cases of Basques insulting Andalusians as 'moriscos' and sending them rosaries so that they might learn to pray in the Catholic fashion.[19]

16 Balthasar de Echave, *Discursos de la Antiguedad de la Lengua Cantabra Bascongada* (Mexico, 1607), fols. 82–4.

17 Echave, *Discursos de la antiguedad*, fols. 64ᵛ, 84; and *El Fvero privilegios, franqvezas y libertads*, fols. 10ᵛ–12ᵛ where it is laid down that since the men of Vizcaya are all hidalgos and of unsullied 'Old Christian' blood, and since no 'New Christian' descendant of converted Moors or Jews, or any person with the blood of Moors or Jews, is permitted to reside in Vizcaya, whoever desires to reside in that province must provide documentary proof of his or her purity of blood.

18 The most celebrated Basque fraternity in Mexico was that of Nuestra Señora de Aranzazu in Mexico City whose main chapel was in the main Franciscan priory; see Vetancurt, *Teatro Mexicano*, part iv, fol. 39ᵛ, and Fray Juan de Luzuriaga, *Paranympho Celeste. Historia de la mystica zarza, milagrosa imagen, y prodigioso santuario de Aranzazu* (Mexico, 1686). This apparently was the only explicitly Basque work published in Mexico in the latter part of the seventeenth century.

19 Guillermo Lohmann Villena, *El Conde de Lemos, Virrey del Peru* (Madrid, 1946), p. 154; see also Mancera to Veraguas in the *Instrucciones que los virreyes dejaron* (1867), p. 259.

This estrangement between Basques and southern Spaniards was paralleled by the ill-feeling between Basques and Creoles. In part this was because the Creoles, and particularly the Mexican Creoles, were by origin and temperament much more closely akin to the Spaniards of southern Spain than to those of the north. Also, almost certainly, it was because Creole blood was regarded as being doubly or trebly impure, having in it a strain of Indian blood as well as of Moorish and Jewish. There were accordingly in sixteenth- and seventeenth-century Mexico numerous manifestations of Basque disdain for Creoles. Fray Gerónimo de Mendieta, who regarded the Creoles as unworthy of responsibility, predicted that the Franciscan enterprise in Mexico would falter and collapse if Creole friars were permitted to gain control of the order in the colony and he advocated drastic action to prevent them from doing so.[20] In the first decade of the seventeenth century, a time of bitter dissension among the Franciscans in New Spain, the friars who were in control of the administrative apparatus of the Franciscan province of Mexico, who systematically excluded Creole Franciscans from priorates and all other provincial offices including curacies, and who restricted the entry of Creoles into the novitiate, greatly offending the Mexico City council in the process, were a camarilla of four Basques—Esteban de Alsua, Juan de Lascano, Pedro de la Cruz, and Juan de Salas.[21] The canon lawyer who ventured to defend the Jesuit Gómez, the slanderer of the Creoles, in 1618 was Antonio de Brámbila y Arriaga, *maestrescuela* of the cathedral of Oaxaca, a man who opposed the Creole party at every turn, who suffered two spells of incarceration for his pains, and who was a Basque of Puebla.[22] Don Juan de Mañozca, archbishop of Mexico (1643—50), was a native of Marquina in Vizcaya and the only archbishop of Mexico in many decades who sided with the viceroy and the bureaucratic party against the Creoles. He has been described by Professor Phelan as being 'harshly hostile to the Creoles as a group, regarding them as little better than people of mixed blood'.[23] Mañozca once remarked that 'although the Creoles do not have Indian blood in them, they have been weaned on the milk of Indian women, and are therefore, like the Indians, children of fear.'[24]

The Creoles understandably tended to be as resentful toward the Basques as the Basques were contemptuous of them. In Mexico, as

[20]See the letter from Mendieta to an unknown correspondent dated 20 Mar. 1574 in *Documentos inéditos del siglo XVI para la historia de México*, ed. Mariano Cuevas, pp. 298—300.

[21]See the report of the Franciscan *visitador* Fray Juan de Ciese dated 27 Feb. 1608 printed in Cuevas, *Historia de la Iglesia en Mexico*, iii. 245—7.

[22]AGI Patronato real 221, r 12, fol. 12.

[23]J. L. Phelan, *The Kingdom of Quito in the Seventeenth Century* (Madison, Wisconsin, and London, 1967), p. 270.

[24]Ibid., p. 266.

Viceroy Mancera pointed out,[25] there was no outbreak of fighting and killing between Basques and Creoles of the sort that marred the life of Potosí and Laicacota for many years in the seventeenth century, but there was always an undercurrent of distrust and a marked tendency for the two groups to take opposite sides in the political battle between enterprise and bureaucracy. The Mexican Creoles were wont to regard the Basques as the arch-*gachupines*, the most arrogant and presumptuous of the Europeans in Mexico,[26] while the Basques evinced at least some hostility toward the Mexico City council and a marked sympathy for even the most unpopular viceroys, including the marqués de Gelves.[27] Like most unpopular but wealthy minorities, the Basques put their main trust and hope of security in the administration, for in aiding and at the same time gaining the favour of a *gachupín* bureaucracy which was under pressure, as they themselves were, the Basques saw their best chance of protecting their position. Besides, the Basques had an obvious temperamental affinity with the *gachupín* element and knew that they could always count on many of their own nation among the high officers of state and Church.

Having reached this conclusion, or working hypothesis, regarding the Basques in Mexico, it is appropriate next to consider the Portuguese, Italians, and other foreigners. One does not find that the enviable position of the Biscayans was shared by the other white minorities, for the Basques were alone in being able to follow their various pursuits in Mexico unimpeded by legal disabilities and official disapproval. Nor indeed were the foreigners as numerous as the Basques; where the latter certainly numbered several thousand, the foreigners may well have numbered less than 2,000 all told. Nevertheless, the foreigners played an important and conspicuous role and cannot be omitted from a balanced analysis of seventeenth-century Mexican society.

The colonization of Mexico had never been an exclusively Spanish enterprise. Even in the Conquest itself, we know that Portuguese, Italians, Frenchmen, and even Greeks had participated.[28] Moreover, this penetration of New Spain by foreigners had continued uninterrupted after the Conquest, despite repeated attempts by Charles V and Philip II to stop it. By the Laws of the Indies, entry to America was denied to all who were not subjects of the crown of Castile, excepting only such as had procured a special royal licence. But these exceptions became an important group in themselves. Various categories of

25*Instrucciones que los virreyes dejaron* (1867), p. 259.
26See, for instance, the *Alegaciones en favor del Clero*, fols. 5ᵛ–6, 28, 83ᵛ–85.
27See the Basque papers relating to the tumult of 1624 in AGI Patronato real 221, r 14.
28*The Conquistadors*, p. 137.

foreigners succeeded in obtaining entry permits and indeed naturalization papers, particularly men with special skills which were in short supply in the Indies. In the exploitation of the newly discovered silver deposits experts in mining technology and smelting were needed, and, although the Basques and some other Spaniards quickly acquired these skills, there is some evidence that non-Spaniards, and especially Germans and Italians, played a part. Even after 1600 when most supervisory jobs in mining and smelting and other activities were securely in Spanish hands, the most specialized jobs frequently remained in the hands of foreigners. In the 1620s, in San Luis Potosí, the two most skilful makers of bellows were Portuguese.[29] The two leading drainage engineers in Mexico City in the early seventeenth century were the German Heinrich Martin,[30] who was also a well-known printer and mathematician, and the Fleming Adriaen Boot,[31] who was also the architect of the fortress of San Diego at Acapulco, constructed in the years 1615–16. Another important category of legally resident foreigners were those personally connected with the viceroys and their retinues. The wife of the marqués de Guadalcázar, Ana von Rieder, vicereine from 1613 until her death in 1619, was Austrian,[32] while the marqués de Cerralvo appears to have had several foreigners among his entourage including one French and one German servant.[33] There were also a considerable number of foreign seamen about in Mexico during the time that the flotas were docked in Veracruz and sometimes for longer periods, and in the years 1600–1 these included the great Frenchman Samuel de Champlain, the future first governor of New France, who wrote a report on what he had seen in Mexico for the French king, Henri IV.[34] Yet another group of legally resident aliens were the foreign clergy. These included the English Dominican friar, Thomas Gage, and the Portuguese Provincial of the Augustinians of Michoacán in the years 1629–34, Fray Pedro de Santa María.[35] Finally, the legally resident foreigners included a small group of wealthy merchants who had been able, particularly during the years of the ascendancy of Olivares at Madrid, to purchase permission to trade in the Indies.

[29] Velázquez, *Historia de San Luis Potosí*, ii. 115.

[30] Leonard, *Baroque Times in Old Mexico*, pp. 67–9.

[31] According to Gibson, Boot was specially dispatched by Madrid, *The Aztecs Under Spanish Rule*, p. 238.

[32] Rubio Mañé, *Introducción al estudio de los virreyes*, i. 240–1.

[33] AGN Inquisición 366, fol. 257^v; AGI México 75, r 2: Miranda to council, 18 Mar. 1633.

[34] Though the authenticity of this work has been challenged; see D. A. Vigneras, 'El Viaje de Samuel de Champlain a las Indias Occidentales', *Anuario de Estudios Americanos*, x (1953).

[35] Basalenque, *Historia*, pp. 387–9.

The vast majority of foreigners in seventeenth-century Mexico, however, entered illegally, by bribing ships' officers on the Atlantic flotas. By all accounts, the risk to unlicensed passengers of detection and arrest was relatively small, unless one gave oneself away like Joseph Ebanacolto, who in 1606 presented Viceroy Montesclaros with a letter from Cosimo di Medici, Grand Duke of Tuscany, in which the grand duke explained that he had sent Ebanacolto to purchase on his behalf sparrow hawks and other rare birds.[36] For having crossed the Atlantic without a licence, Ebanacolto was deported back to Spain without his birds.

Owing to the practice of 'composition' of foreigners, we have some idea of how many illegal immigrants there were in seventeenth-century Mexico, and which nationalities they represented.[37] During the reigns of Philip III and Philip IV, the detection of persons residing in Mexico illegally did not normally lead to their expulsion. Instead, they were 'composed', that is to say registered and permitted to stay after payment of a fine assessed as a percentage of their wealth. 'Composition', a practice begun apparently in 1595, led quickly to mass composition, a device whereby the whole unlicensed resident alien body within the area of the jurisdiction of the *Audiencia* of Mexico was promised lenient consideration from the crown, provided they came forward of their own accord, within a specified space of time, and submitted their names to the authorities together with details of their fortunes for assessment of their fines. Thus Viceroy Guadalcázar initiated a programme of mass composition for the non-Portuguese foreigners of Mexico before 1615[38] and for the Portuguese in the years before 1619,[39] and found that there were then 338 adult male foreigners in New Spain excluding those who had licence to settle, or had previously been composed, or who still concealed their identity. Of these, a little more than half were Portuguese while most of the rest were Italian, the great majority of them Genoese. The remainder consisted of some twenty-seven Flemings, ten Germans, seven Frenchmen, three Scots, three Greeks, and three or four others of uncertain provenience. In 1625, Viceroy Cerralvo carried out a second mass composition, this time for those who had slipped Guadalcázar's net, or had arrived without licence in the meantime.[40] Another seventy aliens

36 AGI México 26: Montesclaros to council, 30 May 1606 (gov.).

37 The practice was accorded royal sanction in 1618 and 1619, the only proviso being that 'composed' foreigners could not reside in the ports or engage in international commerce, *RLI* iii Tit. 27, Law xxi. Indeed, the crown was actually anxious to keep skilled craftsmen and other 'useful' persons in the Indies, ibid., Law x (1621), a typical Olivarist innovation.

38 AGI México 28, r 3: Guadalcázar to council, 25 May 1615 (gov.).

39 AGI México 29, r 2: Guadalcázar to council, 27 Sept. 1619 (gov.).

40 AGN reales cédulas duplicados 50, fols. 122–39.

were placed on the register, nearly three-quarters being Portuguese and the rest mainly Italian, especially Genoese. The pre-eminence of the Genoese among the Italians may be explained presumably by the very special relationship that existed between Genoa and Spain during this period; far behind the Genoese, but in second place, came the Piedmontese with sixteen, and after them the Venetians with eight, and in fourth place the Neapolitans with six. Of course, besides the 400 or so on the composition registers of the four provinces of the *Audiencia* of Mexico, we may take it as certain that there were also some in New Galicia, and some more in the remote frontier areas of the north and far south.[41]

The registers of composed foreigners tell us not only the origin of the immigrants but also their places of residence in Mexico and, in some cases, their occupations. These details are of considerable interest, for in contrast to what the frequent viceregal complaints concerning foreign activity in the silver-mining areas and the ports might lead us to expect, only a very small minority of the foreigners resided in San Luis Potosí, Guanajuato, Pachuca, Taxco, and so forth,[42] or in Veracruz or Acapulco. Of the 171 Portuguese on the list of 1619, for instance, only about a dozen dwelt in areas of silver-mining activity, half of them in San Luis. Twenty-five lived in Mexico City, fourteen in Puebla. The vast majority, nearly 120, resided in and around the secondary towns of central Mexico—Atlixco, Cuernavaca, Tlaxcala, Texcoco, Querétaro, Celaya, Valladolid, Tulancingo, and so on. A high proportion were poor men, cobblers, barbers, carpenters, hosiers, and even vagabonds. Three or four were married to Indian women and many more had native concubines, both of which phenomena were usually signs of poverty. On the other hand, a sizeable number were wealthy merchants and it was really these men who made the foreigners a major political and social issue in the colony.

The preoccupation of the viceroys with the foreign presence in the silver towns was not misplaced, despite the fewness of the foreigners who actually lived in them. The foreigners, as a rule, avoided the mining industry itself. They viewed the silver towns not as a base, but as a valuable market and a source of specie. It was this which particularly

[41] For traces of Italians in seventeenth-century New León, see the *Historia de Nuevo León*, ed. Israel Cavazos Garza (Monterrey, 1961), pp. xxxiii–xxxvii, where señor Cavazos Garza suggests that the author of an anonymous chronicle of New León, of the years 1650–90, was Juan Bautista Chapa (Chapapria), a Genoese who had crossed to Mexico as a young man in 1647.

[42] In Zacatecas in 1605 there were apparently some ten or twelve Italians and Portuguese; Mota y Escobar, *Descripción geográfica*, p. 66, though these foreigners did not figure on Guadalcázar's Registers coming as they did under the jurisdiction of New Galicia.

worried the authorities, for the foreigners were not only traders but specialized in the illicit side of trade.[43] Based on Mexico City and Puebla, and in the case of New Galicia, on Guadalajara, the foreigners dealt in contraband, smuggling merchandise through Veracruz and Acapulco without paying imposts, selling in the silver towns either directly or through brokers, and receiving and exporting untaxed bullion. Frequently they served as brokers for reputable merchants and manufacturers and mine-owners, all of whom were eager to reduce the amounts they paid in tax. Even very minor foreign entrepreneurs, often mere peddlers, participated in this activity, and some petty traders came from as far away as Seville and Cadiz each year to sell off contraband in Zacatecas and San Luis and smuggle out silver on the next flota.[44]

The decisive advantage of the foreign merchant over the Mexican or peninsular entrepreneur in the movement of contraband was the vast international commercial network at his disposal. Seville, Cadiz, and San Lucar, the centres of the Indies trade, were three of Europe's most cosmopolitan emporia. The colonies of Portuguese, Italians, Frenchmen, and Flemings which loomed so large in the life of these ports and which were so important that by the second half of the seventeenth century they were to possess more of the Indies trade than Spanish merchants,[45] dominated commercial exchange between Andalusia and northern Europe. Their business connections embraced virtually the whole of western Europe, especially the great business centres—Amsterdam, Antwerp, Frankfurt, and Genoa. They knew the ins and outs of the flota system as well as any and better than most. Any vessel that docked on the Guadalquivir was vulnerable to their machinations. Naturally these foreign entrepreneurs, many of whom were heavily espanolized and whose sons could often pass for Spaniards, had the closest links with their compatriots in the Indies. And so the commercial techniques developed by non-Spanish capitalists, to counteract the crushing burden imposed on trade by the stifling Spanish tax system, were exported ready-made to the New World.

The progress of the method was facilitated by the creeping decline of bureaucratic standards in Spain and America under the successors of Philip II. Officers, from viceroys to minor ships' officers, became increasingly lax in the exaction of the king's dues and the enforcement

[43] Hence the tendency of many rich aliens to avoid the compositions. AGN ramo de civil has numerous cases of seventeenth-century foreign businessmen in Mexico who had been discovered and were fined for not having come forward.

[44] AGN ordenanzas iv, fol. 36.

[45] Lynch, *Spain under the Habsburgs*, ii. 170–1.

of the king's rules, and more and more self-seeking. Collusion of officials with contrabandists became a usual occurrence just as did willingness to take bribes for the passage of unregistered emigrants. Landeras de Velasco, visitor-general to New Spain in 1606–9, was horrified by the morass of administrative corruption which he uncovered in Veracruz.[46] Pedro de Vergara Gabiria, the *Audiencia* judge who examined the customs machinery in Veracruz in 1620–1, professed to be staggered by the extent of collusion between bureaucracy and smugglers.[47] He told of an unregistered Portuguese ship laden with unregistered Rouen cloth and French metalware which was unloaded under the very eyes of the customs and stowed in the warehouse of Francisco de Texoso, a well-known Portuguese entrepreneur and slave factor. But even those who professed to find the situation shocking were frequently denounced for the very frauds of which they complained. Vergara Gabiria was charged in 1624 with smuggling 100,000 pesos' worth of textiles and wine into Mexico with the connivance of the commander of the flota.[48] Martín de Carrillo y Alderete, visitor-general in the years 1625–8, was similarly accused of gross corruption. Viceroy Gelves, the most puritanical ruler of Mexico in the seventeenth century, charged the whole Mexican bureaucracy and merchant community with defrauding the king continually.[49]

Though the crown repeatedly urged them to act, the viceroys were unwilling or unable to arrest the process. The marqués de Guadalcázar repeatedly deplored the influx of foreign merchants, capital, and goods into Mexico.[50] 'The harm done by foreigners born in Seville and other places in Spain', he declared, 'is almost too great to be imagined.' He singled out for special mention John Rutherford and his two brothers, Scottish merchants with stores in Mexico City, Oaxaca, and San Luis, and contacts as far afield as Genoa and Antwerp. They and dozens like them were cheating the king on a massive scale and undermining the official Indies trade. But at the end of Guadalacázar's term, as both Vergara Gabiria and Gelves emphasize, the position was worse than ever. Gelves, with his unflagging zeal, achieved some temporary improvement, but in a little more than two years he was overthrown by his enemies; moreover, even he, tireless though he was, all but admitted that the task was impossible. Cerralvo, after eleven years of rule,

[46] AGI Indiferente de Nueva España, 77. Landeras de Velasco to council, 4 Nov. 1606.

[47] AGI México 74, r 1: Vergara to council, 30 Oct. 1620, and r 2, 20 Mar. 1621.

[48] AGI Patronato Real 221, r 14: 'Relacion de los subcesos de Mexico . . .', fol. 3.

[49] AGI México 30, r 1: Gelves to council, 23 Feb. 1623.

[50] AGI México 28, r 3: Guadalcázar to council, 31 Jan. 1615 and 25 May 1615.

suggested somewhat disingenuously in 1636 that something ought to be done to stop the dangerous and unimpeded flow of foreigners through Veracruz.[51] Even in 1648, eight years after the breaking away of Portugal from Spain and the onset of war between the two countries, Veracruz was still an easy haven for Portuguese ships and merchants and the crown was rebuking the viceroy for his manifest failure to enforce the ban on trade between Portugal and Mexico.[52]

The foreigners, then, achieved their main inroads into Mexico as a result of bureaucratic corruption and the character of the Spanish tax system which, from the time of Philip II onwards, was among the most oppressive in Europe. The position of the foreigners in Mexico, however, remained vulnerable and was dependent on the continuing favour of a lax administration; for as long as the viceroy and his officers were primarily concerned to fill their own pockets, they had a stake in the unimpeded flow of unlicensed passengers and goods, and in conniving at evasion of Madrid's controls and imposts. The threat to the foreigners came principally from the 'puritans', officers such as Landeras de Velasco and Gelves who put the regulations and the interests of the state first and who were prepared to brave the anger of the foreigners and their allies in doing what they saw as their duty. Thus we may fairly expect to encounter a stress within the Mexican administration between those who took a hard line on the foreigners and those who took a soft, a stress closely related to that between those who took a hard line on the Peru trade and commercial policy, and those who took a soft. The viceroy who took the hardest line on both in the seventeenth century, and angered many of his officers and the foreigners, also took the hardest line with the Negroes and vagabonds. The marqués de Gelves antagonized the Portuguese, expelling them from Zacatecas and San Luis Potosí, even when they were craftsmen engaged in highly specialized tasks,[53] tied their hands in Veracruz and Acapulco to a considerable extent if only very temporarily, and imprisoned a sizeable number of them in Mexico City.[54] There is no cause for surprise, then, when one learns that the Portuguese were conspicuous in the great insurrection in Mexico City of 15 January 1624.[55]

---

[51] Marqués de Cerralvo, *Relación del estado en que dejó el gobierno de la Nueva España*, in *La Nueva España*, p. 245.

[52] AGN cédulas originales iii, fols. 83–4: council to Salvatierra, 4 July 1648.

[53] Velázquez, *Historia de San Luis Potosí*, ii. 115–16.

[54] Antonio de Brámbila y Arriaga, *Relación en favor del marqués de Gelves*, *DRT* ii. 215, 255.

[55] AGI Patronato Real 223, r 5, fol. 109[v]; Juan Gutiérrez Flores and Juan de Lormendi, *Relacion sumaria y puntual del tumulto y sedicion que hubo en Mexico a los 15 de enero de 1624 y de las cosas mas notables que lo precedieron* (Mexico, 1625), fols. 8[v]–9[v].

If the attitude of the bureaucracy to the foreigners was mixed, so also, apparently, was that of the colonists. Doubtless there were numerous entrepreneurs who benefited from the services of the foreign merchants. Apart from any other consideration, it was the Portuguese who brought the slaves from Africa and the Portuguese and other foreigners who supplied commodities from northern Europe which neither Creole nor *gachupín* businessmen could have procured for themselves. But at the same time a great many Mexican entrepreneurs must have suffered at the hands of foreign competition. Seventeenth-century Spaniards were not particularly gifted at commerce, as their performance in Seville and Cadiz amply demonstrates, and foreigners were often able to get the better of them. It is clear that at least some Spaniards laid the principal blame for the shrinking of the Atlantic flotas on the Portuguese,[56] and it cannot be supposed that Spaniards who suffered as a result of the recession in the official trade looked benignly on the prosperity of the foreigners. It has been suggested that a wave of xenophobia, or at least a wave of Lusophobia, swept the Spanish Indies in the 1630s and 1640s.[57] There is, however, little real evidence for this apart from the spurts in Inquisition activity against the Portuguese crypto-Jews, many of whom were merchants, at Lima and Cartagena in the later 1630s, and in Mexico in the years 1642–50. A document of the late 1630s shows that the Mexico City council was then in favour of increasing the number of Inquisition familiars in New Spain,[58] presumably to combat crypto-Judaism; but then this is not necessarily evidence of xenophobia or of bitter trade rivalry between Spaniards and foreigners.

The issue of the foreigners in seventeenth-century Mexico is certainly complicated, indeed inextricably bound up, with the question of crypto-Judaism. It is in fact impossible to determine the position of the non-Spanish white element in Mexican society solely in economic and legal terms, owing to the marked tendency in seventeenth-century Spanish America to confuse Portuguese with Portuguese New Christians and crypto-Jews, to overlook the abhorrence of Portuguese Old Christians for Portuguese New Christians, and to assume that the Portuguese, Jewish and non-Jewish, were united in hatred of the Castilians.[59] Recognition of this brings us to yet another tension in

56 See the short tract of Alonso de Cianca, *Discurso breve . . . en que se muestra la causa que ha enflaquecido el comercio de las flotas* (n.p., n.d. [Madrid, c 1620]).

57 Lynch, *Spain under the Habsburgs*, ii. 112–13.

58 *ACM* xxxi. 70.

59 *DHM* vii. 33–4; appendix xi of García de Proodian, *Los Judíos en América*, pp. 272–4; C. R. Boxer, *Salvador de Sa and the struggle for Brazil and Angola, 1602–1686* (London, 1952), pp. 15, 72, 81.

seventeenth-century Mexican society, that arising from religious intolerance and the mutual detestation of Catholic and Jew.

The Mexican Inquisition, it is important to note, though busily engaged against sorcery, bigamy, drug-taking, blasphemy, and solicitation of women by clergy at confession, reserved its chief effort, especially during the first half of the seventeenth century, for the suppression of Judaism. Cases of Mohammedanism and Protestantism were extremely rare, though neither was unknown, and when they did occur aroused the inquisitors' curiosity rather than their wrath. Solicitation of women by clergy employing Latin and the appurtenances of the faith as methods of seduction, though extremely common,[60] was treated leniently and, as a matter of policy, was as far as possible kept from the public view; even the most debauched clergy such as the Jesuit Gaspar de Villenas, arraigned in 1621 for soliciting ninety-seven women from the confessional and actually having illicit relations with more than thirty, some on church premises,[61] were not publicly disgraced and never appeared in *Autos-de-fe*. Judaism alone aroused violent feelings because, of Spain's traditional religious enemies, only the Jews had slipped, by means of disguise, into the mainstream of Spanish life, and only the Jews were evident to any significant extent in seventeenth-century Spanish America. The traditional antipathy to the Jews reappeared in the New World with full force. 'New Spain seethed with Jews,' wrote the Mexican inquisitor Estrada y Escovedo in 1646, referring to the situation before 1642, 'who, concealing their perfidy with constant deception, used to imitate Catholic conduct outwardly; a cruel nation, whose hatred of all the nations of the world is so great, that, if once the mask with which impatiently they conceal it were cast off, the volcano of its virulent hatred would erupt in the most appalling atrocities.'[62]

That the vast majority of secretly practising Jews, in seventeenth-century Mexico, were of Portuguese origin is quickly shown by a check through the Mexican Inquisition case books. In the three decades 1620–50, for instance, slightly more than 200 Jews were tried by the inquisitors, the bulk of them in the years 1642–6. Of these 200, slightly less than half had been born in Portugal, mainly at Lisbon and Castelobranco; another thirty-five or so were Mexican-born of

---

[60] In peak years, such as 1621, many dozens of clergy were entered on the Inquisition files for solicitation of women at confession; for 1621 see AGN Inquisición 334 and 337.

[61] AGN Inquisición 330. The ninety-seven were a remarkable mixture comprising nuns, young girls and mature women married and unmarried, of all races, white, black, Indian, and mestizo.

[62] Pedro de Estrada y Escovedo, *Relacion sumaria del auto particular de la fee* (April 1646) in *DHM* xxviii. 18.

Portuguese parents, while a further fifteen or twenty had been born of Portuguese Jewish parents in France, Italy, and Peru. Of the remainder, most were the offspring of Portuguese crypto-Jews residing in Spain; scarcely a handful even might have been of Spanish origin and some, even of these, had Portuguese wives or mixed with the Portuguese circle. This overwhelming preponderance of Portuguese among the judaizers sentenced in Mexico demonstrates that in general there was no correlation in New Spain, and presumably therefore also in the rest of Spanish America, between New Christians, or Christians of Jewish descent, and crypto-Jews, or Jews only outwardly simulating Christianity. It may be safely assumed, though it can never be proved, that there were many more Spanish New Christians than Portuguese in Mexico, but that the Spanish New Christians had forsaken the old faith to a much greater extent. This is to be explained by the fact that Portuguese Jewry was largely descended from those Spanish Jews who had refused to convert to Catholicism in 1492, and had left Spain, while the Spanish New Christians were mainly descended from those who had converted, and stayed; also, the Portuguese Inquisition had been rather a feeble instrument in comparison with its Spanish counterpart, until the annexation of Portugal, to Spain in 1580, so that the Portuguese crypto-Jews had suffered only a minimum of pressure until a late stage. The preponderance of Portuguese Jews appearing in Mexican *Autos-de-Fe* in the seventeenth century is paralleled by a similar preponderance, though one not quite so complete, in the *Autos-de-Fe* of Spain itself in this period.[63]

Of the role of the Jews in seventeenth-century Mexican society a certain amount can be ascertained. As with the rest of the foreign community, few of them lived in the silver-mining zones, including less than one-eighth of those arrested by the Inquisition. The three main Mexican Jewish centres were Mexico City, where about half of the Jews lived, and Veracruz and Guadalajara which accounted for nearly two-thirds of the remainder. Curiously, scarcely a handful resided in Puebla. The majority of the Jews were shopkeepers, craftsmen, peddlers, and vagabonds; but the élite of the community, men like Simón Váez Sevilla and Matías Rodríguez de Oliveira of Mexico City, and Francisco de Texoso of Veracruz, were wealthy merchants, some of the wealthiest of New Spain. Simón Váez, a native of Castelobranco, whose business contacts ranged from Manila in the Philippines to Pisa in Italy, where part of his family lived, had shops in Mexico City, Zacatecas, and other Mexican towns, and with over 200,000 pesos was of roughly equivalent worth to Manuel Bautista Pérez, who was head of

63 Henry Kamen, *The Spanish Inquisition* (London, 1965), pp. 216—18.

the Jewish community in Péru until his arrest in 1635.[64] Simón Váez presided over Mexican Jewry until the catastrophe of 1642, in company with his relative Captain Antonio Váez de Castelobranco, a merchant and messianic dreamer who had learned his Judaism in Pisa and who, among his various tenets, and much to the indignation of the inquisitors, denied the existence of hell.[65] Most of the Jewish merchants had built up from small beginnings with remarkable speed, and had travelled and fought for a living in an astounding number of places. Mathías Rodríguez de Oliveira, born in Portugal, had lived in Madrid and Seville, obtained Negroes in Angola in person, taken his Negroes to Mexico and sold them, returned to Spain and then Lisbon, and then in 1630 returned to Mexico, where he amassed a considerable fortune and was one of the leaders of the Jewish community until he was seized in 1642 along with Simón Váez and most of his friends and Jewish associates.[66] Julian de Alvarez, merchant and citizen of Cacacuero in Michoacán, had been born in Amsterdam, and had lived in Holland, Italy, and Spain.[67] Francisco López Fonseca, known in Peru as Francisco Méndez, had lived in Coimbra and La Guardia in Portugal, Valladolid, Madrid, and Seville in Spain, Cartagena, Quito, Guayaquil, Riobamba, and Maracaibo in South America, and Veracruz and Mexico City in New Spain.[68] Melchor Rodríguez López, a cacao dealer of Mexico City who owned a cacao estate in southern Mexico, had lived in various places in Spain, in Tenerife, and for some time in Luanda, in Angola.[69] Pedro Fernández de Castro, a son-in-law of Simón Váez, born in Valladolid, Old Castile, had been in Naples, Rome, Ferrara, Marseilles, Genoa, and various parts of Spain as well as Mexico.[70] Juan de Torres, like Rodríguez de Oliveira, having started in Portugal, set up in Mexico City on the proceeds from a cargo of Negroes that he had purchased in Angola.[71] Diego Pérez de Albuquerque, citizen of Zacatecas, had been raised in Bordeaux, and had lived for periods in Rouen, Seville, and Puebla.[72] Luis Núñez Pérez, a humble peddler of Mexico City and another messianic dreamer, had lived in Portugal, Spain, Angola, Portuguese Brazil, Dutch Brazil, and Cuba as well as

[64] AGN Inquisición 409, fol. 381; Oliveira, apparently, was the second richest, though I have found no estimate of his fortune; Francisco de Texoso had some 70,000 pesos, ADI Palafox papers lxvi, fols. 114ᵛ–115ᵛ.
[65] AGN Inquisición 489, fols. 319, 381ᵛ–382.
[66] ADI Palafox papers lxvi, fol. 114ᵛ.
[67] AGN Inquisición 431, fols. 91–3.
[68] AGN Inquisición 410, fol. 494.
[69] AGN Inquisición 378, exp. 3.
[70] AGN Inquisición 489, fols. 579–83.
[71] AGN Inquisición 433, fol. 538 and *passim*.
[72] AGN Inquisición 348, fols. 511, 517, 531.

Mexico.[73] And so the list might be continued. It emerges from the details of the Jews seized by the Mexican Inquisition that the three areas of Mexican commerce with which Jewish entrepreneurs were most closely involved were the slave trade from Africa, the importing of cacao from Venezuela which first became an important element of Mexican commerce in the 1630s, and, most of all, the trade in Chinese, Spanish, northern European, and Mexican textiles.

Wealthy Jews, despite being Portuguese, could and did acquire social standing in Mexico, despite the fact that all, or nearly all of them, including Simón and Antonio Váez, were of very humble origin.[74] The Portuguese were not popular in Mexico, but provided that Judaism was well enough concealed they could rise up the social ladder.[75] Melchor Juarez, who was given away in 1643,[76] escaped the clutches of the Inquisition chiefly because he was then secretary to the visitor-general, Bishop Palafox. Jorge de Espinosa, alias Jorge Serrano, who had been in many parts of Spain, Brazil, and the Spanish Indies, was *corregidor* of Coatzacoalcos in 1647, despite having been exposed as a Jew by the Peruvian Inquisition and 'reconciled' to the Church in the *Auto-de-Fe* at Lima in January 1639.[77] Captain Antonio Váez de Acevedo had commanded an infantry detachment in Mexico City in 1641 and was *corregidor* of Pampanga, in the Philippines, in 1648, when the Inquisition commissioners seized him.[78] His brother, Captain Sebastian Váez de Acevedo, was appointed purveyor-general of the Armada of Barlovento, the Caribbean battle squadron, in 1640 by Viceroy Escalona. Simón Váez and Mathías Rodríguez, though merchants of humble birth, were reputable enough, according to Guijo,[79] to mix socially with *Audiencia* judges. Simón Enríquez, the Portuguese member of the Mexico City council in the 1620s, despite his certificate purporting to prove that he was a Portuguese *fidalgo* of unsullied Old Christian descent,[80] was very probably of Jewish origin.

Regarding the attitudes of the Mexican Jews, a little can be said. Spanish suspicions of an inter-continental Jewish political conspiracy had, as far as one can tell, little or no basis in fact; apparently there is little to support Bishop Palafox's assertion that Amsterdam and Lisbon

---

[73] AGN Inquisición 412, fols. 416, 534–8ᵛ, 543.

[74] Guijo, *Diario*, i. 47.

[75] Estrada y Escovedo, *Relación Sumaria*, DHM xxviii. 42, 49–51; Guijo, *Diario*, i. 46.

[76] AGN Inquisición 416, fols. 427–8, 466.

[77] AGN Inquisición 416, fol. 539.

[78] AGN Inquisición 430, fol. 593.

[79] Guijo, *Diario*, i. 46–7.

[80] ACM xxii. 246; this quite possibly is the only document in the Portuguese language preserved in the records of the Mexico City council.

were 'the only centres from which the Jews take orders'. The Inquisition, despite its eagerness to expose Jewish subversiveness in all its forms, could find nothing more than an occasional indication that the Jews sympathized with the revolt of Portugal against Spain, and indeed with the Portuguese struggle against the Protestant Netherlands,[81] and that Antonio Váez and Luis Núñez Pérez, the two visionaries of Mexican Jewry, had foretold that a great Armada would come from Portugal, conquer Mexico, and save the Jews from the Spaniards. What is abundantly clear is that Jews put their main trust in the Almighty, and if there was any to spare for the Dutch West India Company, it was very little by comparison.

That the Jews were contemptuous of the Catholics whom they considered 'blind beasts' seems plain enough, and it may also be, as is suggested by an account of Peru left by an anonymous Portuguese Jew in the second decade of the seventeenth century,[82] that they tended to be disdainful of the Creoles, considering them feeble and lethargic, men who 'have no wish to take risks or accept danger by land or sea to gain a living'. The Indians, according to the anonymous chronicler at least, were the 'most cowardly and timid people in the world so that one shout from a Spaniard is enough to make them tremble and a single white man is enough to put a hundred of them to flight'. There is no evidence that any Mexican Jews agreed with the Amsterdam Rabbi Manasseh ben Israel, and a number of Spanish friars, who thought that the American Indians were the descendants of the ten lost tribes of Israel.[83] As regards the religious life of the Mexican Jews, it is clear that their knowledge of Hebrew was very limited, but they were much better acquainted with Jewish laws and customs than is sometimes suggested, owing to the circumstance that six or seven of their leaders had lived in Italy as members of orthodox Jewish communities. Most of the prayers and psalms that they recited were in Spanish and Portuguese.

The question why the Jews remained within the territory of the Spanish Monarchy, taking a risk which in the end brought many or most of them to disaster, is not an easy one to answer. It does seem, however, that economic opportunities for Jews in such safe, or relatively safe, areas as France, Italy, or Brazil, were very limited as compared with the opportunities in Spanish-speaking lands, and that the lure of silver-producing, textile-importing colonies with a weak

---

[81] AGN Inquisición 412, fols. 540–541ᵛ.

[82] See the *Descripción del Virreinato del Peru. Crónica Inédita de comienzos del siglo XVII* ed. Boleslao Lewin (Rosario, Argentina, 1958).

[83] Rafael Heliodoro Valle. 'Judíos en México' in *Revista Chilena de Historia y Geografía*, lxxxi (Santiago de Chile, 1936), pp. 216–20.

native bourgeoisie was a powerful one. It should also be remembered that from 1601 until the mid-1630s in South America, and until 1642 in Mexico, very few Jews were seized by the Inquisition, and that the risk that Jewish settlers in the Spanish Indies were running in the early seventeenth century must have seemed much less than it appears in retrospect. In Mexico the Inquisition sprang into action suddenly, as we shall see in chapter eight, and, beginning in 1642, seized over 150 Jews in the space of three or four years. These prisoners were tortured until they confessed their Judaism and were then publicly 'reconciled' to the Church in a series of *Autos-de-fe,* beginning in April 1646 when forty Jews were presented, continuing in January 1647 with twenty-one Jews presented, and March 1648 with another forty, and culminating in the famous *Auto General de la fe* of 11 April 1649, arguably the most costly and grandiose *Auto-de-fe* ever held outside the Iberian peninsula, when eight Jews were burned and twenty-seven 'reconciled'. In the years 1650–1 most of those who had been reconciled were deported to Spain, for it was felt that it was better to keep them in Spain than leave them in the Indies where it was so much easier to escape from surveillance. As far as one can tell from Inquisition activity, this deportation seems to have ended the main crypto-Jewish presence in the viceroyalty. Nevertheless, cases of Judaism continued to crop up during the rest of the century and even into the early eighteenth century, and more than thirty judaizers were caught and punished between the expulsions of 1650–1 and the mid-1690s. These included some quite interesting personages, notably Domingo Márquez, *alguacil mayor*[84] of Tepeaca, tried in 1660, Captain Matías Pereira Lobo, tried in 1662, Doña Teresa de Aguilera y Roche, wife of a governor of New Mexico, sentenced in 1663 (whose husband, Don Bernardo López de Mendizabal, was probably tried in 1662), Captain Agustín Muñoz de Sandoval, sentenced in 1695, and a Jewish friar tried in 1706, Fray Joseph de San Ignacio.

Such then, as far as one can glean from the Inquisition records, was the position of the Jews in seventeenth-century Mexico; and, with them, the end of the first part of this study is reached. Before proceeding with the second, it may be as well to recapitulate. Of the various stresses and strains in Mexican society in the seventeenth century the most important was the conflict between the Spanish colonists on the one hand, in alliance with the bishops and the secular clergy, and the Spanish, Indian, and mendicant bureaucracies on the other, for control, especially economic control, of the Indian population. This is perhaps equivalent to saying that Mexico was subject to much the same sort of

[84] An *alguacil mayor* was a district police officer.

battle between officialdom and enterprise as many other European and European-dominated societies in the early modern era. The tension between officers and colonists, however, though the main piece, is by no means the only piece in the framework. The conflict between a powerful, privileged, and well-entrenched administrative and ecclesiastical class and the settlers was also, to a large extent, a conflict between peninsular Spaniards and Creoles with the former occupying a favoured position in respect to offices and dignities in the land colonized by the latter. This situation had its similarities to the friction between Dutch and Boers in eighteenth-century South Africa, or English and English Americans in eighteenth-century New England. In addition, there were a number of subsidiary strains of various kinds, the most significant being that between those, both inside and outside the Mexican bureaucracy, who put loyalty to the Spanish state and the interests of the Spanish state first, especially in such fields as taxation and control of trade, conduct, and consumption, and those who, for their own, usually economic, reasons, preferred lax application of the rules. In allowing for the political relevance of this stress, it should be noted that in the final years of Philip III's reign and the early years of that of Philip IV, there was much talk of reform in Spain in certain influential quarters, and a strong demand for a new austerity and a crack-down on corruption, proposals which were strongly resisted by bureaucratic elements, both in Mexico and in Spain.

PART TWO
MEXICAN POLITICS
1620-1670

V

GELVES AND THE INSURRECTION OF 1624

Don Diego Carrillo de Mendoza Pimentel, conde de Priego, marqués de Gelves, *comendador* of Villanueva de la Fuente, was appointed thirteenth viceroy of Mexico by the Spanish government at Madrid in April 1621. The timing is significant, for the recent accession of Philip IV to the Spanish throne had afforded a powerful new impetus to the movement for reform that had begun after the fall of the corrupt Duke of Lerma in 1618. The new king's ministers, led by the brilliant if somewhat erratic Gaspar de Guzmán, conde de Olivares, the figure who was to dominate Spanish policy for the next twenty-two years, were resolved to set the monarchy on a more vigorous and ambitious course than it had taken for more than two decades.

The reign of Philip III, though in many respects the high-point of the Spanish supremacy in Europe, had nevertheless marked a step back from the forceful *Weltpolitik* of the latter part of the reign of Philip II. Spain had disengaged itself from inconclusive wars with France, the United Provinces of the Netherlands, and England, and contented herself with enforcing her will, where and in as far as she could, by diplomacy. However, the benefit that might have accrued to the country from this respite from struggle had not materialized. The government of Philip III's favourite, the Duke of Lerma, though constructive in its policy of peace, had proved a lamentable influence in the economic and social sphere. Little or nothing had been done to halt the decay of Spanish industry and agriculture, or to deal with the problem of racing inflation. Indeed matters had been made worse. The tight controls and relatively high standard of bureaucratic integrity of Philip II's day had been abandoned and corruption and extravagance had spread alarmingly. Furthermore, the court had appeared determined to worry the less, the graver the nation's difficulties had become, preoccupying itself more and more with pleasurable diversions and entertainments, fashion, and art. This state of affairs had generated its own reaction—a body of opinion tired of drift and resolved to turn the country back to the old austerity, discipline, and thrusting foreign policy. Spain, in the midst of its decadence, produced a resolute puritanism of strongly aristocratic and military flavour, a puritanism akin, some might say, to that 'Puritanism of the right', to borrow Professor Trevor-Roper's phrase, which at this time was gaining ground in much of Europe and which in England was later to produce the 'policy of thorough' of Strafford and Laud.

Olivares stood at the head of this movement for reform. His aim was to revive and strengthen Spain, and to achieve this he planned to introduce a whole package of drastic reforms, economic, social, and moral. Moreover, his vision of national revival embraced Spain in the Indies as well as Spain in Europe. He knew that none of his other goals would be attainable if the financial position of the monarchy was not greatly improved, and for this improvement he assigned a major role to the New World. This was not simply because an important part of Spanish wealth came from America, but also because much of it was lost there. In the Indies slip-shod administration, tax evasion, and bureaucratic corruption were even more rife than in Spain itself. If the American administration could be reformed and its officers more effectively disciplined enormous rewards could be expected to accrue to the crown. And so in 1621, when the reform party was in the ascendant at Madrid, the reformers turned part of their attention to the Indies. A specially appointed visitor-general was despatched to Peru, while to Mexico, also provided with special commissions, was sent the marqués de Gelves.

Gelves was a model puritan of the right and a model politician of thorough.[1] He abhorred all vice, waste, and ostentation and regarded it as a sacred duty to reform society. He was sixty-four years of age, an experienced soldier, and a rigid disciplinarian. His career was highly distinguished. He had led the cavalry in the army of the Duke of Alva sent to subdue Portugal in 1580, had held high command in Sicily, and had sailed on the Invincible Armada and been captured and imprisoned by the Dutch. Subsequently he had served in Flanders, on the council of war in Madrid, as commander of the garrison at Milan, and finally, in the years 1614–20, as viceroy of Aragon.

The marquis landed at Veracruz in September 1621 determined to carry out his mission, determined, that is, not just to rule Mexico but to change it. Soon after his arrival, and as if in mockery of his purpose, thieves broke into one of the customs offices in the port and got away with 7,000 pesos of silver. But there was no time to tarry in Veracruz; Gelves left almost at once for Mexico City. Midway between the coast and the capital, he gave the colony a foretaste of the austerity to come. The city councils of Puebla and Mexico were then busy preparing those grand fiestas with processions, lavish display, bull-fights, and fireworks which had in recent years become customary at the reception of

[1] For details of Gelves's career see the report of the council of the Indies, AGI México 2, r 4, fols. 234–5; and also AGI México 29, r 4: Gelves to council, 14 Nov. 1621.

viceroys. Gelves, dismissing such effusions as a waste of time and money, ordered all these intended entertainments and all this pageantry to be cancelled.[2]

When he arrived in the capital, the marquis soon saw that the state of the viceroyalty was as bad as had been feared. There had been a serious split in the secular authority, and a group of three justices of the *Audiencia*—Don Pedro de Vergara Gabiria the chief justice, Galdós de Valencia, and Vázquez de Cisneros—had worked openly against the marqués de Guadalcázar and the officers loyal to him. In the ensuing political battle the group led by Vergara Gabiria had emerged victorious. They had denounced Guadalcázar's 'tyrannical' rule to the council of the Indies with marked effect and obtained a ruling that the *Audiencia* and not the viceroy should, from that time on, appoint the judges to conduct the *residencias* of *corregidores* in the area around the capital.[3] Madrid had reprimanded the viceroy and required him to relinquish office some months before he was due to sail from Acapulco to take up his new post as viceroy of Peru.[4] The executive power, for the interim until the new viceroy arrived, had been assigned to the *Audiencia* under the presidency of Vergara Gabiria.[5] The principal use to which the justices had put their power, which had lasted from March to September 1621, appears to have been that of enriching themselves and their underlings. They had organized, working with the Mexico City council and Don Melchor de Varaez, *corregidor* of Metepec and a friend of Vergara Gabiria, a ruthless racket in maize and wheat which had forced grain prices in the capital up far above their normal level. To clinch their hold over the Mexico City grain market, the magistrates had nominated Varaez, notwithstanding the royal prohibition against holding two district governorships simultaneously, *corregidor* of the capital. The racket in food had been supplemented with other and equally unsavoury operations such as the pilfering of part of the money that had been pigeon-holed by Guadalcázar for the drainage works in progress around Mexico City. Moreover, one need not rely only on the testimony of Gelves and his supporters that the situation was appalling,

---

2 BND 2354, fol. 188; and the *Relacion del estado en que el marqués de Gelves hallo el reyno de la Nueva España*, [Madrid?, 1628?], fol. 1.
3 See the virulent attack on Guadalcázar in AGI México 74, r 1: *Audiencia* to council, 10 Jan. 1620. This was the earliest instance that I have found of the dissension between Guadalcázar and the magistrates.
4 AGI México 74, r 1: council to *Audiencia*, 5 Sept. 1620; during these months Guadalcázar resided in Mexico City as an ordinary citizen, although being insulted several times by Vergara Gabiria, see AGI Patronato real 222, fols. 1294, 1312v.
5 Vergara Gabiria, a Basque whose brother was receptor in the council of the Indies, had come to Mexico as a justice in 1615 having previously held office in the province of Quito, see AGI México 2, r 5, exp. 109.

for Archbishop Pérez de la Serna himself, the man soon to become Gelves's foremost enemy, informed the council of the Indies that the *Audiencia*'s rule was so bad that after it 'it seemed easier to conquer New Spain over again than correct the abuses that flourished there'.[6] Gelves, for his part, reported to the council that it was impossible to describe conditions in the colony, they were so wretched.[7]

Gelves was not only a puritan but, as he soon showed, resourceful and genuinely anxious to relieve the sufferings of the poor. Again and again in subsequent years the viceroy and his supporters were to refer to his sympathy for the lower classes, and there is no reason to doubt the sincerity of it. In a matter of weeks he broke up the food racket and brought down the price of maize and other basic foodstuffs in Mexico City by more than half.[8] This done, he proceeded to take further measures to suppress illicit economic activities on the part of privileged groups,[9] though here his concern was less for the people than for enforcing the king's regulations and increasing the yield to the king's treasury. He tightened up the customs machinery in Veracruz and Acapulco, confiscated consignments of unregistered merchandise including at least one very valuable cargo of silk in Acapulco,[10] and disciplined numbers of officials and *corregidores*.[11] He also put an end to the arrangements by which some city councils, notably that of Zacatecas, had been paying the tax on sales at a rate far below that which was actually due from them. Zacatecas had been paying *alcabala* at 4,000 pesos annually since 1607; in July 1622 the viceroy auctioned the tax to a junta of merchants for over 9,000 pesos.[12] As the consequence of all this delving and straightening out, royal income shot up dramatically during the years of Gelves's rule,[13] the remittance to the crown in 1622 rising to 600,000 pesos as against 509,000 pesos for 1621, and showing another hefty increase in 1623, though one should bear in mind the possibility that Gelves's stringency helped bring about, or at least hasten, the trade recession which was now making itself felt.

[6] AGI México 29, r 5: Pérez de la Serna to council, 16 June 1622.

[7] AGI México 29, r 4: Gelves to council, 14 Nov. 1621.

[8] Ibid.; see also Rosa Feijóo, 'El Tumulto de 1624', *Historia Mexicana*, xiv (1964), 44–8, and BND 2354, fol. 188ᵛ.

[9] AGI México 30, r 1: Gelves to council, 23 Feb. 1623 and 7 June 1623; see also the lengthy account in Antonio de Brámbila y Arriaga, *Relacion en favor del marques de Gelves*, DRT ii. 213–90.

[10] Flores-Lormendi, *Relacion sumaria*, fol. 2ᵛ.

[11] Gelves was perhaps the only viceroy of the period to criticize the *corregidores*, see AGI Mexico 29, r 5: Gelves to council, 26 Feb. 1622.

[12] Bakewell, *Silver Mining and Society*, p. 103.

[13] AGI México 5, r 4: Gelves to council, 16 June 1622; and also Gelves to council, 7 June 1623 in the *Anuario de Estudios Americanos*, xiii (1956), 378.

But the economy was not the viceroy's only sphere of action. The marquis entered the social and moral arena as energetically as he did the economic. We have already seen something of the measures that he adopted to restrict the Negro community and dampen the spirit of that people. His drive against bandits and other criminals made an even greater impression. 'It was generally reported', records Thomas Gage, 'that since the Conquest unto those days of his, there had never been so many thieves and malefactors hanged up.'[14] The prisons were quickly filled literally to overflowing despite the willingness of Vergara Gabiria and his colleagues, presumably bought, to release some of the multitude of the viceroy's prisoners including, according to Gelves, an infamous rapist. The marquis also banned the possession of firearms without licence, especially pistols, and, much to the irritation of some of his critics, achieved at least some measure of success in enforcing the ban. In addition, the viceroy took steps to clear prostitutes from the streets and shut down many of the more objectionable brothels and gambling houses in line with the policy then being implemented in Spain.

The zeal of the new viceroy, as one would perhaps expect, soon upset and antagonized major sections, and particularly the upper sections, of Mexican society. There was friction between the viceroy and the *Audiencia* almost from the outset with the magistrates taking umbrage at what they considered the marquis's high-handed manner.[15] It appears that Gelves did try to humour Vergara Gabiria and draw him into his ruling circle but to no avail. The chief justice obstructed the viceroy at every turn and on occasion was as rude to him as he had been accustomed to be to Guadalcazar. The breach between them became final when an order came through from Madrid reprimanding the *Audiencia* for having conferred two district governorships on Varaez and fining the justices 100 ducats each. Gelves then took the resounding step of actually collecting the fines, and from that moment on, relations between viceroy and *Audiencia* deteriorated rapidly until Gelves lost all patience with the chief justice, and on 22 August 1622 had him suspended from office and placed under house arrest.[16] A few days later the same steps were taken against Galdós de Valencia. Meanwhile various other important office-holders had fallen out with the viceroy; Matheo de Aróstegui, secretary for Indian tribute, and the treasurer, Alonso de Santoyo, and both the Mexico City council and

14 *Thomas Gage's Travels*, p. 78.
15 AGI México 74, r 2: *Audiencia* to council, 11 Nov. 1621.
16 AGI México 2, r 4: Gelves to council, 23 Aug. 1622; Madrid, when it heard the news, ordered Gelves to release the two magistrates and reinstate them, but the viceroy ignored the order and the two men were still confined to their homes on the morning of 15 Jan. 1624.

the *consulado*[17] were becoming increasingly hostile. The feud between Gelves and the city fathers, having started with the tussle over food prices, intensified as the viceroy's economic measures began to bite, and reached a climax when the *regidores* publicly affronted the viceregal dignity by walking out of a ceremony in the cathedral at which the viceroy was present. Gelves retaliated by carrying out the threat he had made to expel them from the city.

Gelves, with his imperious rigidity, was not afraid to alienate powerful elements of the bureaucracy and the Creole *haute bourgeoisie*. His willingness to do so and his general heavy-handedness may seem, particularly in view of the fact that he had very few troops at his disposal, surprising in a man with almost fifty years military and civil experience in the king's service, but one must be careful not to exaggerate the extent of the danger to which the viceroy was exposing himself by pursuing the policies he did. He had known that there would be opposition. Madrid too had known that resistance was likely, and for precisely that reason had asked Archbishop Pérez de la Serna to stand loyally by him in the king's interest.[18] Though it is true that Gelves and his government were overthrown by revolution on 15 January 1624, it is very doubtful whether this would have happened had the secular clergy not sided with the disaffected party. Even the combined forces of discontented officers and Creoles would never have dared bring down a viceroy without highly effective clerical cover. Gelves's downfall, though rooted in the discontent of sections of the laity, was actually brought about by Archbishop Pérez de la Serna.

Juan Pérez de la Serna, before being made archbishop of Mexico in 1612, had been teaching philosophy at the university of Sigüenza in Old Castile. Despite his academic background, he soon showed, on taking up his post in Mexico, that he was skilful in the handling of men. Indeed there were some who considered him too worldly for a churchman. Gelves, when he had arrived in the capital, had been shocked to learn that the prelate operated a meat-store in an annex to the archiepiscopal residence to sell off the meat made over to the Church in payment of the tithe, and, much to Pérez de la Serna's displeasure, had secured its closure. Madrid, in 1620, had reprimanded the archbishop for attending certain theatrical performances which were considered by some to be unseemly. But Pérez de la Serna's

[17] Gelves himself states that he was opposed by both the *corregidores* and the Mexico City council and *consulado*, see AGI Patronato Real 221, r 13: Gelves to council, 8 Nov. 1622, and AGI Mexico 29, r 4: Gelves to council, 26 Feb. 1622.

[18] See the *Cedulario de los Siglos XVI y XVII*, ed. Alberto María Carreño (Mexico, 1947), *cédula* no. 101, p. 247: council to Pérez de la Serna, 11 May 1621.

worldliness also included a strong awareness of social problems and of the needs of Mexican society. His letters reveal profound consternation at the phenomenon of economic depression, dismay at the bankruptcy of merchants and the fearful plight of the poor, and determination to find more livings for the growing number of diocesan clergy under his wing. Above all, he regarded himself as the champion of the people. We have already made note of his role in the Gómez affair of 1618, and his readiness to jump to the defence of Creole honour; his support and enthusiasm for the cult of the Virgin of Guadalupe,[19] almost certainly, has a similar significance. Though at times he was something of a demagogue, there is nothing to suggest that he did not sincerely believe in the rightness and urgency of the causes that he took up.

In 1619, Pérez de la Serna had clashed with Guadalcázar over the issue of episcopal rights in the Indian parishes under mendicant control, having previously obtained from Madrid a *cédula* granting him power of veto over the curates put forward by the mendicant orders and the power to examine the fitness of such curates especially with regard to morals and competence with Indian languages.[20] The friars, and particularly the Franciscans, had opposed the archbishop's attempt to implement the *cédula*, for they regarded his attempt, not at all unreasonably, as a first step toward the dismantling of the Indian Church of the friars and the replacement of mendicant parochial clergy with secular priests. Guadalcázar, being, as we have said, a staunch ally of the regulars, refused, despite the clear instruction from Spain, to permit the implementation of Serna's order. When the archbishop, in July 1620, issued an edict commanding the friars to submit their curates for examination by his staff, the Provincials of the orders, backed by the secular arm, were able to defy him openly.

In the spring of 1621, following Guadalcázar's departure from office, Pérez de la Serna had resumed his campaign and delivered an ultimatum requiring the friars to comply with his orders within sixty days or else face the appropriate ecclesiastical penalties. The Franciscans and the others had thereupon decided on concerted defensive action and appealed to the *Audiencia* for help. Vergara Gabiria, who was on bad terms with the archbishop, had promptly condemned Pérez de la Serna's action and ordered that Madrid's instructions be suspended indefinitely. Pérez de la Serna, checked again, had then vented his fury by sending off orders to Texcoco and other Indian centres calling on the *corregidores* and Indian town councils to forbid the Indians to attend the friars or receive the sacraments from them, and to prevent

19Cisneros, *Sitio, naturaleza, y propriedades de la ciudad de Mexico*, fol. 109v; Florencia, *La Estrella de el norte de Mexico*, p. 23.
20*Cedulario de los siglos XVI y XVII*, pp. 232–3.

them making donations to mendicant funds.[21] At the same time Pérez de la Serna's deputy, the diocesan coadjutor Garcés de Portillo, brought out a printed tract threatening the orders with further chastisement.[22] Predictably, neither move had any effect.

Pérez de la Serna's disgust with Vergara Gabiria and the *Audiencia* was not solely the result of their disagreement on Church matters. Pérez de la Serna, the defender of Creole honour and patron of the Virgin of Guadalupe, was also a leader of the Creole campaign against corrupt and oppressive bureaucracy. Indeed, he regarded the secular administration as the worst of all the ills besetting the viceroyalty. 'I consider it undeniable', he wrote to the council of the Indies, 'that the root and stem of all the difficulties of the colony, and of the losses to the royal treasury, is the arrogance of His Majesty's officers, an arrogance which might be disregarded were it simply a matter of abuse of jurisdiction, but which cannot be countenanced, being as it is the cause of colossal corruption.'[23] The archbishop, it is clear, disliked the regime of the *Audiencia* as much for its general policy as for its ecclesiastical. And so, though Gelves showed no particular affection for the secular clergy, Pérez de la Serna was at first inclined to support and indeed congratulate him; for anyone who sought to curb the excesses of the bureaucrats met with his approval. It is surely one of the significant ironies of the conflict of 1621–4 in Mexico that the heads of both parties considered corruption in high places the chief cause of discontent in the colony, and that both liked to think of themselves as acting on behalf of, and as being loved by, the common people.

Where Pérez de la Serna and Gelves ceased to see eye to eye was over the rest of the latter's policy and particularly his attitude to the Mexico City council and the merchants. Gelves considered the Creole leadership to be no better than the corrupt bureaucrats and treated entrepreneurs and office-holders with equal severity. Pérez de la Serna, however, stood by all the Creoles including the very rich and disapproved strongly of the viceroy's treatment of the Mexico City *regidores*, his bullying of other city councils such as that of Zacatecas, and the stringent measures that he took to suppress commercial fraud. Pérez de la Serna also took offence at Gelves's prying into the economic activities of the diocesan authorities and of his own servants, and, to complete his estrangement from the marquis, was infuriated by the latter's decision on the matter of the Indian parishes held by the friars.

[21] BNX 1510, exp. 5: Pérez de la Serna to *corregidor* of Texcoco, 2 Sept. 1621.

[22] See Pedro Garcés de Portillo, *Cerca de lo que se ha dudado si el ilustrisimo senor arzobispo de Mexico pueda descomulgar a los religiosos que tienen curas de almas . . .* (Mexico, June 1621).

[23] AGI México 29, r 5: Pérez de la Serna to council, 12 June 1622.

At first Gelves had reserved judgement; but then, swayed perhaps by the pen of Juan de Torquemada, he came out in favour of the mendicants.

This last development had taken place late in July 1622. Earlier in the summer, the archbishop's party and the party of the *Audiencia* had begun to move together to form an alliance against Gelves. Early in July, a month before the suspension of Vergara Gabiria and Galdós from office, the *Audiencia*, in a remarkable display of inconsistency, had reversed its judgement of the previous year on the ecclesiastical question and come out in favour of the seculars.[24] Thus Vergara Gabiria and his colleagues cleared the way for Serna, for a time, to proceed with his campaign. The test case had been fought over the Franciscan parish of Santa María la Redonda, the north-western part of Mexico City, and Vergara Gabiria now ordered the prior of the convent of Santa María to submit his candidate for the curacy to the archbishop for examination in languages and morals. Serna, eager to make the most of his opportunity, organized a whole procession of clerics to accompany him to the friary to obtain the prior's submission. The procession had the desired effect, but at the friary Pérez de la Serna suddenly and inexplicably fainted, much to the dismay of his followers and the delight of his foes, and had to be carried back to his residence by litter without having accomplished his object.[25] In subsequent days, the archbishop's staff pursued the recalcitrant prior with some vigour but again without effect. Pérez de la Serna then issued an ultimatum, and on finding that it was ignored, issued another this time replete with the direst threats he could muster. Finally, a few hours before the expiry of this second ultimatum, the viceroy, anxious to put a stop to the agitation, overruled the *Audiencia* and announced that the royal *cédula* on the examination of mendicant curates was suspended for the time being.[26] The friars were greatly relieved and filled with gratitude; the seculars were furious and showed their displeasure. Nowhere was the viceroy to receive a better press in subsequent years than in the chronicles of the friars, and nowhere a worse one than in the publications of the secular clergy.

Late in 1622, with archbishop and *Audiencia* co-operating increasingly, a new twist was given to the political situation with the arrest of the unscrupulous *corregidor* of Metepec, Don Melchor de Varaez. Varaez was brought to Mexico City under guard and charged with having extorted crops from the Indians of Metepec,[27] paying

---

24 *Cedulario de los siglos XVI y XVII*, p. 263.
25 García, *Crónica Augustiniana*, pp. 180–1.
26 *Cedulario de los siglos XVI y XVII*, pp. 269–72.
27 Evidently Varaez had payed the Indians only one-third of what the crops

them only a fraction of what the food was worth and selling the produce in the capital at great profit to himself and his accomplices. The case came before justice Vázquez de Cisneros who contrived to drag out the trial for months without coming near to a decision. At length Gelves lost patience, and taking the case out of the hands of the *Audiencia* altogether, an unheard of procedure, constituted a special court to finish the business under a magistrate then supposed to be in transit from Manila to Panama, Don Juan de Alvarado. That did the trick. Varaez, seeing that the trial was going against him and anxious to avoid prison, fled, sword in hand, to seek sanctuary in the chapel of the Dominican priory. Shortly afterwards Alvarado pronounced him guilty, clapped a huge fine on him, and sentenced him to perpetual banishment from the Indies.

Varaez remained in the priory undisturbed until October 1623. Then when the rumour spread that he was about to try to escape to Veracruz and evade his fine, and board one of the ships preparing to sail for Spain, Alvarado, acting in Gelves's name, posted soldiers in the cloister to guard his cell. To this the Dominican friars, being on close terms with the Gelves administration, raised no objection. Pérez de la Serna however did. The archbishop condemned the step as an infringement of the right of sanctuary and of ecclesiastical privilege, and informed Alvarado that he had two days in which to withdraw the arquebusiers. Alvarado, with the viceroy behind him, answered that Varaez was not legally entitled to seek sanctuary having in effect broken gaol, and made it clear that the soldiers would stay where they were. At this Pérez de la Serna proceeded to excommunicate Alvarado, one or two other functionaries, and also the unfortunate guards.

Relations between viceroy and archbishop now began to deteriorate rapidly. Serna demanded of Cristobal Osorio, an old enemy of his from the time of the Gómez affair and now one of Gelves's closest advisors, that he should hand over to his staff certain papers relating to the Varaez trial. The archbishop wished to check the proceedings personally. Osorio, at the marquis's order, refused. At this Pérez de la Serna peremptorily excommunicated Osorio and one or two others of the viceroy's entourage and despatched a cleric to the viceregal palace to announce publicly these fresh severities. With the cleric went a band of indignant secular priests who, on being denied entry to the palace, caused a disturbance outside. This led Gelves to make an example of the cleric, who alone had been admitted, and whom he now sentenced to be deported to Spain. The archbishop's reaction to this was to

---

were worth, BND 2354, fol. 192ᵛ: 'Principio de las disenciones que huvo en Mexico entre el Virrey marqués de Gelves de una parte y el arzobispo y chancilleria de la otra'.

declare Gelves an enemy of the Church and to add his name to his rapidly growing list of excommunicates. With the viceroy excommunicated, something that had never before happened in the colony, Mexico found itself in the midst of a major political crisis.

Gelves at once challenged the competence of the archbishop of Mexico to excommunicate the viceroy and called upon the *Audiencia* to deliver judgement on the matter. The duty of the justices in such a situation was of course to try to reconcile the heads of state and Church in the viceroyalty in the interests of the king and public order. But this evidently was not the consideration which was now uppermost in the magistrates' calculations. As if purposely seeking a means to widen the split in authority, they informed the viceroy that they were unable to come to any decision for the time being as they had not had sufficient time to study the point.[28] Gelves was compelled to turn elsewhere. He next assembled a carefully selected body of clergy and university dons, and put the great question of the moment to them. Could the archbishop excommunicate the viceroy? Predictably enough, a majority of the assembly, headed by Gelves's confessor, Fray Bartolomé de Burguillos, a man who had once led an embassy to Japan, came out in the viceroy's favour and rejected the archbishop's decree of excommunication. In support of Burguillos, as one would expect, were the Franciscans, Dominicans, and Augustinians, and also the vicar-general of the Mercenarians, a friend and ally of Gelves, and foe of the Mercenarian faction that had received favours from Galdós de Valencia. The opposition, the minority that preached the ultimate supremacy of the ecclesiastical arm over the secular, included of course the secular clergy, and also the Jesuits and discalced Carmelites.[29]

The opposition of the Carmelites to Gelves is not especially surprising. The Carmelites, unlike the other mendicant orders in Mexico, had little landed property and no Indian parishes and tended to disapprove of the friars who did. Throughout the period of the Mexican crisis of the seventeenth century the Carmelites were to support the secular clergy, and in the 1640s, as we shall see, they were among the closest allies of Bishop Palafox. But how is one to account for the role of the Jesuits? Had they not been at odds with Pérez de la Serna in 1618, not only over the Gómez affair but also over the disputed Otomi Indian parish of Tepotzotlán?[30] Furthermore, the chief Jesuit

[28] Ruiz de Cabrera, *Algunos Singulares Sucesos*, fol. 6.
[29] Ibid., fol. 6; for a statement of the majority's findings see the printed tract by Fray Bartolomé de Burguillos in the BL, see also the anonymous *Memorial de lo sucedido en la ciudad de Mexico desde el dia primero de Noviembre de 1623 hasta el quince de enero de 1624* (not in Medina or Andrade) (Mexico, 1624) (BO), fol. 6[v].
[30] Alegre, *Historia de la Compañía*, ii. 384-5.

spokesman at the viceroy's conference, Juan de Ledesma, was the most renowned Creole Jesuit in Mexico. Why should a predominantly *gachupín* order choose a Mexican Spaniard to speak for them? These are important questions, for there was nothing haphazard about Jesuit policy. The Society was fully committed to the opposition to Gelves,[31] and on 15 January 1624 gave its backing to the Pérez de la Serna-Vergara Gabiria coalition. Indeed, the Jesuits were to continue to snipe at the marquis for years afterwards and even into the eighteenth century.[32] It is clear that the Jesuits acted thus partly for economic reasons. Gelves, in his drive to curb illicit practice on the part of employers, had shown no more deference for the Jesuits than for any other vested interest, and had not only halted the acquisition of property by the Society in line with orders from Madrid, but had pried into Jesuit methods of obtaining Indian labour and had objected to their practice of locking up some of their Indians in their workshops at night.[33] But there were also other considerations behind Jesuit policy. The events of 1618 had been the first serious check to the growth of Jesuit influence in Mexico since the Society had been established there four decades before, and in the wake of their compromise with Serna, the Jesuits seem to have decided that they had blundered badly by departing from their former close association with the Creoles and the secular clergy. The need for a renewed association with the popular party was underlined by two sensational trials in 1619 and 1620 in the wake of which Jesuit prestige had suffered fresh blows. The Inquisition had tried two Jesuits for sexual crimes. This in itself was not unusual in seventeenth-century Mexico, for dozens of clergy were found guilty of soliciting women from the confessional during these years,[34] but the scale of the misconduct certainly was. As related above, one of the Jesuits, Father Gaspar de Villenas, was charged with having solicited from the confessional, over a period of eight years, in Puebla and Mexico City, ninety-seven women, girls, and nuns, often in the most scandalous circumstances.[35] Despite measures by Inquisition and

[31] See the account by an anonymous Jesuit in the BL; 'Relacion de un estupendo y monstruoso caso que ha sucedido en esta ciudad de Mexico', in 'Mexico y sus Disturbios', ii 651 ff.

[32] Alegre, op. cit., ii. 151.

[33] *Relacion del estado en que el marqués de Gelves*, fol. 6; and BND 2354, fol. 191.

[34] It is a curious phenomenon that in the years 1620–1 there was a wave of fierce Inquisition puritanism in Mexico; they were years in which the Inquisition renewed its ban on the use of the drug peyote and collected statements against over eighty clergy, regular and secular, for soliciting women at confession and other sexual crimes; see AGN Inquisición 289, 295, 327, 331, and 334.

[35] AGN Inquisición 330, fols. 1–600.

Jesuits to cover up the story, word had seeped out and spread consternation in Mexico and even in Rome.[36] Nothing seemed more necessary to the Mexican Jesuits in 1623 than policies that would restore their reputation and popularity. It is also noteworthy that Juan de Ledesma was renowned as an expert in Nahuatl and Indian studies and was a leader of that group of Jesuits that wished to see the Society more actively engaged among the Indians;[37] for it was widely rumoured, among those favourable to Gelves at least, that there was a secret deal between Perez de la Serna and the Jesuits by which a share of any Indian parishes wrested from the mendicants would go to the Society.[38]

Gelves, once he had obtained the decision he needed from his assembly of clergy and scholars, turned to the coadjutor of the diocese of Puebla, the Papal representative in New Spain, Dr. Moreno, and called upon him to ratify the judgement and order the archbishop to withdraw the sentence of excommunication. Moreno complied willingly enough and directed Pérez de la Serna to absolve both the viceroy and his officers. The archbishop answered that he would do no such thing and declared that the business lay entirely outside the limits of the coadjutor's sphere of competence. At this, Moreno produced the usual threats and nominated a Dominican friar as his deputy in Mexico City. The friar perambulated the capital escorted by a detachment of his excellency's arquebusiers tearing down his eminence's posters. This served only to provoke the archbishop to renew his sentence of excommunication on the viceroy and to put up a fresh lot of posters.

Meanwhile the tension in Mexico City was mounting and there were various small incidents. On New Year's Day 1624, there was a commotion in the Dominican friary following a sermon by Fray Luis Barroso in which the friar had defended Gelves's actions, argued for the ultimate supremacy of the secular arm over the ecclesiastical in the worldly sphere, and ventured to make certain other remarks derogatory to the archbishop. His utterance of his views produced an angry reaction in his congregation, part of which ran to the Inquisition and exhorted the inquisitors to rouse themselves and punish the friar's heretical utterances against true doctrine.[39] On 3 January, Pérez de la Serna let it be known that a *cesatio a divinis*, a Church strike, was pending and caused a great tolling of bells that went on for hours and

36 Astrain, *Historia de la Compañía*, v. 320—1.

37 Andrés Pérez de Ribas, *Historia de los triumphos de nuestra santa fee entre gentes las mas barbaras y fieras del nuevo orbe* (Madrid, 1645), pp. 452—5.

38 BND 2354, fol. 191, and the *Relacion del estado en que el marqués de Gelves*, fol. 5.

39 *Memorial de lo sucedido*, fol. 23.

plunged Mexico City into tension and gloom. But after this there was a lull. During the week 3–10 January, the tension eased and the chances of a serious disturbance seemed to recede. Then on 11 January the archbishop performed what was to be the most dramatic and famous of all his public acts. He walked, head bowed and with an air of great humility, surrounded by one hundred priests and a multitude of the laity, to plead his cause in person before the *Audiencia*. Gelves, when he learned what was afoot, summoned the magistrates to his presence and gave explicit instructions as to how they were to handle the affair. The justices then returned to the *Audiencia* chamber, cleared the crowd from the building, heard Pérez de la Serna's plea, and then, as they had been instructed, asked the prelate to return to his residence until his points had been considered and a decision reached. Pérez de la Serna refused. Nothing, he declared, would induce him to leave until justice was seen to be done. At this the justices imposed a fine on him for contempt and once again admonished him to go. Still the archbishop refused. Finally, following a second conference with the viceroy in which either Gelves forced the *Audiencia* to take extreme action or else the *Audiencia* tricked Gelves into it, the archbishop was sentenced to be expelled from Mexico and to be deported to Spain.[40]

That afternoon, Pérez de la Serna was placed in a carriage and escorted by troops through Mexico City on the first stage of his journey to Veracruz. An immense, sullen multitude followed the procession as far as the shrine of Guadalupe where the archbishop contrived to delay for some time, celebrate mass, and despatch orders to his clergy to renew the notices of excommunication against the marquis and his officers and to prepare to put the *cesatio a divinis* into effect.[41] Mexico City was now in a state of intense excitement. According to sources favourable to Pérez de la Serna, the Indians were particularly wrought up; later certain secular priests were to make use of this fact in their polemics against the viceroy's party, accusing it of the very crime that the friars laid at their own door—that of putting at risk the Christian faith of the Indians.[42] According to the secular clergy, the Indians were so extremely devoted to the archbishop, and so shaken by his expulsion, that they began asking their curates if Christianity had come to an end.

That night the justices of the *Audiencia* met without Gelves's knowledge and considered how they might withdraw the sentence that

[40] See AGI Patronato real 223, r 1. 'Testimonio de como los oydores dixeron a su excellencia que tenia boto y le persuadieron que botase en la expulsion del arzobispo', signed by Cristobal Osorio and apparently accepted as truthful by the council of the Indies.

[41] BL 'Tumultos de Mexico', p. 163, *Memorial de lo sucedido*, fol. 13v.

[42] DRT i. 348–71.

they themselves had imposed on the archbishop.[43] First they despatched secret orders to the officer in command of the cortège taking Pérez de la Serna to Veracruz, bidding him proceed only very slowly. Then on the morning of 12 January, seeing that they now had either to take the plunge and defy Gelves openly or else accept the banishment of the archbishop and with it any chance of bringing serious pressure to bear on the viceroy, the magistrates suspended the sentence and dispatched orders recalling the archbishop to the capital.[44] Gelves, when he heard, flew into a terrible rage and ordered the immediate incarceration of the three justices who had defied him, in the palace. That put the total number of *Audiencia* magistrates now under arrest at five. Only one remained at his duties. News of the imprisonment of the justices brought an angry rabble into the Plaza Mayor, the great square at the centre of Mexico City bounded by the viceregal palace, the cathedral, and the city hall. The rabble proceeded to demonstrate noisily in front of the palace, and Gelves ordered out the guard which was commanded by his nephew, Don Francisco Pimentel. The soldiers quickly dispersed the mob, without firing or killing anyone, and cleared the plaza. Two leaders of the demonstration, a mestizo and a Filippino, were seized and then flogged in the public view.[45]

The following morning, that of 13 January, with tension rising higher than ever, the cathedral and churches of Mexico City were packed to overflowing. One would have supposed that it was Holy Week, declared one observer of the scene, had it not been for the strange hush, uneasy tête-à-têtes, and incessant whispering. Word was spread that the clergy were preparing their stroke and that the dreaded *cesatio a divinis* would shortly be put into effect. At midday there was an incident in the cathedral.[46] Three functionaries interrupted mass to read out a proclamation signed by the viceroy absolutely forbidding the diocesan authorities to declare an interdict, whatever their instructions from the archbishop, and warning them that they would be severely punished if they disobeyed. The crowd in the cathedral, encouraged, according to our source, by the priests among them, jeered at the proclamation and began to hiss and spit at the officers, who, fearing more material hurt, hastily departed.

On 14 January Archbishop Pérez de la Serna, who was then at San Juan de Teotihuacán where the cortège had stopped for several days in

43 Possibly in the house of Vergara Gabiria, see AGI, Patronato real 222, fol. 1314.

44 *DRT* 1. 248–9.

45 Ruiz de Cabrera, *Algunos singulares sucesos*, fol. 13.‘

46 AGI Patronato real 221, r 4: 'Ynformacion de lo que paso en la catedral de Mexico el dia 13 de enero . . .'

defiance of the viceroy's orders, a mere twenty-five miles or so from Mexico City, completed his plans for the *cesatio a divinis* and dispatched orders to his staff in the capital to put the strike into effect early the following morning.

At 7 o'clock on 15 January the diocesan chapter proclaimed the *cesatio a divinis* in the cathedral, and immediately after groups of secular priests set off in all directions to close down the city's churches.[47] In every quarter officiating clergy, secular and regular, either stopped abruptly or were interrupted and prevented from continuing with the mass. The Dominican chronicler, Alonso Franco, who was conducting a service at the time, reports that his congregation simply vanished.[48] When the prayers had ceased, candles were extinguished, the churches cleared, church doors bolted, and groups of women left wailing on outside steps. Apparently, every belfry in the city fell silent except for that of the Mercenarians who alone defied the archbishop's ban. According to sources favourable to Gelves, the secular priests, in addition to closing the churches, also did something more: they deliberately and maliciously spread rumours designed to inflame and provoke the people;[49] in particular they put it about that Gelves had sworn to kill Pérez de la Serna should he persist in refusing to move on from Teotihuacán. Sources hostile to Gelves, while denying that the secular clergy had anything to do with the spreading of these dangerous rumours, agree that such reports were spread and that they drove the people to a new pitch of fury.[50]

A short while after the *cesatio* had been proclaimed and while there was still a substantial crowd in front of the cathedral, Cristobal Osorio entered the Plaza Mayor in an open coach and started across it towards the viceregal palace on the opposite side. The faces about him ranged from sullen to menacing. Suddenly a small band of fruit and vegetable sellers, mostly Indian and mestizo boys, started shouting and calling Osorio 'enemy of the Church, Lutheran heretic, and Jewish Moorish excommunicate dog'. One of the urchins threw a cabbage in Osorio's face. At this, he was unwise enough to stop his carriage, and set his Negro coachmen on the boys. Stones began to fly. A mob gathered round. The shouting turned into an uproar. Osorio, taking fright and urging his coach on again, just made it through the palace gates ahead of an incensed rabble.

[47]Flores-Lormendi, *Relacion sumaria*, fol. 8; *Memorial de lo sucedido*, fol. 20.
[48]Alonso Franco, *Segunda parte*, p. 420.
[49]Ibid., p. 420; Jerónimo de Sandoval, *Relacion del levantimiento que uvo en Mexico contra el virey, lunes 15 de enero de 1624*, *DHM* x. 12; and the *Relacion del estado en que el marqués de Gelves*, fol. 13ᵛ.
[50]See particularly *DRT* i. 437–8.

Gelves, who was still in bed when the tumult began, speedily dressed and took up his sword and captain-general's baton. Once appraised of the situation, he ordered out the guard as he had done three days before. But this time the soldiers, being only twenty or so strong, were too few to disperse the mob. They pressed the crowd back somewhat, but could do no more. More rioters appeared. Again stones began to fly, and the guards were thrown back inside the palace. The gates were closed and everyone within, soldiers, gentlemen, and servants, rushed to arms. The rabble grew with every second. Gelves, too angry to reason calmly, was for sallying forth in person at the head of his men to attack the mob. From this reckless course, he was dissuaded by the admiral of the fleet recently arrived from Spain, Don Jerónimo de Sandoval, the conde de Santiago Calimaya, and other noblemen who were with him. They pointed out that he would be betraying the king's trust by exposing his person to such danger and advised him to hoist the king's standard from an upper window, sound the alarm from the palace roof, and bring out the city militia to his aid. The standard was then raised and the trumpet sounded. However, this, as Thomas Gage records, 'prevailed not, none stirred, all the chief of the city kept within doors'. In this way the Creole citizenry of the capital made its move: it did nothing. Instead of bringing help, the trumpet blasts only drew more and more rioters into the plaza.[51]

The mob was of very mixed composition.[52] It is clear that the mass of the rioters were Indians, backed by large numbers of mestizos, Negroes, and mulattoes. But it also included a considerable number of whites. All the accounts favourable to Gelves and some of those that oppose him assert that a good many Spaniards were to be seen. The difference between the two sets of narratives is that those that are hostile to the viceroy insist that those whites that took part were renegades, vagabonds, and other riff-raff and included no citizens of the better sort, while the accounts sympathetic to Gelves hold that the rioting Spaniards were not only of the disreputable type but included many of the more substantial citizens. Also, as we observed in chapter five, it was noticeable that a number of Portuguese joined in.

But although the mob was so various in composition, it displayed, throughout the commotions of that day, a remarkable degree of co-ordination and sense of purpose. This would suggest that the insurrection was, to some extent at least, led and directed. The pro-Gelves sources are very emphatic on this point and insist that the multitude was incited and urged on by secular priests and by the

[51] *Memorial de lo sucedido*, fol. 20ᵛ.
[52] Ibid.; Flores-Lormendi, *Relacion sumaria*, fol. 8ᵛ; Ruiz de Cabrera, *Algunos singulares sucesos*, fol. 16; *DRT* i. 284, 289, 313.

archbishop's servants.[53] It was the priests, asserted the *Gelvistas*, who stirred up the Indians by calling to them in Nahuatl that 'they no longer possessed their God, for the viceroy had killed him'. It was the priests who prompted the mob to yell ' ¡ *Viva el rey y viva Cristo, y muera el hereje luterano! ¡ Viva la Iglesia, viva la fe, viva el rey, muera el mal gobierno, muera ese hereje excomulgado, Prendan al virrey*! '[54] The archbishop's party, of course, afterwards went to great lengths to prove that no priest or servant of the archbishop had been involved in the disgraceful affair and produced an elaborate document complete with a set of statements by eye-witnesses given under oath in support.[55] It is perhaps impossible to be sure, but the balance of evidence does suggest that the lower secular clergy did urge on and to some extent lead the insurgents, and, it is important to note, this was the finding of the special investigator, Don Martín de Carrillo y Alderete, afterwards sent out by Madrid to investigate the rising.[56] There are various reasons for doubting the assertions of the archbishop's adherents, not the least of which is the fact that among the eye-witnesses who swore that no priest had taken part were some rather dubious personages, including a secular priest, Antonio González, who was later tried for his part in the rising and found guilty of inciting the mob to rebellion and treason.

From about nine o'clock, it became clear that the viceroy was facing a full-scale insurrection. The plaza was filled with a multitude of rioters. A ladder was brought up from the construction site around the cathedral and placed under the window from which the royal standard had been hoisted; a cleric or theology student bounded up the ladder, sword in hand, cut loose the standard and, to thunderous applause, brought it down.[57] The banner was then hoisted from the top of the cathedral. Soon afterwards a group of Indians seized the matting being used for shade by some fruit and vegetable women who were watching the spectacle from the plaza's edge and, heaping this material together with some empty crates started a sizeable fire against the palace gates. At about the same time, Antonio González made a spectacular entry into the plaza on horseback clutching a large crucifix in one hand and a machete in the other, at the head of a column of mestizos and Negroes

[53] Flores-Lormendi, *Relacion Sumaria*, fol. 8ᵛ; *Relacion del estado en que hallo el reyno el marqués de Gelves*, fol. 13ᵛ; BND 9390, fol. 170; AGI Patronato real 222, fol. 489.

[54] *DRT* i. 92; Soria, *Relacion verdadera*, fol. 2; Sandoval, *Relacion del Levantimiento*, p. 13.

[55] *DRT* i. 278–341.

[56] See pp. 172–3.

[57] Flores-Lormendi, *Relacion sumaria*, fol. 9; AGI Patronato Real 221, r 5, fol. 25ᵛ.

wielding sticks, swords, knives, and pistols.[58] One part of the mob went to the Inquisition and called on the inquisitors to come out with the emblems of their office in support of the people. Gelves had been on bad terms with the Inquisition and was later to accuse the Mexican tribunal of having contributed, behind the scenes, to his overthrow;[59] but whether the inquisitors had a hand in the business or not, they had no intention of doing anything foolhardy. They could scarcely stay indoors, being the Inquisition, with Church and state in uproar, and so they appeared in full inquisitorial garb and uplifted crosses and proceeded to the plaza. When the Inquisition appeared, the mob ceased its cries and hurling of stones and fell respectfully quiet. The inquisitors then bade the people extinguish the fire, which they did, and then entered the palace by a minor entrance.

Inside the inquisitors found a heated argument in progress with Vázquez de Cisneros, the only *Audiencia* magistrate still at liberty, and a number of other persons begging the viceroy to save himself and his adherents, and rescue the king's interest from danger, by yielding to the demands of the people, that is to say by bringing back the archbishop from Teotihuacán and releasing the five captive magistrates of the *Audiencia*. If he refused, they declared, there would be a fearful catastrophe. The inquisitors at once threw their weight behind Vázquez de Cisneros. The noise of the tumult in the plaza reinforced their warning. At length, Gelves gave way. The three justices held in the palace were set free, the confinement of Vergara Gabiria and Galdós de Valencia to their homes was formally ended, and an order was signed for the recall of Pérez de la Serna from Teotihuacán. When this was done, the viceroy and the noblemen with him, the inquisitors and justices, ascended to the palace roof and appeared before the multitude which soon ceased its yelling and fell silent. An official then announced that the *Audiencia* was free and that the archbishop was on his way back. The concessions were enough to satisfy part of the mob but not apparently all. There was a moment of general confusion in which the issue of continued disturbance or peace hung in the balance; but then stones began to fly once more and the palace roof was deserted. In a few minutes the people were as furious as they had been before the viceroy's concessions. The rubbish piled against the gates was set alight again and more ladders were brought up from the building site.

In desperation, Gelves now tried a different expedient. He ordered the four magistrates with him to go out of the palace and into the plaza on horseback and by whatever means they could calm the multitude.

---

[58] Ibid., fol. 9ᵛ; AGI Patronato real 224, r 4, fol. 3; *Relacion del estado en que hallo la Nueva España el marqués de Gelves*, fol. 13ᵛ.
[59] AGI Patronato real 223, r 5, fol. 7ᵛ.

The justices therefore appeared alone among the people. One was hit by a stone before they were recognized, but once they were, the crowd fell again to silence. The justices made their way across the plaza to the city hall on the far side from the cathedral, and as they went they addressed the people. Whether they made a serious attempt to stop the tumult or not, it seems impossible to say. What is clear is that the justices were joined in the town hall, almost at once, by their colleagues Vergara Gabiria and Galdós de Valencia, who were now free, and by the Mexico City council.[60] To show their approval of this development, the mob fetched the royal standard from the cathedral and raised it over the city hall. At this juncture there rode into the Plaza Mayor a column of gentlemen headed by the chief Creole noble, the marqués del Valle, Don Pedro Cortés, who, though racked by gout, had risen from his bed to do his duty and stand by the king's lieutenant. As a Cortés, Don Pedro was revered by Creoles, Indians, and half-castes alike, and his appearance in the plaza produced an effect similar to that earlier produced by the arrival of the Inquisition.[61] There was a respectful silence. Don Pedro made a short speech, the character of which we can only guess at, and then entered the palace by the side entrance in order to place himself at the viceroy's service. Some minutes later he reappeared in the company of the marqués de Villamayor and his gentlemen, and the Inquisitors, announcing that they were riding to Teotihuacán to bring back the archbishop.

At this the crowds at last seemed satisfied or at least the hard core of rioters began to waver. A column of some forty or fifty Franciscans appeared, headed by Fray Juan de Lormendi and bearing a banner and uplifted crosses, and circulated round the plaza calling in Nahuatl to the Indians to fall in behind them.[62] This was by far the most effective move to empty the plaza made yet. Two or three secular priests answered the friars in Nahuatl, calling them heretics and foes of the Church and exhorting the Indians to ignore them, but to no effect. No one ventured to harm the friars and the great bulk of the Indians followed them out of the plaza. The residue of the mob, consisting mostly of mestizos and Negroes, now moved off toward the Dominican

[60] And various other prominent Creoles and office-holders, notably Juan de Cervantes Casaus, knight of Santiago and *contador* of the *tribunal de cuentas*; see AGI Patronato real 223, r 4: 'Testimonio de los Autos fechos por los sseñores oydores de la rreal audiencia de Mexico estando en las casas del cabildo de la dicha ciudad . . .', fols. 1, 6; see also Ruiz de Cabrera, *Algunos singulares sucesos*, fol. 18.

[61] *Memorial de lo sucedido*, fol. 21.

[62] AGI Patronato real 222: the trial of Vergara Gabiria (1626), fol. 454; *DRT* ii. 146; Mexico City *cabildo* to council, 19 Feb. 1624; and Flores-Lormendi, *Relacion sumaria*, fol. 9ᵛ.

priory shouting as they went that they were going to free Melchor de Varaez.[63] When they arrived, they started shouting that they would burn the gates down unless the prior opened them. The prior ordered the gates to be thrown open. The crowd now ransacked the building searching for Fray Luis de Barroso, the friar who had derided the archbishop on New Year's Day, and intent on setting Varaez free, smashing doors and windows as they went. They failed to find the friar, who had concealed himself well, but did succeed in chasing off the arquebusiers and releasing Don Melchor. It was now mid-morning, between ten and eleven. Vergara Gabiria and his friends were free and the archbishop was on his way back to the capital. The Plaza Mayor was all but deserted.[64]

Gelves, dazed but still in command at the palace, used the four-and-a-half-hour respite that now ensued, in as far as he could, to strengthen his position. Some, though very few, reinforcements were found. Gunpowder and shot were made ready. A friar brought in a supply of cord for the muskets and arquebuses.

The lull ended at about 3 o'clock, though how or why it ended it is difficult to say. The sources conflict. According to accounts favourable to Pérez de la Serna,[65] the resumption of the tumult was the viceroy's own doing, for, at a time when the plaza was beginning to fill with people once more, chiefly the curious and perplexed, he is said to have either lost his nerve or succumbed to a desire for revenge, and ordered his men to open fire. The volley killed a few people but provoked the rest to a furious new attack on the palace. Authors sympathetic with Gelves, however, say that the order to fire was given only as a last resort when the rabble were already attacking the prison wing of the palace.[66] This perhaps is the more plausible version, for as a military man Gelves knew perfectly well that the score or so arquebuses at his disposal were far too few to enable him to clear the plaza by firing. And indeed the firing served only to provoke the mob. The cry went up that the viceroy must be killed. A band of Negroes and mestizos appeared on horseback carrying every kind of weapon including firearms. The shots from the palace began to be answered by reports from the square.

By 4 o'clock the situation was extremely grave. The soldiers that the marquis had positioned on the palace roof suddenly came under fire from a score or so arquebusiers who had taken up position on the roof

[63] AGI Patronato real 222: the trial of Vergara Gabiria, fol. 489; BL m–m 236: 'Tumultos de Mexico', p. 174; Alonso Franco, *Segunda parte*, p. 421.

[64] *Memorial de lo sucedido*, fols. 22^V–23^V; Flores-Lormendi, *Relacion Sumaria*, fol. 9^V.

[65] See for example Ruiz de Cabrera, *Algunos sucesos singulares*, fol. 19.

[66] See, for instance, Sandoval, *Relacion del levantimiento*, p. 16.

of the archbishop's residence nearby. Pérez de la Serna was afterwards to produce documents complete with sworn statements purporting to show that these mysterious gunmen had no connection whatever with himself or any of his associates.[67] But however that may be, there is no doubting the effectiveness of their firing. The viceroy's men suffered casualties and were soon driven from their position. With the palace roof deserted, the mob was able to advance right up to the palace again and kindle a new fire against the gates.

At this juncture, the *Audiencia*, acting with the Mexico City council and the Creole nobility, made its move.[68] Whether the justices had planned to overthrow Gelves if possible all along, as Gelves believed,[69] or whether, as seems more probable, they merely seized the opportunity when it came, they now publicly announced that they had resolved, in view of the emergency and the threat to life and property, to assume the executive power and all the viceroy's functions. Vergara Gabiria was proclaimed captain-general of New Spain and commander of the militia, and orders were despatched to every part of the city, summoning the citizenry to arm and assemble behind the town hall. The justices later sought to justify their action by pointing out that the viceroy had lost control of the state and that it was therefore their duty to take over in order to restore order and safeguard the interests of king and Church. Moreover, they were to claim to have delayed their action for as long as possible in the face of threats from the people to kill them if they did not assume power.[70] The Jesuits later lent a hand in polishing up the points of the argument.[71]

Towards 5 o'clock the Creole militia, some 4,000 strong,[72] was drawn up, banners flying, under the orders of Vergara Gabiria. Numerous key members of the Creole nobility and *haute bourgeoisie* were at hand,[73] as were also, to give moral support, a number of secular clergy and some twenty Jesuits. Some time was spent in organizing the command. The standard of the city was carried by Andrés de Valmaseda, a prominent member of the city council, and one of those who had been most embroiled with the viceroy over the matter

[67]*DRT* i. 433–63.
[68]AGI Patronato real 221, doc. 7, and doc. 10, section 9.
[69]AGI Patronato real 223, r 5: 'Declaraciones del marqués de Gelves'
[70]AGI Patronato real 221, r 5: *Audiencia* to council, 27 Feb. 1624.
[71]Ibid., r 8: 'Ynformaciones hechas por el lcdo. Alonso V..zquez de Cisneros . . .' fols. 13, 19–22.
[72]*DRT* i. 149. Mexico City council to council, 19 Feb. 1624: AGI Patronato real 221, r 10, fol. 11.
[73]AGI Patronato real 222, trial of Vergara Gabiria, fols. 497^V, 501^V, 527, 530; AGI Patronato real 221, r 11, fols. 8^V, 10, and r 8: 'Ynformaciones hechas por el lcdo. Vázquez de Cisneros', fol. 29.

of maize prices. Appointed *maestre de campo* and second in command to Vergara Gabiria was Don Juan de Cervantes Casaus. Among the captains of the various detachments were Jerónimo de Cervantes Casaus, Juan's brother, Hernán Carrillo Altamirano, the author of the tract questioning the *corregidores* and the *repartimiento*, Matheo de Aróstegui, *contador de tributos*, Diego Cano Moctezuma, Don Felipe de Sámano Turcios, and two other *contadores*.

When all was ready Vergara Gabiria made what was to be the most controversial move of the whole day: he bade the militia march off in the opposite direction from the hard-pressed palace and form up at the Franciscan priory. The militia did precisely this. The *Gelvistas* were afterwards to single out this manoeuvre as the most brazen act of teachery committed on that day, but here again the *Audiencia* had an answer ready.[74] The manoeuvre, explained the justices, was a last resort following three unsuccessful attempts to reach the palace and following the decision that it might be fatal to oppose the plebeian masses by force; it was designed to draw off the crowds from the Plaza Mayor and relieve the pressure on the palace while at the same time countering the threat from Tlatelolco whence, it was rumoured, several thousands of agitated Indians were on their way, armed with spears, bows, and arrows. If the *Audiencia* and the city council had not taken the precautions they did, it was declared, the whole of Mexico City might have been sacked and pillaged, and its churches and convents razed to the ground.[75]

While the forces of the citizenry were forming up at the friary, the rioters in the plaza were breaking their way into the prison wing of the palace. Several more fires were started. Gelves, in desperation, decided to open the cells and let the 300 prisoners through into the palace proper; and as they poured through, he offered them pardon, freedom, and arms, in the hope that in return they would fight for him against the main rabble. But the prisoners, knowing perfectly well that the mob would set them free in any case, quickly switched sides. The defenders of the palace were now at the end of their strength. The defence was on the point of crumbling. At this moment Vergara Gabiria led the Creole militia back into the Plaza Mayor. The Creole citizenry appeared at such an ambiguous moment that it is impossible to say whether, as Vergara Gabiria was to hold, his forces were just too late to save the viceroy, or whether, as Gelves was to maintain, the convergence of rioters and militia in the plaza gave the decisive impetus to the storming

74*Puntos breves en defensa del Lic. Pedro de Vergara Gaviria* ... (Madrid?, *c.* 1630) (Bodl.), fol. 5; AGI Patronato real 224, r 10,: Vergara Gabiria to council, 18 July 1626.

75Ibid; and Soria, *Relacion verdadera*, fol. 4v.

of the palace. Certain eyewitnesses who sympathized with Gelves afterwards asserted that even some of the militia captains, notably Hernán Carrillo Altamirano, took part in the final assault, and accused Vergara Gabiria of having had a hand in it and of having ordered that the marquis be taken alive rather than dead.[76] But the evidence for the involvement of the militia in the storming of the palace is slight; it seems implausible that Vergara Gabiria and his associates should have exposed themselves so openly and so unnecessarily. Vergara Gabiria himself later claimed to have made one last attempt to save the viceroy, sending two of his Augustinian friends to the palace with a spare habit to disguise him in, but that the density of the multitude was such that they were unable to make their way through.

As the militia entered the Plaza Mayor, the viceroy's gentlemen were being beaten back along the corridors and up the staircases of the palace. In another moment the resistance had collapsed. It seemed certain that the viceroy was done for. The mob, wrought up to a frenzy and avid for plunder, was screaming for the viceroy's blood. But Gelves, in his moment of greatest danger, displayed a remarkable coolness. Taking off his suit and his all too conspicuous spectacles, and putting on the clothes of a servant, he darted adroitly into the crowd as it hurtled through his rooms and shouted 'Kill the Viceroy!' together with those around him. Mingling with the multitude and aided by the dusk, he made his way out of the palace and across the plaza, and then on to safety in the Franciscan priory.

Behind him he left a scene of pillage and destruction. Some of his soldiers and servants lay dead; most, including his nephew and a mulatto slave Lucas, who, evidently, had fought more bravely than anyone and was the hero of the day, had escaped. The palace was ransacked; the rooms and chapel wrecked. Furniture, mattresses, and everything movable including the horses and mules in the stables, were carried or led away. Certain persons removed the entire corpus of the viceroy's papers and files. A portrait of Gelves was set alight and thrown out into the plaza for the people to jeer at and trample on. Only the royal strongbox, by far the most valuable item in the palace, was left untouched, perhaps because of its formidable size and locks. Fray Bartlomé de Burguillos, the viceroy's confessor, was found cowering in the garden while the plants in it were being uprooted, and was carried off, still wearing his breastplate, to the archbishop's gaol. Alvarado, also found among the shrubs, seeing that he was about to be torn to pieces, went down on his knees and begged his assailants not to

---

[76] AGI Patronato real 222, trial of Vergara Gabiria, fols. 523, 527, 530, 543, 1342.

kill a man who was still under the sentence of excommunication; he was spared and dragged off together with three or four other prisoners to the *Audiencia*'s gaol.

Meanwhile, the militia was dispersing the crowds in the plaza. Most of the people quickly drifted away though a remnant stayed together and moved off to attack the residence of Alonso de Herrera, the official whom Gelves had placed in charge of his drive against vagabondage, and wrecked it.[77] They then visited in turn the homes of Alvarado and others of the *Gelvista* circle and left them in a shambles too. Finally, they were halted at the house of Cristobal de Osorio, who, having barricaded himself in with the help of relatives, slaves, and friends, successfully held them off.

By sundown, both the Plaza Mayor and the palace were virtually empty. Beacons were lighted at key points in the city centre and squads of Creole gentlemen and citizens patrolled the streets, as they continued to do all night,[78] dispersing remaining groups of Indians and other plebeians. Then, at about 9 o'clock, the city centre came alive again as the shops and stalls[79] opened and the townspeople poured into the streets to discuss the day's events. Word went round that Archbishop Pérez de la Serna with Don Pedro Cortés and a column of Creole nobles, secular clergy, Jesuits, and inquisitors in his train, was nearing Guadalupe. Excitement mounted. Then, at about midnight, the archbishop, passing through streets lit by torches, lanterns, and fireworks, and acknowledging the cheers of the multitude from his open carriage, reached the city centre. The bells of the city's churches rang out, women sobbed for joy, and the Indians tossed flowers.

77*Memorial de lo sucedido*, fols. 26v–27.

78*DRT* i. 150.

79An important point that emerges from the sources is that there was no looting or pilfering of food. Even the stalls heaped with fruit and vegetables, which stood around the Plaza Mayor when the rioting began, were left wholly untouched; see Soria, *Relacion verdadera* fol. 5, Franco y Ortega, *Segunda parte*, 421, BL, 'Tumultos de Mexico', p. 170, *Memorial de lo sucedido* fol. 27; this is significant both in itself and because the American historian Chester L. Guthrie, who in the 1930s undertook a study of the tumult, argued that the chief cause of the insurrection was something quite different from the complicated social and political tensions that have been considered in this chapter—that the chief cause was in fact chronic food shortage. The complete and well-attested absence of looting and pillaging would appear to militate strongly against his argument. For Guthrie's case, first expounded in his doctoral dissertation, 'Riots in seventeenth-century Mexico City: a study of social and economic conditions' submitted at Berkeley, see C. L. Guthrie, 'Riots in seventeenth-century Mexico City' in *Greater America: essays in honour of Herbert Eugene Bolton* (Berkeley, California, 1945), pp. 245–53.

Thus ended the tumult of Monday 15 January 1624.[80] The rising, one must admit, was no great revolution. There were fewer than seventy dead and wounded all told and only six or seven hours of actual rioting at the most. And yet, in a certain sense, it was a revolution: a viceroy had been brought down by the people for the first time in the history of the Indies, and by his overthrow, as we shall see, a whole programme of reform, initiated originally in Madrid, was halted and destroyed.

[80]It is a curious phenomenon, well known to historians of the English and French Revolutions, that Monday was a particularly popular day for uprisings, presumably because the preceding rest-day allowed time for recuperation of energy and general preparation.

VI

CERRALVO (1624-1635)

On the afternoon of 15 January commenced the term of the sixth ruling *Audiencia* of New Spain and certainly the most dubious in law. Presiding over it was the man who had headed the fifth *Audiencia* and become the acknowledged leader of the anti-Gelves party, Pedro de Vergara Gabiria. Although its term was to be short—eight months only—it was eventful and of a significance for our subject which warrants detailed attention.

The weeks following the insurrection were the heyday of those who had wanted the viceroy's overthrow. Vergara Gabiria, the archbishop, and the other leaders basked in their victory and were greeted everywhere by cheering crowds and general applause. Since it was in the interest of the new government to gratify those whom the marquis had offended, there was now a systematic promotion of everyone and everything that he had cracked down on. Official corruption, according to Brámbila and other sources, soon became rife again.[1] The controls on the black population, on vagrancy, gambling, and prostitution were relaxed. The Portuguese and other foreigners went back to the silver mines and their old practices. The situation in the ports became chaotic once more. No effort was made to recapture any of the criminals who had escaped from the viceregal prison or to punish any of those who had had a hand in the sacking of the palace. Quantities of virulent lampoons and indecent rhymes attacking Gelves circulated freely on paper and by mouth and appeared on walls. Arquebuses and pistols were again carried openly in the streets. And Melchor de Varaez, whose 70,000 peso fine was now suspended, toured the capital triumphantly in an expensive new coach.

The *Audiencia*, at the same time as it jettisoned Gelves's reform programme, took steps to strengthen its hold on the administration. The palace was repaired and stocked with arms and ammunition, and Vergara Gabiria, Vázquez de Cisneros, and Juan de Ibarra, another of the justices, moved in to become its new occupants.[2] Several detachments of infantry, amounting to about 300 men, were raised and

[1] Brámbila, *Relación en favor del marqués*, DRT ii. 260–3; BM George IV 215, doc. i, fols. 35–6; this is the manuscript version of Flores-Lormendi which contains passages omitted from the printed version.

[2] AGI Patronato real 222, fols. 1, 326; Brámbila, op. cit., DRT ii. 281–90.

placed on a standing basis, and a strong guard was posted in the palace. Vergara Gabiria himself, apparently somewhat nervous, took fifty armed men with him wherever he went. Officers sympathetic to Gelves, notably Don Carlos de Luna, *corregidor* of Tlaxcala, were stripped of their posts and replaced with those whom the marquis had dismissed or otherwise offended.[3] Don Juan de Benavides, commander of the flota then in harbour at Veracruz, and a business accomplice of Vergara Gabiria, secured the port of Veracruz for the new regime and persuaded the commander of the fortress of San Juan to surrender his charge. The new commander chosen by the justices was the archbishop's nephew, Francisco de la Serna. On being informed that Gelves had absented himself from his post and disappeared, the commander of the fortress of San Diego at Acapulco also agreed (though he was afterwards to change his mind) to surrender his charge to an officer appointed by the *Audiencia*.

It was some days before the regime discovered the viceroy's whereabouts. When it was learned that he was in the Franciscan priory, guards were posted at all its entrances ostensibly to protect the marquis from the popular fury, but in fact to keep him where he was, isolate him from those outside, and intercept all communications to and from him.[4] In effect, Gelves was a prisoner and was to remain so for the next nine months, having for company only the friars, four pages, and a cook.

Once it had secured its *de facto* position, the *Audiencia* sought to improve its legal position, especially when it was learned that Gelves was demanding through various clergy that he be restored to power. The only plausible option open to the *Audiencia* was to seek formal approval for its actions from as many institutions and personages of standing as possible, and this, beginning on 22 January, is what it now endeavoured to do. In the space of two or three days, the justices summoned to the palace the Mexico City council, the diocesan council, the Inquisition, *consulado*, treasury, religious orders, titled lords, university, and representives of the nobility and commonalty,[5] and demanded of all these that they express their views on the situation; they were told that his excellency was asking to be returned to his post and asked to say whether they felt the *Audiencia* should comply with

[3] AGI Patronato real 221, r 11: 'Puntos que se an de adbertir . . .' fol 11; Brámbila, op. cit., p. 281.

[4] AGI Patronato real 221, r 14: 'Relacion de los subcesos de Mexico . . .', fol. 4.

[5] AGI Patronato real 223, r 4, fols. 16–24: 'Autos y pareceres de los tribunales reales, ynquisicion, tribunal de cruzada, cabildos eclesiastico y secular, unibersidad, religiones, señores de titulo, caballeros, republicanos de la ciudad en razon de que no combiene que buelba al gobierno el señor marques de Gelves'.

his demand or retain power in its own hands. Since these interviews were held in the palace under the eyes of the guard, and it was well known that Vergara Gabiria was not a man to be trifled with, it is not surprising that all those interviewed answered, or were taken as having answered, that in view of the general situation and in the interests of order, Gelves should remain in the priory and the *Audiencia* should retain power. The response was less uniform, however, when the persons concerned were asked to put their views in writing in order to clarify the situation to the government at Madrid. Some, notably the Mexico City council and the Jesuits, were willing enough, but the conde de Santiago Calimaya quietly absented himself from the city and Don Pedro Cortés and, one presumes, the friars simply refused.

Certainly the most difficult task confronting the *Audiencia* was justifying itself to Madrid. It was decided in consultation with the archbishop that the best chance of putting their case over convincingly would be if Pérez de la Serna himself led the delegation to Spain and this he agreed to do, despite the fact that it was unprecedented for an archbishop or bishop in Mexico to return to Spain without instructions or permission to do so from Madrid. To back up the archbishop, it was decided that the eloquent Christobal de Molina, the author of the tract questioning the *corregidores* and *repartimiento*, should go, on behalf of the Mexico City council, and, on behalf of the Creole nobility, the author of that other tract attacking the *repartimiento*, Hernán Carrillo Altamirano.

Madrid received the news of the January rising with consternation mixed with bafflement. No one doubted the seriousness of what had occurred; the problem was to grasp what exactly had. Even before Pérez de la Serna had completed the last leg of his journey, from Seville to Madrid, all kinds of theories were circulating at court. On arrival, the prelate was ushered into the presence of Olivares (14 June) whose questions he answered, in his own opinion at least, most satisfactorily.[6] He was also summoned before the king, and, on subsequent days had several meetings with the marqués de Cerralvo, captain-general of Galicia, the man whom the king had chosen to replace Gelves as viceroy of Mexico and who was then at court. On the strength of these meetings, Pérez de la Serna came to the conclusion, mistakenly as it turned out, that matters were going well for himself and his allies. In his letter to Mexico City, he dismissed the efforts of Gelves's friends on behalf of the marquis as ineffective and vouched for Cerralvo's 'sanctity, honesty, prudence, and courage'; he did not think that

6 AGI Patronato real 223, r 1: Pérez de la Serna to *Audiencia*, Madrid, 22 June 1624.

Cerralvo was likely to have much sympathy for Gelves despite the fact that the two were distantly related (having been acquainted with Cerralvo for many years, Serna may well have known that Cerralvo in fact disliked Gelves). Pérez de la Serna did not even feel any real concern that it had been decided that there should be a thorough investigation into the overthrow of Gelves, to be undertaken by Martin de Carrillo y Alderete, member of the supreme council of the Inquisition, and inquisitor of Valladolid.

In Mexico meanwhile, Gelves was busily passing messages by means of his friars to various institutions and dignitaries, accusing Vergara Gabiria and his friends of treason and other crimes and exhorting all who were loyal to work for his restoration. The *Audiencia* countered this by accusing Gelves of sedition and stirring up trouble, and at the same time exploited it in an attempt to frighten Madrid into supporting them against Gelves. The council of the Indies was informed that Gelves, in league with the friars administering the Indian parishes encircling Mexico City, and various Indian caciques, was plotting his revenge; should he succeed, they warned, he would certainly slaughter his enemies and cause a bloodbath.[7] At the same time, the foes of Gelves published at least two accounts of the tumult of 15 January and the events that had preceded it, designed to show Gelves in the worst possible light. One of these tracts, the *Algunos singulares y extraordinarios sucesos* was composed by a secular priest, Cristobal Ruiz de Cabrera, and the other, the *Relacion verdadera de la commocion popular* by a Castilian underling of Vergara Gabiria, recently appointed *corregidor*, Don Martín de Soria.

In addition to the passing of messages and the publication of tracts, there was also at least one vicious brawl between opposing factions of Mercenarian friars, one for Gelves the other for Vergara Gabiria, which only broke up with the intervention of Don Juan de Cervantes and a force of infantry. But perhaps the most interesting occurrence was the imbroglio over the fortress of San Diego at Acapulco. The commander of the fortress, Don Pedro de Legorreta, a Basque, had, as we have seen, agreed originally to surrender his charge to the *Audiencia*. When, however, Legorreta learned that Gelves was being kept in the Franciscan priory in Mexico City against his will, and that he was calling on those loyal to him to stand by him against the *Audiencia*, he not only refused to hand over the fortress, but gathered in stocks of

---

[7] AGI México 74, r 3: 'Autos hechos por los señores pressidente y oydores de la real audiencia de Mexico sobre que el señnor marques de Gelves con ayuda de los religiosos de las ordenes de San Agustin, San Francisco, Santo Domingo, y la Merced y de los yndios quiso bolber a governar la Nueva España amenasando que a de cortar cavezas y haziendo otras amenasas' (February 1624).

arms, ammunition, and supplies with the aid of the pro-Gelves *corregidores* of Tixtla and Iguala and seized the sails of two vessels that had been about to sail for Peru, laden with silks and taffetas belonging to Mexico City merchants and members of the Vergara Gabiria circle.[8] Such defiance, of course, greatly angered the *Audiencia*. But there was not a great deal to be done. San Diego was a strong position, recently strengthened as a precaution against the Dutch, and very difficult to seize. The justices had no choice but to try to bargain. The consequent talks are of interest particularly in one respect—the light that they throw on the role of the Basques in the events of 1624. It will be remembered that the Basques in Mexico displayed a marked tendency to adhere to the bureaucratic and *gachupín* party. How then, one asks, did they react to the insurrection of the 15 January? The opposition to Gelves, though it embraced the Creole party, included also important elements of the administration. Indeed several of the leaders of the opposition were themselves Basques, notably Vergara Gabiria, Juan de Ibarra, and Matheo de Aróstegui, *contador de tributos*. Furthermore, Vergara Gabiria, in his quest for support, had made a point of appealing to Basque sentiment and had assigned to the Basques their own infantry detachment which he placed under the command of Aróstegui. Nevertheless, while some Basques did support Vergara Gabiria, the signs are that the great majority remained sympathetic to Gelves and hostile to his enemies. The author of the 'Relacion de los subcesos de Mexico . . .', himself a Basque, states emphatically that the mainstream of Basque opinion, even in the militia, ran strongly against Vergara Gabiria and his friends.[9] One hundred and thirteen Basques of Puebla were later to come forward with a mass declaration loud in its dislike for Vergara Gabiria, and still more for the Mexico City council, and full of praise for Gelves and for his policies.[10] In another instance, Pedro de Bolívar y Mena, a Creole-Basque lawyer, was to publish a similar representation, of similar content, on behalf of the Basques of Mexico City.[11]

8 AGI Patronato real 223, r 9: Vergara Gabiria to Legorreta, 25 May 1624.

9 AGI Patronato real 221, r 14: 'Relacion de los subcesos de Mexico', fol. 4v.

10 AGI Patronato real 221, r 12: 'Memorial hecho y firmado por ciento y trece Bascongados con voz y cauzion del comun de los demas leales de la dicha nacion donde rrepresentan al S. Visitador Don Martin Carrillo Alderete en contra oposicion de los traidores las loables acciones del govierno del exmo. señor marques de Gelves . . .' One of the signatures is that of Antonio de Brámbila.

11 Pedro de Bolívar y Mena, *Protestacion de los Vizcainos de la Nueva España hecha al visitador Don Martin Carrillo sobre el govierno del virey marques de Gelves y Sobre no haber tenido parte en la sedicion y tumulto de Mexico.* (Mexico 1625?). I have not been able to trace a copy of this tract. Toribio de Medina had not seen it either, but, taking note of its existence from Beristain, includes it in his list (no. 360).

To the stubborn Legorreta, Aróstegui, acting for Vergara Gabiria, dispatched a suitably guipuzcoan emissary, one Iregui, bearing letters imploring him in the name of Basque solidarity[12] to submit to the new captain-general. Aróstegui asserted that Legorreta was acting to the 'dishonour of the nation' by supporting the marquis, and reminded him that among the Basques it had always been the rule that they sustain one another. To reinforce his plea, Aróstegui offered Legorreta the vacant *corregimiento* of the Villa de los Valles. But neither the appeal to sentiment nor the offer of an alternative post had any effect. Legorreta simply answered that he would obey no orders save those of the king and the viceroy, the king's lieutenant.[13]

If the *Audiencia* failed to win the allegiance of the Basque community, or at least of the greater part of it, it also failed, the indications are, to gain the long-term support of the ordinary people. While the Mexico City council and the merchant class remained tied to the *Audiencia*, the lower classes were soon alienated and driven to renew their affection for Gelves. It was the secular clergy after all who had won mass support for the justices, and once the manoeuvres of the archbishop, so impressive to the poor and superstitious, had ceased to occupy the centre of the stage, there was nothing to counteract popular discontent with what was happening on the economic front. On the contrary, there was much to foment it. Racketeering, accompanied by its sister evils, price inflation and food shortage, and aided by the effects of a severe drought,[14] was teaching the poor to look back fondly on the days of Gelves's rule. Evidently the cheering and applause with which the populace of Mexico City greeted the marquis when eventually he reappeared before them on 30 October 1624 marked a genuine change of heart.[15]

Tension between *Audiencia* and the *Gelvistas* rose as the moment of Cerralvo's arrival approached. On 1 September Gelves's representatives presented the Mexico City council, diocesan chapter, Inquisition, university, and other bodies with a proclamation asserting that the justices had sought, by means of lies, to blacken Gelves's name and to dissuade the responsible elements of the viceroyalty from recognizing him as viceroy, by spreading word that he was intent on avenging himself on those who had opposed him; while in fact all that the

---

[12] AGI Patronato real 223, r 9: Aróstegui to Legorreta, 25 May 1624 and Vergara Gabiria to Legorreta, same date.

[13] AGI Patronato real 223, r 9: Legorreta to Vergara Gabiria, no date.

[14] Gibson, *The Aztecs*, p. 454.

[15] AGI Patronato real 221, r 12: 'Dos testimonios de la entrada y salida del señor marques de Gelves de las casas reales y gobierno . . .'; IAH col. PT, leg. 49: 'fragmento del diario del Br. Gregorio Martín de Guido (Guijo?), fol. 284.

viceroy demanded was to be returned to the government, and he swore that there would be no reprisals.[16] Two days later, Vergara Gabiria replied with a counter-proclamation reminding the tribunals concerned that the question of who was to rule, pending the arrival of the marqués de Cerralvo, had been put to them already and that they had decided unanimously that the magistrates of the *Audiencia* should rule and not the marqués de Gelves. There was now another round of discussion and, in the case of the university at least, a vote; but in the end the decision was the same as before, that the *Audiencia* should retain the executive power for the interim. Later in the month, as the flota bearing the viceroy-elect neared Veracruz, a powerful Dutch force, the rump of the Nassau squadron, appeared off Acapulco bay.[17] When the news reached Mexico City, the justices immediately assembled a council of war. It was decided to prepare an expedition to reinforce the garrison of the fortress of San Diego. Gelves, however, who with some justice, claims to have avoided until this moment making any move that might be construed as an attack on the *Audiencia*, so as to reduce the risk of renewed disorder, now decided that his first duty was to fight the foreign and heretic threat. Aware of the differences between Legorreta and Vergara Gabiria and considering that reinforcements from among his own supporters would be more welcome than any sent by the *Audiencia*, the marquis bade his nephew raise a body of men. On learning of this, Vergara Gabiria, either taking the move to be a serious threat or else making use of it as a handy pretext, had Francisco Pimentel and a number of his men seized, and put it out that a dangerous conspiracy to overthrow the *Audiencia* had been narrowly thwarted.[18] Meanwhile, the Dutch, under Admiral Schappenham, blockaded Acapulco.

On 14 September, in Veracruz, Francisco de la Serna welcomed ashore the fourteenth viceroy of Mexico, Don Rodrigo Pacheco Osorio, marqués de Cerralvo, and his wife, the sixth vicereine, Doña Francisca de la Cueva, daughter of the sixth Duke of Albuquerque. Vergara Gabiria's policy, it soon became apparent, was to ingratiate himself in as far as he could with the new viceroy, and indeed it is hard to see

16 Cristobal Bernardo de la Plaza y Jaén, *Crónica de la real y insigne Universidad de México de la Nueva España desde el ano 1553 hasta el de 1687* (2 vols., Mexico 1931), i. 280–3.

17 'Relacion de los subcesos de Mexico ...' fol. 6ᵛ; the Nassau Squadron was the largest Dutch force to enter the Pacific in the seventeenth century but it was a great fiasco. It blockaded Callao without result, attacked Guayaquil without taking it, and blockaded Acapulco, again ineffectively; see Phelan, *The Kingdom of Quito*, pp. 104–5.

18 AGI Patronato real 221, r 14: 'Relacion de los subcesos de Mexico ...', fols. 8ᵛ–9ᵛ.

what likely alternative he had: the arguments used to exclude Gelves from power could scarcely be used against his successor. Anything but instant submission would have amounted to plain and undisguised rebellion. But Vergara Gabiria and his associates had as yet no reason to suppose that they were lost. Cerralvo's reputation was of a man of fashion, not a puritan. Archbishop Pérez de la Serna had vouched for his prudence, and there was every reason to believe that the lesson that had been taught one viceroy would not be quickly forgotten by his successor. Besides, it was apparent that Madrid had resolved to tread with caution, for the visitor-general, the inquisitor of Valladolid, was not on the fleet, having been purposely kept back for the following year. Furthermore, Cerralvo was all smiles and, like the diplomat he was, did everything to allay the fears of those in positions of responsibility. He spent a whole month on the journey between Veracruz and Mexico City, biding his time and exchanging courtesies and compliments, and did not finally arrive in the capital until 17 October.

Cerralvo's first interview with Vergara Gabiria went off smoothly enough. It was clear that there was to be no sudden change in the administration or purge of the enemies of Gelves.[19] Just to make sure, however, that the marquis was fully aware of the feelings of those who were against Gelves, a demonstration was staged a few days after Cerralvo's arrival in Mexico City, in which an effigy of Gelves was burned in the city centre and a crowd shouted insults outside the Franciscan and Dominican friaries.[20] But Cerralvo's main concern at this stage was not the *Audiencia* or Gelves, but the Dutch. His first significant action, apart from removing the arquebusiers from the Franciscan friary, was to raise some hundreds of men and to send them together with instructions and compliments to Legorreta.[21]

On 21 October Cerralvo visited the Franciscan friary for his first interview with Gelves. The meeting was long, though not particularly cordial, and was followed by an exchange of letters and then a second meeting.[22] The two marquises violently disagreed. Cerralvo's cautious approach and apparent friendliness toward Vergara Gabiria offended the older man, as did his plan for returning Gelves to power for just one day, as a gesture to signify that no representative of the king could be

19 AGI, Patronato real 221, r 11: Gelves to council, 22 Jan. 1625.

20 AGI Patronato real 223, r 8: 'De todo lo sucedido en este reyno cerca de la rebelion de Mexico desde que partio la flota de Junio deste ano hasta los siete de Septiembre (1624) . . .' (by Gelves himself), fol. 2ᵛ.

21 AGI Patronato real 221, r 14: 'Relacion de los subcesos de Mexico . . .' fol. 9ᵛ.

22 AGI Patronato real 221, r 11: Cerralvo to Gelves, 29 Oct. 1624, Gelves to Cerralvo, 30 Oct. 1624, and Cerralvo to Gelves, 30 Oct. 1624.

removed by the people. Cerralvo made it plain that Gelves would not have the slightest chance to settle scores with his foes and insisted that in the ceremony which was to accompany his purely symbolic return to power, Gelves should ride in procession with the *Audiencia*, Mexico City council, diocesan chapter, and the rest of his enemies. This, protested Gelves, was humiliation; but Cerralvo was adamant. He ordered Gelves to make the sacrifice in the greater interest of the king. The two marquises did agree, however, to keep their differences private lest news of them prejudice the stability of the colony.

The restoration of Gelves on 31 October, despite its circumstances, was in at least one respect a triumph for him: the multitude gave him a reception matching those that had been bestowed upon Pérez de la Serna. He rode at the head of the *Audiencia*, and his other enemies, under triumphal arches of flowers and linden to the sound of fanfarades, fireworks, and thunderous applause. He was greeted as 'father and protector of the poor, and scourge of the proud and overbearing'.[23] When the procession entered the Plaza Mayor, for Gelves no doubt the scene of bitter memories, there was a salute of guns and a great display of fireworks.

Gelves spent the one day of his second term as viceroy brooding, being powerless to do anything else, over the hypocritical salutations of those who had overthrown him and sullied his reputation and honour In the evening of 1 November, in another ceremony, he formally relinquished the viceregal office and then proceeded, accompanied by Cerralvo and the Creole nobility, to Tacuba where he lived during the rest of his time in Mexico.

The 2nd of November was a day of interim, and on the 3rd Cerralvo was formally installed as the fourteenth viceroy. From that day for the next ten months, the new viceroy was engaged in building his own power base, a task which he accomplished gradually so as to cause a minimum of alarm.[24] His aim was to manoeuvre himself into a position of political dominance in New Spain by the autumn of 1625, when the visitor-general, Don Martín Carrillo, was due to arrive from Spain. Cerralvo refrained from dismissing any of the officers appointed by the *Audiencia* from their posts, but as vacancies appeared he filled them with his own relatives and friends, a policy which, though unpopular with the Creoles and theoretically illegal, was nevertheless the only effective way for a viceroy to ensure his power. Thus, making no overtly hostile moves, Cerralvo whittled away Vergara Gabiria's influence as surely as if by a purge. Meanwhile, Madrid had forbidden

---

23 AGI Patronato real 221, r 12: 'Dos testimonios . . .'
24 AGI México 74, r 16: *Audiencia* to council, 17 Jan. 1625.

Pérez de la Serna[25] to return to Mexico, thereby depriving the secular clergy of their leader and removing Vergara Gabiria's greatest asset from the scene, and 'promoted' Galdós de Valencia to a post in Peru, thereby weakening him further.

At this stage, virtually everything seemed to militate against Vergara Gabiria. Cerralvo, being a man of fashion, noted for the sumptuousness of his household and entertainments, was not the sort to reintroduce Gelvesian austerity. His suavity enabled him to convince those who had profited from the policies of the *Audiencia* that they had nothing to fear from him, and he also robbed Vergara Gabiria of support by exploiting the nervousness of the Creole leadership and its anxiety to retrieve its reputation for obedience and loyalty. Indeed, fear of the consequences of 15 January, and of losing standing in Madrid, had virtually muted the Creole party. The viceroy was able to seal his success by appropriating an instrument which his predecessors, including Gelves, had lacked—a force of troops. Finding the 300-man force raised by the *Audiencia* at hand, he quietly changed its officers and gained it for himself.[26]

Carrillo landed at Veracruz in September 1625, to find the viceroyalty quiet, but somewhat tense and nervous. Almost at once a number of persons slipped quietly away from the capital, including several secular priests,[27] at least one of whom repaired to New Galicia, while a number of anonymous threatening notes were directed to Carrillo. The *visitador*'s first impression was that virtually the whole colony was divided on political lines between *Gelvistas*, as the supporters of the unfortunate viceroy were popularly known, and the supporters of Vergara Gabiria and Pérez de la Serna. Carrillo carried instructions to delve into the circumstances of the rising, apportion blame and guilt, and inflict due punishment. He was also empowered to report on the general condition of the colony and provided with secret documents naming him as temporary governor of New Spain should Cerralvo die or cease to act as viceroy for some other reason.[28] This was important, for it shows the extent of Madrid's new-found distrust of the *Audiencia* that it should thus deprive it of one of its

[25]Serna was not only forbidden to return to Mexico but treated with coolness for some time; it was only after the intervention of the Pope who was anxious that, as a defender of ecclesiastical privilege, Serna should be protected, that he was eventually assigned the Castilian bishopric of Zamora; see Urban VIII to Philip IV, Rome, 6 Sept. 1625, ADI Palafox papers xxxvii, fol. 42.

[26]AGI Patronato real 224, r 3: Carrillo to council, 15 Nov. 1625.

[27]AGI Patronato real 224, r 4, fol. 3; and r 3: Carrillo to council, 15 Nov. 1625.

[28]BM Eg. 322: 'Consultas del consejo de estado tocantes a Indias, 1627', fols. 87–8.

most significant functions—that of assuming the executive power in the event of an interim between viceroys; moreover the step was to prove to be a permanent constitutional change, for henceforward it was usual for Madrid to appoint substitute governors, or temporary prelate-viceroys,[29] to fill in the gaps between viceroys: the coming to power of the seventh ruling *Audiencia* in 1649 occurred, as we shall see, only because of the death of the temporary bishop-governor, Torres y Rueda.

Carrillo's first impression of Cerralvo (he was later to be at odds with him) was most favourable. The viceroy, he reported to the council of the Indies, had handled the difficult situation in Mexico with admirable skill and tact and acted quite properly in maintaining the force of infantry, despite the considerable expense that it involved. 'I consider it essential to maintain, and possibly even to increase, this force,' he wrote, for without it 'it would be difficult to govern and administer this city, for it is full of riff-raff of limited reason and few responsibilities who know now the means by which to cast off from themselves the yoke of justice.'[30]

The *visita* had a slow start, owing to the *visitador*'s ill-health, but at length, on 6 November, the beginning of both the *visita* and Gelves's *residencia* was announced. After a month of preliminary work, Carrillo proceeded to hear Gelves. Starting on 2 December, he spent two hours with the marquis daily for two months assessing his story and considering his evidence. Gelves contended that the rising was the result of an elaborate conspiracy planned and put into operation by a broad combination of social groups and administrative bodies which included all those who were rich and powerful and resented what he had tried to do to relieve the sufferings of the poor; in particular, he accused the *Audiencia*, the Creole city councils, the bishops, Jesuits, treasury and other administrative staff, *consulado*, nobles, Inquisition, and *corregidores*.[31] The fact that the marquis was given so much time with the *visitador* was taken to mean, particularly by those who were against him, that Carrillo was on his side; and indeed, although Carrillo did not accept Gelves's view without some qualification, it emerges plainly from his reports that he was. By 26 January, even before he had spent much time with Gelves's opponents, Carrillo was informing Madrid that

29 Enrique Sánchez Pedrote discusses the phenomenon of the rise of reserve viceroys in his article 'Los Prelados Virreyes', *Anuario de Estudios Americanos* vii (1950), 211–53, but in relation to Peru; he does not mention the developments of 1624–5 in Mexico, and provides no real explanation for the introduction of prelate-viceroys possibly for that reason.

30 AGI Patronato real 224, r 3: Carrillo to council, 15 Nov. 1625.

31 AGI Patronato real 223, r 5: 'Declaraciones del m. de Gelves hechas ante el ldo. Don Martín Carrillo visitador que fue de la Nueva España'.

though he did not believe that there had been a deliberate, pre-meditated, conspiracy to overthrow the viceroy, there had indeed been a premeditated attempt to cause enough trouble to defeat or impede his policies, and that as regards the 15 January, the *Audiencia* and Creoles had betrayed the viceroy by making no effort to save him from the mob and had 'rejoiced at what happened that day'.[32] All the evidence showed that it was a case of deliberate treason. After the commotion, no one had made the slightest effort to restore Gelves to power or punish those who had taken part in the rising and the sacking of the palace. Furthermore, he affirmed, there could be no question but that the secular clergy had incited the masses to rise.

Hostility to Carrillo increased as his sympathy for Gelves became more evident, and fear of the consequences of the *visita* grew as first the searches and investigations, and then the arrests began. By 30 January, there were 224 names on Carrillo's list of guilty or suspected persons, 36 of them being already under arrest.[33] Popularly, it was assumed that Vergara Gabiria and his supporters had been broken by Carrillo and Gelves in league with Cerralvo, for nothing was known publicly of the true state of relations between the two marquises or of Cerralvo's lack of enthusiasm for the *visita*.[34] In fact, relations between them were becoming worse as Vergara Gabiria's position disintegrated, for Madrid, wishing to minimize the risk of further turmoil in New Spain, had instructed Gelves to depart for Spain in the spring of 1625, an order which Cerralvo, being anxious to be rid of Gelves, wanted to see respected, but which Gelves ignored.[35] Moreover, Gelves, backed by Carrillo, was threatening to break with Cerralvo openly, a move which would have put the viceroy in the position of appearing to sympathize with Vergara Gabiria and oppose the *visita*; Cerralvo was thereby forced to acquiesce in a thorough pursuit of corrupt and guilty officials with which he was not in sympathy. On 9 March 1626 a sensation was caused in Mexico City when Vergara Gabiria himself was arrested and his belongings, including his library of 700 books, seized.[36]

By the summer of 1626, Carrillo felt that he had verified the full extent of the treason and was considering what policy he ought to recommend to Madrid. He was caught in a dilemma, for though he believed that the guilty should be punished and in principle that the

[32] AGI Patronato real 224, r i: Carrillo to council, 26 Jan. 1626.
[33] AGI Patronato real 224, r 3: memorandum of 30 Jan. 1626 of Carrillo's secretary, Miguel Guerrero.
[34] BM Add. MS. 13, 975, fols. 294–5.
[35] BM Eg. 321, doc. 40; AGI Mexico 3, r i: *consulta* of the council of the Indies, 9 Jan. 1626, and Gelves to Cerralvo, 9 May 1625.
[36] AGI Patronato real 222, fols. 4, 9v.

facts should not be swept under the carpet, he also believed that the facts had to be swept under the carpet if further trouble was to be prevented—which was Madrid's foremost preoccupation—and the reputation of the Church safeguarded. His list of implicated persons now involved no fewer than 450 names[37] including those of the Mexico City councillor Andrés de Valmaseda (who was already behind bars), Hernán Carrillo Altamirano (the enemy of the *corregidores* who was then in Madrid), Pedro Garcés de Portillo (the coadjutor of the archbishopric), Cristobal Ruiz de Cabrera, Jerónimo de Aguilar (the archbishop's major-domo), Archbishop Pérez de la Serna himself, that other enemy of the *corregidores*, Cristobal de Molina, Galdós de Valencia, Pedro de Vergara Gabiria, Vázquez de Cisneros, Juan de Ibarra, Mateo de Aróstegui, Fray Juan de Lormendi, eight Jesuits including Juan de Ledesma and Guillermo de los Ríos (head of the main Jesuit college in Mexico City and a personage particularly close to Viceroy Cerralvo, being his confessor), and ten other secular priests, including the bellicose Antonio González. In the upshot, Carrillo advised that the crown show great leniency and grant a general pardon, for if there was no general pardon, he explained, the colony would be plunged afresh into dissension and disorder. He recommended that everything possible should be done to calm the Creoles, that the evidence against all but the most guilty be suppressed, and that even though he was one of the most guilty, no action should be taken against the archbishop. 'I do not believe,' wrote the *visitador* to the council of the Indies, 'that his Majesty in his holy zeal would wish to have recorded in writing particulars likely to bring the reputation and authority of a prelate of the Church into disrepute, however true and justified they may be.'[38]

Gelves's enemies now seemed as humbled as Gelves had been. But Vergara Gabiria's resources were not yet exhausted. As Carrillo admitted, the senior justice had, with his great intelligence and legal expertise, cloaked most of his doings so effectively that there was considerable doubt as to whether the case against him would stick. Moreover, his supporters, in Mexico and Spain, were doing their best on his behalf and were meeting with at least some success.[39] It was being put about, not wholly implausibly, that the senior magistrate was being expended to redeem the marquis's honour, that Vergara Gabiria was being used as a scapegoat to divert attention from the reckless mistakes

37 AGI Patronato real, r 4: 'Testimonio y relacion de las personas eclesiasticas, seculares, y regulares, que quedan presas por mandato del lic. Don Martín Carrillo y Alderete, visitador-general de la Nueva España'.
38 AGI Patronato real 224, r 3: Carrillo to council, 20 July 1626.
39 AGI Patronato real 224, r 10: Vergara Gabiria to council, 18 July 1626.

and arrogant foolhardiness of Gelves which were the true causes of the insurrection. Carrillo they depicted in their complaints to Madrid as the unscrupulous lackey of the two marquises whose intention was to feather his own nest at the expense of justice and truth. In Mexico the more active opponents of the *visita*, including Juan de Pareja, successor to Garcés de Portillo as coadjutor of the archbishopric, Melchor de Varaez, and a new arrival, Bishop Cañicares of New Cáceres in the Philippines, the brother of Vergara Gabiría's wife and ostensibly *en route* from Spain to the Far East, were agitating to some effect. The bishop, coming higher in the hierarchy than Carrillo, could not be silenced by the latter, and declared in his sermons that Mexico was being wickedly oppressed by an overweening triumvirate consisting of the two marquises and Carrillo whose goal was to pervert justice, deceive the king, and ensnare the innocent.[40] Pareja, aided by the bishop and his friends, brought out a pamphlet or two of similar tone and content to Cañicares's sermons, and there was also at least one minor disturbance caused by the bishop outside the Inquisition building.

The council of state in Madrid, which superseded the council of the Indies when American affairs were deemed sufficiently serious, was dismayed and angered to discover that Mexico was not yet restored to its former tranquillity.[41] It was resolved that everything possible to end the Mexican agitation should be done at once: Pareja, Bishop Cañicares, and Gelves were to be recalled to Spain. Mexico City and the Creoles were to be pardoned for the rising of 15 January and declared guiltless. The appointment of Lucas de Vergara Gabiria, Pedro's brother and a veteran of the Spanish Flanders army, as commander of the garrison of Manila was cancelled. And it was decided to scrutinize Carrillo's work on the circumstances of the tumult, in other words to hold an investigation into the investigation.[42] Don Francisco de Manso y Zúñiga, a churchman and experienced member of the council of the Indies, was commissioned to convey the general pardon to Mexico City, cancel those of Carrillo's measures which seemed too harsh, take Carrillo's place as standby for the executive power should anything befall Carralvo, and succeed Pérez de la Serna as archbishop of Mexico.

However, the belief that Manso, who had always looked to the crown for advancement and was well versed in Mexican affairs, would restore peace to the colony was quickly shown to be ill founded. If Manso had put the royal interest first before, and it is difficult to see how he can

40 AGI Patronato real 224, r 3: Carrillo to council, 20 July 1626 and 22 July 1626.
41 BM Eg. 320: 'Consultas de consejo de estado tocantes a Indias, 1627', fol. 45.
42 BM Eg. 320: 'Consultas de consejo de estado', memorandum of 29 May 1627, fols. 87-8, and AGI Mexico 3, r 2, doc. 31.

have been chosen if he had not, he certainly did not do so now. No sooner had he landed in New Spain than he showed, by the alacrity with which he courted Creole favour and support, that he intended to be Pérez de la Serna's successor in more senses than one. In December 1627, even before he reached Mexico City, he was haughtily demanding of the viceroy that Carrillo's *visita* be halted, that all investigations into the tumult except those conducted by himself cease, and that Gelves be restrained.[43] On arriving in the capital, he caused a storm of excitement by threatening Carrillo with severe penalties if he did not stop the trial of Vergara Gabiria, which was then in progress, and immediately surrender the senior magistrate to his keeping; he also instructed that all proceedings against those on Carrillo's list, with only some seven or eight exceptions, should be dropped, and Carrillo's prisoners released. Carrillo and Gelves reacted furiously and pressed on with redoubled urgency with arrangements for the trial of Vázquez de Cisneros. Viceroy Cerralvo, though extremely irritated by Manso's arrogant attitude and partiality for the Creoles, saw in the newly arrived archbishop the perfect means of ridding himself of Gelves and Carrillo without assuming the responsibility for ending the *visita*. He had particular reason for wishing to be rid of Carrillo, who had been informing Madrid that he was corruptly sanctioning irregularities in the import and export of oriental silks through Acapulco and engaging in other peculations.[44] Accordingly the viceroy swallowed his annoyance with the archbishop, forbade investigations into the tumult to continue, and publicly humiliated the *visitador* by stopping the trial of Vergara Gabiria.

On 20 January 1628 Archbishop Manso, with the full support of the Viceroy, published the general pardon. The archbishop's position at the head of the Creole party and the secular clergy was now assured. Mexico City and the Creoles were jubilant. Carrillo, however, responded by intensifying his *visita*.[45] He had the residence of Don Pedro Cortés and those of several other prominent Creoles searched, and entered into a quarrel with the Mexico City *cabildo* over whether or not he had right of access to its records. The Creoles protested indignantly to the archbishop, declaring that Carrillo was ignoring the pardon conceded to Mexico City and 'causing great distress to its citizens';[46] Manso responded by calling on the viceroy to disperse Carrillo's staff and expel the *visitador* from the capital. Cerralvo, though unwilling to go so far as

43 AGI Patronato real 225, r 1: Cerralvo to council, 4 Jan. 1628, and BM Add. MS. 13, 975, fols. 291ᵛ–292.
44 AGI Mexico 92, r 3: Carrillo to council, 5 March 1627.
45 BM Add. MS. 13, 975, fols. 293–4.
46 Ibid., fol. 293ᵛ; *ACM* xxvi. 224–6.

that, still put his abhorrence of Carrillo before his detestation of Manso, and ordered the *visitador* to suspend everything and prepare to depart for Spain on the flota of that spring. Carrillo had no choice but to submit. Gathering up his papers and nursing his resentment, he proceeded in the company of Gelves, Vergara Gabiria, and his six or seven remaining prisoners to Veracruz to await embarkation. That was not quite the end of the luckless story of Martín Carrillo's *visita*, for the fleet on which he and Gelves sailed was the very same that was intercepted by the Dutch West India squadron under Piet Heyn off the Cuban coast at Matanzas, routed, driven ashore, and plundered. Carrillo, Gelves, and their party, though they did subsequently make their way back to Spain, were apparently only able to complete their journey some time later.

With Carrillo out of the way, the viceroy was free, as he thought, to proceed unhampered with his peculations; while Archbishop Manso was free to consolidate and increase his newly won influence with the Creole party. The publication of the general pardon had brought him great popularity. González Peñafiel, one of the new magistrates of the *Audiencia* of Mexico, records that 'the people, governed as they always are by what they see, without giving a thought to anything else, gave thanks to the archbishop, attributing to him personally what they really owed to the goodness of the king, acclaiming him *padre de la patria*, and promising themselves that good times lay ahead.'[47] Despite the ending of the *visita*, Manso continued to concern himself with the tumult of 1624, particularly in his reports to Madrid,[48] for he knew that Carrillo and Gelves would soon be close to the ear of the king and that their arguments and their resentment were still a threat to himself and his supporters. Accordingly, he persisted with his attack on the *visita*, accusing Carrillo of every sort of misconduct including that of having plundered 90,000 pesos of the king's money in Mexico City, with the connivance of the viceroy, under pretence of reimbursing himself for his official expenses. The tumult of 1624, declared the archbishop in his letters to Madrid, had been a spontaneous, leaderless outburst, a rising of the ignorant masses, and of the masses alone, against a regime which was generally and rightly detested on account of its brutal and oppressive policies and its insolence towards the Church. If a chief cause for the mishap had to be found, he asserted, then it was the weakness and obstinacy of Gelves which had enabled a clique of treacherous, selfish men to dominate and ruin him. Those who were really guilty were not Vergara Gabiria or Galdós de Valencia, still less

    47 AGI México 74, r 4: González Peñafiel to council, 9 Nov. 1630.
    48 See three letters, AGI Patronato real 225, r 2: Manso to council, 20 Jan., 29 July, and 13 Oct. 1628.

Archbishop Pérez de la Serna, but Cristobal de Osorio, Juan de Alvarado, Bartolomé de Burguillos, and Antonio de Brámbila.

While Manso continued his offensive against Carrillo and Gelves, he also busied himself with a variety of new issues. Of these, one of the most pressing was the labour question and particularly the question of the Indian share-out. Manso consulted various hacienda owners as to their situation and needs, including the conde de Santiago Calimaya, and expounded his opinions in no uncertain terms in a letter to Madrid.[49] The policy that he recommended corresponded exactly to that advocated by Hernán Carrillo Altamirano, Cristobal de Molina, Juan Fernández de Vivero, and the Mexico City council.[50] Referring to the chronic shortage of Indian labour which he stressed by quoting Matheo de Aróstegui's figures for Indian tributaries, according to which their number had decreased by over 14,000 in the quadrennium 1624–8, and referring also to the wastefulness and inefficiency of the prevailing system of labour exploitation, he argued that the *repartimiento* system in Mexico had either to be dismantled or radically reformed. Labour, he asserted, was now so scarce that the viceroy's officers had the power of petty despots. Not only did they reap vast profits from their control of the Indians, but they could make or break virtually any Spanish landowner as they pleased. The solution, he urged, was to curtail the powers of the *corregidores* and to establish an entirely new labour system, without the *repartimiento*, 'leaving the Indians free to work as they please, at whatever work they please, and to go to those employers who offer the best conditions of employment'. In that way the Indians would be happier, would suffer less disruption, social and personal, would receive better treatment, and enter into a closer and more personal relationship with their Spanish employers.

Another cause which received the archbishop's blessing was the opposition of influential Creoles to the force of regular infantry at the viceroy's disposal in Mexico City. The troops had by 1628 become a major grievance, particularly with the Mexico City council which regarded them, naturally enough, as an unwelcome instrument of coercion, as a heavy and unnecessary expense, and as a slur on its honour and on the honour of all the Creoles of New Spain.[51] The city council tried again and again to sway the viceroy and obtain the disbandment of the force, claiming that the soldiers were lowering the

[49] AGI Patronato real 225, r 2: Manso to council, 10 May 1628.

[50] Apart from Carrillo Altamirano's tract, the hostility of the Mexico City council to the *repartimiento* in this period is made clear in AGI México 31, r 1: 'Copia de parezer de la ciudad de Mexico sobre el repartimiento de yndios' (15 Nov. 1632).

[51] *ACM* xxvi. 47, 136, 144–6.

moral tone of the city with their drunkenness, their rapacity, and their women, but always Cerralvo refused to yield. The marquis declared that in all the realms of the Spanish Monarchy, the executive power had troops at its disposal, and that in New Spain the natural position for troops was Mexico City, since Mexico City was the strategic centre of the viceroyalty and the obvious base from which to defend the coasts against the Dutch. In as far as the force also served to maintain order in the capital, he added, there was no need whatever for the respectable citizenry to feel apprehensive, for it was or should be apparent to all that the soldiers were not intended as a precaution against them but against the dangerous mass of Negroes, mestizos, and mulattoes. Dissatisfied, the Mexico City council turned to the archbishop, who, of course, was only too glad to help. He wrote to Madrid declaring that the infantry was an affront to New Spain, an instrument maintained by Cerralvo for no other reason than to further his own despotic designs. 'The soldiers are totally unnecessary', he affirmed, 'and serve only to perpetrate crime, commit outrages, and start brawls, and this in a city in which hardly a sword is drawn the whole year round.'[52]

The viceroy, like the Creoles, was quick to recognize in Manso the successor to Pérez de la Serna. As early as January 1628, he warned Madrid that the prelate was showing disturbing signs of becoming an obstacle to his government.[53] He hinted that it had been unwise of Madrid to appoint as archbishop a man who, as a member of the council of the Indies, had a ready pretext for interfering wherever he pleased; moreover, the archbishop's obstinate attitude had already served to stiffen the resistance of the Mexico City council to his attempts to manipulate it and had encouraged the *regidores* to oppose his power. But, as the archbishop noted and deplored, Cerralvo was, even so, having a much easier time with the Mexico City council than he might have had; for, by a judicious application of carrot and stick, the viceroy had infiltrated the council in a way that Gelves had never attempted to do.[54] Relying on the *escribano mayor* Don Fernando Carrillo, whom Manso called the 'curse of this republic', and the *regidor* Pedro Díaz de la Barrera, brother-in-law to his close associate and accomplice Antonio Urrutia de Vergara, Cerralvo was still able to bend the council, if not entirely to his will, then at least to a considerable extent.

The chief instance of Cerralvo's twisting of the Creole councillors in the period after Manso's arrival is the debate over the Union of Arms of 1628–9. The Union of Arms, the most famous of Olivares's schemes

[52] AGI México 3, r 3: Manso to council, 3 July 1628.
[53] AGI Patronato real 225, r 1: Cerralvo to council, 4 Jan. 1628.
[54] AGI México 3, r 4: Manso to council, 7 Nov. 1629.

for the strengthening of the Spanish Monarchy, was a proposal that involved every section of the Spanish imperium from Italy to the Philippines and was designed to ease the burden of military and financial effort then being born by Castile, by sharing this burden more equitably through the empire. According to the plan, every state in the Monarchy would vote funds to support part of a common military reserve fixed in proportion to the resources of that state, the whole of which reserve could be used for the defence of any part of the empire that was attacked. The peripheral parts of the Monarchy, in other words, were being asked to pay more towards the cost of the Castilian hegemony. In 1626, the proposal had been laid before the *cortes* of Aragon, Valencia, and Catalonia, though with only very limited success. Afterwards, the Union had been put to the *cortes* of Castile and then, one by one, to the representative institutions of the other states of the empire. When it was put to the American viceroyalties, the form of the Union was modified, for Mexico and Peru were unable to contribute men; their contribution was assessed entirely in cash.[55] It shows perhaps how far the decline of Mexico was now acknowledged in Madrid that the Mexican contribution was fixed at 250,000 ducats annually for fifteen years, for although this was much more than the sums voted by Aragon, Valencia, or Catalonia, it was 100,000 ducats less than the amount asked of Peru.

Although Mexican representative institutions in 1628 were far too weak to make possible resistance of the sort that had been put up by Aragon or Catalonia, there was, all the same, some resistance. When it first became known that the viceroy was about to lay the Union of Arms before the city councils of New Spain, Mexico City, Puebla, and the other towns appealed to the viceroy to convene a special assembly of delegates representing all the Spanish towns of the viceroyalty to discuss and consider the proposal. This, as Cerralvo himself averred, was tantamount to a demand for a Mexican *cortes* on the model of that of Castile. Cerralvo, knowing that the *cabildos* were much easier to handle singly than together, was all against the idea, and knowing that Madrid would also be against it, rejected the proposal out of hand. He then proceeded to lay the Union before the city councils, commencing with that of Mexico City which was the most susceptible to his machinations. The *regidores* tried to secure a deal, the subsidy in return for concessions, but the marquis, in no mood to give ground, applied maximum pressure and before long Mexico City's resistance collapsed.

[55] See the *Razonamiento que el excellentisimo senor Marques de Cerralvo Virrey desta Nueva España hizo al cabildo de Mexico sobre la Union de Armas en 19 de Octiubre de 1628* (Mexico, 1628); and Elliott, *The Revolt of the Catalans*, pp. 217 ff.

Fernando Carrillo robbed the opposition faction, which was still being led by Andrés de Valmaseda, of enough votes to obtain a majority for the Union, without conditions.[56] Then, seeing how small was the resistance put up by the capital, most of the other towns of the viceroyalty—Zacatecas, Guadalajara, Antequera, and Veracruz—yielded also. But Puebla held out. The Puebla city council, the largest and most determined in New Spain, was, as usual, the most difficult to handle and stood its ground for some months.[57] Eventually, however, after some shrewd activity, the marquis obtained Puebla's consent also. Cerralvo does not mention in the relevant letter to the council of the Indies how he won round the aldermen of Puebla, but we know from a different instance the sort of methods that the viceroy employed in dealing with the Puebla *cabildo*. In 1631–2, when he was again obstructed by Puebla, the viceroy went to work at its most sensitive point—the labour needs of its *regidores*. Cerralvo gave a model demonstration of the political uses of bureaucratic control of the labour supply, instructing the *corregidores* of Atlixco, Tlaxcala, Cholula, and Tepeaca not only to cease assigning *repartimiento* labour to all estates belonging to the *regidores* of Puebla, but to permit no Indians whatever to go to work on their estates.[58] Puebla held out for three months, but then gave way.

A new phase in the contest between Cerralvo and Manso began in 1629, the year of the most terrible of the inundations of Mexico City. Mexico City, situated precariously on the waters of Lake Texcoco, had long suffered from floods, but neither before nor since 1629 did it ever suffer the like of the floods of that year. The catastrophe was so appalling that the news of it struck a note of terror even in the midst of the Thirty Years War in far-away Frankfurt-am-Main.[59] On 21 September the capital of New Spain was lashed by winds, rain, and the raging of Lake Texcoco which shattered the city's dikes and flood defences. The streets quickly filled with water and were to remain impassable to everything save boats and canoes for months. Thousands of flimsy abodes were swept away and hundreds of people and livestock drowned, especially in the outlying Indian quarters of the city. The friars, Jesuits, and secular clergy exerted themselves to relieve the suffering of the Indians, care for the sick, and bring food to the starving, but understandably with only limited success. Religious services were held on the roofs of the city's churches and friaries day

56*ACM* xxvi. 356–9 and xxvii. 5–20; Fernando Carrillo, in this matter as in his contribution to the debate over the *repartimiento*, consistently opposed the Creole party.

57AGI México 30, r 1: Cerralvo to council, 25 May 1629.

58*FHT*, vi. 540–1, 560, 567.

59Where a news-sheet was published in 1630 describing the catastrophe in Mexico City and claiming the destruction of 8,000 houses and 4,000 people.

and night for weeks. The Virgins of Los Remedios and Guadalupe were brought from their respective sanctuaries and placed in the cathedral where they were to remain for more than four years. Commerce and industry came to a standstill. The markets and corn exchange all but ceased to function. By December, of the 340 licensed taverns that had enlivened Mexico City before the flood, only twenty-seven were still in business. A great part of the Spanish population of the city moved out to the lake-side townships, especially Coyoacán, Tacuba, and Tacubaya, often dispossessing Indian caciques and principals of their residences in the process, or migrated to Puebla and other towns including Pachuca and San Luis Potosí.[60] And although much of this Spanish population reverted to the capital after the receding of the waters in 1634, part of it did not, so that even as late as 1654 Mexico City was still to have between a quarter and a third fewer white inhabitants than it had had before the floods in 1629.[61] During the inundation, and to a lesser extent after it, districts in the 'Spanish' city centre vacated by Spaniards and their Negroes were filled with Indians fleeing from the outskirts and Tlatelolco.[62]

The inundation of 1629, whatever else it did, did not induce the political factions to forget their differences, even for the duration of the disaster. In the very same report, of November 1629, in which he detailed the extent of the catastrophe, Archbishop Manso intensified his campaign against the viceroy.[63] Though the people were suffering from the effects of the floods, avowed the prelate, they were suffering even more from the despotic rule to which Cerralvo had subjected them. The first priority for Mexico, he asserted, was an entirely new administrative structure that both reduced the size of the viceroy's bureaucracy and reduced its powers. The whole system of *corregidores* was rife with corruption and should be abolished excepting only some 'five or six in the regional capitals who should be paid sufficient salaries and appointed by Your Majesty' (that is, in Madrid and not in Mexico City), the sufficient salaries being to obviate the necessity of corruption.[64] In the same report, Manso spoke of the evil consequences of Cerralvo's efforts to infiltrate the Mexico City council and *Audiencia* and recommended that the council of the Indies consider means by which to free those institutions from the web of bribery and

60 BND 2396. fols. 267–8; AGN Indios x, fol. 89v.
61 See pp. 30, 40 above.
62 AGN Historia 413, fol. 16; AGN Indios xii, fol. 149.
63 AGI México 3, r 4: Manso to council, 8 Nov. 1629.
64 It is interesting to compare this plan with the less drastic recommendations that Manso had put forward eighteen months before, AGI México 3, r 4: Manso to council, 26 May 1628, in which he proposed merely that Madrid should appoint more of the *corregidores*, and the viceroy fewer.

intimidation in which the viceroy had them caught. Moreover, whilst Manso was writing to Madrid in this vein, numerous lampoons and satirical sheets were circulating in the capital attacking the viceroy and his policies.[65] The Creoles were accusing Cerralvo of having neglected the flood defences of the city. Where Gelves had had the drainage channels checked and cleaned regularly, Cerralvo had allowed them to deteriorate. Where Gelves had sought and followed expert advice in his drainage projects, Cerralvo was said to have wasted 100,000 pesos on utterly unsound schemes, letting much of the money seep into the pockets of Fernando Carrillo and the Jesuits.[66] Furthermore, the viceroy was said to have remarked that if the Creoles wanted to have the flood water drained, they should drink it.

Another effect of the flood was to increase the tension between diocesan and mendicant clergy. As Archbishop Manso saw it, the migration of whites, Negroes, and mixed bloods from the capital rendered the old boundaries between the different spheres of ecclesiastical jurisdiction in Mexico obsolete. In his view, it was the duty of the secular clergy to follow where their flock led, just as the Dominicans saw it as their duty, since they administered Oaxaca, to tend the Oaxacan Indians, Mixtecs, and Zapotecs, even in Mexico City and Puebla.[67] It was a doctrine that was bound to lead to trouble and, in the viceroy's opinion,[68] was formulated for precisely that purpose. The archbishop dispatched secular priests to various lakeside towns to supervise their scattered parishioners and administer the sacraments, and the friars, especially the Dominicans, who were all in favour of the principle when it suited their interests but all against it when it did not, reacted angrily. At Coyoacán there occurred an ugly incident so injurious to the dignity of the clergy that it was said to have caused the vicereine, Doña Francisca, when she heard the news, to burst into tears.[69] A young secular priest named Esteban de Riofrío, having been told to conduct a service at Coyoacán, asked permission to do so of the Dominican Provincial who was then at the Coyoacán friary. The Provincial was understod as having given his consent. Two days later, the priest appeared in Coyoacán accompanied by two or three diocesan functionaries and a Filipino servant and proceeded to celebrate mass in

65 BND 2 362, fol. 268ᵛ; AGN Inquisición 363, leg. 38.

66 AGI México 3, r 4, exp. 166: 'Ruina y desolacion de la ciudad de Mexico por la inundacion . . .', fol. 7; Cerralvo, in sharp contrast to Gelves, was closely allied with the Jesuits, and had as his confessor none other than Father Guillermo de los Ríos; Alegre, *Historia de la Compañía* ii. 153.

67 AGN Indios 11, fols. 98ᵛ–100ᵛ; AGN Historia 413, fols. 16, 30.

68 AGI México 3, r 4, exp. 140: Cerralvo to council, 25 Aug. 1630.

69 AGN Inquisición 366, leg. 19, fol. 258; and also AGI México 3, r i: Cerralvo to council, 26 Jan. 1630.

a disused chapel crowded with Creoles, Negroes, and mestizos. Suddenly, five or six Dominican friars, clutching sticks and supported by Indians, broke into the chapel and interrupted the service shouting and insulting the young priest, according to the Inquisition records, as *un ydiota cleriguillo desvergonsado*. However, Riofrío displayed remarkable coolness and, raising his voice, continued intoning his text. At this the friars rushed at him, tore the missal from his hands, emptied the communion cup on the floor, and then informed the congregation that they were all excommunicated for the offence of having attended a priest who had no authority to celebrate mass in that place. When Riofrío persisted and took up the holy wafer, the friars flew into a terrible rage, seized the wafer, crushed it and hurled it to the floor, kicked and punched the priest and tore the vestments from him. When part of the congregation seemed about to intervene, Riofrío begged them to stand back and to disperse and this they did. At length the chapel emptied, the altar was demolished by the Indians at the bidding of the friars to prevent its being used again, and Riofrío, bruised and battered, made his way back to Mexico City.

The incident was followed by an acrimonious dispute which engaged the attention of clergy and laity alike for several weeks. Archbishop Manso excommunicated the five Dominicans and tried to have them arrested and bade his clergy denounce the friars from the pulpit. The *Audiencia* took charge of the legal aspects of the case while the Inquisition, disturbed by what had happened, undertook its own special investigation. The Jesuits, who were now in close alliance with Cerralvo and the bureaucratic party and therefore also with the mendicant orders, contributed two tracts defending the Dominican action and blaming Archbishop Manso for the scandal.[70] The *Audiencia* was sharply divided, with one faction for the viceroy and the other for the archbishop, but with the viceroy's party the stronger, it at length arrived at its decision and declared that it was indeed the archbishop who was at fault,[71] a decision which made the friars jubilant and put Manso and the secular clergy in an impotent fury.

Meanwhile, even before it received the news of the inundation of Mexico City and the bitter wrangling of the autumn of 1629, the council of the Indies in Madrid had begun to urge the king to remove Cerralvo, preferably in 1630, or by 1631 at the latest.[72] Weighing

[70] AGN Inquisición 340, leg. 13.

[71] See the *Audiencia*'s summing up, *En el pleyto que se trata entre el ordinario y sagrada religion de Sancto Domingo sobre el conocimiento del excesso que dicen cometieron ciertos religiosos de dicha orden en la villa de Cuyuacan . . .* (n.p., n.d. [Mexico, probably 1630]).

[72] AGI México 3, r 4, exp. 131: council *consulta* of 7 Sept. 1629.

against the marquis, apart from the complaints of Archbishop Manso and the Creoles, were several considerations, among them one relating to the fortress of San Juan de Ulúa at Veracruz. In 1627 Madrid had resolved, in view of the occurrences of 1624 in Veracruz, to transfer control of the garrison of San Juan from the hands of the viceroy to its own hands; however, when the garrison commander appointed by Madrid had presented himself before the viceroy, Cerralvo had ignored him and entrusted the fortress to one of his own underlings, thereby retaining his freedom to interfere discreetly in matters relating to the port, including the flow of trade. Furthermore, it had come to light that in the year 1628 there had been grave irregularities in the way the cargo of the Manila galleons had been registered and taxed, irregularities in which the viceroy was involved; and that the viceroy was also implicated in certain highly irregular arrangements for the exploitation of the salt deposits of Peñol Blanco and Santa María in the region east of Zacatecas, deposits from which came the salt used in the processing of silver ore.[73]

Furthermore, the council of the Indies soon came to the conclusion that it was necessary to remove Archbishop Manso as well. By May 1630 it seemed to Madrid that the prelate had abandoned all consideration of government and was taking his feud with the viceroy to the most extraordinary lengths;[74] he had received a royal *cédula* impressing on him the growing seriousness of the Dutch threat in the Caribbean area and asking him to co-operate closely with the viceroy so as to ensure the safe dispatch of the treasure fleet, and had interpreted this as meaning that Cerralvo was now obliged to confer with him on all matters relating to defence and shipping. When Cerralvo refused, the archbishop had turned the matter into a public controversy and appealed to the Mexico City council and the *consulado* and other bodies for their support. Cerralvo, who had now put up with two and a half years of Manso, was asking in his letters to Madrid that the archbishop be recalled to Spain, claiming that the viceregal authority in New Spain, already seriously weakened by the manoeuvres against Guadalcázar and the overthrow of Gelves, was in serious danger of collapse.[75]

Removing Cerralvo and Manso from Mexico, however, proved to be slow work. The king accepted that Cerralvo should go and appointed

---

[73] Ibid. For the relevance of salt to silver production, see Bakewell, *Silver Mining and Society*, pp. 147–9; Thomas Gage referred to Cerralvo as the 'best monopolist of salt that ever those parts knew', *Thomas Gage's Travels*, p. 77.

[74] AGI México 3, r 4, exp. 117: council *consulta* of 4 May 1630.

[75] AGI México 30, r 3: Cerralvo to council, 24 Jan. 1630, and AGI Mexico 3, r 4, exp. 140: Cerralvo to council, 25 Aug. 1630.

Don Felipe Fernández Pacheco, duque de Escalona, to succeed him, but there was uncertainty as to when the Duke would be able to take up his new post.[76] In February 1631 the council submitted a fresh memorandum to the king in which it repeated that it was essential to remove both Cerralvo and Manso as soon as possible.[77] It transpired, however, that Escalona was unable to go and the plan to remove Cerralvo had to be put off, though Manso was ordered to return to Spain in 1631.[78] But Manso simply ignored the order and from that year on, for the next three years, sent back pretext after pretext for putting off his departure[79] (there is some reason to believe, as we shall see, that one of his reasons was the opportunity he enjoyed in Mexico for making money). Cerralvo's departure was also delayed until 1635, though it is difficult to see why; Gage suggests that Cerralvo was able to bribe his way by showering Olivares and his subordinates with lavish gifts,[80] and whether or not there is any truth in this, it is clear that Cerralvo dispatched a bumper silver remittance to the crown in 1631 of 1,447,858 pesos and at least one magnificent gift consisting of six solid gold nuggets.[81]

In general, the period 1630–5 in Mexico was one of gloom and deepening depression. Mexico City remained flooded until 1634, and the effects of this, combined with the sharp recession in trans-Atlantic and local Caribbean trade in the aftermath of Matanzas[82] (a disaster which struck a heavy blow to the merchants of Mexico City as well as those of Seville and their foreign suppliers) and the stepping up of Dutch pressure on the Spanish Main, caused a severe contraction in at least some sections of the Mexican economy. Furthermore, even worse in some ways than the floods and the Dutch was the serious loss of life that resulted from the spread of disease from Mexico City in 1629 and the need to mount a massive public works programme to drain the stricken capital. The *cocoliztli* of 1629–31 ravaged the whole valley of Mexico, hitting Texcoco and Teotihuacán particularly severely,[83] and

76 AGI México 3, r 5, exp. 177, and r 4, exp. 140.
77 AGI México 3, r 4, exp. 140.
78 AGN reales cédulas originales i, fol. 128.
79 AGI México 3, r 5, exp. 215: Manso to council, 16 Sept. 1631; ibid., Manso to council, 6 March 1633, and the council *consulta* on these and three other similar letters.
80 *Thomas Gage's Travels*, p. 77.
81 AGI México 31, r i: Cerralvo to council, 20 March 1632.
82 According to Pierre Chaunu, 'les quatre ou cinq ans qui vont de Matanzas à 1634 resonnent, pour l'économie de l'Atlantique espagnol, comme des années de marasme et de défaite.' Chaunu, *Séville et l'Atlantique*, viii. 2 (1), p. 1673, and also pp. 1643, 1654, and *passim*.
83 AGN Indios x, fols. 229, 275; Gibson, *The Aztecs*, pp. 449–50.

in 1634 spread to Tlaxcala and Puebla,[84] and this, together with the sudden need for an enormous public works *repartimiento*, severely disrupted the labour system in much of the Mexican heartland.

Cerralvo, in a difficult situation, had to take drastic action.[85] Maintaining the huge ecclesiastical *repartimiento* as it was, and the *repartimiento* for the mines, he abolished the share-out for Spanish agriculture in line with the long-neglected royal instructions of 1601 and 1609,[86] and brought Indians in large numbers from as far away as Puebla, Tlaxcala, Cuernavaca, and Toluca to dig fresh channels and build dikes and sluices to control the flow of water from the various small rivers of the valley of Mexico into lakes Texcoco and Chalco. Although there is little reason to suppose that the viceroy would have abolished the agricultural *repartimiento* when he did had it not been for the inundation of the capital and need for public works, he claimed credit, in his report to Madrid, for being an obedient servant of the crown and a notable benefactor of the Indians.[87] The Creoles and the Indian workers certainly welcomed the abolition of the agricultural share-out,[88] but in view of the unfavourable circumstances and the further reduction in the labour supply, it is unlikely that it made much difference in practice. The Indian communities remained as firmly under the thumbs of the *corregidores* as ever, and anyhow the *repartimiento* was retained for the friars (which caused particular bitterness),[89] for the mines, and for public works. Certainly there is no sign of a slackening off in the tussle for Indian workers between officers and colonists in the years 1633–5.[90] If the Creoles had won a victory, it was a barely perceptible one.

Politically speaking, the last four years of Cerralvo's term were characterized by a rather sterile and uninteresting protraction of the viceroy's feud with the archbishop. Cerralvo himself saw the split as remaining constant, neither narrowing nor widening.[91] There were no more major issues. There was just a constant dissension between the administration and the secular clergy: Manso invariably failed to consult Cerralvo, as he was supposed to do on various matters

[84]ACP xviii, fol. 56; Gibson, *The Aztecs*, p. 450.

[85]*Descripcion de la Nueva España*, p. 227; *FHT* vi. 394–7, 616.

[86]Gibson, *The Aztecs*, pp. 233, 235.

[87]AGI México 31, r 2: Cerralvo to council, 25 Jan. 1633.

[88]Ibid., 'Copia de parezer de la ciudad de Mexico sobre el repartimiento de yndios', 15 Nov. 1632.

[89]ADI Palafox papers lxiii, fols. 202, 836.

[90]*FHT* vii. 4–10; one of the hacienda owners who became embroiled with Cerralvo's officers in 1633 was a *regidor* of Atlixco.

[91]AGI México 3, r 6: Cerralvo to council, 30 Aug. 1633, and AGI México 31, r 2: Cerralvo to council, 21 Mar. 1634.

concerning Church administration and preferment, and encouraged his subordinates to criticize the viceroy from the pulpit. There were also a number of minor altercations. In one incident the *corregidor* of Mexico City seized a mulatto thief, claimed by the secular clergy to be under their protection, and proceeded to hang him; whereupon a band of secular priests supported by members of the public recovered the prisoner from the very foot of the gallows and whisked him to safety in clerical quarters.

Probably the most serious question was that of ecclesiastical jurisdiction, stemming from the royal *cédula* of September 1624[92] confirming the decision of 1618 which assigned to the bishops the power to examine mendicant curates in Indian languages and morals and inspect Indian parish premises and services. Manso began his campaign to have the ruling implemented with some propaganda criticising the orders for the low quality of their parochial work and reminding king and public that he had 451 lower secular clergy in the archbishopric alone, besides dozens of students aspiring to the clerical profession, and all too few benefices for them.[93] Then, in August 1631, having prepared the ground for his offensive and presented the *Audiencia* with his *cédulas*, he summoned the Augustinian curate of the Indian quarter of San Sebastián Atzacualco in Mexico City to appear before his staff within two days. Cerralvo judged it best to go along with Manso initially, not wishing, perhaps, to disregard crown policy too openly. The friar was obliged to submit to examination, as also, during the next weeks, were a number of other mendicant curates in the Mexico City area. Then in November 1631 Manso set out on a tour of his diocese examining the friars and their work in a considerable number of Indian towns and districts, so that by February 1632 he had examined more than forty mendicant curates, finding nearly all of them unworthy of their posts. Meanwhile, Cerralvo was working to strip the archbishop of his jurisdictional gains. The regulars appealed against Manso's actions to the *Audiencia* which, predictably enough, split into two factions. The majority sided with the bureaucratic party, and judged the archbishop's tour to be unlawful. The viceroy then immediately confirmed the decision and ordered the archbishop to drop his investigations. Manso was outraged but powerless. He could

92 *Cedulario de los siglos*, pp. 296–8.
93 *El Dr Diego Guerra ... dice que los arzobispos y obispos de las Indias Occidentales pretenden que V.M. les haga merced ... para que los religiosos ... que ... exercen officio de curas ... esten subordinados immediatemente a los ordinarios en la visita y examen en ciencia y idioma ... y en defecto de cualquier de estas dos cosas los puedan remover ...* (Mexico, 1631) (UTL). Guerra was the treasurer of the diocesan council of Mexico, afterwards sent by Manso to Madrid as procurator of the bishops of Mexico.

only denounce the *Audiencia* as a tool of the viceroy. 'This dispute', he wrote to the council,[94] 'is not between crown and regulars but between crown and viceroy, with the latter controlling the *Audiencia* judges . . .' Dejectedly he predicted, correctly as it turned out, that Cerralvo would continue blocking royal policy until he, the archbishop, left Mexico, when the whole question would be quietly shelved.

Manso finally departed for Spain early in 1635, leaving Cerralvo the unchallenged master of Mexico for the last few months of his term. In Madrid, Manso received a reception nearly as cool as that which had been accorded to his predecessor Archbishop Pérez de la Serna. Like Pérez de la Serna, he was demoted from archbishop to bishop, being assigned the see of Cartagena in Murcia. The council of the Indies stood by him, however, and advised the king in 1637 that he deserved elevation to a higher post. Eventually he became archbishop of Burgos. At his death in 1655, his belongings were seized by the crown, his gold, silver, and pearls, alone being found, according to Guijo, to be worth more than 800,000 pesos.[95]

Cerralvo completed his rule much as he had begun. According to a secret report of 1634 from the customs officers of Veracruz, corruption was then more rife than ever. Cerralvo had recently dispatched one of the judges who supported him in the *Audiencia* to Veracruz, ostensibly to suppress fraud, but in fact to organize a racket in Caribbean trade in which viceroy, *Audiencia* judges, and various *corregidores* were all involved.[96] The Creoles, one may presume, were only too pleased to hear the news in July 1635 that Cerralvo's successor, the Marqués de Cadereita, had landed, and with him the new *visitador*, the judge entrusted with Cerralvo's *residencia*, Don Pedro de Quiroga y Moya. Now at last there was at least a faint chance of bringing Cerralvo and his subordinates to account.

What is one to conclude from the events of 1624—35? First and foremost, it is clear that the political battle of 1621—4 did not end with the coming of Viceroy Cerralvo, but continued uninterrupted until 1635; the battle between the parties of Gelves and Pérez de la Serna became, albeit with certain important differences, the battle between the parties of Cerralvo and Manso. Moreover, it was no coincidence that churchmen led the opposition in both cases, for the opposition to the viceroys came from the colonists only indirectly. If the Creoles were politically timid before the tumult of 1624, and determined to take no risks unless shielded by clergy and peninsular office-holders, they were more timid still after 1624 when they took fright at the prospect of

94BM Add. MS. 13, 974, fols. 111—112ᵛ: Manso to council, 1 Feb. 1632.
95Guijo, *Diario*, ii. 61.
96AGI México 4, r 6: Veracruz customs officers to council, 15 Dec. 1634.

being found responsible for the tumult, and would venture virtually nothing other than support for the secular clergy and the archbishop. And indeed the secular clergy and the archbishop were the Creoles' only plausible recourse, for with even their own city councils at least partially gagged they had no other prospect of positive leadership. And yet the opposition to the viceroys was nevertheless in some sense the work of the colonists: for the political strength of the secular clergy and the source of their appeal to the Creoles was that they were both clergy and Creole. Clergy, because only the clergy could defy the viceroy with virtual impunity and only the clergy were socially so well entrenched that they could afford to cause disturbances, and Creole, because it was precisely the Creole character of the secular clergy which appealed to the colonists and enabled them to act as spokesmen for the white population of the colony. Thus Manso backed almost every Creole demand and particularly the great Creole demand for the reduction of bureaucracy in the interests of enterprise, and was therefore with good reason, like Pérez de la Serna before him, called *padre de la patria* by the Creoles. But Manso was also a churchman, and therefore restricted as regards methods of opposition to the viceroy, ecclesiastical questions and points of ecclesiastical jurisdiction being the sphere in which he had most leverage. And so ecclesiastical politics became, in a sense, a substitute for direct confrontation over social and economic issues; the impulse to oppose was provided by the weight of Creole grievances, but the arms and armour of opposition were Church law and clerical privilege.

VIII

CADEREITA, ESCALONA, AND PALAFOX
(1635-1642)

The fifteenth viceroy of Mexico, Don Lope Diez de Armendariz, marqués de Cadereita, was the second who was technically a Creole (the first being Luis de Velasco II); but though he was born at Quito in South America, where his father, a Navarrese nobleman, was president of the *Audiencia*, he was raised and educated in Spain and was in effect a peninsular Navarrese gentleman. He was sixty years of age when he became viceroy and had spent the greater part of his career as a naval officer holding high command on the Atlantic convoys.

Cadereita's term (1635–40), though troubled in various ways, and particularly by Creole discontent, passed without any of the unseemly Church-state quarrels which had marred the terms of Gelves and Cerralvo. One reason for this was that under Cadereita the Mexican diocesan clergy were virtually leaderless.[1] Archbishop Manso had gone, and his appointed successor, Francisco Verdugo, died before leaving Spain; after Verdugo's death, the archbishopric remained vacant for several years. The bishop of Puebla, Bernardo de Quirós, an elderly Asturian churchman, who might have acted as *de facto* head of the secular clergy, as Bishop Palafox was to do in the 1640s, chose, for whatever reason, not to play that role. The consequent comparative calm of the secular clergy in Cadereita's term had the effect of precluding any official, publicized disputes; for, as we have seen, in Mexico only the clergy could oppose the viceregal authority openly. The resulting lack of printed polemics for Cadereita's years led the great nineteenth-century historian of Mexico, H. H. Bancroft, to assume that 'little of note occurred during his rule' and that under Cadereita, 'affairs progressed to the general satisfaction'.[2] This, however, appears to be a mistaken view, for as we shall see, the signs are that despite the lack of Church-state friction, affairs in fact progressed under Cadereita entirely to the general dissatisfaction.

Cadereita began his rule amid a general mood of pessimism and gloom.[3] Caribbean trade was in a state of disruption with the intensification of Dutch activity in the area in these years marked by

[1] Sosa, *El Episcopado Mexicano*, i. 181–7; Cuevas, *Historia de la Inglesia en México*, iii. 139.

[2] Bancroft, *History of Mexico*, iii. 94.

[3] AGI México 31, r 3: Cadereita to council, 11 Apr. 1636.

the sacking of the Honduran port of Trujillo in 1633 and the seizure of Curacao in the following year. Prices of Caribbean products in Mexico, especially Venezuelan and Guatemalan cacao, were soaring wildly. Trade between Mexico and Peru was prohibited completely by the royal *cédula* of November 1634, news which came as a severe blow to the merchant guild of Mexico City. To add to these misfortunes, Indians were still dying in some numbers of *cocoliztli* and supplies of mercury for the silver mines were shorter than ever. Cadereita himself had little relish for his job, being both old and in increasingly bad health; early in his term he wrote to Madrid asking to be relieved of his duties on the grounds that ill-health was preventing him from discharging his duties as promptly and efficiently as he would wish.[4]

The one fillip for the Creoles was the vigorous investigation that was now undertaken into the viceregal conduct of Cadereita's predecessor, Cerralvo, and the activities of various of his officers. Cadereita, whether through desire to court Creole opinion, or whether, as Palafox suggests,[5] out of dislike of Cerralvo, broke sharply with the previous administration, declining even to consult Cerralvo on the state of the colony, as was the usual practice at the transfer of office from one viceroy to another, or to keep up the common courtesies. Moreover, he moved close to Don Pedro de Quiroga, the *visitador* entrusted with the investigations into Cerralvo's conduct, who was known to be a friend of Archbishop Manso.[6] This of course greatly re-assured the Creoles and angered Cerralvo who had the mortification of seeing his *residencia* pursued vigorously and denunciations of his rule made without fear or hindrance. For a time it seemed that Cerralvo and Urrutia de Vergara would be successfully indicted on various counts and would suffer serious damage both to their reputations and their pockets, but in the end Cerralvo's luck held. Quiroga went down with fever while investigating fraud in Acapulco, and soon died, thereby causing Cerralvo's *residencia* to be suspended. Cadereita pressed Madrid to send a replacement as speedily as possible to continue and complete Quiroga's work,[7] but Madrid, where Cerralvo's accusations, and possibly bribes, were having a remarkable effect, sent word that there would be no replacement and that Cerralvo's *residencia* would remain suspended until Cadereita was succeeded by another viceroy. Cerralvo was given permission to return to Europe and take up his new post on the staff of the Cardinal-Infante at Brussels, news which doubtless greatly exasperated both Cadereita and the Creoles.

4 ADI Palafox papers xxxiii, fol. 181: crown to Cadereita, 24 Dec. 1638.
5 ADI Palafox papers lxxviii, fols. 75–6.
6 AGI México 32, r 4: Mexico City council to council, 2 May 1636.
7 ADI Palafox papers xx, fol. 21; ibid. xxii, exp. 2.

Yet Cadereita, despite his dislike of Cerralvo and corrupt govern-ment, his liking for Quiroga, a run of good harvests, and his success in stabilizing prices in central Mexico and Mexico City,[8] failed in the long run to avoid trouble with the colonists. One must not be deceived, as arguably the Chaunus were,[9] by the temporary rally in Mexican Atlantic commerce in the years 1635–8, into thinking that Cadereita's term was a period of some economic improvement; probably the short-lived Atlantic advance was no more than a reaction, a change in the pattern of investment due to the closing-down of the Mexico-Peru trade during these years, a closing-down which Cadereita and Quiroga had to a large extent themselves effected. Furthermore, it is clear from the position at Zacatecas[10] and Durango that the recession in Mexican silver mining was now becoming more marked. 'Just to think what is being lost in this viceroyalty', wrote Cadereita to Madrid in 1638, 'pains me, and all the more so when I consider that the Almighty blessed this land with so many silver mines. All could be saved if we had more mercury and more labour, and it is worth pondering that my predecessors always had these resources in abundance while I am so sorely starved of them that returns from Guadiana (Durango), Zacatecas, and Guadalajara, are down this year, on the average in past years, by more than two-fifths.'[11] But worst of all was the political task before him. It was a task which was next to impossible. For he had to try to reconcile Creole interests with the interests of the crown, at a moment when the crown was desperate for funds with which to stave off disaster in Europe and the Creoles were no less desperate to stave off economic disaster at home. If Cadereita was to put the necessity of the monarchy first, which it was his duty to do and which he did, then the interests of the Creoles had to be sacrificed to that greater necessity and the Creoles were bound to turn against him. And not only the Creoles. Some officers of the crown could be expected to join the opposition, especially those of the sort that had opposed Gelves. For the whole political situation of the later 1630s was reminiscent of the early 1620s, always bearing in mind that the diocesan clergy were now not involved and that Cadereita was much more selective in his targets than Gelves had been.

The year 1635, the year of Cadereita's arrival in Mexico, was also the year of the entry of France into the Thirty Years War in Germany and the beginning of the climax of the great struggle between Spain and France which had been brewing in Europe for three decades and more.

8 AGI México 35, r 2: Cadereita to council, 6 Dec. 1641; *ACM* xxxi. 180.
9 Chaunu, *Séville et l'Atlantique*, viii–ii–i, pp. 1733, 1744–5.
10 Bakewell, *Silver Mining and Society*, pp. 164, 242.
11 AGI México 34, fols. 81–2: Cadereita to council (Hacienda), 12 July 1638.

The climax was to end after five years of bitter conflict in Spain's *annus terribilis*, the year of the revolts of Catalonia and Portugal and the consequent crippling of Spanish power. But during the five years of this climax, years that corresponded exactly to those of Viceroy Cadereita's term in Mexico, Spanish armies were engaged in Flanders, France, Germany, Switzerland, Italy, and the Pyrenees, and the whole edifice of Spain's economy and administration was creaking ominously under the strain. But while Spain itself bore the brunt of the burden, other parts of the monarchy, including Mexico, were heavily involved too. New Spain, however little she could afford to pay more, was confronted with demands that she could not evade.

Among Cadereita's first moves in the fiscal sphere was an attack on French capital, in accordance with instructions that he had brought with him from Madrid. The viceroy's officers seized funds in the hands of Frenchmen in Mexico, and, more important, in the hands of brokers holding money belonging to French merchants in Seville and Cadiz. The operation was clumsily handled, allowing time for much of the cash to be concealed,[12] but some 116,000 pesos were confiscated in Mexico City and a further 47,000 in Veracruz.[13] Of this wealth, 31,000 pesos belonged to one Pedro de la Farxa, described as a French merchant of Seville, and 20,000 to François de Sandier of the same city. This stroke was accompanied by a general tightening up of trade controls and customs machinery in Mexico and a clamp down on the contrabandists. Quiroga, during his spell in Acapulco, appears to have confiscated large amounts of unregistered silk and other merchandise,[14] with the approval of the viceroy. In Puebla, the viceroy confiscated at least one hefty consignment of unregistered cloth despite an appeal from the Puebla city council that he be lenient with the city in view of its present difficulties.[15] The proceeds from all this activity were considerable. Cadereita informed the council of the Indies in July 1637 that the eastbound flota of that year was carrying 1,230,000 pesos of silver for the crown which he claimed was more than 500,000 pesos more than the average remittance of previous years.[16]

These blows to the Mexican business community were followed by word that Mexico was to be subjected to a new burden of tax to provide money for the projected Armada of Barlovento.[17] This battle squadron, planned to consist of twelve heavily armed men-of-war and

[12] AGI México 31, r 3: Cadereita to council (Franceses), 17 Apr. 1636.
[13] Ibid.; see the list of sums confiscated, fol. 11v.
[14] AGI México 33, fol. 194. Cadereita to council, 22 July 1637.
[15] ADA Cadereita papers 7b–cn–3: Puebla *cabildo* to Cadereita, 29 Aug. 1637.
[16] AGI México 33, fol. 185: Cadereita to council, 22 July 1637.
[17] Parry, *The Spanish Seaborne Empire*, pp. 262–4.

two or three lighter support craft, was Madrid's answer to the long-standing Dutch challenge on the Spanish Main and the newer French challenge. The cost of the Armada was to be borne jointly by all the Spanish colonies of the Caribbean and Gulf of Mexico, but owing to the small resources of most of these colonies the principal burden, inevitably, had been assigned to New Spain.

Cadereita knew that the task before him would be difficult. To finance the building and maintenance of the Armada, funds in the order of 500,000 pesos per annum would be needed and this sum had to be asked of a Creole population already weighed down by misfortune and muttering with discontent. Aware that the Creoles would demand more than a few concessions as the price for their consent, Cadereita prepared his approach carefully. Emulating the tactics that Cerralvo had adopted over the Union of Arms, he laid Madrid's scheme before the Mexico City council first, encouraging that body to pose as spokesman and guardian of all Mexico and hinting that the capital would secure the lion's share of the commercial and manufacturing business that would accompany the assemblying of the Armada. The viceroy ignored Puebla, much to the indignation of that city,[18] for a whole year, despite the fact that Puebla traditionally had been far more closely connected with the maintenance of fleets than Mexico City.

Mexico City, like Puebla in the following year, accepted at once that the Armada was necessary both to the Spanish monarchy and to Mexico; the capital also agreed that it should pay 200,000 pesos annually toward the upkeep of the force. At the same time, however, the *cabildo* warned that the money could not be found unless the viceroy acted to reflate the economy, and suggested that the contribution that New Spain was to make deserved recognition in the form of a favourable response to various long-standing Creole desires. Indeed the city, acting in consultation with the *consulado*, drew up a list of demands and submitted them to the viceroy;[19] shortly afterwards, the most important of these demands also appeared in print.[20] Cadereita, wishing to place himself in as accommodating a light as possible, thereupon appointed a special committee of *Audiencia* justices, churchmen, and treasury officials to meet the city, consider its demands, and consider what could be done.

[18] ACP xviii, fol. 252.

[19] *ACM* xxx. 212: memorandum of 21 July 1636; and *ACM* xxxi. 70.

[20] *Consulta de la Ciudad de Mexico al excellentissimo senor, Virrey, marques de Cadereyta sobre que se abra la contratacion del Piru, se comersie libremente con este reyno por las causas expressas* (Mexico, 1636); see also the *Consulta de la ciudad de Mexico al excellentissimo senor Virrey Marques de Cadereyta sobre quatro puntos que miran a la conservacion deste reyno* (Mexico, 1636).

The demands were certainly sweeping. The city council wanted its territorial jurisdiction extended to a radius of five leagues so as to put the city on a par with several of the chief cities of Castile. Such an adjustment would have meant a considerable reduction of the area under the direct control of the viceroy's officers in the valley of Mexico, cutting back several *corregimientos* quite drastically and doing away with that of Tacuba altogether; at the same time it would have given the city a much greater degree of control over the several sizeable Indian communities settled around the capital. Another demand was that the provisions for the Armada of Barlovento be supplied by Mexico City and that the officers, or at least a high proportion of them, be Creoles. Another was that the officers of the infantry detachments sent almost annually to the Philippines be Creoles. Another asked that the remaining *encomiendas* in New Spain be granted and guaranteed to their holders in perpetuity. Another requested that there be a reduction in both the scale and frequency of public celebrations and religious fiestas, particularly those held at the expense of the city. Another asked that a cacao exchange be established in Mexico City in order to stabilize the market and reduce the scope for racketeering in that basic commodity.

This was a good deal, but it was by no means all. The city council also wanted to see the terms of office of the *corregidores* reduced and fixed in future at a maximum of two years, and the system of *residencias* for *corregidores* thoroughly overhauled. In addition, it asked that the *consulado* be abolished, a most interesting demand aimed presumably at achieving more freedom for the merchant body, and that the number of Inquisition familiars in Mexico be increased. Further, the *cabildo* desired that half the seats on the *Audiencias* of Mexico, Guadalajara, Guatemala, and Manila, be filled from that time on by Creole justices, or rather Mexican Creole justices. There were also one or two prestige items. The city wished to be recognized as the third secular authority of New Spain, after the viceroy and *Audiencia*, and to be graced with the title of, and addressed by the viceroys as, the *señoría*.

Though principally concerned with secular matters, the city council did not neglect Church affairs. It complained that the number of regular clergy in Mexico was excessive, since most of the Indians had perished leaving the friars little to do, and asked that the mendicant establishment be reduced. Especially, the council wanted the crown to cease financing the passage of mendicant missions from Castile to Mexico. In addition, the *cabildo* wished to see the restrictive quotas placed by most of the mendicant provinces in New Spain on intake of Creoles removed and the passage of peninsular Spanish friars to the

Philippines stopped, this last so as to give Mexican Creole friars the ascendancy in the Far Eastern missions as well as in Mexico. Further, the *cabildo* expressed the opinion that in New Spain there were too many nuns. It requested that no more convents be built, and also, as it deemed Mexican convent life at that time insufficiently strict, that more discipline be imposed. Finally, the city council wanted the economic expansion of the religious orders in Mexico halted and the appetite of the regulars, and particularly of the Jesuits, for haciendas curbed.

The most urgent appeal of all made by Mexico City, however, we have kept for last. It related, as one would expect, to the most pressing economic issue of the day in the Indies—Madrid's prohibition, or rather attempted prohibition, of all trade between Mexico and Peru. Mexico City wanted the Mexico-Peru run to be legalized again and to be placed on a more secure footing in law than it had been in the past, and for Mexican merchants to be permitted to ship more silver each year to Manila with which to purchase silk from the Chinese. The council did its best to convince Madrid that the argument that Pacific trade damaged Castilian manufactures and Andalusian exports was false and defective. The *consulado* of Seville was cited as the villain of the piece and taken to task for filling the king's ears with nonsense concerning the state of Spanish commerce. Mexico City argued that there had been no real decline in Atlantic trade, only a change in its character. The number of ships sailing in the flotas of the 1630s, it agreed, was considerably less than the number that had sailed in most years before 1620, but this, it held, was because the vessels on the Spain-Mexico run had increased in size and, more importantly, because there had been a shift of emphasis from bulky but comparatively unprofitable cargoes such as wine, oil, soap, and hardware, to less bulky but more valuable wares, principally high-quality fabrics. Moreover, asserted the *cabildo*, it was impossible that Mexican enterprise could injure the Spanish, for the two sets of merchants dealt in quite distinct commodities; in textiles, for example, Seville plied Peru with European silks, velvets, linens, Rouen cloth, and Castilian woollens, while Mexico City traded in Chinese silks, damasks, and brocades, and grograms and cottons for the poor, all fabrics beyond the scope of Sevillean merchants. The argument, if not particularly convincing, was made vigorously. The opening of the Peru trade was seen as the panacea for all Mexico's ills. Mexico City entrepreneurs, armed with capital once again, would somehow achieve the revival of the mines of Zacatecas and San Luis, and of the *obrajes* of Puebla; and thus would work be provided for the idle and vagabondage cease. But if the Peru trade was not opened up, the consequences would be disastrous. The colony would remain in the grip of economic depression and would be incapable of supporting the Armada of Barlovento or helping the Monarchy in any significant way whatever.

The demands of the Puebla city council, drawn up in the summer of 1637,[21] were broadly similar to those of Mexico City. There was the same insistence on the pre-eminent importance of the Peru trade and of making Peruvian silver accessible to Mexican businessmen, the same desire to see more offices, military and judicial, assigned to Mexican Creoles, the same request that the territorial jurisdiction of the city be extended. The only significant disagreement between the two cities was the conflict in their views regarding each other. Puebla declared that she would not be pushed into the background by Mexico City and emphatically rejected Mexico City's claim to speak for all the Creoles of New Spain.

Cadereita, though apparently not unsympathetic to the Creole position, conceded little. The great question of Pacific trade was entirely out of his hands and for Madrid alone to decide, though he did agree to raise the issue with Madrid.[22] Cadereita, together with his committee and his confessor, Fray Juan de Grijalva, came out strongly, though hardly unexpectedly, against the proposal to extend the territorial jurisdiction of Mexico City. For the rest, the committee offered only vague promises, and mainly promises on relatively marginal questions. Nothing was conceded regarding the *corregidores*. Still, the effort that Mexico City had put in did achieve something. If the setting up of a cacao exchange in 1638 counted for little, the crown was soon to prohibit further ecclesiastical building in Mexico and further acquisition of land by the religious orders. Still more important, the crown decided to have the Pacific trade question and every other major issue thoroughly investigated by the visitor-general to be sent out at the end of Cadereita's term. It is hard to say exactly how much bearing the Creole demands of 1636–7 had on the decision to send Juan de Palafox to Mexico in 1640, but in view of Palafox's special commission to examine Pacific trade and the sweeping powers with which he was provided, it seems improbable that they did not have at least some.

In December 1636, unable to refuse to contribute to the war, Mexico City agreed to pay 200,000 pesos annually toward the financing of the Armada of Barlovento, and soon the other cities of New Spain followed suit, the contribution of the ailing Zacatecas being pegged at 10,000

21 ACP xviii, fols. 256–62.

22 AGI México 31, r 3: 'Lo proveido a las condiciones y capitulaciones de esta ciudad ...' fol. 1; AGI México 34, fols. 235–7: Cadereita to council, 12 July 1638.

pesos. The money was to be raised by increasing the tax on sales. Never had the outlook for Mexican business been gloomier. To darken the picture still further, the Dutch West India Company now stepped up its activity in the Caribbean and Gulf of Mexico and in the three months of the spring of 1637 seized fourteen merchantmen in the area. Cadereita, though he had his money, was meeting with considerable difficulty in his work of assembling the Armada. The work proceeded excruciatingly slowly. By the summer of 1639, the galleons under construction at Havana and Campeche were still uncompleted, as also were the hundred guns ordered from the foundries of Manila. A large consignment of cash sent by Cadereita to Spain for the purchase of additional ships had been appropriated by Olivares and put to a different use.

Meanwhile Cadereita's regime, with its zeal for collecting tax and willingness to confiscate unregistered merchandise, was facing increasing opposition. The Creole *cabildos* and *consulado* were seething with discontent, and though they dared take no drastic step, they quietly supported the faction in the *Audiencia* that was at odds with the viceroy, particularly Andres Gómez de Mora, the forceful fiscal of the *Audiencia*, a man whom Cadereita came to regard as a major nuisance.[23] The situation became worse after Antonio Urrutia de Vergara broke gaol in the summer of 1637 and sought refuge in the Dominican priory, the same as had once housed Melchor de Varaez. The parallel was somewhat ominous, for Urrutia de Vergara's seeking of sanctuary, it appears, heralded an alliance between Creoles and disaffected officers which was similar to that which had brought down the marqués de Gelves.

By December 1638, Madrid had decided that Cadereita should soon return to Spain, in accordance with his own wishes. It seems clear that the marquis's ill-health was the chief reason for this,[24] though at the same time Madrid was beginning to feel that some basic changes were needed in New Spain. Although the council of the Indies can have been neither surprised nor impressed by the evidence of Creole discontent, since Castile itself at that time was groaning under a much greater burden of misfortune, it was rather worried by the conflicting reports of Cadereita, on the one hand, and of Cerralvo, who was then in Madrid, on the other, regarding the role of Antonio Urrutia de Vergara and a whole collection of lesser persons associated with him and with the former viceroy.[25] According to the one side, Urrutia de Vergara

23 AGI México 34, fols. 203–8: Cadereita to council, 12 June 1638.
24 ADI Palafox papers xliii, fol. 181: crown to Cadereita, 24 Dec. 1638.
25 For Madrid's concern and confusion over Urrutia de Vergara, see ibid., fol. 199: crown to Cadereita, 24 Dec. 1638 and fol. 188: crown to Cadereita, 3 Oct.

was an evil genius, according to the other, an innocent victim. Whatever else was unclear, the Council could see that the feuding between the two viceregal factions in Mexico was a political danger and had to be stopped. In October 1639 Cadereita was instructed to cease all action against Urrutia de Vergara and to leave the whole business and other related matters for the visitor-general to sort out.

During the last year and a half of Cadereita's term, the opposition to his rule appears to have grown appreciably. Urrutia de Vergara, Gómez de Mora, Fernando Carrillo, and their circle did the actual work of harassing the viceroy, by all kinds of small but significant manoeuvres behind the scenes, while taking care not to soil their hands or take any real risks. The conde de Santiago Calimaya, Juan de Cervantes Casaus, the Mexico City council, and the rest of the Creole leadership gave them support,[26] as also did three *Audiencia* justices, Mathías de Peralta, Francisco de Rojas, and Agustín de Villavicencio. Cadereita, clearly, was discomfited by the harassment he received and referred more than once in his letters to Madrid to his fear that there might occur 'a popular commotion'.[27] By the time the marquis's term reached its end, abuse was being lavished on his name from virtually every quarter.

In June 1640 the flota from Spain brought to Mexico two men, one the viceroy, the other the visitor-general, whose prominence in Spain, in one case by reason of birth, in the other by virtue of merit, demonstrates the importance now attached by Madrid to the task of putting its Mexican house in order. To revive the viceregal authority, now wilting somewhat following the treatment received by Guadalcázar and Gelves and the feuds which had embroiled Cerralvo and Cadereita, Madrid had chosen as sixteenth viceroy a grandee of Spain, the first ever to rule Mexico. He was Don Diego López Pacheco y Bobadilla, marqués de Villena, duque de Escalona, a relative of the Duke of Braganza, the man who was to become, in December 1640, the rebel

1639; for the concern that Urrutia de Vergara was causing Cadereita and his officers, see AGI México 35, r 1: Cadereita to council, 15 Mar. 1639 and Juan de Miranda to council, 25 Feb. 1639.

26 Cadereita later accused the Creoles of base and deceitful opposition, owing to the abrupt way in which they came out against him openly as soon as he had stepped down from office and even before his *residencia* had begun; see AGI México 35, r 2: Cadereita to council, 16 Sept. 1640; see also the legal defence of Cadereita at his *residencia*, ADI Palafox papers xxii: 'Por parte de el señor Marques de Cadereita . . .', esp. exp. 11.

27 ADI Palafox papers xx, fols. 21–2. Cadereita to conde de Castrillo, 27 Sept. 1638; AGI México 35, r 1: Cadereita to council, 28 Feb. 1639.

King João IV of Portugal.[28] The visitor-general, Juan de Palafox y Mendoza, was a protégé of Olivares, one of the most brilliant men of his generation, and author of several religious and political writings which had made some impression in Spain.

Palafox is probably the most interesting, and arguably the most important, single figure in seventeenth-century Mexican history. He was the illegitimate son of an Aragonese marquis by a young widowed noblewoman of Zaragoza.[29] Raised by his father who provided him with the best education then available in Spain, he spent several years at the universities of Salamanca and Alcalá de Henares. In 1626, at the age of twenty-six, he sat with the Aragonese nobility at the famous *cortes* of Monzón, assembled by Philip IV and Olivares to debate the Union of Arms and revise Aragon's contribution to the resources of the crown. In the ensuing debates, Palafox, unlike most of the Aragonese aristocracy, displayed a marked zeal for the interests of the monarchy and an ardour for Olivares's schemes which attracted the attention of the king's favourite and launched him on his career. His obsession with loyalty, an obsession related quite possibly to his illegitimacy, which was a serious stain in the Spain of his day, and his ardour for great designs were to remain with him for the rest of his life.

Palafox was exactly the kind of dependent valued by Olivares: lacking a secure place in society, burdened by the circumstances of his birth, he was entirely dependent on royal favour for his advancement and correspondingly diligent in the king's service and that of his chief minister. His intelligence and assiduousness were rewarded with rapid advancement in both the secular and clerical bureaucracies, and in 1629 he was appointed to the clerical staff of the Infanta Maria who was then preparing for her journey to Vienna for her marriage to her cousin, the Archduke Ferdinand. Palafox accompanied the entourage of the Infanta on its progress through Italy to Vienna and, when he had discharged his duties in the Austrian capital, set out on a European tour through Bohemia, Germany, Flanders, and France, returning to Madrid in 1631.[30] During the next eight years he served on the councils of Aragon and the Indies, and in 1637 was one of the junta of judges that acquitted Pedro de Vergara Gabiria finally of the charges of treason made against him by Gelves and Carrillo.[31] He also found time to write various tracts on the religious and political state and prospects of Spain, and in 1638 published his long account of the Fuenterrabía campaign

---

[28] Rubio Mañé, *Introducción al estudio de los virreyes*, i. 246.

[29] Genaro García, *Don Juan de Palafox* (Mexico, 1918), p. 13.

[30] BND 3048, fol. 34^v; it is possible that Palafox also visited Sweden, see García, op. cit., p. 51.

[31] BM Add. MS. 13, 975, fol. 276.

and the state of the Franco-Spanish war which was then in its third year. In 1639, at the age of only thirty-nine, he was appointed visitor-general of New Spain and, at the same time, preferred to the bishopric of Puebla de los Angeles.

The social and political ideas of Palafox relate closely to the historical context of the Spain of his day, to the last phase of Spanish greatness; but they also relate, in a significant way, to the general seventeenth-century European reaction to courtly extravagance, corruption, and waste. Palafox was in fact a leading proponent of that social and political puritanism which is so significant a feature of the seventeenth century, and his thought bears numerous points of resemblance to that of such other political churchmen of the epoch as Archbishop Laud, and later Bishop Bossuet. His outlook, austerely religious and in some respects mystical, was nevertheless nothing if not worldly and intimately bound up with government and war. In his mind, religion and politics, morality and administration were all closely linked. In one sense his political goal was like that of Machiavelli: he wished above all to maximize the effectiveness of the state, and its military and administrative appurtenances, and to enable the state to defeat its enemies: but he believed, unlike Machiavelli, that the key to efficacy was religion. Indeed, he saw his task as a God-given duty to refute Machiavelli (and Bodin)[32] who, as it appeared to him, had wickedly insinuated, even affirmed, that Christianity and Christian doctrine were irrelevant, even harmful, to successful political and military action. Palafox aspired, turning Machiavellianism on its head, to show that in reality Christian doctrine and morality were nothing less than the essential, indispensable basis of all effective action. Power he defined as the will of God in the world. Only those who served Him could ultimately succeed. From this it followed, in Palafox's view, that the only great state was the Spanish monarchy, for Spanish monarchy was in his day the pillar of the Catholic Church and the Church's intentions for society. From this it followed in turn that the chief goal of modern political thought was to show how to arrest the decline of Spain and restore the Spanish ascendancy in Europe and the world at large. The means for the achievement of this goal, prescribed by political theory according to Palafox, was the suppression of vice, the godly ordering of government and administration, and the proper adjustment of the clergy to society. Neglect, complacency, and failure to reform, he admonished his countrymen, were the formula for disaster; if Spain was not lifted from its moral decadence, the Spaniards would soon follow in the wake of the ancient Persians and Romans.

---

[32] Juan de Palafox, *Historia real sagrada, luz de príncipes y subditos* (written in Puebla, 1641–2) in Palafox *Obras* (12 vols., Madrid, 1762), i. 293.

'The triumph of licence in a state', he wrote,[33] 'not only destroys the spiritual well-being of that realm, but undermines its worldly effectiveness.' Again and again he returned to this theme. No sooner does a state decline into vice, than 'prowess itself withers and so does the nation's will'. A kingdom without virtue, and by virtue he meant Christian virtue, 'is like a body without blood'.[34] Palafox's view of wealth followed from his general approach.[35] Riches were necessary, nay essential, not for purposes of luxury—that would be fatal—but as the means with which to confront and confound the heretic and the rebel. Money was needed on the one hand to buy armaments, and on the other, and no less important, to provide the churches, seminaries, schools, orphanages, hospitals, libraries, and houses of correction for former prostitutes, which he believed to be the material foundation of the godly society. The resources of a nation had to be properly managed lest they be misused, managed by upright and godly officials. Hence the overwhelming need in any state for honest officers and the need for vigilance and checks to ensure that they remained honest. Palafox, at the crux of his political philosophy, might have paraphrased Machiavelli's 'the sinews of war are not gold but valiant soldiers' with 'the sinews of war are not gold but upright and meticulous administrators'.

It might seem that Palafox was heading for trouble bringing notions such as these to New Spain. Mexico had no love for puritans, as Gelves had discovered to his cost. But Palafox was not Gelves. His puritanism was to work in a quite different way. The bishop did not remain aloof from the Creoles as the marquis had done; rather, he did his utmost to enter into and influence their lives. Moreover, as we shall see, on most political and social issues he was, though often not for the same reasons, in agreement with the Creoles. Altogether, far from being resented, Palafox became the most genuinely popular leader of the Creoles not only of his own time, but of the whole seventeenth century; and this is precisely what he had wished for: no word was used more ardently or frequently by Palafox than the word *amor*; all his life long he had wished fervently to cherish and be cherished, and in this, as we shall see, he succeeded.

One of the major factors which helped Palafox was his view of the Church. The bishop had a distinctive approach to ecclesiastical questions deriving from his belief in the organic wholeness—Palafox

---

[33] Juan de Palafox, *Diversos dictamenes espirituales, morales, y políticos*, no. xli in *Obras*, x.

[34] Ibid., no. clv.

[35] Juan de Palafox, *Diálogo político del estado de Alemania, y comparación de España con las demas naciones*, in *Obras*, x. 80–2.

constantly uses the metaphor of the body when describing society—of the Catholic state. He envisaged the Church as the head of the nation, inseparable from it, vital to it, its guiding force. For this reason he believed that that section of the clergy which came nearest to the laity, the secular clergy, was much more important than the regular clergy. For Palafox, the diocesan clergy were the essential part of the priesthood; the rest of the clergy he considered marginal. The secular clergy alone shared the life of the people, the secular clergy alone could show the people the godly way. It was imperative, therefore, that the seculars should be well schooled, of immaculate morals, and devoted to prodding the laity to its duty. And nowhere more so, he added, than in the Indies where the white population was deficient in discipline and obedience compared with that of Europe, since most of it had migrated to America in search of riches and self-advancement, thereby forsaking worthier objects.[36] At the head of the secular clergy, and therefore with respect to discipline, obedience, morals, and the proper ordering of society at the head of the laity also, were the bishops. Palafox's lofty conception of the episcopal office was central to his political thought.[37] The bishops, he believed, were, or rather should be, the guardians of society upholding the platform, the firm basis, on which the state and the secular administration could function effectively and successfully. He was highly critical of the actual bishops of his day, particularly of their failure to take their dioceses properly in hand. He deplored careerism among the bishops and asserted that bishops should stick to their dioceses as closely and for as long as possible, resisting transfer and promotion; for in his view movement from bishopric to bishopric broke the delicate ties between bishops and their congregations, left many bishoprics vacant for lengthy periods, which he regarded as an appalling irregularity, and made impossible that intimate, emotional relationship between bishop and community which he regarded as absolutely essential and desirable. 'The constant rule', he declared, 'is that a bishop should live and die in his first diocese just as a husband must with his lawful wife, and in the same way as it is adultery when a husband leaves his wife and lives with another woman, so it is spiritual adultery when a bishop leaves his first see for another, except when he is transferred by the hand of God, that is by the Pope.'[38]

36 Juan de Palafox, *Carta pastoral a la venerable congregacion de San Pedro de la ciudad de los Angeles y a los reverendos sacerdotes de todo el obispado* (Mexico, 1640), fols. 16–18.

37 Juan de Palafox, *Respuesta y discurso sobre las frecuentes translaciones que se hacen de los señores obispos de unas a otras iglesias*, in *Obras*, iii. 1 i, pp. 416–69.

38 Ibid., p. 419.

Palafox frequently referred in his writings to the diocese of Puebla as his spiritual spouse and habitually called the diocese his 'Rachel'.

Plainly such principles as these were likely to smooth Palafox's path, enabling him, while sticking to his ideals, to play the bishops' traditional part in Mexican politics, to put himself at the head of the secular clergy and champion the popular cause. They also make it possible to see how it was that Palafox, fearful of discord though he was, was so ready to censure the regular orders in Mexico, for they, far from avoiding property, wealth, and influence—which was Palafox's ideal for mendicants and Jesuits alike—were richer, and in many areas more powerful, than the diocesan clergy itself, a circumstance, Palafox admonished Madrid, which was injurious to Church and laity alike.[39] Palafox's views on Mexican politics were, to a considerable extent, formed even before he left Spain. He had been through the issues often enough in the council of the Indies, had several times revealed his sympathy for Archbishops Serna and Manso, and had, as we have seen, been one of the junta that had acquitted Pedro de Vergara Gabiria.

But to return to the year 1640. Never did New Spain put on a more lavish display than when it greeted its first grandee-viceroy, the duque de Escalona, in July of that year. The dances performed by the mulatta girls were, it is said, particularly splendid.[40] The duke's upturned mustachios, which to the modern eye lend his countenance a rather ludicrous look, were deemed magnificent by the admiring masses that gathered to see him. 'With such a fine face,' declared the people, according to Gutiérrez de Medina, 'you will certainly accomplish fine things.' The duke entered Mexico City alone, for Palafox had remained behind in Puebla, preferring to spend his first months in Mexico becoming acquainted with his diocese rather than beginning straight away with his *visita* in the capital. During these first months the new viceroy concerned himself chiefly with Cadereita or rather with the bad odour in which Cadereita's term had ended. Escalona informed Madrid that his predecessor had intimidated and imprisoned so many prominent persons that the colony was seriously affected by anxiety and unrest.[41] When Cadereita had left the viceregal palace, as he himself had affirmed, he had met with a hail of insults and other manifestations of dissatisfaction. However, the situation offered Escalona an excellent opportunity to get off to a good start with the Creoles, and he took it, releasing those whom Cadereita had

[39]Juan de Palafox, *Cartas reservadas al rey*, *BAGN*, ser. i, ii. 506–20.
[40]Nicolás de Torres, *Festin hecho por las morenas criollas de la muy noble y muy leal ciudad de Mexico al recebimiento del exmo. senor marques de Villena* (Mexico, 1640) (HSA).
[41]AGI México 35, r 1: Escalona to council (gov.), 25 Nov. 1640.

incarcerated on political and some other grounds, and inviting those whom Cadereita had forced to flee from the capital to return. Of course, by such action the duke incurred the enmity of Cadereita, but this mattered little since the Duke was already on bad terms with him. Cadereita, violating accepted convention, had continued to fill administrative vacancies, promoting dependents of his own, after learning that Escalona was on his way and even after the Duke's landing at Veracruz. One of the new viceroy's first actions therefore, was to cancel Cadereita's latest appointments and replace the dismissed Cadereita men with his own.

Escalona's other chief concern in this period was the Armada of Barlovento. He seems to have achieved a marked speeding-up in the assembling of the force.[42] On learning that insufficient ships were under construction in the shipyards of Campeche and Havana, he bought, and in some cases hired, a number of additional vessels. He placated the gunpowder manufacturers who had been at loggerheads with Cadereita and persuaded them to resume work. The furnishing of supplies and munitions he placed in the capable hands of the Portuguese-Jewish merchant Sebastian Váez de Acevedo. A batch of heavy guns were moved from Acapulco to Veracruz and orders for additional ordnance were placed in Spain and with the foundries of Puebla and Manila.

Palafox finally arrived in Mexico City on 12 October. At once he commenced work on the *visita*, preparing offices and moving into them the judicial legacy of his predecessor, Quiroga—four carriage-loads of papers. He appointed secretaries, the chief of whom was the Portuguese *converso* Melchor Juárez, and began collecting information from every source relating to the rule of Viceroys Cerralvo and Cadereita and the conduct of their associates, and relating to the *Audiencia, corregidores*, taxation methods, and the Peru trade. Also, having prepared the ground, he started to hold trials beginning with those of Urrutia de Vergara and Gómez de Mora. Of these, the former was found guilty of sedition, fined the remarkably small amount of 2,000 ducats, and banished from New Spain, while the latter was acquitted.[43] These trials were followed by dozens of others. Among those found guilty of corruption and abuse of power were the *corregidores* of Texcoco and Tepeaca; both were heavily fined. In all, in a little more than a year,

---

[42] AGI México 35, r 1: Escalona to council (gue), 25 Nov. 1640; see also the *Relacion de todo lo sucedido en estas provincias de la Nueva España desde la formacion de la Armada real de Barlovento, despacho de Flota, y sucesso della, hasta la salida deste primer aviso del año de 1642* (Mexico, 1642); the flagship, the *Santissimo Sacramento*, had twenty-six heavy guns.

[43] ADI Palafox papers li, fol. 110: Palafox to council, 24 June 1641.

Palafox dispatched 100 cases.[44] Mexico had not witnessed such a burst of judicial activity since the hectic days of Gelves.

The conclusions reached by Palafox at this early stage of his investigations were generally such as to please the Creoles. He was highly critical of the judicial system in the colony and considered the administration thoroughly defective. 'In the higher tribunals', he reported to Madrid, 'some semblance of justice is upheld, but in [the courts of] the *corregidores,* little or none.'[45] The sway of the *corregidores* in most of the country, he averred, was so oppressive that the colonists were virtually forced to concentrate in just one or two areas where they were less obstructed by bureaucracy, leaving most of Mexico short of Spaniards. The viceroys turned a blind eye to the violence and rapacity of their officers, and neglected the interests of Spaniards and Indians alike, because their power depended on the *corregidores.* Altogether, there was not the slightest doubt, Palafox concluded, that the viceroyalty was sorely in need of thoroughgoing reform.

Gradually, as Palafox and his staff proceeded with their work, they were drawn into conflict with the viceroy.[46] Both visitor-general and viceroy were reluctant to become involved in a political imbroglio. Escalona was well aware that he had nothing to gain by antagonizing so formidable a personage as Palafox while, for his part, the bishop claims to have deliberately slowed down his investigations and avoided making certain arrests in the hope of preventing a serious split. But the inexorable logic of the situation forced both their hands. Escalona had to protect his officers if his power was to remain intact; Palafox had to press for reform if he was to remain consistent with his general beliefs and his conclusions regarding Mexico.

The friction between Escalona and Palafox, having begun in the course of Palafox's pursuit of certain *corregidores,* intensified when Palafox became embroiled with the friars over the Indian parishes of his own diocese of Puebla. It was of course quite unacceptable to Palafox that the greater part of his diocese should be under the ecclesiastical guardianship of the mendicants. His plans for a reformed secular priesthood, a priesthood that would be the guide and conscience of the community of the diocese, were merely words on paper until the seculars were in practice the secular clergy and until the seculars had adequate support and livings. There were in 1640 over 600 secular

[44] ADI Palafox papers xlix, fols. 30–40: 'Resumen de las sentencias pronunciadas por el excelentisimo señor Don Juan de Palafox . . .'
[45] ADI Palafox papers lxxx, fols. 35–8: Palafox to council, 10 July 1641.
[46] ADI Palafox papers xlix, fols. 198–9: 'Auto secreto sobre los impedimientos que puso a la vissita el señor marques de Villena' (14 Feb. 1642).

priests in the bishopric of Puebla, the majority of whom regarded themselves as being inadequately provided for.[47] Moreover, as Palafox informed Madrid, the secular clergy, so long as they remained the most discontented group among the privileged elements of Mexican society, were the most serious threat to its stability.[48]

In December 1640 Palafox was back in Puebla preparing his moves against the mendicants. The moment seemed opportune: it was evident that the viceroy would try to stay out of it, while the Puebla city council and the cathedral chapter were solidly behind him[49] as were the Creoles generally. Late in December the priors of thirty-seven mendicant establishments administering Indian parishes in the diocese of Puebla, including those of Tlaxcala, Cholula, Tepeaca, Huejotzingo, Tehuacán, and Orizaba, were informed that they must yield their curates for examination in morals and languages by the bishop's staff within a short stipulated period or face the confiscation of their parishes. Thirty-six of the priors replied that it was impossible for them to comply within the stipulated time limit, since it was not in their power to act without first receiving permission from the Provincials of their orders in Mexico City. Palafox refused to wait. He ordered the parishes to be seized. The operation began with the 'taking of Tlaxcala' on 29 December and continued until 8 February 1641.[50] The towns seized were declared 'parishes of Spaniards', parochial administration was taken over by the diocesan authorities, and livings for more than 150 secular priests were allotted.[51] The Franciscan friars bore the brunt of the confiscations, losing thirty-one parishes; the Dominicans were stripped of three and the Augustinians of two. One mendicant parish, that of the Indian suburbs of Atlixco, being the only one whose prior had complied with the bishop's ultimatum, was spared.

The high-point of the episode was undoubtedly the start, the 'taking of Tlaxcala'.[52] At two o'clock of the morning of 29 December, a party of horsemen, lay and clerical, most brandishing weapons, some arquebuses, entered the town awakening everyone with their clatter. Arms were required, according to the Creole side, because there had been reports that the Franciscans would attempt to organize resistance among the Indians.[53] In fact, the friars abandoned Tlaxcala to their

[47]Alegaciones en favor del clero, fols. 3, 5ᵛ; La Puebla de los Angeles, p. 53.

[48]Palafox, Cartas reservadas al Rey, BAGN, ser. i, ii. 508–10.

[49]ACP xviii, fol. 207ᵛ.

[50]Francisco de Ayeta, Crisol de la verdad en defensa de su provincia del Santo Evangelio (n.p., n.d. [Madrid, c. 1693]), fol. 59.

[51]BND 3048, fol. 37.

[52]Luis de la Palma y Freites. Por las religiones de Santo Domingo, San Francisco, y San Agustin . . . (Madrid, 1644), fols. 24ᵛ–27; Vetancurt, Teatro Mexicano, part iv, fols. 14–16.

[53]Alegaciones en favor del clero, fol. 69.

adversaries without thought of resistance and barricaded themselves in their priory. The town was declared a 'parish of Spaniards', church bells were rung, and mass, at which apparently Bishop Palafox was present, was celebrated. The Tlaxcaltecs were told that from that time on they had to come to the secular clergy for mass and the sacraments and that they would be punished severely if they did not break their ties with the friars. The Indian *cabildo*, outraged but powerless, was made to surrender its building so that it might be used to house the new curate and his assistants. The only instance of violence occurred the following day when a friar carrying a sack of flour to the friary was set upon and beaten, apparently by some Indian supporters of the new curate.

Palafox's seizure of thirty-six Indian parishes caused delight among the Creoles and rage among the bureaucratic party; it also caused an eruption of clerical strife which lasted throughout 1641, and in a somewhat gentler form for years afterwards. The Franciscans delivered sermon after sermon attacking Palafox,[54] commissioned canonical texts in support of their case,[55] and appealed to the viceroy for his help. They also launched a counter-attack on the ground. Hoping to deprive the secular clergy of the indispensable aesthetic base of the Indian church, they moved all the Indian virgins, images of Jesus and the saints, and holy ornaments that they could from the parochial churches of the Indian towns into their own conventual chapels,[56] seeking in this way to retain the spiritual allegiance of the Indians. After 8 February, when the last of the thirty-six parishes was seized, the friars kept up their resistance. There were various incidents. On 22 July, in one of the most notable, a dozen Franciscans, wielding knives and sticks and breaking doors and windows as they went, broke into a parochial chapel in Cholula, where they seized a famous Virgin much venerated by the Cholultecs, complete with silver tiara and gems, and, cutting the belfry ropes as they left to prevent the alarm from being sounded, made off with her.[57] Occurrences of this sort were accompanied by a general tug-of-war throughout the bishopric, for the allegiance of the Indians. The secular clergy, in their effort to persuade the Indians to abandon the friars, declared that sacraments administered to Indians by friars would no longer count in the eyes of God and that Indian marriages consecrated by mendicants would not be valid.[58] Despite this propaganda, at least some Indians did frequent or try to frequent the mendicant chapels rather than their parochial

---

[54]*AGN* cédulas originales i, fols. 540–1.

[55]The most important being Francisco López de Solis, *Compendio de lo mucho que esta escrito en defensa de los religiones* . . . (Mexico, 1641).

[56]AGN cédulas duplicadas lvii, fols. 46^v–47.

[57]ADI Palafox papers lxiii, fols. 340–1.

[58]BNX 1066, fols. 3–5, 69^v–70, 72.

churches. In some cases, Indians were forcibly prevented from going to the friars and subjected, as indeed the friars had subjected them in cases of religious offences, to corporal punishment. The friars retorted by urging the Indians to ignore the secular clergy and shift the focus of their religious life over to the priories.[59] Occasionally there were fights between the Indian supporters of the two clerical factions.[60]

This prolongation of the clerical strife forced the viceroy to abandon his initial neutrality. Little by little, the gulf between Escalona and Palafox widened. In Oaxaca a bitter contest had flared up between the bishop of that diocese and the Dominicans, and tension was rising in the dioceses of Mexico and Michoacán, and also in New Biscay where the bishop eventually followed Palafox's lead and seized a number of Franciscan parishes.[61] The viceroy, convinced that the visitor-general was causing far more problems in New Spain than he was solving, now came out openly against Palafox and declared that he would allow no more transfers of mendicant parishes to take place. The friars, who had been expecting a fresh *Palafoxista* offensive, breathed again. Palafox was furious. Escalona followed up his initiative by giving support to the beleaguered Franciscans in Palafox's own diocese.[62] He authorized the *corregidores* to frustrate Palafox's efforts to stop the assignment of *repartimiento* labour to the friaries, thus ensuring that the friars continued to receive Indians to do their chores. However, Escalona soon had to face Madrid's displeasure at the line he had taken: by February 1642 he was being rebuked by the crown for opposing the visitor-general and for obstructing measures which were, as Madrid put it, echoing Palafox's phrase, 'so desired by both Spaniards and Indians'.[63]

In the latter part of 1641, the controversy over the Indian Church was eclipsed, as a political issue, by the sudden rise of the Portuguese question. After the autumn of 1642, when the Portuguese question was settled, other issues moved to the fore. But although the clerical conflict lost its urgency, it did not cease; rather it continued to nag in the background of Mexican politics, with occasional manifestations of a violent kind such as that at Calpa in 1644 when a diocesan priest was assaulted in his home by the local Franciscan prior and three other friars, and seriously injured.

---

[59] ADI Palafox papers lxiii, fol. 336; *Cedulario de los Siglos XVI y XVII*, p. 364.
[60] BNX 1066, fols. 54–55v.
[61] Fernando Ortiz de Valdés, *Defensa canonica por la dignidad del obispo de la Puebla de los Angeles* (Madrid, 1648), fol. 191v.
[62] ADI Palafox papers lxiii, fol. 836; Palafox, *Cartas reservadas al Rey* BAGN, ser. i, ii. 515.
[63] AGN cédulas originales i, fol. 531: crown to Escalona, 10 Feb. 1642.

The Portuguese question of 1641–2, which in origin had little to do with Mexico, was the issue that settled the conflict between Escalona and Palafox. In April 1641 Escalona received word from Madrid that Portugal had revolted against the monarchy in the previous December, attempted to sever its link with Spain, and proclaimed the leader of the Portuguese aristocracy, the Duke of Braganza, King João IV of Portugal. News of this blow to Spanish pride, coming in the wake of the news of the revolt of the Catalans, spread consternation and dismay in Mexico as it did in the rest of the Spanish overseas empire. It was also somewhat embarrassing for Escalona personally, whose dead wife was a sister of the upstart, Braganza. At first, however, there was little sign that the Portuguese rebellion would cause a major crisis in Mexico. Madrid sent the viceroy instructions regarding precautions to be taken to obviate any risk of Portuguese sedition in the colony: no more Portuguese were to be admitted into Mexico; entry of Portuguese ships into Mexican ports was prohibited; correspondence to and from Portuguese merchants operating in the viceroyalty was to be intercepted.

During the summer of 1641 there developed in New Spain an ominous tension between the Spanish and Portuguese populations. Spaniards and Portuguese had, traditionally, tended to dislike each other, and as we have seen, in the New World this distrust was accentuated by the general tendency among the Spaniards to associate the Portuguese with crypto-Judaism. Now, in addition to this and the earlier news of the revolt of Portugal itself, came the news of the revolts of Madeira and Brazil and of the Portuguese conspiracy or, if there was no conspiracy, of the great scare, in Cartagena of the Indies.[64] The news was spiced with tales of massacres, and it was said in Mexico City that the Portuguese in Brazil had slaughtered 3,000 Spaniards. Palafox took the lead in asserting that Mexico was also in danger, and in this he received support from the Mexican Inquisition which reported to the Inquisitor-General in Spain that Mexico City, Puebla, and Veracruz were in the grip of tension and fear and that the Mexican Portuguese were believed to have built up stocks of firearms and ammunition.[65] Palafox reminded the crown that Escalona was a relative of the Braganza.[66]

In November 1641 the situation developed into a tussle between Palafox and Escalona, with the former accusing the latter of failing to take the necessary steps to prevent a Portuguese insurrection in Mexico

64 AGN Inquisición 489, fol. 85: Palafox to Escalona, 20 Nov. 1641.
65 AGN Inquisición 407, fols. 439–42.
66 AGI México 4, r 6, exp. 281: Palafox to council, 19 June 1641.

and of putting the colony at risk.[67] In his communications with the viceroy, the bishop painted an alarming picture contending that the Portuguese were drunk with the successes of their compatriots against Spain, that everywhere there was talk of the possibility of a Portuguese rebellion, and, with patent exaggeration, that the Portuguese had bought up all the firearms in the colony. He also claimed, again with evident exaggeration, that there were more Portuguese than Spaniards in the port of Veracruz, the 'key' to New Spain, and that, in the event of an insurrection, the Portuguese might easily be able to seize it. He deplored the fact that the Portuguese Sebastián Váez de Acevedo was still *purveedor general* of the Armada of Barlovento, and had therefore access to large quantities of weapons and supplies, and that his brother was in command of an infantry detachment in Mexico City, and that other Portuguese officers were in command of other units at Veracruz and Campeche. He warned that the Portuguese had numerous slaves and mulatto employees who were always loyal to them and ample money with which to promote their plans. Escalona replied icily[68] that the visitor-general had been misled by irresponsible informants into exaggerating the dangers of the situation out of all proportion to what they were in reality. He defended the brothers Váez de Acevedo as loyal officers with many years in the king's service and assured the bishop that all Madrid's instructions had been carried out. Everything, he declared, was under control.

However, Palafox's efforts may well have persuaded the Duke to take some further precautions, in his own interest as well as that of the king, for he must have suspected that Palafox might try to use his Portuguese connection against him. A week after his reply to Palafox, Escalona issued a decree that all the Portuguese of Mexico City, including the Creole Portuguese, had to register with the *corregidor* within three days and surrender their fire-arms.[69] Similar orders were dispatched to the *corregidores* outside the capital for general implementation throughout New Spain. In the capital, 419 adult male Portuguese registered,[70] evidence of just how numerous and prominent they were, and sixteen fire-arms, which of course is very few, were handed in. At the same time as he communicated these findings to Madrid, the viceroy went onto the offensive against Palafox. He accused him of abusing the powers conferred on him by Madrid and of being consumed with such ambition that he secretly desired to be viceroy himself. He both advised

67AGN Inquisición 489, fols. 85–88ᵛ: Palafox to Escalona, 20 Nov. 1641.
68AGN Inquisición 489, fols. 93–6: Escalona to Palafox, 20 Nov. 1641.
69AGI México 4, r 6, exp. 305: printed decree dated 27 Nov. 1641.
70AGI México 4, r 6, exp. 306, fols. 4–6ᵛ: Escalona to council, 30 Dec. 1641.

and requested that the bishop be stripped of his commissions and called back to Spain as soon as possible.

By this time both viceroy and visitor-general were angling in Madrid, each trying to secure the removal of the other. Palafox did not go so far as to accuse the viceroy of treason and complicity with the Portuguese, but he did charge him with having failed to take adequate steps to prevent a rebellion, and insinuated that the Duke may have been sympathetic to Braganza. In January 1642 the conflict between Escalona and Palafox intensified when the *corregidor* of Veracruz arrested a Carmelite friar who was trying to smuggle letters onto the fleet for Spain, letters from Palafox to Madrid urging the recall of Escalona to Spain.[71] But although this denunciation of Escalona failed to get through, others did, and when it came to weighing the evidence in Madrid, the cards were stacked heavily in favour of Palafox. The Duke came far higher in the social hierarchy than the bishop, but that fact cut little ice with Olivares, who had always been suspicious of great aristocrats and was now in a state of paranoia since the revolts of Catalonia and Portugal and the turning against him of virtually the whole Castilian aristocracy. Palafox was a trusted servant of the crown and when he counselled the recall of Escalona, his warning was certain to be taken seriously. Accordingly, while urging the Duke to maintain maximum vigilance, Olivares had secret *cédulas* dispatched to the bishop empowering him to dismiss the viceroy when and if this should seem necessary and authorizing him to take the Duke's place as temporary viceroy.[72] At the same time, as further signs of the king's favour, Palafox was entrusted with Escalona's *residencia*, on top of those of Cerralvo and Cadereita, and informed that he had been preferred to the archbishopric of Mexico.

Tension between Spaniards and Portuguese continued through the spring of 1642, and so, when Palafox received his *cédulas*, it was not difficult for him to justify his use of them. On the evening of 9 June, the bishop revealed his documents to the *Audiencia*, the Mexico City council, and the Inquisition, and having obtained their recognition that he was authorized to act against the viceroy, made arrangements to carry out the deposition. At dawn on 10 June the bishop entered the viceregal palace at the head of a column of *Audiencia* officials, secretaries, and soldiers and roused the startled Duke from his bed. The King's orders were read out and Escalona acquiesced almost without protest.[73] Dazed, the Duke left the palace only half dressed, abandoning his rooms, keys, personal and government papers, and other effects to the bishop. He rode out to the friary of Churubusco with the prior of which he was on good terms and where he was to reside for the next months.

Juan de Palafox, visitor-general and interim viceroy of New Spain, bishop of Puebla de los Angeles and archbishop-elect of Mexico, was now at the zenith of his power and prestige. He commenced his brief term as viceroy by taking a number of measures against the Portuguese and purging his enemies, or at least some of them, from the administration.[74] All Portuguese with military or administrative posts in Mexico were dismissed excepting only Sebastián Váez de Acevedo whose particular talents were found to be indispensable. The Portuguese community of Veracruz was ordered out of the port, only one Portuguese being allowed to stay, a native of Tangier[75] excepted on the ground that that colony, unlike the rest of the Portuguese empire, had remained loyal to Spain; some of the Veracruz Portuguese moved to Puebla, others to Mexico City, and at least one prominent group of Veracruz Portuguese Jews to Orizaba.[76] The *corregidor* of Veracruz was accused of plotting rebellion with the Portuguese and imprisoned in the fortress of San Juan, and a number of other Escalona men were stripped of their positions and in some cases imprisoned.

Escalona meanwhile was seeking to vindicate himself and damage the bishop. He formally accused Palafox of having coveted his office, of having contrived his downfall with wicked skill, and of persecuting him and his associates, blackening the name of a grandee of Spain by treating him like a traitor, spying on him and imprisoning his servants.[77] He appealed against the decision to put Palafox in charge of his *residencia*, objecting, with ample justification, that the bishop should not be his judge, being his declared enemy. He protested his innocence of even sympathy with traitors and vigorously repudiated the idea that he might have been plotting rebellion, pointing out that Mexico was a land in which he was without relatives, wealth, vassals, arms, or private strongholds.[78] He also warned Madrid not to trust

[73] AGI México 4, r 6, exp. 311.

[74] See Palafox's dispositions in (surprisingly) AGN cedulas duplicadas lxii, fols. 4^v 9, 29–31, 51^v, 67^v: García, *Don Juan de Palafox*, p. 116.

[75] AGN Inquisición 397, fol. 471^v; AGN reales cédulas duplicados lxii ('libro de gobierno de Don Juan de Palafox') fol. 67^v; the Portuguese of Tangiers, Diego Méndez Merino, was afterwards arrested by the Inquisition for judaizing.

[76] AGN reales cédulas duplicados lxii, fols. 28–32.

[77] *Declaración del duque de Escalona de como dejó la gobernación de la Nueva España, DHM v, 147–50.*

[78] AGI México 4, r. 6, exp. 312: Escalona to council, 30 June 1642.

Palafox and declared that it was a great mistake as well as a violation of precedent to assign both the highest secular authority and the supreme ecclesiastical office in Mexico to the same man. But if Escalona bitterly attacked Palafox, there were other prominent figures in Mexico who vigorously supported him. Alonso de Villalba, for instance, one of the judges of the *Audiencia*, wrote to Madrid praising Palafox and avowing that Escalona was far too inept a man to be left in control of New Spain in such dangerous times.[79]

Palafox lost no time in attacking vice and moral laxness in the capital. He launched a determined drive against prostitutes, drove them from conspicuous places, and founded a house for reformed whores named La Magdalena.[80] He also endeavoured to suppress licentious dances, immodest dress, and the employment of scantily clad mulatta girls to entice passers-by into *pulquerías*. He reformed the convents of the capital, as he had reformed those of Puebla, and compelled the mothers superior to accept and impose exacting new rules. He also prodded the secular clergy of the capital into a more austere frame of mind and, threatening the friars of the diocese of Mexico with the punishment he had meted out to the friars of Puebla, he forced them to yield on a number of points of jurisdiction.[81]

Probably the outstanding event of Palafox's brief viceregal term (June to November 1642) was the uncovering by the Mexican Inquisition of the so-called *complicidad grande* or 'great conspiracy'. This was the exposure of the main network of crypto-Jewish groups in Mexico and the beginning of a series of arrests, on 13 July, which was to continue for some three or four years and take in about 150 Jews in all. Whether the Mexican Inquisition really discovered the existence of the main crypto-Jewish community at this time, however, is a moot point. One wonders whether it is possible that Escalona, who favoured at least some Portuguese New Christians, notably Sebastián Váez de Acevedo and Matías Rodríguez de Oliveira,[82] and who himself had at least some New Christian blood in his veins,[83] might have restrained the Inquisition or at least encouraged its inactivity under the corrupt senior inquisitor Marcos de Bohórquez, while Palafox, being more in tune with popular opinion, more puritanical and therefore in sympathy with Bohórquez's enemies among the Inquisitors, and strongly anti-Portuguese, enabled or at least encouraged the Inquisition to act. What is clear is that Palafox strongly disapproved of the fact that Jews had

---

[79] ADI Palafox papers, xiii, fol. 85: Alonso de Villalba to council, 21 July 1642.
[80] BND 3048, fol. 47; ADI Palafox papers xii, fols. 230-1.
[81] Vetancurt, *Teatro Mexicano*, part iv, p. 16.
[82] ADI Palafox papers lxvi, fol. 114[v].
[83] Kamen, *The Spanish Inquisition*, p. 20.

previously been able to buy protection[84] and applauded the sudden Inquisition offensive in the second month of his rule.[85] Palafox also thought that it was right that the Jews should lose their money, in the first place because it had been made at the expense of the crown, and secondly to prevent it from seeping through to Lisbon and Amsterdam. Moreover, it is undeniable that the tightening up of the Inquisition and the exposure of the *complicidad grande* in the summer of 1642 fitted in neatly with Palafox's own drive against corruption and against the Portuguese.

Palafox's brief term, then, witnessed the beginning of the destruction of the crypto-Jewish community in Mexico, if not exactly at his bidding, then at least with his blessing. About fifty Portuguese Jews were seized during the last three months of his term, including Simón Váez Sevilla, Mathías Rodríguez de Oliveira, Francisco de Texoso, Antonio Váez Castelobranco, and their families. Dozens more were arrested after 1642. As we have seen, some remained undetected after 1650, but the arrests of the summer of 1642 broke the back of crypto-Judaism in Mexico. Much of the wealth of the prisoners was apparently never found by the inquisitors. Simón Váez Sevilla, the richest of the Mexican Jews, successfully concealed much of his fortune, though what was seized was valued at more than 100,000 pesos. The trials of the prisoners by the Inquisition continued in the background of Mexican public life through the 1640s, and the trials were followed by the series of *Autos-de-Fe* staged in Mexico City in the years 1646–9; by that time, however, Palafox and the Mexican Inquisition had fallen out; Palafox had become a notable critic of the Inquisition, and at least some of the Portuguese New Christians in New Spain, as a result, took Palafox's side in the political struggle of 1646–9.

Palafox's rule, though brief, was vigorous. It was also, in several respects, a significant interruption in the pattern of viceregal government as practiced by Viceroys Cerralvo, Cadereita, and Escalona. For it was characterized by signs of Palafox's willingness to respond to Creole desires. The Mexico City council was delighted by his approach, especially by his determination to curb the excesses of the *corregidores* [86] and by his indifference to the segregation policy. The *cabildo* was also pleased with Palafox's reform of the Mexico City militia and his

[84] ADI Palafox papers v, fol. 57.

[85] Ibid., fols. 56–8, 75: however, Palafox does appear to have defended his New Christian secretary, Melchor Juarez, against the Inquisition much to the Inquisition's annoyance, AGN Inquisicion 416, fols. 427, 466.

[86] AGI Patronato real 244, r i: Mexico City *cabildo* to council, 25 July 1642; see also Palafox's report to his successor Salvatierra, in Juan de Palafox, *Ideas políticas*, selection by José Rojas Garciidueñas (Mexico, 1946), pp. 161–4.

policy of assigning more militia commissions to Creoles. It is also reasonable to assume, in view of Palafox's expressed belief that more district governorships should be given to Creoles,[87] that he acted as he preached and appointed a number of Creole *corregidores*. In addition, Palafox was notably helpful to hacienda owners and other proprietors who wished to extend the system of debt-peonage and increase their permanent Indian work force, thus reversing the policy of his predecessors who had consistently sought to impede entrepreneurs in this respect.[88] It is also clear that Palafox was in favour of giving the Mexican Creoles the full benefit of the Armada of Barlovento, particularly the contracts for construction, maintenance, and provisioning, which Cadereita and Escalona had tended to assign to others, and of allotting the Creoles a high proportion of the officers' positions in the fleet. Altogether, it may be fairly said that Palafox's viceregal term marked a brief ascendancy for the political forces of the colonists and secular clergy and a significant if only temporary reverse for the Spanish, Indian, and mendicant bureaucracies.

87 Ibid., p. 163.
88 Chevalier, *Land and Society*, p. 285.

VIII

SALVATIERRA, TORRES DE RUEDA AND THE DISTURBANCES OF THE LATER 1640's

Palafox, the seventeenth viceroy of New Spain, was succeeded in November 1642 by the conde de Salvatierra who governed Mexico for some five and a half years until May 1648, years which were among the most disturbed in the history of the viceroyalty. One aspect of this tumoil, the struggle between Bishop Palafox and the Jesuits, has traditionally attracted a good deal of interest in and outside of Mexico;[1] indeed echoes of that remarkable conflict have continued down to the present day. But the very factors which have tended to bring out this side of the subject, the interest of the French Jansenists in Palafox's writings and the implacable hostility to Palafox of the Jesuits, have also tended to obscure the specifically Mexican context of the struggle and to emphasize its ecclesiastical aspects at the expense of the social and political. However, a strictly historical approach to the question, it may be argued, merely by placing the commotion squarely

[1] See C. E. P. Simmons, 'Palafox and his critics: re-appraising a controversy', *HAHR* xlvi (1966) 394–408; Genaro García, *Don Juan de Palafox*, pp. 149–94, is, as one might expect, very much for Palafox; H. E. Bolton, in his review of this book in the *American Historical Review*, xxv (1919), 127, says that García's conclusions on Palafox are 'marred by a manifest bias, a partizanship which perhaps reflects the present day political struggles of Mexico'; Father J. Brodrick in *The Economic Morals of the Jesuits* (London, 1934) regards Palafox as 'patently unbalanced, a headstrong, domineering man who had no capacity at all for government' and who suffered from 'persecution mania'; for other Jesuit accounts, highly critical of Palafox, see Alegre, *Historia de la Compañía*, vol. ii; Cuevas, *Historia de la Iglesia en México*, iii. 307–37, and Astrain, *Historia de la Compañía*, v; for samples of the abuse poured on one another by Jesuits and Carmelites at the time of the proposed canonization of Palafox, a canonization which the Jesuits succeeded in blocking, see the writings of Father Butrón, AHN *códices* 188–b on the dispute between Palafox and the Jesuits over Jesuit missionary practices in China, see J. S. Cummins, 'Palafox, China, and the Chinese Rites Controversy', *Revista de Historia de América* (1961), 397–427; for Palafox and the Jansenists see the *Lettre de l'illustrissime Jean de Palafox ... Evesque d'Angelopolis dans l'Amerique ... Au Pape Innocent X, contenant diverses pleintes de cet Evesque contre les entreprises e les voilences des Jesuites, et leur maniere peu evangelique de prescher l'Evangile dans les Indes* (Paris, 1659) and the other seventeenth-century French renderings of Palafox's writings; see also the anonymous *Vie du venerable Dom Jean de Palafox, Evêque d'Angelopolis et ensuite Evêque d'Osme, dediée a Su Majesté Catholique* (Cologne, 1767).

in its Mexican situation, will almost inevitably remove the emphasis from the ecclesiastical and bring out a good deal of relevant material which has hitherto been overlooked or ignored. Here, it might be as well to explain at the start, it will be contended that not only must the conflict between Palafox and the Society of Jesus be assessed primarily in social and political terms if it is to be rightly understood, but that the conflict was really only part, as far as Mexico was concerned, of a wider struggle between an alliance of elements headed by Palafox and a rival combination which included the Jesuits. The *Palafoxistas*, as they were called, were, broadly speaking, the Creoles, and the allies of the Jesuits, the bureaucratic party.

The first part of the story, the controversy of 1642–3, is the simplest. In essence, it was a dispute between diocesan clergy and Jesuits over the apportioning of church wealth. By 1640, little more than half a century after their appearance in Mexico, the Jesuits had acquired so much landed property in the colony that the colonists had ventured to protest and the bishops had become extremely concerned. Madrid too had become concerned and, as we have seen, had sought to prohibit further Jesuit expansion. However, none of the viceroys with the exception of Gelves, seems to have taken the regulations very seriously and acquisition of land by the Society in Mexico had continued unabated.[2] Although the colonists were chiefly worried by the Society's amassing of land as such,[3] the diocesan authorities were more troubled by the adverse impact of Jesuit expansion on diocesan income from tithes, the church tax on agricultural produce. For the Jesuits, like the Dominicans, Augustinians, and Mercenarians, though not the Franciscans who had not engaged in acquisition of land, claimed benefit of clergy and exemption from the diocesan tax—an exemption which the bishops did not acknowledge—and refused to pay tithes. This had not greatly mattered early in the century, for at that time the landed property held by the regular orders in Mexico had not been especially extensive; by 1642, however, the Society had been bequeathed and had otherwise obtained such a number of ranches, sheep haciendas, and plantations, that it had significantly reduced the area in Central Mexico on which tithes were paid. The loss to diocesan chests was rendered all the more galling to the bishops in that the Jesuits, being, as is well known, assiduous and efficient proprietors, invariably increased the value and yield of the properties they acquired. Moreover, the Mexican bishops were, or claimed to be, far more

---

2Chevalier, *Land and Society*, pp. 239–50.

3*Informes sobre el pleito que la catedral de Puebla siguio con los Padres de la Compañia sobre los diezmos*, five tracts composed and printed at Puebla in the years 1642–4 (in the BP), fol. 108.

dependent on their income from tithes than their counterparts in Spain,[4] and it is certainly true that the financial strength of the Mexican dioceses was roughly in proportion to their agricultural wealth; thus Puebla, having within its limits the most intensively cultivated land in the viceroyalty, was twice as rich as the archbishopric of Mexico and several times richer than most of the other bishoprics. In 1624 there had commenced what was to become one of the most protracted suits in Spanish legal history, the combined attempt of the diocesan chapters of Mexico and Peru to force the religious orders in the Indies to pay tithes. In 1636 the dispute had begun in earnest when the cathedral chapters of Mexico City and Lima had been permitted to send representatives to plead their case in Madrid.[5] But though they concentrated on tithes, the bishops did not forget to question the right of the orders to acquire property in the first place.

The Jesuits were not only the wealthiest order in Mexico, they were also the most eager to refute the criticisms of the colonists and the bishops. The friars disliked discussing tithes for they were shy of admitting that they were interested in property and had acquired valuable lands; but the Jesuits were not in the least embarrassed by their holdings. As they saw it, Jesuit wealth was not only justifiable but positively necessary and essential.[6] As true standard-bearers of the Counter-Reformation, the Jesuits interpreted their work and activities in quite a different way from that in which the mendicant orders with their thirteenth-century constitutions and vows of poverty professed to interpret theirs. The Society had been founded to strengthen the Church, stiffen the morale of the faithful, and direct the counter-attack on the heretic; and to perform this role, as its members had always avowed, it needed the weapons of the world, influence and money. The tendency of Jesuit theologians generally to conceive of a close, immediate, dialectical relationship between the Holy Spirit and the material world was strongly echoed in the theory and practice of the Society in Mexico. Provided the wealth of a religious order was held in common and not spent on the comfort of its individual members, asserted the Jesuits, there was every justification for its seeking to increase its property. If the Jesuits were not wealthy, they asked, how could they maintain their colleges, schools, and missions?

---

4 Juan de Palafox, *Carta segunda a Inocencio Décimo, Pontífice Máximo*, in *Obras*, xi. 32.

5 *Cedulario de los siglos xvi y xvii*, 304–8, 345–6, 352–7; W. Borah, 'Tithe collection in the Bishopric of Oaxaca, 1601–1867', *HAHR* xxix (1949), 505.

6 Padre Alonso de Roxas, *Al Rey por la Compañía de Jesús de la Nueva España en satisfación de un libro de el visitador obispo don Juan de Palafox y Mendoza* (n.p., n.d. [Madrid?, 1645?]), pp. 44, 83, 89–90, 99.

The original clash between Palafox and the Jesuits stemmed from a dispute between the Puebla diocesan chapter and the Society which had occurred in 1639.[7] The disagreement began when a wealthy prebendary of the diocesan chapter, named Hernando de la Serna, made known his intention to be patron of the new college which the Jesuits were proposing to establish at Veracruz and to endow it with a sheep hacienda worth, according to Palafox, 70,000 pesos. The rest of the diocesan chapter, headed by its executor, Juan de Merlo, a personage who was to be closely associated with Palafox, responded to this by warning the prebendary not to bequeath the property without first ensuring that it would continue to be liable to the tithe. However, Serna completed the transaction without making any such stipulation, thereby depriving the diocesan chest of a significant annual income. Merlo, extremely annoyed both by the loss and the affront to diocesan dignity, thereupon declared Serna responsible for the lost tithes and placed his remaining property under distraint pending payment. The Jesuits responded by taking legal action in defence of their man and tempers were rising when the new bishop arrived.

The first effect of Palafox's arrival, as far as the diocesan dispute with the Jesuits was concerned, was to restore calm. The tithes issue was quickly relegated to the background, as Palafox turned the attention of the secular clergy to a dozen other matters and began almost at once to implement his particular brand of reformation.[8] The cathedral and churches of the city were scrubbed and cleaned. The secular clergy of Puebla took to wearing simpler costume and to removing their beards in emulation of their prelate. Dozens of new rules relating to services, procedure, and discipline were laid down. The nunneries were reformed, prostitutes cleared from the plazas, and so forth.

But though Palafox made several friendly gestures toward the Society in the period 1640–1,[9] the Jesuits could not help but feel uneasy. What was the meaning of the Palafoxian reformation? Would the reform and revival of the secular clergy involve an increase or reduction in Jesuit influence? The signs, from the Jesuit point of view, were not good. Although the Society was not directly affected by the 'taking of Tlaxcala' and the other mendicant *doctrinas* in the diocese, it was natural that the Jesuits should be worried: if the bishops were despoiling the friars of their curacies in Central Mexico today, might

[7] Juan de Palafox, *Carta al Padre Horacio Caroche*, *Obras*, xi. 134–6; Alegre, *Historia de la Compañía*, ii. 340–1.

[8] BM Add. MS. 13, 974, no. 21: 'Relacion del viaje del obispo de la Puebla de los Angeles desde Veracruz a dicha ciudad', fol. 109ᵛ; Ortiz de Valdés, *Defensa Canónica*, pp. 207–13; BND 3048, fols. 36–43.

[9] Cuevas, *Historia de la Iglesia en México*, iii. 311.

they not try to do the same with the Jesuit missions of New Biscay tomorrow? No less alarming were Palafox's ideas about education and training the clergy. The Jesuits had monopolized higher education in Puebla and most of the rest of New Spain for so long that they had come to conceive of education as their particular territory; besides, education was one of the keys to Jesuit influence and power, for it was the Jesuits who had trained the clergy, lawyers, and noblemen of the day. Now Palafox was founding the college-seminaries of San Pablo and San Juan, colleges under diocesan control designed to perform almost exactly the same function as the two Jesuit colleges in Puebla, Espíritu Santo and San Ildefonso.[10] The result was a rivalry of educationalists which, within a year or two, was to become bitter, mounting to a crescendo in the later 1640s with the diocesan colleges getting the better of the struggle and winning the lion's share of popular support.[11] Besides, it was obvious that the Palafoxian reformation would be costly and this alone seemed likely to induce Palafox to cast hostile glances at Jesuit wealth and take a hard line on tithes. Apart from the huge sums that Palafox had begun to spend on schools, churches,[12] and orphanages, and on providing new vestments and organs, he had, in accordance with royal instructions,[13] restarted work on Puebla cathedral which had been at a standstill since 1618, and plunged the construction site into feverish activity. Moreover, Palafox made no secret of the fact that not only would the cathedral be finished but that it would be greatly embellished. He intended it to be a symbol of his reformation, the finest architectural structure in the Indies and a match for the finest in Europe.

Although therefore the years 1640–1 were a time of peace between the secular clergy and the Jesuits in Puebla, likely areas of friction were in fact increasing and the tithes issue, which was of some if not great importance, went unresolved. Palafox, while doing his utmost to appear less rigid than his deputy, Merlo, nevertheless upheld his policy in substance. Serna's property was freed from distraint, but Palafox declared categorically that cathedral chapters had the right to ensure that tithes continued to be paid on estates bequeathed to religious foundations, and it was precisely this principle that the Jesuits refused

10 Diego Antonio Bermúdez de Castro, *Theatro Angelopolitano. Historia de la Ciudad de la Puebla de los Angeles* (Puebla? , 1746), p. 185; *La Puebla de los Angeles*, pp. 139–40: Palafox to Council, 27 Sept. 1641.

11 BNX 890: Leonardo de Saldaña, 'Cartas escritas a un amigo', fol. 20; Ortiz de Valdés, *Defensa Canónica*, fol. 102.

12 According to Bermúdez de Castro, Palafox, during his nine years in Mexico, built or repaired, in the whole diocese, more than fifty churches, *Theatro Angelopolitano*, p. 186.

13 *La Puebla de los Angeles*, pp. 150–1.

to accept. Accordingly, having waited until Palafox had relinquished the government of the colony to the conde de Salvatierra in November 1642, the Society brought a suit before the *Audiencia* against the cathedral chapter of Puebla, of which, it should be noted, Palafox remained head, having decided to decline the archbishopric of Mexico, in accordance with his ideals regarding episcopal loyalty, and stay with his 'Rachel'.

There now ensued a remarkable contest between bishop and Jesuits in the exercise of influence with the *Audiencia*.[14] The Society was rich and powerful, but Palafox too had leverage with the *Audiencia* since one of the commissions Madrid had assigned to him specifically empowered him to investigate and reform the tribunal.[15] The result was that the *Audiencia* judges split evenly into Jesuit and Palafoxist camps, argued bitterly, and twice suspended the case without reaching a decision. Palafox published a tract expounding his position in the dispute, while two prominent Jesuits, Andrés Pérez de Ribas and Francisco Calderón, replied on behalf of the Society.[16] Finally, after bringing in more judges on the case, the *Audiencia* settled the dispute in favour of Palafox.

The Jesuits were undoubtedly angry, but despite this, for the next two years they remained virtually silent. They refused to accept that the bishops could reserve tithes on properties acquired by the Society, but there was now no way that they could challenge the principle without first overcoming the visitor-general's power, and the Jesuits alone, for all their money and influence, were not strong enough to accomplish that. Their only likely allies in the years 1643–5, the mendicant orders, were naturally wary of further entanglements with Palafox at least without firm prospect of victory. There now ensued, accordingly, the two quietest years, politically speaking, of the decade.

The tracts published by Palafox and the Jesuits in 1643 show very plainly that the area of disagreement between them was, at that stage, very limited; indeed, it was restricted entirely to the tithes issue. Palafox declined even to make an attack on the economic policies and wealth of the Society, let alone on its theology, political attitudes, and philosophy of education. Consequently, in 1643, and for as long as the tithes issue remained the main bone of contention between Palafox and the Jesuits, which is to say for another three years, the dispute between them was very narrowly defined and therefore not especially important. It was only after the advent of new factors in the period 1644–6,

---

[14] Palafox, *Carta al padre Horacio Caroche*, Obras, xi. 136.
[15] For Palafox's *Audiencia* ordinances see BND 2940.
[16] These were the *Informes sobre el pleito* referred to above.

factors which pushed the tithes issue far into the background, that the area of disagreement between Palafox and the Jesuits widened and they became engaged in a major political battle. The years 1644–6 in New Spain witnessed the formation of a new political combination the purpose of which was to destroy the Palafoxian reformation in all its manifestations. But, and this is the crucial point, it was the viceroy who was to create this combination and swing the balance of political forces against Palafox, and it is in the secular and not the ecclesiastical sphere that one must seek the underlying causes of the commotions of 1647–9.

The origins of the strife between Salvatierra and Palafox reach back to the first months of the conde's term as viceroy. Almost at once, Salvatierra had shown himself a good friend to the Franciscans, had taken their side in the diocese of Puebla, and had helped them shore up what remained of their influence there.[17] He backed the Franciscans partly owing to personal preference but also under pressure from the *corregidores*, who in the Puebla area and elsewhere were the one group with whom Palafox had been on the worst possible terms since the moment of his arrival.[18] The *corregidor* of Tlaxcala had declared, in a letter to the viceroy, that the secular clergy had usurped a great part of his authority since Palafox had placed his curates in charge of the Indian parishes of the district, and that they had even taken it upon themselves to send Indian labourers to work on local haciendas.[19] The *corregidor* of Huejotzingo had made a similar complaint to the viceroy, declaring that the *Palafoxistas* had reduced his authority almost to nothing.[20] Never was the mutual dependence of *corregidores* and friars more clearly displayed than at this time.

In the period 1644–6, relations between Palafox and the viceroy and *corregidores* deteriorated. Several incidents testify to the growing tension, among them a sharp tussle between viceroy and visitor-general over the *corregidor* of Huejotzingo.[21] The affair began when Palafox summoned the *corregidor* to arrest a Spaniard who had insulted an Indian functionary appointed by the new curate of Huejotzingo; the

17*Alegaciones en favor del clero* pp. 122, 126, 158.

18ADI Palafox papers lxxx, fols. 35–8: Palafox to council, 10 July 1641; an exception apparently was the *alcalde mayor* of Puebla itself; it is perhaps significant in this connection that the *alcaldía mayor* of Puebla in the years 1644–5 was held by a nobleman belonging to a family with strong Creole traditions, Gonzalo Gómez de Cervantes, knight of Santiago.

19AGI México 35, r 3: 'Informes echos al virrey por los justicias del modo que son administrados los yndios' (1644), fol. 6: *Corregidor* of Tlaxcala to Salvatierra, 29 Nov. 1643.

20Ibid, fols. 9ᵛ–11; see also the papers in AGI Patronato Real 244, r 2.

21AGI México 35, r 3: Salvatierra to council, 20 Sept. 1644, no. 1.

corregidor, instead of seizing the Spaniard, seized the Indian and two of his underlings. Palafox responded to this by excommunicating the *corregidor* and calling on the *Audiencia* to have him and his deputies arrested. Salvatierra who, naturally, was concerned to shore up the secular administration, tried to force the *Audiencia* judges to reject the bishop's request. However, the magistrates, in the very presence of the viceroy, divided three to two in favour of the bishop. Salvatierra had suffered a major rebuff; the unfortunate *corregidor* and his men were arrested and some of their possessions confiscated. This incident was quickly followed by another, again a clash between Palafox and a *corregidor*.[22] According to Salvatierra, one of the new curates had made advances to the wife of the *corregidor* at confession, and she, being a virtuous lady, had resisted and exposed the clergyman's evil designs to her husband; this had led to unpleasantness between the *corregidor* and the curate which in turn had led to the clergyman accusing the *corregidor* before the Puebla diocesan council; in the upshot, Palafox had had the *corregidor* seized, fined, and sentenced to expulsion from the viceroyalty. This was followed by an ugly scene in one of the churches of Cholula between Palafox in person and the *corregidor* of that town,[23] and acute friction between the *corregidor* and the new curate, one of Palafox's closest associates, Antonio de Peralta, a clergyman who had come from Spain with him. Salvatierra reacted to all this by complaining bitterly to the council of the Indies. He accused the Mexican bishops of wanting to be masters of the viceroyalty,[24] he passed on the complaints of the *corregidores* that Palafox's clergy were helping the hacienda owners to obtain Indians,[25] he charged Palafox with wanting to break utterly the traditional links between the friars and the Indians,[26] and accused the bishop of having forcibly seized religious images and *retablos* from Franciscan priories and having put them in Indian parish churches administered by secular clergy.[27] He also placed in detention Alonso de Villalba, the most pro-Palafox of the *Audiencia* judges.

Relations between viceroy and visitor-general deteriorated further from September 1644 when Palafox returned to Mexico City from Puebla to resume work on his *visita* which had made little progress since 1642.[28] Salvatierra and Palafox were in conflict on every point; authority was hopelessly split and administrative officers threatened

22 Ibid., fols. 2ᵛ–3.
23 Ibid., fols. 3ᵛ.
24 AGI México 35, r 3: Salvatierra to council, 20 Sept. 1644, no. 1, fol. 2ᵛ.
25 'Informes echos al virrey', fol. 4.
26 AGI México 35, r 3: Salvatierra to council, 20 Sept. 1644, no. 7, fol. 4ᵛ.
27 Ibid., letter no. 4.
28 ADI Palafox papers liv, fol. 233.

again by the *visita* were clamouring for the viceroy's protection. It was at this juncture that the conde decided that if he did not soon rid Mexico of Palafox the viceregal authority would melt to nothing. Accordingly, he wrote to Madrid revealing his resentment against the bishop, avowing that Palafox was rendering government impossible, and accusing him of frequenting the chambers of the *Audiencia* 'more frequently than would appear necessary'.[29] Salvatierra also encouraged all those who opposed Palafox to send their own petitions to Madrid declaring that the bishop was 'too upright' and would, if he were not stopped, reduce everything to chaos;[30] and in this he met with ready co-operation from all the religious orders except the Carmelites. However, as Salvatierra saw, the co-operation of the religious orders and the administration was not enough. To induce Madrid to suspend the *visita* and withdraw Palafox, the impression had to be given that everyone of consequence was against Palafox, and that he was genuinely and generally resented. To this end, the viceroy set to work on the Mexico City council, the mouthpiece of the Creoles, for if he could induce Mexico City to condemn the visitor-general, he believed, his hand would be immensely strengthened. Aided by the *corregidor* of Mexico City, Don Diego Orejón, he put maximum pressure on the city councillors, intimidating some and bribing others.[31] One councillor, Diego de Monroy, was promised that he would be made *corregidor* of Guanajuato. At length, the viceroy and his colleagues had their way and Mexico City wrote to Madrid criticizing Palafox and asking that he be recalled.

This fact has been pounced upon by some modern Jesuit historians eager to prove that Palafox was disliked by nearly everyone in Mexico.[32] The fact that the Mexico City council joined in the campaign against the bishop, it has been argued, is a sure sign that Palafox had the weight of public opinion against him. But the argument does not stand up to critical scrutiny. When Salvatierra left Mexico in the spring of 1648, the Mexico City council immediately sent word to

[29] AGI México 35, r 4: Salvatierra to council, 20 Feb. 1645.

[30] ADI Palafox papers ix, fol. 68: Palafox to council, 21 Dec. 1646; BM Add. MS. 13, 976, no. 47: 'Relacion sucinta de lo sucedido en la Nueva España entre los señores conde de Salvatierra virrey y el obispo de la Puebla, visitador-general, sobre las diferencias que han tenido por sus puestos; hecha por persona despasionada y que ha visto lo que en ello ha Pasado', fol. 301.

[31] BM Add. MS. 13, 976, no. 47: 'Relacion sucinta de los sucedido', fol. 301ᵛ; Guijo, *Diario*, i. 17.

[32] Astrain, *Historia de la Compañía*, v. 359–61, quotes the denunciation triumphantly and cites it as proof that Palafox was unpopular, domineering, and corrupt and that he secretly wished to be viceroy; see also Cuevas, *Historia de la Iglesia en México*, iii. 309.

Madrid declaring that its denunciation of Palafox had been forced and was utterly spurious. Indeed, the council reversed its former position, expressing enthusiastic support for Palafox and condemning the conde. The letter was afterwards published together with similar expressions of support for Palafox from the Puebla city council:

The city of Mexico, capital of New Spain, . . . declares before Your Majesty . . . that in the year 1646, some of its councillors denounced . . . the bishop of Puebla . . . at the instigation of certain officials and associates of the viceroy, the conde de Salvatierra, who were themselves in trouble in connection with the *visita* and the investigations of the bishop . . .

. . . and it should be known that the policy [of Palafox] which was the cause of this irregularity was the most popular and necessary that it was possible to formulate, ensuring the security, benefit, and reform of these provinces whose sufferings are caused by the rapacity and avarice of the *corregidores*. The conde, however, saw the matter in a different light, siding with them and bringing soldiers into the city of Puebla . . . which was the origin of all the dangerous events that followed. Nor was there any human remedy in the Indies, for in addition to silencing the royal *Audiencia*, the viceroy made himself master of all the tribunals and institutions. Accordingly, some of those who had a hand in the denunciation of the bishop are not guilty, for anyone who did not yield to the conde exposed himself to great danger.[33]

The year 1646 was undoubtedly one of sharp division within the Mexican body politic. Palafox did not hesitate to lead the opposition to Salvatierra any more than he had hesitated in 1641–2 to lead the opposition to Escalona. He received notable support from Don Bartolomé de Benavente y Benavides, bishop of Oaxaca, a keen *Palafoxista* who was at loggerheads with the Dominicans and *corregidores* of the south, and from Francisco Diego de Evia y Valdés, bishop of New Biscay, as well as inconspicuous background support from the Creoles generally; Benavente actually joined Palafox in requesting Madrid to withdraw Salvatierra from the government of New Spain.[34] Palafox indeed wrote no less scathingly respecting the viceroys than did the viceroy regarding the bishops. He warned the Council of the Indies that respect for royal enactments in Mexico had sunk so low since Cerralvo's time, that if nothing were done to arrest the process the position would soon be reached in which Madrid's wishes would carry

---

[33] *Copia de las cartas que las ciudades de Mexico y la Puebla escrivieron a la real persona y a sus conseios de estado y de las Indias informando de la verdad de lo que sucedio en la Nueva España* (Mexico, 1648) (BNX, not in Andrade or Toribio de Medina); see also ADI Palafox papers vii, fols. 2, 9, 57ᵛ, which give additional proof of the support of the Creole leadership for Palafox, and Guijo, *Diario*, i. 17.

[34] ADI Palafox papers xxxvii, fols. 94, 132.

no weight at all. Already, he asserted, in reference to the notorious submissiveness of the viceroy to his wife, the condesa and her ladies had more influence on the conduct of government in New Spain than the king.[35] In another letter, he declared that the king's decrees could scarcely be taken less notice of if they came from the king of France. A principal cause of the evil, in Palafox's pro-Creole view, was the highly defective system of administrative appointments and *corregidores*. 'In New Spain', he wrote, 'His Majesty appoints only five or six senior officers, the viceroys appoint one hundred and fifty.'[36] Unless Madrid greatly increased its share of such administrative appointments, he concluded, there would be no remedy and the poison of bureaucratic corruption would prove fatal. Furthermore, Palafox, like Manso before him, argued that the majority of the *corregidores*, that bureaucratic group to which he was most hostile, should be done away with, since they fulfilled no useful purpose and served only to oppress the people, and that the *alcaldes ordinarios*, the elected chief aldermen of the city councils, should be left to preside over local government.

But although there was a deep split in the Mexican body politic in the years 1644–6, there was not yet any commotion of the sort that occurred in 1647. The reason for this, it may very well be, is that in 1644–6 Salvatierra lacked the clerical cover without which nothing of a drastic nature could be accomplished. The viceroy could hardly try to lay hands on Palafox over matters relating to the *visita*, the *corregidores*, or the *Audiencia*, without blighting his own reputation and career. The viceroy could go onto the offensive when, and only when, appearances suggested that he was not responsible for the consequent commotion, that is to say when enough elements of the clergy were prepared to shield him; for in Mexico only the clergy were secure enough to be able to set off disturbances. Now it so happened, most inconveniently for Salvatierra, that the years 1644–6 coincided with a notable lull in ecclesiastical politics. The Mexican Franciscans had recently been brought to heel by a general chapter of their order at Toledo in Castile, which had decided to resign its claim to the Indian parishes lost in 1641[37] and to mend its fences with Palafox; and to enforce this policy, the Franciscan General had selected the most peaceable and conciliatory Spanish friar available to be commissary--general of New Spain. This person, Fray Bonaventura de Salinas y

35 ADI Palafox papers xxxv, fol. 21: Palafox to Francisco Zapata, 9 Sept. 1646.
36 ADI Palafox papers ix, fols. 56–62: Palafox to Council, 30 Nov. 1646; see also ADI Palafox papers xxxv, fols. 71–80: Palafox to the conde de Castrillo, 7 Sept. and 7 Oct. 1646.
37 ADI Palafox papers xlvii: 'Renunciacion que la religion de San Francisco a hecho' (1645).

Córdoba, succeeded in his mission, and gained warm praise from Palafox in the process.[38] Curiously, at this very same conjuncture the Mexican Jesuits had similarly been taken to task by their European brethren.[39] The Jesuit General in Rome, desiring to improve relations with the visitor-general of New Spain, had assigned to the Mexican province of the Society, as its new Provincial, Father Juan de Bueras, a person as competent and peaceable as Salinas y Córdoba. Consequently, the Jesuits too in the mid 1640s were in a noticeably less aggressive mood than they had been earlier. Certainly the Augustinian friars were at this time in a great fury with Palafox for trying to reduce their influence at the university[40] while reforming the constitutions of that seat of learning, the reform of the university constitutions being another of Palafox's numerous commissions; but that was a comparatively minor squabble, useless as a smokescreen for the viceroy.

But although the bureaucratic party was deprived of the support of the Franciscans and Jesuits in the mid 1640s, it did make one significant advance in the ecclesiastical sphere at this time: it won the support and allegiance of the new archbishop of Mexico, Don Juan de Mañozca. Mañozca had been consecrated archbishop by Palafox in 1644, and had briefly been quite close to him; soon, however, disagreement had caused a breach between the two. On the reason for this one can only speculate. We have noticed already that Mañozca was a Basque who was prejudiced against Creoles. Probably he also took umbrage at Palafox's unassailable position as de facto head of the Mexican secular clergy. It may also be relevant that Mañozca was an inquisitor by training and inclination,[41] that he virtually controlled the Mexican Inquisition during his time as archbishop by virtue of his special commission to reform the tribunal,[42] and that his first loyalty was very much to the Inquisition and not to the episcopal hierarchy; for it may possibly be that Palafox had already begun to criticize the Mexican Inquisition as a corrupt body interested only in laying its hands on money and therefore in seizing Jews—and oblivious to its duty to discipline the people and preside over morals. Be that as it may, a major consequence of Mañozca's adherence to the bureaucratic party was the intervention of the Inquisition in Mexican politics on the viceroy's side, with the archbishop's hold over the tribunal being

[38] ADI Palafox papers xxxv, fol. 80: Palafox to Castrillo, 6 June 1646.

[39] Palafox, *Carta al padre Horacio Caroche, Obras*, xi. 143.

[40] ADI Palafox papers ix, fol. 68; though Salvatierra did intervene to help the friars block the Palafox constitutions, see the *Efemérides de la real y pontificia universidad de México segun sus libros de claustros*, ed. A. M. Carreño (Mexico, 1963), i. 207–9.

[41] Sosa, *El Episcopado Mexicano* i. 230.

[42] AGN Inquisición 416, fol. 476.

SALVATIERRA, TORRES DE RUEDA

reinforced by the latest member to join it. This was his cousin, Don Juan Sáenz de Mañozca, another Basque and possibly the most virulent inquisitor to serve in Mexico in the seventeenth century.

In February 1646 the peaceable Jesuit Provincial, Father Bueras, died suddenly, and by his decease greatly strengthened the hand of the anti-Palafox coalition. The person chosen to succeed Bueras was the aristocratic Pedro de Velasco, a native of Mexico City and the first Creole ever to become Jesuit Provincial of New Spain.[43] He was a nephew of Viceroy Velasco II, had spent fourteen years in the Jesuit missions of Sinaloa in New Biscay, and, according to Alegre, knew the whole of Saint Thomas Aquinas by heart. Politically, he was closely associated with Francisco Calderón, Andres Pérez de Ribas, and Juan de San Miguel, the extreme anti-Palafox wing of the Society in Mexico, and consequently, from the spring of 1646 onwards, relations between the Jesuits and Palafox began to become more strained.

Nevertheless, another whole year was to pass before the start of the disturbances. It was a year of mounting tension but also a year of hesitation. The Jesuits, or rather the anti-Palafox wing of the Society, hoped to use the viceroy and the secular power against Palafox, just as the viceroy and the secular power hoped to use them. Both elements wanted the other to take the risks and the blame. Meanwhile Palafox was content to remain on the defensive. Accordingly, between February 1646 and March 1647, there was in Mexico a static confrontation in which the two sides offended each other only with words, published tracts, rhymes, and pasquinades.[44] The Jesuits displayed their usual eloquence at the pulpit, at the expense of Palafox, and Juan de San Miguel went so far as to admonish New Spain not to dabble with heresy lest she follow on the heels of Germany and England and bring down the wrath of the Almighty upon herself.[45] Francisco Calderón, according to Palafox, declared before a gathering of thirty Jesuits in Mexico City in November 1646 that they should 'commend New Spain to God, for from the provocation that the bishop of Puebla had given viceroy and *Audiencia*, an even bigger tumult was to be expected than that of the 15 January'.[46] And the more the conde held back, the more impatient the Jesuit extremists became. They

[43] Alegre, *Historia de la Compañia* ii. 207.

[44] Including a scurrilous tract which dilates at length on the sexual relations of Fray Marcos Ramírez del Prado, the Franciscan and anti-Palafox bishop of Michoacán who apparently was detested by a large number of the 300 secular clergy of his diocese, with the prioress of the convent of Valladolid, ADI Palafox papers liv, fols. 362–73; see also AGN Inquisicion 424, legajos i and 2; BM Add. MS. 13, 976: 'Relacion sucinta', fol. 303.

[45] *Sermon que predico el Padre Iuan de San Miguel* ... (Mexico, 1646).

[46] Palafox, *Carta al padre Horacio Caroche, Obras*, xi. 148–9.

enlisted the aid of the condesa, a domineering woman and a good friend to the Society, to help increase the pressure on her husband.[47] Father Juan de San Miguel, who, according to Palafox, was kind neither to his enemies nor his friends, is even said to have disparaged the viceroy as a 'Galician coward who is too scared to seize Palafox and throw him out of here'.[48]

In Mexico City, where the majority of the population were on Palafox's side, satirical sheets and verses circulated heaping ridicule on the conde and condesa and on the archbishop and Inquisition. These sheets enfuriated Mañozca and the inquisitors, who issued edicts warning that it was a crime against the faith to make insinuations about inquisitors, and an especially infamous crime at a time when the Inquisition was in the thick of Christ's battle against Judaism. Mañozca ordered the secular clergy of the capital to extract seditious papers from their parishioners and surrender them to the Holy Office. A number of persons suspected of composing and circulating such sheets were arrested and there commenced a special series of trials.[49] The records of these trials testify vividly to the tension building up in Mexico City and demonstrate the political terms in which the confrontation between Palafox and his enemies was understood by ordinary people and the common clergy. Bernardo de Quesada, to take one example, a cleric attached to Mexico City cathedral, lamented before the inquisitors that what Palafox had accomplished in the capital had been undone and obliterated by his enemies. All virtue had gone, he declared, the administration had become thoroughly corrupt again, and the nunneries had reverted to their old laxness. Archbishop Mañozca, his own superior, he ventured to call an indolent rascal who neglected his duty. Altogether, he summed up, 'I believe that the remedy for this land would be for my lord [Palafox] to govern it for say three years; and with that he would stop the practice of selling high office to the highest bidder, put virtuous men in administrative positions, revive justice, arrange everything in the service of God and the king, and reduce the government to a Christian one'.[50] Late in 1646, certain influential persons ventured to protest that the Inquisition was moving outside its proper sphere of competence, particularly when Alonso de Villalba, the leader of the Palafox faction in the *Audiencia*, was charged with having a hand in the insults against the viceroy, vicereine, archbishop, and Inquisition.[51] At this, the Jesuits and Dominicans promptly came forward with canonical proofs

[47] UTL G106: 'Relacion de lo occurido en Puebla', section 2, p. 11.
[48] Palafox, op. cit., p. 150.
[49] AGN Inquisición, vols. 424 and 429.
[50] AGN Inquisición 424, fol. 20ᵛ.
[51] Ibid., legajo i.

confirming that criticisms of inquisitors were offences against the faith.[52]

On 2 March 1647, five days before the commencement of the commotion, the Inquisition issued another edict condemning those who criticized the government and Inquisition, and this time, to underline its point that such people were heretics, it ordered a special ceremony to be conducted in all the parish churches of Mexico City.

'We command [ran the edict] that whilst our censures are being read [to the people], priests should hold a lighted candle in either hand and the holy cross should be draped in black as a sign of mourning; . . . and when the reading of the censures is done, we command that the said priests plunge the lighted candles in the holy water saying thus as the candles are extinguished in this water, so may the souls of such obstinate rebels [as write tracts attacking the viceroy, archbishop, and Inquisition] perish and be buried in hell." '[53]

On 6 March 1647, either succumbing to provocation or more probably deciding that his enemies' challenge had to be taken up, Palafox suddenly abandoned restraint and retaliated against the Jesuits,[54] who had been delivering some virulent sermons against him in recent weeks. Merlo, acting on Palafox's instructions, asked to see the preaching licences of the Jesuits of Puebla. They refused to present them, claiming special privilege. On 8 March the Jesuits were handed an ultimatum from the diocesan chapter which again was ignored. Finally, on 10 March drastic measures were taken against the Society within the jurisdiction of the diocese of Puebla:[55] the Jesuits were forbidden to preach, absolve, or fulfil any priestly function, and laymen were forbidden to attend the Jesuits under pain of excommunication. By this step Palafox unleashed the forces of conflict that had been pent up for so long.

When he heard the news, the Jesuit Provincial, Pedro de Velasco, held a series of meetings with his colleagues and also with representatives of the other religious orders in Mexico City, and prepared his reply. This was the election, by an old privilege of the orders, of two prominent Dominican friars, Agustín de Godines and Juan de Paredes (prior of the Dominican friary of Mexico City), as *jueces conservadores* or special ecclesiastical judges to adjudicate in the dispute between the Society and the bishop. The Dominicans, who were in one of their *gachupín*

---

52 Ibid., fols. 125–38.
53 Ibid., a printed sheet, fol. 151ᵛ.
54 Cuevas, *Historia de la Iglesia en México*, iii. 312–13.
55 UTL, Genaro García collection no. 105: 'Relación verídica de lo acaecido en la ciudad de la Puebla de los Angeles en el año de 1647 entre el Ilmo. exmo. y venerable sr. Don Juan de Palafox y Mendoza y los religiosos de la compañía' (1647 and 1649) (20th-century copy), pp. 6–7.

quadrennia at this time,[56] had for a year or two been the most militant of the mendicant orders. They had lost three Indian parishes to Palafox in 1641, but their chief reason for joining in the attack on the bishop at this stage was their anxiety for their extensive interests in Oaxaca which were threatened by the *Palafoxista* Bishop Benavente.[57] Having chosen their special ecclesiastical judges, the Jesuits then called upon the viceroy to acknowledge the validity of the election and prevent Palafox from trying to block it by means of the *Audiencia*. Salvatierra, satisfied at last that the clergy were doing enough to protect him, agreed. The *Audiencia* was bypassed and the validity of the election of *jueces conservadores* in the dispute with Palafox upheld by viceregal order.[58] Palafox, seeing the Dominicans, of all elements of the clergy, in alliance with the Jesuits, was outraged by the hypocrisy and political opportunism that it implied. In Europe and in China, as he pointed out,[59] the two orders were, by tradition and theological tendency, arch-enemies. Even the Jesuits, or at least the European Jesuits, were to agree with Palafox on this. When the Castilian province of the Society learnt of the alliance of their Mexican brethren with the Dominicans, they communicated their disapproval in no uncertain terms.[60] Meanwhile, in Mexico City, Archbishop Mañozca too had declared in favour of the *jueces conservadores* and had incarcerated Juan Bautista de Herrera, Palafox's diocesan representative in the capital, who had ventured to protest at the recognition of the judges, in the archiepiscopal gaol.[61] Another dissident, don Francisco López de Solís, lecturer in canon law at the University and perhaps the most prestigious Mexican Creole lawyer of the day, was imprisoned by Salvatierra. [62]

On 2 April 1647 the special ecclesiastical judges reached their decision on the dispute over preaching licences and came out, predictably enough, in favour of the Society. Palafox was given six days in which to drop his case and revoke the censures that he had imposed under pain of excommunication and a heavy fine. However, on 6 April Palafox beat the judges to the mark, and in a solemn ceremony in

---

[56] Franco y Ortega, *Segunda parte*, 519.

[57] González Dávila, *Teatro eclesiástico*, i. 232.

[58] BM Add. MS. 13, 976, no. 47: 'Relacion sucinta' is the document which declares most explicitly that Salvatierra and his officers were using the Jesuits and Dominicans as a political instrument with which to 'finish with the bishop and the *visita*', fol. 302; but see also Palafox, 'Quejas contra Salvatierra' BNX 1216, fols. 15–22; UTL G 105: 'Relación verídica', p. 12, and Guijo, *Diario*, i. 10.

[59] Palafox, *Carta al Padre Horacio Caroche, Obras*, xi. 185.

[60] *Copia de una carta que el padre provincial y los padres de la Compania de Jesus de Castilla, escribieron al padre provincial y Compania de la Nueva España* (1647), in García, *Don Juan de Palafox*, p. 304.

[61] UTL G 105: 'Relación verídica', p. 13.

[62] Ibid.

Puebla cathedral excommunicated the judges and forbade anyone under his diocesan jurisdiction, clerical or lay, to recognize the *jueces conservadores* as true *jueces conservadores*, or to read or listen to any of their proclamations under pain of excommunication. At the same time, Palafox took the opportunity to excommunicate several more of the most prominent Jesuits of Puebla and put out a fresh call to the citizens of Puebla to transfer their sons from the Jesuit colleges of the city to his own, a call which appears to have had, as we have noted already, a marked effect.

On 8 April the special judges excommunicated Palafox and Merlo and threatened with excommunication any who questioned their competence to excommunicate the bishop. However, as was quickly apparent, the declaration had only a very limited force so far as the city and diocese of Puebla were concerned owing to the fact that the special judges had no way of promulgating their decree in that city. Consequently, the *Palancas*, as the *Palafoxistas* called the viceroy's party,[63] or at least the viceroy, condesa, and archbishop, decided to dispatch a special Inquisition commission to Puebla to enforce promulgation of the judges' censures. This mission, headed by the former chaplain of the duque de Escalona, Gutiérrez de Medina, and a Basque secular priest, Miguel Ibarra, entered Puebla on 18 May 1647 and took lodgings and offices in the Augustinian friary. In the next few days, these functionaries affixed copies of the judges' censures and special Inquisition posters threatening those who might be inclined to disturb those of the judges, to walls and gates all over the city.[64] The Inquisition forbade criticism of the *jueces conservadores*, declared that it was a religious offence to deride the Jesuits, forbade anyone to question whether such rulings were within the competence of the Inquisition, and banned all printing in Puebla for a period of four years.[65]

The next few days in Puebla were very tense.[66] Some of the posters of both Inquisition and Dominican judges were torn down; others were spattered with mud and spat upon. Obscene daubings appeared on the walls of friaries and convents and virulent political verses circulated more than ever. There was also some trouble in the nunneries. For years, the 600 nuns of Puebla, like the 1,000 nuns of Mexico City, had

63 UTL G 105: 'Relación verídica', pp. 56–7 the Salvatierra party, apparently, called themselves the *realistas* (royalists), BM Add. MS. 14, 012, fols. 65–7.

64 AGN Inquisición 429, fol. 411ᵛ; Juan de Palafox, *Carta al Inquisidor General ... en que se queja de los atentados cometidos contra su dignidad y persona por el tribunal de la Inquisicion de Mexico* (10 August 1647) (1st edn. Cadiz, 1813), pp. 5–8.

65 Ibid.

66 AGN Inquisición 429, leg. 15; UTL G 105: 'Relacíon verídica', p. 16.

been sharply divided, for the Palafoxian discipline and against.[67] Most of the mothers superior appear to have been against, and in the nunneries affiliated to the religious orders, except, as always, in that of the Carmelites, the Inquisition functionaries were given a polite welcome when they came to read out the censures and decrees to the assembled nuns. However, in the nunneries under the bishop's jurisdiction, that is in nunneries with secular priests as confessors, there were a number of incidents. Palafox, apparently, had instructed the confessors to instruct the mothers superior to bid the sisters flee to their cells and refuse to listen should the Inquisition officers come to read out their edicts. In two or three cases, however, the plan went awry and the mothers superior denounced the priests to the Inquisition who had them hauled away.

The Inquisition commissioners, annoyed by their reception in the city, soon began arresting secular priests and other partisans of Palafox and detaining them in a special gaol that had been prepared in the Augustinian friary. The arrest which caused most stir was that of Antonio Xuarez Maldonado, a well-known and popular parish priest who was afterwards dragged away in chains and taken under guard to Mexico City where his arrival caused a minor disturbance with groups of youths noisily blaming the scandal on the archbishop.[68] Xuarez was charged with having said that the Inquisitors were biased against Palafox and that they were profligate and slept with women; he was also charged with having called the archbishop an old fool and with having said that there would be fighting if the viceroy dared to send officers and soldiers into Puebla.[69] In addition to Xuarez, some thirty other prisoners, lay and clerical, ranging from close associates of the bishop to a mestizo caught throwing mud at an Inquisition poster, were despatched for trial in the capital.[70] One of the prisoners, a servant of Palafox, was charged with having insulted and threatened the prioress of one of the nunneries of Puebla for having permitted the Inquisition censures to be read to her nuns. Another, a New Christian lawyer attached to the *Audiencia* whose father had been 'reconciled' by the Peruvian Inquisition for judaizing, was charged with slandering the viceroy, archbishop, and Inquisitors as 'common thieves'. Another, Antonio Aguilar, a parish priest, was charged with saying that the Inquisition had no right to do what it was doing, and that if the viceroy dared to send his men into Puebla there would be a terrible tumult and that after it not a hair of the Jesuits would remain.

67 AGN Inquisición 429, fol. 407.
68 BNX 890, fol. 4ᵛ; UTL G 105: 'Relación verídica', p. 16.
69 AGN Inquisición 429, fol. 404.
70 Ibid., fols. 402–16.

On 7 June 1647 there occurred an incident which was subsequently to play a crucial role in the controversy over the Puebla troubles of 1647; there was a popular demonstration in support of Palafox. According to the *Palafoxistas*, who obviously had an interest in making as little of the incident as possible, very little happened;[71] Palafox simply appeared in the Plaza Mayor, the cathedral bells were rung as always happened when Palafox appeared, and a huge crowd had gathered, as a spontaneous expression of the love and affection which the people felt for their prelate. However, according to the viceroy, Inquisition, and Jesuits, there was a lot more to the incident than that.[72] As they saw it—or as the *Palafoxistas* believed, concocted it—Palafox had arranged the whole affair as a means of impressing his enemies with his power to disturb the stability of the viceroyalty and had toured the city in a magnificent carriage to shouts of 'Palafox for viceroy!' The Inquisition sought to depict Palafox as a menace to order and either believed or pretended to believe that a rising was likely.[73] According to the Inquisition, a gang of mulatto thugs were kept in the bishop's residence along with a store of guns and ammunition

... and in general it was spread abroad that the bishop's residence was stocked with guns ... and that his servants went armed with pistols and other arms ... moreover, the *corregidor* of Puebla, Don Agustín de Valdéz y Portugal reports [to the Inquisition] that the bishop's servants are spreading the word that there will be a tumult or popular rising. The Inquisition commissioner replied that he could not imagine such a thing as there were so many loyal and noble persons in the city as would be seen at the first blast of the trumpet (calling out the militia). The *corregidor* replied that there was nothing to fear from the noble and loyal elements, but that the commissioner should realize that there were many Negroes, mulattoes, mestizos, and secular priests in the city.[74]

According to the anonymous author of the 'Relación verídica' and other pro-Palafox tracts, Salvatierra and his associates were deliberately concocting lies in an attempt to blacken the reputation of the visitor-general.[75] Probably, it would be more accurate to say that the viceroy was merely making political capital out of the fact that the city of Puebla was in a state of considerable excitement. For there can be no doubt that *Palafoxistas* as well as *realistas* feared that there might be a

71 UTL G 105: 'Relación verídica', p. 20.
72 AGN Inquisición 416, fols. 475V–493: Mexican Inquisition to Inquisitor General in Madrid, 15 Aug. 1647; and the passage from the 'Relacion ajustada', a Jesuit manuscript in the Bibl. Vitt. Eman. in Rome, quoted in Astrain, *Historia de la Compañía*, v. 380.
73 AGN Inquisición 416, fols. 475V–493 and 429, fols. 409–10.
74 AGN Inquisición 416, fol. 484.
75 UTL G 105: 'Relación verídica', p. 20.

popular commotion. 'What limits would there have been to the commotion?' asked Leonardo de Saldaña, a pro-Palafox Creole citizen of Puebla, in a letter to a friend.

How many deaths . . . would have resulted from such a tumult which would have been provoked by the Jesuits in order to lend feasibility to their lies had not Providence ordained another course and had not the bishop foreseen that if the worst came to the worst, the common people would rise up in his defence? For there was great risk to those who were behind the trouble, especially the Jesuits, for were the common people let loose, and in Puebla they consist of Indians, Negroes, mulattoes, and mestizos, with the Spaniards making up less than a fifth of the population, the city's churches and convents would have been in great danger of being sacked and burned.[76]

The demonstration of 7 June and other evidence of the agitated state of Puebla persuaded Salvatierra that it was time to suppress the *Palafoxistas* by force. A special expedition was made ready and placed under the command of Don Diego de Orejón, *corregidor* of Mexico City, and Agustín de Valdéz, *alcalde mayor* of Puebla. On 9 June an edict was proclaimed in Puebla which had already been published in the capital a fortnight earlier, announcing that the king and his council of the Indies had acknowledged the *jueces conservadores* and threatened with severe punishment any who dared question the legitimacy of their actions. The document, purporting to be a royal *cédula*, was in fact a forgery authorized, one presumes, by the viceroy.[77] Palafox, his diocesan chapter, and the Puebla city council, in a last-minute effort to mollify the conde despatched representatives to the capital to offer concessions, but it was now too late to resolve the crisis by negotiation. Salvatierra refused even to see the Puebla delegates.[78]

Palafox now found himself in the most difficult quandary of his career. He was to relive the experience many times in subsequent years and discuss it several times in his later writings.[79] If he resisted the viceroy, or caused others to resist, he would have been guilty of

[76] BNX 890 fol. 6[V].

[77] BNX 1216, Palafox, 'Quejas contra Salvatierra', fols. 7, 41[V]; *Razon qve da a vuestra magestad el obispo visitador don Iuan de Palafox*, fol. 5; and for the document itself, see Francisco González Cossio, *La Imprenta en Mexico* (additions to Toribio de Medina) (Mexico, 1952), pp. 66–77, *Testimonio de una provision del rey en que se imparte plenamente el real auxilio a la legitima jurisdiccion apostolica de los muy r. p. jueces delegados conservadores de la Compania de Jesus en el pleito con don Juan de Palafox*.

[78] BM Add. MS. 13, 976: 'Relacion sucinta', fol. 303[V]; UTL G 105: 'Relación Verídica', p. 17.

[79] BNX 1216, Palafox 'Quejas contra Salvatierra', fols. 28–40; Juan de Palafox, *Cargos y satisfacciones*, in *Obras*, xi. 231–3; *Razon qve da a vuestra magestad el obispo visitador Don Iuan de Palafox*, fols. 16–19.

treason, have threatened the stability of the viceroyalty, risked everything that he had worked for, and, probably, wrecked his own career. On the other hand, if he submitted, he would have destroyed his own work or at least consented to see it destroyed, betrayed his ideals, and denied his Creole flock and, as he saw it, the Almighty Himself. What then could he do? He resolved to disappear. On the night of 14 June he suddenly left Puebla and wrote, on the following day, from Tepeaca, explaining his action to his diocesan council. Then, with only two companions, he vanished into the sierra, leaving no sign as to his whereabouts.

The disappearance of the visitor-general was, of course, regarded as a most extraordinary event. In the short run, it proved disastrous for his cause. The *Palafoxistas* were utterly dismayed while the viceroy's party was jubilant. But in the long run, Palafox was shown to have been right. By refusing either to provoke a disturbance or give in, he both preserved his own position and rendered matters difficult for his enemies. At least one of the viceroy's supporters tried to argue that the very quietness in Puebla that followed Palafox's flight from the city proved that he was responsible for the previous agitation,[80] but the authorities in Madrid and Rome, as we shall see, were not taken in by this line of argument. Palafox's confidence that, sooner or later, Madrid would rescue him and his reformation was to prove well founded.

In the days following Palafox's disappearance, Puebla was the scene of some spectacular happenings. Salvatierra's special force arrived with its secretary, Melchor Juárez, the New Christian who had been Palafox's secretary some years before; he had fallen out with Palafox, joined with the bishop's adversaries, and, by a fine twist of irony, become secretary to Archbishop Mañozca.[81] In the wake of the viceroy's and archbishop's men, the Jesuits and Dominicans staged a grand entry of their own, the two special judges leading the way in an extravagantly adorned coach escorted by their own guards. The Puebla Jesuits and their supporters, bearing uplifted crosses and chanting *Te Deums*, turned out in force to greet them. The next few days, as far as the anti-Palafox elements were concerned, were devoted largely to festivities, junketings, and the overthrow of Palafoxian austerity.[82] The religious orders gave a series of lavish banquets to which they invited one another and their friends. The special ecclesiastical judges, followed by a train of smiling friars and Jesuits, toured the city, visited the baths of Atoyaque, enjoyed sumptuous picnics in the Puebla alameda, and were danced to by mulatta girls. The theatre and other entertainments

---

[80] AGI México 76, r 1: Pedro Melián to council, 19 Aug. 1647.

[81] BM add. MS. 13, 976: 'Relacion Sucinta', fol. 305; Guijo, *Diario*, i. 10.

[82] BM add. MS. 13, 976: 'Relacion sucinta', fols. 305v–306; BNX 890, fols. 7v–8: Saldaña, first letter.

of which Palafox had disapproved were revived; there was music and dance on all sides, the nunneries relaxed, and prostitutes once more abounded.

While the viceroy's party rejoiced, the *Palafoxistas* were plunged in gloom and subjected to a systematic repression conducted by Orejón and Valdéz. Palafox's residence was seized and ransacked and his papers, including the bulk of the documents relating to the *visita*, removed.[83] The colleges of San Pedro and San Juan were occupied by soldiers and the city was patrolled, according to one account almost as if it were enemy territory. A number of houses and other buildings were searched for traces of Palafox, including the Carmelite priory.[84] Spies and informers were kept busy reporting to the *corregidores* and Inquisition on known sympathizers of Palafox, and the city was daubed with anti-Palafox slogans. A number of nuns who ventured to protest at the abandonment of the Palafoxian rule were punished and at least one was stripped of her veil and set to scrub the kitchens. The general atmosphere, according to the pro-Palafox texts, was one of utter dejection. The entire Negro and mulatto population of the city demonstrated its resentment at the way Palafox had been treated by suspending indefinitely the music, dances, and games, which it was accustomed to perform on Sundays and holidays.[85] In the streets, people were too frightened even to mention the name of Palafox. The author of the 'Relación Verídica' records that his one consolation during that evil hour when Palafox and his supporters were so sorely oppressed was to see that of those who opposed the bishop only a few were natives of New Spain.[86]

Among their various activities at this time, Orejón and Valdéz were busy collecting evidence, or what they accepted as evidence, against the visitor-general. In particular, they took statements from dozens of witnesses to the effect that Palafox and his friends had been planning to provoke a popular commotion. Most of this material, according at least to the Puebla city council[87] and other pro-Palafox sources, was utterly bogus, for most of the witnesses represented in the *corregidores'* records as Spanish gentlemen were in fact Negroes, mestizos, and other 'disreputable persons'. Some of these witnesses, according to the Puebla city council, were swayed by Jesuit coin, others were tortured, while a number of Negro slaves were promised their freedom if they would

83 ADI Palafox papers xc, fols. 78–9: Salvatierra to Agustín de Valdéz, 9 and 18 July 1647.
84 Guijo, *Diario*, i. 12.
85 UTL G 105: 'Relación verídica', p. 47.
86 Ibid., p. 23.
87 ACP xxii, fols. 169v–172.

assent and denounce the bishop. Altogether, concluded the *cabildo*, the affair was a disgraceful slur on the 'reputation of one of the most noble and loyal cities that His Majesty has in his monarchy'.

Another feature of the repression of these months was the declaration that the diocese of Puebla was a *sede vacante*, that Palafox was no longer bishop. The viceroy's party had to work hard to extract this declaration from the diocesan chapter and there was some delay before it was obtained.[88] The method used to overcome the resistance of the council was simple, if somewhat crude. Don Juan de Merlo, who in Madrid had just been chosen as the new bishop of Honduras, was arrested, dispatched to Mexico City, and imprisoned. Alonso de Cuevas y Dávalos and three or four other members of the chapter were threatened with arrest and forced into hiding. The rest of the chapter were either intimidated, or, as apparently in the case of Juan de Vega, the *gachupín* dean, bribed.

The campaign against Palafox in Puebla continued throughout the summer of 1647 and was punctuated by a number of fairly memorable incidents. One such was the ceremony on the night of 21 July when Pedro de Velasco and the special ecclesiastical judges presided over the return of their preaching licences to the Jesuits of Puebla;[89] it was apparently a splendid occasion at which the viceroy, archbishop, *Audiencia*, and all the mendicant orders were represented, only the Carmelites being conspicuous by their absence. But by far the most remarkable demonstration in Puebla during the months of Palafox's absence was the masked procession put on by the Jesuits on the day of Saint Ignatius Loyola. This, according to the pro-Palafox sources, was an utterly disgraceful affair;[90] it certainly caused a scandal which was to be remembered for more than a century. A column of masked students, Negro slaves, and others specially hired by the Society, protected by officers and soldiers, paraded through the centre of the city with a grotesque representation of Palafox and a triumphal float bearing Saint Ignatius. Another group of masqueraders, dressed like secular priests and wearing masks crudely representing various of the bishop's associates, were subjected to mockery. The whole affair, according to the *Palafoxistas*, was characterized by extreme irreverence and lewdness, with some of the masqueraders carrying 'lewd instruments' with which they made indecent gestures at the women and girls looking down from the windows above. However, the Almighty

---

88 BNX 1216: Palafox, 'Quejas contra Salvatierra', fols. 85v–87.

89 UTL G 105: 'Relación Verídica', p. 38.

90 BNX 890: Saldaña, second letter, 18 Nov. 1648, fols. 20–21v; Juan de Palafox, *Carta (Tercera) . . . al sumo Pontífice, Inocencio Decimo* (8 Jan. 1649) (3rd. edn., Madrid, 1768), pp. 73–5.

punished the Jesuits for their insolence, we are told, for as the procession neared its end, the head of Saint Ignatius fell off.

The summer months of 1647 in Puebla did not pass without at least some *Palafoxista* counter-demonstrations. In particular, there were the four days of disturbances beginning on 24 September. According to the Inquisition, which made much of the episode,[91] the rioting started with the ringing of the cathedral bells and the gathering of a large crowd in the city centre, and led to a certain amount of stone-throwing and shouts of 'Viva Palafox, viceroy and visitor-general! ' and 'Muera the Galician! ' (meaning Salvatierra). Groups of rioters ran through various streets, stoned the residences of Agustín de Valdéz and the dean, Juan de Vega, and abused the Jesuits as 'Lutheran heretic dogs' and the Augustinians as 'tale-bearers and Inquisition gaolers'. The demonstrators also smashed part of the choir-loft of the Jesuit college of the Espíritu Santo. According to the author of the 'Relacion veridica', however, the scale and significance of the disturbances was greatly exaggerated by the viceroy's party for their own ends, the incidents really being of only a very minor character.[92]

Towards the end of October 1647, the period of Palafox's eclipse at last came to an end and the situation in New Spain was completely transformed by the arrival in Veracruz of word from Madrid. Palafox had won the battle for the ear of the king.[93] The conde de Salvatierra, it was learned, was removed from the government of Mexico and 'promoted' to that of Peru. To succeed him, temporarily, until a new viceroy came from Spain, Madrid had appointed Don Marcos de Torres y Rueda, bishop of the Yucatán, a personage who would certainly side with Palafox against the Salvatierra party. Puebla turned overnight from despondency to jubilation.[94] The Inquisition commissioners, suddenly quietened, returned to the capital. Palafox, after an absence of four months and twenty-four days, returned to his 'Rachel', on 10 November, arriving in the middle of the night so as to avoid too great a demonstration of popular joy. Then on 25 November Puebla was at last given over to thanksgiving, music, dancing, and illuminations.

For the next six months or so, the political combinations in New Spain were in a state of equilibrium. Bishop Torres y Rueda arrived in Veracruz from Campeche on 24 November, and in Mexico City a few weeks later; on arrival, he discovered that the conde was not yet ready

91 See the report based on statements from thirty 'eye-witnesses': AGN Inquisición 416, fols. 495–496ᵛ: Mexican Inquisition to Inquisitor General, 12 Nov. 1647.
92 UTL G 105: 'Relación verídica', pp. 45–6.
93 Guijo, *Diario*, i. 13.
94 BNX 890: Saldaña, 2nd letter, fols. 25ᵛ–28; Guijo, *Diario*, i. 14.

to relinquish office.[95] Much to his annoyance, the bishop was forced to move into a residence at Tacuba where he was kept at the conde's expense until the following spring. During this period, the *realistas*, as they termed themselves, in no position to resume their offensive, remained on the defensive, while the *Palafoxistas*, similarly constrained, had to put off their hopes of revenge.

In May 1648 the period of suspense ended with the coming of fresh word from Spain. This time Madrid was much more emphatic.[96] Salvatierra was ordered to hand over the government to Bishop Torres at once. Archbishop Mañozca and the Jesuit and Dominican Provincials were rebuked in no uncertain terms for their conduct, and the *jueces conservadores* were instructed to cease their activities immediately. Bishop Torres was asked to take steps to ensure that the conflict between the parties now came to an end, and in particular to do nothing to obstruct the passage of the conde to Acapulco and on no account to conduct a purge of pro-Salvatierra *corregidores* and other officers. Palafox was asked to do his utmost to help bring the trouble to an end and ordered to cease interfering with Jesuit educational activities in Puebla.[97]

However, the royal hope that New Spain would now be restored to tranquillity was to go unfulfilled. Bishop Torres took over the government with the title of bishop-governor on 13 May 1648 and the long-awaited purge of *Palancas* began almost at once. On 15 May Don Diego de Orejón and several of his deputies were dismissed from their posts in Mexico City and compelled to take refuge in the Jesuit college of Saint Gregory. The conde's assessor, Mateo de Cisneros, was also dismissed and punished with a massive fine. Evidently Torres, in direct contradiction to his orders from Spain, was soon 'changing all the *alcaldes mayores*, *corregidores*, deputies, and officers in the colony'.[98] The purge was particularly effective in Puebla, where it began on 28 May. The recently appointed pro-Salvatierra *corregidor*, Diego de Villegas, was replaced with Don Juan Manuel de Sotomayor. Juan de Vega and two or three other members of the Puebla diocesan council who had co-operated with Salvatierra and the Jesuits in the declaration of *sede vacante* were forced to flee to Mexico City where they found

95 AGI México 36, r 2: Salvatierra to council, 21 Dec. 1647; AGI México 76, r i: *Audiencia* to council, 20 Dec. 1647 (one can discern Salvatierra's hand behind this letter).

96 AGN cédulas reales originales iii, fols. 29–50; Guijo, *Diario*, i. 14.

97 AGN cédulas reales originales iii, fol. 39.

98 Guijo, *Diario*, i. 15; AGI México 76, r. 3: Pedro Melián to council, 26 May 1649.

refuge in the Jesuit college of Saint Peter.[99] Agustín de Valdéz was arrested in Tepeaca, of which jurisdiction he had recently become *corregidor*, imprisoned for a time in Palafox's college of San Juan in Puebla, and then moved to Mexico City to be tried by the *Audiencia*.

For the rest of 1648 the *Palafoxistas*, under the well-disposed if somewhat corrupt gaze of Bishop Torres, enjoyed a clear ascendancy though their opponents still continued to resist. The leadership of the anti-Palafox coalition had now devolved upon Archbishop Mañozca, who though elderly was not lacking in that obstinacy so characteristic of his nation. In fact, he seized on every opportunity to snub his enemies, even causing the bells of Mexico City cathedral to be rung when he was informed of the safe arrival of the conde and condesa in Peru. More importantly, he and his cousin put up a stout resistance to Bishop Benavente of Oaxaca who had been assigned powers to investigate certain aspects of the Inquisition by Madrid, when that prelate repaired to the capital in July, intent on destroying the hold of the Mañozcas over the institution. After some weeks of moves and counter-moves in and out of the *Audiencia*, and at least one popular demonstration against the archbishop,[100] Bishop Benavente was forced to retire to Oaxaca having accomplished nothing.

The most important aspect of the continued tension of 1648 was the development of the feud between Palafox and the Jesuits. In September a group of the bishop's representatives and other clerical functionaries returned from Rome bringing with them the text of Pope Innocent X's bull of 14 May 1648, in which most of the points, or at least ecclesiastical points, at issue between the Society and the bishop were settled in favour of the bishop.[101] But even with the Pope against them, and with remarkable sang-froid, not to say disregard for their own professed principles, the Jesuits refused to accept the verdict, pointing out that the Papal bull was yet to be ratified by the royal council of the Indies.[102] By the end of 1648 the prospect of peace between Palafox and the Jesuits was more remote than ever. Palafox was now using every means at his disposal to lessen Jesuit influence in Puebla. The battle over education was in full swing and according to

[99]BNX 890 fols. 40–41ᵛ: Saldaña, 3rd letter.

[100]Guijo, *Diario*, i. 19–20; UTL G 105: 'Relación verídica' fols. 85–9.

[101]Guijo, *Diario*, i. 21.

[102]Andrés de Rada to Palafox, 14 Apr. 1649 in *Cartas del venerable siervo de Dios Don Juan de Palafox y Mendoza, obispo de la Puebla de los Angeles, al R. P. Andres de Rada, Provincial de la Compania de Jesus en Mexico, y de este a su excelencia ilustrisimo y otros documentos* ed. Thomas Vasconsellos (Rome, 1700), p. 15; Juan de Palafox, *Al Rey nuestro señor, Satisfacion al memorial de los religiosos de la Compañía del nombre de Jesus de la Nueva España. Por la dignidad episcopal* (Madrid, 1652), pp. 12–13.

Andrés de Rada, Velasco's successor as Jesuit Provincial, the diocesan council of Puebla was even refusing to receive graduates of Jesuit colleges into the secular clergy.[103] Palafox also persuaded at least one Indian lay brotherhood to move its chapel from the Jesuit Church to a parish Church under his own jurisidiction, a move that incensed the Jesuits.

Palafox also began to broaden the scope of his criticism of the Jesuits. Already by the spring of 1647 he had ceased to restrict his remarks to such ordinary matters as that of the tithe. In his second letter to the Pope, the bishop had ventured to condemn Jesuit wealth as such and had expressed his dislike of the way the Jesuits created a spiritual flock for themselves out of those who worked on their haciendas and in their factories and kept their workers away from the parish churches.[104] But even in his second letter Palafox was still restricting the terms of the argument, criticizing only what he regarded as the bad practices of the Society in Mexico. It was not until after the events of the summer of 1647 that the bishop started to attack the Society and criticize its tendencies and traditions in a general sense. 'What other religious order', asked Palafox in his third epistle to the Pope, 'has been such an obstacle to the progress of the Church and filled Christendom with so much dissension?'[105] The Society of Jesus, he declared, has so strange a character that it belongs neither with the secular clergy nor with the regular.[106] On the one hand the Jesuits threaten the integrity of diocesan administration by usurping the functions of the secular clergy, while on the other they eschew the goals of the cloister, of self-mortification and poverty of the spirit. Worse still, he continued, the Jesuits had maimed and twisted holy doctrine, even the very essence of Christianity, to suit themselves and their own sordid ends;[107] in China they had distorted the teachings of the Church beyond recognition. Furthermore, as a consequence of the extravagant notions of the Jesuits, the Jesuit ascendancy over Catholic education had become one of the foremost perils facing the Church. The Jesuits were undermining both the faith and the morals of the young. In short, he affirmed, Jesuit doctrines were 'not only bad, but very dangerous and prejudicial to the Christian commonwealth'.[108]

---

[103] Cartas (Palafox-Rada), p. 29.

[104] Juan de Palafox, Carta segunda a Inocencio Decimo, Pontifice Maximo (25 May, 1647), Obras, xi. 34–5, 48, 52, 58.

[105] Carta del venerable siervo de Dios Don Juan de Palafox y Mendoza al sumo Pontifice Inocencio Decimo (8 Jan. 1649) (3rd edn., Madrid, 1768), p. 141.

[106] Ibid., p. 140.

[107] Ibid., pp. 142–82.

[108] Ibid., p. 151.

The letter ended with Palafox asking the Pope to do away with the Society in its existing form and either merge it with the rest of the regular clergy by changing its constitutions, or with the secular clergy by putting it under the bishops.[109]

Naturally enough, this great widening of Palafox's critique of the Society caused a sharp about-turn in the position of the European Jesuits on developments in Mexico. Hitherto, the European Jesuits had thought that their Mexican brethren were in the wrong and had been prepared to assert that nothing was to be gained by prolonging the dispute with Bishop Palafox. The Jesuit General in Rome, Vincenzo Caraffa (1645–9), writing in January 1648, had sharply rebuked the Mexican province of the Society for its role in the events of 1647.[110] In 1648, however, as the European Jesuits learned of the fresh developments in the feud, their attitude changed. They saw the bishop's position for what it had now become, a full-scale assault on the Society. By the beginning of 1649, all possibility of a *rapprochement* had gone and Palafox and the Jesuits were implacable foes everywhere and constantly.

The continuation of the trouble in Mexico and Palafox's disobedience to the crown in persisting with his feud with the Jesuits resulted in the decision to suspend his *visita*, which was by no means yet approaching completion, and to recall him to Spain. He received instructions in the autumn of 1648 to sail on the flota of 1649. Probably, Palafox's star at court had been in partial decline for some time owing to the fall of Olivares in 1643, the rehabilitation of his enemy the Duke of Escalona, and also the disturbances of 1647; his credit had still been good enough to enable him to get the better of Salvatierra, but with the continuing dissension of 1648, Madrid judged it politic to recall him. Apparently, Palafox was greatly dismayed by the order. It made him sad that he was required to leave so much unfinished and to leave also his beloved Puebla.[111]

Still, a short period remained to Palafox from the autumn of 1648, time enough to advance his work a little further. His chief priority in these final months was the completion of Puebla cathedral. He intended it to be the monument to his endeavours in Mexico, the symbol of his reformation, a purpose for which its harmonious but austere outlines eminently befitted it. The architect and sculptor to whom he entrusted

---

[109] *Carta del venerable siervo de Dios* pp. 182–3.

[110] *Carta de reprension que el R. P. Vincencio Caraffa, Preposito General de la Compania de Jesus dirigio al P. Pedro de Velasco, Provincial de la misma en la Nueva España*, (Rome, 30 Jan. 1648) in *DHM* vii.

[111] Palafox to Pope Innocent X, 8 Jan. 1649, in *La Puebla de los Angeles*, pp. 159–61.

direction of the last stages in the construction of the great edifice was his fellow Aragonese, Mosen Pedro García Ferrer, an artist whose aesthetic ideas harmonized well with his own. The amounts of labour and money needed to finish the cathedral in time were prodigious, but the Puebla city council, eager to get a step in front of Mexico City, contributed handsomely, labourers toiled day and night, and at length the building neared completion. Plans were prepared to celebrate its consecration with the utmost magnificence on 18 April 1649.

The consecration of Puebla cathedral of course had political as well as religious and artistic significance. However one looked at it, it was a victory for Palafox, a means of perpetuating his influence and his memory, and of making a deep impression on the common people. Moreover, it was regarded as a challenge by the Mañozca party, a challenge which that party was determined to meet. By the beginning of 1649, archbishop, Inquisition, and Jesuits were hard at work devising a scheme for rubbing the shine off Palafox's triumph, for staging an event of equal or, if possible, greater magnificence. Their idea was to stage a gigantic *Auto-de-fe*, by far the largest that had ever been held in Mexico, using up the main body of the remaining Jewish prisoners in the Inquisition dungeons in one go, so as to achieve maximum effect. The scheme was bound to succeed, indeed it was the one sure way to bring out the whole population of Mexico City and make it bow in reverence before the Mañozcas and their colleagues. The date for the celebration of this giant *Auto General de la Fe* was fixed, with eloquent sense of timing, for Sunday 11 April, one week before the opening of Puebla cathedral. To ensure success, the inquisitors gave the event an elaborate build-up. On 11 January archibishop, inquisitors, and Jesuits paraded through the centre of Mexico City with the Mexico City council and nobility trailing dutifully behind, making the appropriate announcement.[112] This was followed up by the publication in Mexico City of a full-length epic poem celebrating the downfall of Judaism before the Holy cross.[113]

Meanwhile, the political situation had been made additionally complicated by the policies of Bishop Torres and the husband of his niece, his right-hand man Juan de Salazar. By all accounts the bishop was extremely corrupt[114]—it was later revealed that he and his relatives had pocketed upwards of half a million pesos during his brief term—and

[112]Guijo, *Diario*, i. 28.

[113]Francisco Corchero Carreño, *Desagravios de Christo en el Triumpho de su cruz contra el Judaismo, poema heroico* (Mexico, 1649); Corchero Carreño was the chaplain in the viceregal prison.

[114]AGI México 76, r 3: Bañuelos to council, 26 May 1649; ibid., Pedro Melián to council, 23 May 1649; Guijo, *Diario*, i. 48–50.

doted on his niece, Doña Petronila de Torres, apparently a most extravagant young lady. Altogether, the bishop was so preoccupied with profit that he quickly exhausted the good will that he had gained with the Creoles by his purge of Salvatierra's men: he fell out with Palafox who refused to tolerate his colleague's lax ideas, and as has been seen,[115] became embroiled with the Mexico City council and with Don Jerónimo de Bañuelos, the recently arrived, Madrid-appointed, pro-Palafox[116] *corregidor* of Mexico City. When the bishop arrested Bañuelos on the first day of January 1649 and appointed Andrés Pérez Franco in his place, the break between Torres and the *Palafoxistas* became final. At the same time, he remained sharply at odds with Archbishop Mañozca and the Inquisition. The stage seemed to be set for a battle of three prelates.

April 1649 was certainly an extraordinary month in Mexican history. Two days before the celebration of the *Auto General*, Bishop Torres fell seriously ill and was soon in a critical condition. On Saturday the 10th the archbishop, inquisitors, Jesuits, and Dominicans staged a special preliminary ceremony in Mexico City with the Mexico City council and nobility once again following deferentially behind. On Sunday the 11th, while the bishop-governor lay dying in the viceregal palace, the *Auto General* was celebrated in the Plaza del Volador whither 500 carriages brought the notables of the capital and where a vast multitude of the common people were gathered. Judging by the long and detailed description left by its official chronicler, the Jesuit father Mathías de Bocanegra,[117] it was a very imposing affair and was certainly the most memorable *Auto* ever to be held outside the Iberian peninsula. A considerable number of judaizers were presented to the people, apparently about forty, and they included the élite of Mexican Jewry, Simon Váez de Sevilla, his wife, Doña Juana Enríquez, Captain Antonio Váez Castelobranco, Captain Sebastián Váez de Acevedo, and Mathías Rodríguez de Oliveira. Thirteen of the forty, eight women and five men, were burned at the stake, twelve after being reconciled for the second time and strangled first. One, Tomas Treviño de Sobremente, a merchant of Antequera, died a martyr for his faith, being burned alive after being gagged to stop his defiant utterances.[118] The consecration

[115] See p. 98.

[116] AGI México 76, r 3: Torres to council, 3 Jan. 1649; ibid., Bañuelos to council, 26 May 1649.

[117] Mathías de Bocanegra, *Auto General de la Fee, celebrado . . . en la muy noble y muy leal ciudad de Mexico, 11 de Abril de 1649* (Mexico, 1649); see also Guijo, *Diario*, i. 39–47.

[118] He is mentioned as a martyr by the Jewish authors Menasseh ben Israel and Miguel de Barrios, but the claim has been disputed, see Cuevas, *Historia de la Iglesia*, iii. 186.

of Puebla cathedral a week later, on Sunday the 18th, was similarly magnificent. The ceremonies, presided over by Palafox in person, began at six in the morning and lasted for the whole of that day, and intermittently for several days afterwards. A vast gathering of the common people and some 1,200 clergy were present at the festivities which included the usual services, Indian and Negro dances, games, and a dazzling display of choral music by the Puebla choir, then the best in the Americas, conducted by Juan Gutiérrez Padilla, New Spain's most eminent composer.[119] The festivities were certainly a great success for Palafox, but none could deny that at least some of the shine had been rubbed off it by the triumph of the Inquisition the week before. On 22 April Bishop Torres expired leaving power in the hands of the *Audiencia*, an eventuality which Madrid had consistently sought to avoid since 1624. Five days later, the six residing magistrates were sworn in as Mexico's seventh ruling *Audiencia*.

The period from late April to June 1649, the final phase of Palafox's presence in Mexico, was a period of continued but confused and desultory friction. The six magistrates of the *Audiencia* were sharply divided over various matters, usually three against three,[120] and took no positive action in either Palafox's or Mañozca's favour. There was some intense bickering between the Dominicans and Bishop Benavente in Oaxaca,[121] and a certain amount of political skirmishing in the capital, but that was all. In May, Palafox wound up his immediate affairs in Puebla, bade farewell to his friends and his spiritual flock to both of which, characteristically, he left a good deal of advice,[122] put Merlo in charge of his diocesan council, and descended to Veracruz. The *flota* sailed on 10 June, carrying Palafox away from the land in which he had spent a fortnight less than nine years and in which he had made his greatest effort to realize his ideals. He sailed with the hope that one day he would return, leaving, in the words of Andrés Pérez Franco, 'the whole colony disconsolate on account of the love that it bore him'.[123]

119 For a detailed description of the ceremonies see Antonio Tamariz de Carmona, *Relacion y descripcion del templo real de la ciudad de la Puebla de los Angeles en la Nueva España* [Madrid?, 1650?], for details on the development of music in Puebla at this time, see R. Stevenson, 'The "distinguished maestro" of New Spain: Juan Gutiérrez de Padilla' *HAHR* xxxv (1955), 363–73; on Palafox's great interest in his choir, see Ortiz de Valdés, *Defensa canónica*, fol. 210ᵛ, and *Reglas y ordenanzas del choro de esta santa iglesia cathedral de la Puebla de los Angeles* (2nd edn., Puebla, 1711) (Composed by Juan de Palafox),.

120 AGI México 76, r 3: Pedro Melián to council, 23 May 1649.

121 Ibid., r 3: *Audiencia* to council, 21 July 1650.

122 *Puntos que el señor Don Juan de Palafox dexa encargados a las almas de su cargo al tiempo de partirse destas provincias a los reynos de España* (Puebla, 1649).

123 AGI Patronato real 244, r 3: Pérez Franco to council, 4 May 1649.

IX

ALVA DE LISTE, ALBUQUERQUE, AND BAÑOS
(1650-1665)

In July 1649, a month after Palafox's departure, the pro-Salvatierra faction among the magistrates, led by Mathías de Peralta, president of the *Audiencia*, and Andres Gómez de Mora, seized the initiative in the *Audiencia*.[1] Don Diego de Orejón was acquitted of the charges against him and provided with a new administrative post. Agustín de Valdéz, shortly afterwards, was likewise cleared and restored to the administration of Tepeaca. Indeed, before long most of the pro-Salvatierra officers who had been dismissed by Bishop Torres had been returned to their posts or provided with new ones.[2] In the *Audiencia*, the opposition to Matías de Peralta was finally defeated in October after a violent quarrel between Peralta and Alonso de Villalba, which ended with Villalba being suspended from his duties and placed in confinement.[3]

By December 1649, it was clear to everyone that the tide, in the strictly political sphere at least, was running strongly against the friends of Palafox. The *Audiencia* dispatched a special force to Puebla under the command of Juan Manuel de Sotomayor, knight of Calatrava and *alcalde del crimen*, to seize the royal shields that had been placed by Palafox either side of the central *retablo* in Puebla cathedral.[4] The *Audiencia* was acting on the suggestion of Archbishop Mañozca, the Inquisition, and the fiscal of the *Audiencia*, Pedro Melián, a fierce enemy of Palafox. It was proclaimed that Palafox had commited a grave offence by placing the royal arms of Aragon in a place of priority over the arms of Castile, and by including on the shields a mysterious quarter—red cross with green tree—unknown to heraldic experts in Mexico City and presumed to have some connection with the Palafox family.[5] Sotomayor, without first informing either the city or diocesan council, removed the shields from the cathedral, causing a considerable

---

[1] Guijo, *Diario*, i. 59–61.
[2] AGI México 76, r 3: *Audiencia* to council, 21 July 1650, fol. 6v.
[3] Guijo, *Diario*, i. 68–9.
[4] Ivan Alonso Calderón, *Memorial historico ivridico politico de la santa iglesia cathedral de la Puebla de los Angeles en la Nueva España* (n.p., n.d. [c. 1651]) fols. 1v, 4, 7v–8, 9v, 86; Guijo, *Diario*, i. 75.
[5] Calderón, *Memorial historico invridico politico*, fols. 5v–6, 20v.

disturbance in the process, and locked them up in the Augustinian priory, actions which caused the Puebla diocesan council to send a delegation to the capital to voice a strong protest. Sotomayor also took the opportunity, again acting on the orders of the *Audiencia*, to remove the Asturian *corregidor* of Puebla appointed by Bishop Torres, García de Valdés Osorio, and put in his place Don Diego de Villegas, an old enemy of Palafox, who had been dismissed from the same post by Bishop Torres in 1648.[6]

The beginning of 1650 brought little comfort to the *Palafoxistas*. In the final months of their rule, the *Audiencia* magistrates were as distinctly anti-Palafox as ever. In May there was a remarkable wrangle among the Dominican friars, with the Dominicans of Puebla trying to prevent the election as Provincial of Juan de Paredes, the former special ecclesiastical judge against Palafox; but the Dominicans of Mexico City, with the aid of the *Audiencia*[7] and to the joy of the Jesuits, overrode them, and Paredes was elected, despite still being under sentence of excommunication by the bishop of Puebla.

A year and a month after the death of Bishop Torres, the new viceroy, Don Luis Enríquez de Guzmán, conde de Alva de Liste, marqués de Villaflor, disembarked at Veracruz in the company of Pedro de Gálvez, magistrate of the *Audiencia* of Granada, the new *visitador* sent to complete the *visita* of Palafox, at a salary of 6,000 pesos. Immediately the *Palafoxistas*, hopeful of improving their position now that the *Audiencia*'s term was ending, took heart, and on 22 May Merlo excommunicated twenty-three of his foes including a number of Jesuits and Dominicans.[8] However, on 4 June, Gálvez, whose sympathy for the *Palafoxistas* and succession to Palafox's *visita* gave him influence in Puebla, was able to persuade Merlo to withdraw the sentences of excommunication for the time being.[9]

Alva de Liste was sworn in as nineteenth viceroy on 28 June 1650, the event being celebrated with the usual bull-fights, music, and dance, and then quickly settled down to the business of government. His first step was to please Archbishop Mañozca, the Inquisition, and the Jesuits, by giving support to the archbishop's ruling that Juan de Vega and the other ex-members of the Puebla diocesan council should be freed from the penalties placed on them by Palafox and Merlo and be restored to their positions on the Puebla diocesan council.[10] But it was not the conde's intention to exploit ecclesiastical dissension in the way that Salvatierra had tried to do. The new viceroy had no Palafox to contend with and nothing to gain by attacking his supporters. Gálvez, the new *visitador*, though Palafox's successor, politically speaking, and

6 Guijo, *Diario* i. 76–7.   7 Ibid. i. 96–9; ACP xxiii, fols. 113ᵛ–121ᵛ.
8 Guijo, *Diario*, i. 101–2.   9 Ibid. i. 103.   10 Guijo, *Diario*, i. 108–9.

on good terms with the *Palafoxistas*, was essentially a man of compromise who particularly desired to cool tempers down.[11] This suited Alva de Liste admirably, for his intention was the same. His concessions to the Mañozca party, accordingly, were carefully balanced by favours to the other side.[12] If he humoured Mañozca, the Inquisition, Dominicans, and Jesuits, he also left the Indian parishes in the bishoprics of New Biscay and Puebla in the hands of the secular clergy, fined the *Audiencia* magistrates 200 ducats each for their action in seizing the royal shields from Puebla cathedral, and helped to maintain Palafox's colleges. Almost from the first, Alva de Liste had considerable success in reducing the level of tension; in this, almost certainly, he was helped by the death of Archbishop Mañozca in December 1650, only a few months after the beginning of his term.[13] The conde's culminating achievement as a peacemaker in the clerical sphere was his success, in February 1652, in arranging a compromise between Merlo and the Jesuits by which the Jesuits in the diocese of Puebla agreed to present their preaching licences to be confirmed by the diocesan authorities, which they had always refused to do in the time of Palafox, while in return Merlo consented to lift the restrictions that had been imposed on them.[14]

Alva de Liste's only serious brush with a section of the clergy was his quarrel with the diocesan council of Mexico over a point of precedence relating to the Corpus Christi day procession on 8 June 1651. The viceroy wished to put six of his pages in a certain prominent position customarily taken by the diocesan council and became caught up in an argument which led his shouting at the master of ceremonies and making certain unseemly gestures, which according to Guijo greatly scandalized the assembled people and clergy. The procession was held up for several hours, causing considerable popular excitement, but in the end the proceedings went ahead with the viceroy having his way.[15]

Alva de Liste, unlike Velasco, Cerralvo, Escalona, and Salvatierra, but rather like Cadereita, was on good terms with his *visitador*, Pedro de Gálvez. The *Audiencia* magistrates hated Gálvez, and one of their number, Pedro Fernández de Castro, asserted in a letter to Madrid that

11 AGI México 92, r 3: Gálvez to council, 15 Apr. 1653; AGI Patronato real 244, r 3: Gálvez to council, 23 and 24 Apr. 1651.

12 Manuel Rivera Cambas, *Los Gobernantes de México* (2 vols., Mexico, 1872–3), i. 182–4.

13 After falling sick in October, see Guijo, Diario, i. 131, 138.

14 ADI Palafox papers lxxii fol. 20: Alva de Liste to Merlo, 29 Dec. 1651; AGI México 37, r i: Alva de Liste to council, 23 Mar. 1652 (no. 8 ecel.); Guijo, *Diario*, i. 190–1.

15 AGI México 36, r 4: Cuevas Dávalos to council, 14 July 1651; Guijo, *Diario*, i. 203–4.

the new *visitador* was at one with the *Palafoxistas* and a more relentless meddler even than Palafox;[16] but the viceroy found the *visitador* very much to his taste and was on such close terms with him that their friendship caused numerous eyebrows to be raised, including those of the conde's successor, the duque de Albuquerque.[17] Whether the co-operation between the two, which was also much valued by Gálvez,[18] was of an essentially corrupt nature, is difficult to determine, though it seems likely that it was. Albuquerque certainly thought so. Moreover, Gálvez, though he did venture to criticize the *corregidores* in one report to Madrid,[19] made no attempt to get at the viceroy's officers *à la Palafox*, he concentrated all his powers on the *Audiencia*, with which the viceroy was not on close terms, arraigning the senior magistrate, Mathías de Peralta, on eighty charges and suspending him and Gómez de Mora from their duties and stopping their salaries;[20] but then, by proceeding thus, since his commissions related particularly to the *Audiencia*, he was only sticking closely to his brief. But also it is clear that at least some of Alva de Liste's staff were highly corrupt. Ventura Garin, for instance, secretary to the viceroy, had amassed 50,000 pesos in the thirteen months up to his death in August 1651,[21] or more than eight times the salary of the *visitador*, a fact which speaks for itself. A corrupt secretary probably means a corrupt viceroy, and in any case it is hard to see how anyone who prized compromise and accommodation in the Mexico of the 1650s could have been otherwise than corrupt.

Towards the end of Alva de Liste's term, in December 1652, the *Palafoxistas* had the satisfaction of seeing the Dominican election of 1650, by which Juan de Paredes had become Dominican Provincial, quashed by an order of Madrid implemented by the viceroy. This was a defeat for the *Audiencia* and the Jesuits and a severe blow for Paredes who was now hounded by his Dominican opponents to such an extent that he besought the Jesuits to help him leave his order and sustain him against the *Palafoxistas*.[22] In the final months of Alva de Liste's rule, from January to July 1653, little happened of note, apart from

16 AGI Patronato real 244, r 3: Fernández de Castro to council, 24 Apr. 1651.

17 ADA a15c17 (1653): Albuquerque to Luis Méndez de Haro; Albuquerque seems to have thought Gálvez rather unintelligent.

18 AGI Patronato real 244, r 3: Gálvez to council, 15 Mar. 1652.

19 Ibid., Gálvez to council, 23 Apr. 1651.

20 AGI México 92, r 3: Gálvez to council, 5 Apr. 1653; Guijo, *Diario*, i. 133–4, 181, 196–7; it is noteworthy that Gálvez also found fault with another magistrate, Antonio de Ulloa, for being too favourable to Palafox.

21 Guijo, *Diario*, i. 169.

22 BND 1869–74: Juan de Paredes to Julian de Pedraza, 15 Mar. 1653; Guijo, *Diario*, i. 203–4.

the severe drought which struck central Mexico at that time and an outbreak of smallpox in Mexico City. Alva de Liste was preparing for his move to Peru whither he had been promoted, and Mexico was looking forward to its second grandee, the duque de Albuquerque.

The eleven-vessel flota bearing Don Francisco Fernández de la Cueva y Enríquez de Cabrera, eighth duke of Albuquerque, and with him Don Marcelo López de Azcona, former abbot of Roncesvalles, the new archbishop of Mexico, docked at Veracruz early in July. On 13 July, in preparation for the transfer of power, Alva de Liste moved from the viceregal palace into the residence of the marqués de Villamayor. With the flota, there also came rumours that Don Juan de Palafox would not be returning to Mexico, despite the great hope in many sectors that he would, and that he was about to accept, or had already accepted (as in fact he had), the mitre of Osma, one of the poorest bishoprics of Castile;[23] however, mixed with these rumours there also came denials originating, apparently, with Palafox himself,[24] and renewed affirmations that he would soon return, all of which caused considerable confusion in Puebla. Furthermore, there also arrived with the flota orders from the Inquisitor General, published by the Inquisition in the churches of Mexico City on Sunday 20 July, that is immediately, to the effect that all portraits of Bishop Palafox were to be surrendered to the Holy Office and that in future it was forbidden to make portraits of the bishop.[25] Plainly the Inquisition, even in Castile, was disturbed by the growing cult surrounding Palafox. On 15 August Albuquerque was sworn in as the twentieth viceroy of New Spain and moved into the viceregal palace with his wife, Juana Francisca, marquesa de Cadereita, daughter of the fifteenth viceroy.

Albuquerque is certainly one of the more interesting viceroys of seventeenth-century Mexico as well as being one of the most eminent socially. His father, the seventh duke, had been one of the toughest, most rigorous, and successful of the viceroys of Catalonia in the early seventeenth century and had specialized in the suppression of disorder.[26] The eighth duke was only thirty-four when he came to Mexico but was already a noted soldier, having distinguished himself in

[23] ADA a15c17 (1653): Dean of Puebla diocesan council to Albuquerque, 11 Sept. 1653.

[24] *DHM* vii. 153: Albuquerque to council, 10 Nov. 1653; it does seem that there was a systematic effort by the *Palafoxistas* to prolong the general hope that Palafox would return, for Madrid had decided that he would not return as early as June 1651, BM Add. MS. 14, 012, fols. 63ᵛ–67, following reports from the bishop's enemies that the split between *Palafoxistas* and *realistas* was still causing tension in Mexico.

[25] *DHM* vii. 151; Guijo, *Diario*, i. 220.

[26] Elliott, *The Revolt of the Catalans*, pp. 116–26.

several battles against the French in Flanders, commanded the cavalry at the disastrous battle of Rocroy and excelled in the defence of Tortosa.[27] He displayed, almost from the first, a very stern sense of duty. He was appalled by the state in which he found the viceroyalty and accused his predecessors of having scandalously neglected their responsibilities, collected far less tax than was owed to the crown, and allowed the machinery of justice to become rotten with corruption.[28] With a fine flourish, he asked of the king's favourite, Méndez de Haro, whether it was desired of him that he rule in the perfunctory style customary in Mexico or in the more robust manner to be expected of a member of his family, for in Mexico, he avowed, he had found in all departments an indolence and carelessness to which he would never be one to adjust his conscience.

Albuquerque's first package of ordinances appeared in September 1653.[29] He was gravely dissatisfied with the state of the people, the prevalence of alcoholism and delinquency, and the freedom permitted to Negroes and mulattoes, and these ordinances were designed as a corrective to what he regarded as some of the worst abuses. One of his principal targets on this occasion was the *pulque* business which, he believed, had been encouraged and exploited by Spanish officers since Escalona's time in a shameful way to the injury of both the Indians and wine imports from Andalusia. He endeavoured to stop the manipulation of Indian *pulque* producers and sellers by Spaniards and Negroes and to prevent the sale of doctored and strengthened forms of the drink. He also sought, in various edicts, to prevent or reduce interference with Indian fruit, vegetable, wood, and charcoal sellers and to enforce the official restrictions on the black population, especially the ban on the possession of arms, restrictions which in the past, as the duke noted, had generally not been enforced. Interestingly, the duke also ordered that tavern-keepers might no longer dress in black or wear the golilla, that is to say, socially respectable dress. According to Guijo, these decrees were stringently enforced and a considerable quantity of dubiously obtained produce was confiscated from Spanish vendors and Negroes.

In the field of economic control and taxation, Albuquerque's regime was, from the beginning, meticulous and exacting. Only two months after taking office the duke arrested and confiscated the possessions of

27Rubio Mañé, *Introducción al estudio de los virreyes*, i. 250; Francisco Fernández de Bethencourt, *Historia genealógica y heráldica de la monarquía Española, casa real, y grandes de España* x (Madrid, 1920), pp. 285–91.

28ADA a15c17 (1653): Albuquerque to Méndez de Haro, 20 Nov. 1653.

29ADA a15c17 (1653): group of letters from Albuquerque to Méndez de Haro dated 4 Nov. 1653; Guijo, *Diario*, i. 229–30.

the Mexico City *Regidor* Felipe Morán, and subjected the prior and consuls of the merchant *consulado* to the same treatment on account of various irregularities;[30] during the years that followed he made strenuous efforts to reform the financial administration of the colony, and dispatched special commissioners to check the work of officials in the provinces and collect tax arrears. Some of these swoops, apparently, were highly effective. Pedro de Oroz, for instance, sent by Albuquerque to Zacatecas at the end of 1654, had, by the time of his death six months later, extracted 400,000 pesos' worth of arrears on mercury transactions, and in Guadalajara the duke's agents appear to have had a similar success.[31] According to Albuquerque's own reports,[32] and Guijo confirms that the 1654 remittance to the crown was quite exceptionally large,[33] he was markedly more successful in collecting taxes and dues than most of his predecessors. Also the duke introduced a number of innovations designed to reduce opportunities for fraud, the most important being his simplification of the distribution of mercury to the silver-miners; by selling directly to the miners, rather than distributing the mercury by means of local treasury officials and *corregidores*.[34]

Albuquerque's dissatisfaction with the state of the colony extended to the clergy as well as all sections of the laity. Early in 1654 he summoned the Provincials of the mendicant orders into his presence and demanded to know why laxness prevailed among the friars in Mexico.[35] He lectured the Provincials on their responsibilities social and moral and sharply criticized the willingness of priors to allow their brethren to stroll about the capital individually, and permit the gates of their priories to remain open until late into the evening. He also treated the vicar-general of the Mercenarians to a special rebuke for allowing one of his friars to keep his own carriage within the priory walls. The Provincials had to agree to introduce a new austerity and to close their priories, from then on, at dusk. Shortly after the meeting, Albuquerque wrote to Madrid requesting the dispatch of more *gachupín* friars, particularly Augustinians, so as to impede Creole influence in the orders more effectively and help to halt what he regarded as the process of moral deterioration.

30 Guijo, *Diario*, i. 232, 236, and ii. 54–5.
31 Ibid. ii. 21: ADA a15c16–2, no. 22: Albuquerque to Haro, 10 June 1655.
32 ADA a15c17 (1654): Albuquerque to Méndez de Haro, 1 Mar. 1654, letter no. 9; ADA a15c17–2, no. 39: Albuquerque to Méndez de Haro, 31 May 1655.
33 Guijo, *Diario*, i. 250–1.
34 Bakewell, *Silver mining and society*, p. 177.
35 ADA a15c17–3 (1654): Albuquerque to Méndez de Haro, 1 Mar. 1654, letters 2 and 8.

In the field of justice, Albuquerque was as good or nearly as good as his boast, displaying a zeal reminiscent of that of his father in Catalonia. The number of hangings in Mexico City during the years of Albuquerque's regime, one notes from Guijo's diary, was considerably more than usual, and Albuquerque was able to claim, in a letter to Méndez de Haro of December 1656, that banditry in central Mexico had been all but suppressed.[36] Regarding the *Audiencia*, Albuquerque reported that five of the magistrates were satisfactory, but that the remaining two definitely were not. Andrés Pardo de Lago he thought old, ignorant, and foolish, and Gaspar Fernández de Castro intelligent but corrupt; both, he declared, were in league with Don Antonio Urrutia de Vergara who was at the summit of his wealth and influence at this time and who, in the viceroy's view, was the leader of those who sought to corrupt administration in Mexico.[37] It is interesting that Albuquerque, like his father-in-law Cadereita, but unlike Cerralvo and Alva de Liste, was on the worst terms with Urrutia de Vergara, though he acknowledged him to be the 'greatest merchant in the Indies',[38] and even advised Madrid to find Vergara a post in the West Indies so as to get him out of Mexico once again.[39]

Aside from Urrutia de Vergara, Albuquerque met with almost no opposition in the first three years of his rule. In more than one letter to Méndez de Haro, the duke spoke of the docile temperament of the Mexican Spaniards and their pleasing willingness to obey and conform in everything except their tax obligations, where they had to be treated with a firm hand.[40] Certainly the Creoles, by comparison with the Catalans or Flemings, were easily governed. Nevertheless, as Albuquerque himself was soon to discover, the political tranquillity which he enjoyed in the years 1653–6 was due as much to the absence of likely leaders of opposition as to his skill as a ruler. Archbishop López de Azcona had died in November 1653, a mere four months after his arrival, and was not replaced by Archbishop Mateo Sagade Bugueiro until July 1656, a circumstance which left the secular clergy without a head, for the bishopric of Puebla was also vacant, Palafox not having returned, and was to remain so until the arrival of his successor Don Diego Osorio de Escobar y Llamas in the company of Sagade Bugueiro

---

36 ADA a15c15: Albuquerque to Méndez de Haro, 23 Dec. 1656.

37 ADA a15c17 (1654), no. 29: Albuquerque to Méndez de Haro, 18 Mar. 1654 ; ADA a15c16–1: Albuquerque to Méndez de Haro, 6 Apr. 1656.

38 AGI México 38, r 4: Albuquerque to council, 17 Sept. 1659.

39 ADA a15c17 (1654), no. 29: Albuquerque to Méndez de Haro, 18 Mar. 1654.

40 ADA a15c17 (1654), no. 9: Albuquerque to Méndez de Haro, 1 Mar. 1654; ibid., no. 31: Albuquerque to Méndez de Haro, 6 Apr. 1656.

in 1656. Meanwhile, the *visitador*, Pedro de Gálvez, had left Mexico early in 1654 and Bishop Benavente had died.

Albuquerque, who had not been at all anxious to see Palafox return, fearing a resurgence of clerical strife and popular excitement,[41] was as relieved when the reports that Palafox would not be returning were confirmed as the *Palafoxistas* were despondent. Though one might suppose that Palafox would have approved of much of Albuquerque's policy, the duke appears to have disliked Palafox and his cause and to have shown a marked preference for his enemies,[42] being especially partial to Juan Manuel de Sotomayor, for whom he was full of praise, Agustín de Valdéz, whom he made *corregidor* of Mexico City in December 1654 and afterwards captain of his guard, and Diego de Orejón, whom he appointed *alcalde mayor* of Puebla, of all places, in 1655. Of Puebla, the viceroy remarked in a letter to Méndez de Haro that the negligence in government and tax-collection, which had in recent years been evident there, had ended under the efficient administration of Orejón.[43] But whatever Albuquerque's opinion of Palafox, he can hardly have disapproved of the bishop's final message to his Mexican supporters blaming himself in part for the dissension of previous years and beseeching those who loved him to forsake agitation and seek instead peace and reconciliation, all alike being children of one father, the Almighty, one mother, the Church, and members of one mystical body, that of Christ.[44]

One further aspect of the first part of Albuquerque's rule was the completion, in January 1656, of Mexico City cathedral. For this work the duke had evinced, since the moment of his arrival, a notable ardour, so much so that he took to inspecting the progress of the work almost daily. He spent large sums on the structure and kept the workmen and artists busy day and night. Guijo remarked approvingly that in two years the duke accomplished more with the edifice than had any other viceroy since the building was begun.[45] The consecration of the cathedral was celebrated with great pomp, some 2,000 clergy attending, on 1 February.[46] The viceroy, being a proud man, was the more gratified, one may presume, in that there was then no archbishop to

[41]*DHM* vii. 153: Albuquerque to council, 10 Nov. 1653; ADA a15c16–2, no. 14: Albuquerque to Méndez de Haro, 5 May 1655.

[42]ADA a15c17: Albuquerque to Méndez de Haro, 15 Nov. 1653; Guijo, *Diario*, i. 264, and ii. 115–16; *La Puebla de los Angeles* p. 71.

[43]ADA a15c16–2, no. 13: Albuquerque to Méndez de Haro, 5 May 1655.

[44]Juan de Palafox, *A los fieles de el obispado de la Puebla de los Angeles. Juan indigno obispo electo de Osma* (8 Sept. 1653) (Madrid, 1653), esp. pp. 232–3.

[45]Guijo, *Diario*, ii. 46; ADA a15c17, no. 26: Albuquerque to Méndez de Haro, 16 Mar. 1654.

[46]Guijo, *Diario*, ii. 47–54.

share in the honour of having completed the cathedral. Furthermore, it is likely that the knowledge that everything relating to the completion of his immense cathedral was settled in a rush by the viceroy just a few months before his arrival added to the subsequent pique of Sagade Bugueiro.

In the summer of 1656, the beginning of the second part of Albuquerque's term, the viceroy's feud with the Mexican bishops began. As the public saw it, the contest between Albuquerque and Sagade Bujueiro originated in an argument over precedence in a religious procession rather like that which had marred the Corpus Christi procession of 1651,[47] but evidently this disagreement, which took place in the autumn of 1656, was merely a sign of a deeper rift. Albuquerque, who believed strongly that humility and deference to the secular authority were the qualities proper in bishops,[48] had for several years been complaining to Méndez de Haro of the meddlesomeness and arrogance of bishops in the Indies,[49] though the only significant trouble during the first part of his rule was the bickering between Evia y Valdés, the new bishop of Oaxaca (1654–6), and the Dominicans in alliance with the southern *corregidores*, an imbroglio which culminated in the excommunication of the *corregidor* of Antequera by Bishop Evia.[50] In the summer of 1656, almost from the moment Sagade Bugueiro arrived, viceroy and archbishop were at loggerheads. Sagade Bugueiro, who had strong feelings on the English invasion of Jamaica which had taken place following the repulse of Penn and Venables's force from Hispaniola in April 1655, had no sooner taken up his mitre than he began pressing the viceroy to dispatch a relief expedition against the English,[51] advice which the duke seems to have resented keenly (in fact Albuquerque's relief expedition did not sail until August 1657). Albuquerque's haughty manner and partiality for an obscure Portuguese secretary named Mezquita, 'a man who was not enthusiastic for Church interests', so irritated the archbishop that he began openly to snub the viceroy, whom he described slightingly as a 'youth', while the duke became so angry that in a letter of November 1656 to Méndez de Haro he accounted the archbishop the 'hardest, most rigid and obstinate man in his opinions that there is'.[52]

---

[47] Guijo, *Diario*, ii. 66–7.

[48] ADA a15c16–1, no. 30: Albuquerque to Méndez de Haro, 25 July 1656.

[49] ADA a15c16–2, nos. 43 and 47: Albuquerque to Méndez de Haro, 5 May 1655.

[50] ADA a15c16–4, no. 25: Albuquerque to Méndez de Haro, 16 July 1656.

[51] Armando Cotarelo Valledor, 'Don Mateo Segade Bugueiro, Arzobispo de Méjico, obispo de Cartagena (1605–72)', *Revista de Indias*, iii (1942), 307.

[52] ADA a15c15, no. 2: Albuquerque to Méndez de Haro, 30 Nov. 1656.

At the same time Albuquerque fell out with the new bishop of Puebla, Osorio de Escobar, a friend and compatriot of Sagade Bugueiro who may have been specially chosen for the diocese of Puebla on the strength of his affection for the Jesuits. The viceroy had ordered, in accordance with certain royal *cédulas*, that the procedure for receiving the new bishop should not include certain particular honours which had been allowed in the special case of Bishop Palafox; however, the viceroy's orders were disregarded and Osorio de Escobar was received as Palafox had been. This made the duke utterly furious. In the letter in which he recounted the incident at Puebla, he accused the whole body of Mexican bishops, with his usual tendency to exaggerate, of wilfully obstructing the progress of the king's affairs[53] and asked that Osorio de Escobar be recalled to Spain or at least made an example of. By November 1656 the duke was more annoyed than ever, informing Méndez de Haro that it was impossible for any statesman in Spain to comprehend what the Mexican bishops were like, 'how they proceed and the disruption they cause, for they are here what the dukes of Savoy, Mantua, and Parma and the government of Venice are in Italy, and what the neighbouring kings and princes are in Flanders with this difference, which makes them worse, that these bishops proceed under the cloak of ecclesiastical privilege which they only use for starting quarrels and feuds against the interest of his Majesty'.[54]

In 1657 and for part of 1658 relations between Albuquerque and the bishops were patched up. The bitter wrangling which had gone on in Oaxaca during 1656 ended in December of that year with the death of Bishop Evia; Osorio de Escobar refrained from offending the viceroy further while Sagade Bugueiro and the viceroy made what proved to be a temporary peace. Indeed in January 1658 Don Benito Fosino Bugueiro, the archbishop's nephew, having resigned as priest, was made captain of the viceroy's guard a few days before being married to the daughter of the conde de Santiago Calimaya and presented by his uncle, the archbishop, with 40,000 pesos' worth of cash and jewels. But by the second half of 1658 Albuquerque and Sagade Bugueiro were at odds again, with the archbishop punishing the Carmelite nuns for their intimacy with the duquesa, Albuquerque's wife, and offending the viceroy, according to the viceroy himself, at every opportunity.[55] In 1659, moreover, the wrangling became worse, the two heads snubbing each other at every turn.[56] Madrid, not being particularly sympathetic to either disputant, admonished both viceroy and archbishop, in

53 ADA a15c16–1, no. 30: Albuquerque to Méndez de Haro, 25 July 1656.
54 ADA a15c15, no. 2: Albuquerque to Méndez de Haro, 30 Nov. 1656.
55 ADA a15c15, no. 10: Albuquerque to Méndez de Haro, Dec. 1658.
56 ADA a15c15–12, 20: Albuquerque to Méndez de Haro, 23 Oct. 1659.

cédulas discreetly bearing the same date, to conceal their differences as far as possible and on no account to use them as a pretext for open political dissension.[57] This, to a considerable extent, judging by the lack of references to the feud in Guijo, the two heads succeeded in doing.

Despite the friction between Albuquerque and the bishops, the people remained as quiet in the second part of the duke's term as they had been in the first. Sagade Bugueiro made no effort to exploit or cultivate popular opinion in the manner of Pérez de la Serna, Manso, and Palafox, and for their part the people showed none of that excitement in the disputes of 1656–9 that they had shown earlier. Altogether, the 1650s were much quieter than any of the three previous decades, and those disputes that did arise, with the exception of the strife in Oaxaca which was essentially a continuation of the conflict of the 1640s, were narrower and pettier than those that had arisen before. As to why the resistance to Albuquerque's austerity and tax-collecting methods was so slight one can only speculate. As so often with periods of calm, the historian has little to go on. Possibly the Creoles, who were the main victims of the duke's policies, were essentially defenceless against a determined and unified administration without the help and assistance of the secular clergy and the poor. For the 1650s, as well as being a comparatively peaceful time regarding relations between the secular and regular clergy, were also a time of comparative abundance and cheap food,[58] owing partly to a succession of good harvests and partly to Albuquerque's determination to protect the populace of Mexico City from food racketeers, even to the extent of arresting the *corregidor* of Mexico City and four or five *regidores* for taking bribes from the bakers.[59] Furthermore, Albuquerque's austerity appears to have been shrewdly selective, especially as far as his *corregidores* were concerned. Indeed, if one excepts the two points upon which the duke was adamant—collection of taxes in full and suppression of food and drink racketeering in Mexico City—he seems to have given his officers a fairly free hand, especially in the provinces, at the expense of the settlers.[60]

Apart from an incompetent attempt by a young soldier to assassinate the viceroy in the cathedral, in March 1660,[61] for reasons unknown,

[57] ADA a15c–a9, legajo 5: Crown to Albuquerque, 24 Aug. 1659.

[58] ADA a15c17 no. 23: Albuquerque to Méndez de Haro, 1 Mar. 1654; note also the absence of droughts or crop failures in the years 1654–60, Gibson, *The Aztecs*, p. 454.

[59] Guijo, *Diario*, ii. 119.

[60] ADA a15c15–13: 'Cargos y descargos y sentencia de residencia del duque de Albuquerque', cargo no. 3.

[61] Guijo, *Diario*, ii. 131–2.

and the rising of the Indians of Tehuantepec against their cruel and rapacious *corregidor*, Juan de Avellano,[62] the final months of Albuquerque's term slipped by quietly. In September 1660 he transferred power to his successor, the twenty-first viceroy and the last to be considered in this study in detail, Don Juan Francisco de Leyva y de la Cerda, marqués de Labrada, conde de Baños, a military man who had distinguished himself against the French at the raising of the great siege of Lérida.[63] Baños was to rule Mexico for the next four years, though the real ruler of the viceroyalty during that time, according to his enemies at any rate,[64] was his sickly but strong-willed wife, Doña Mariana Isabel, the tenth vicereine. Moreover, the conde ruled badly and his term came to an ignominious end. He was remembered as one of the most oppressive of all the viceroys of Mexico,[65] except by the bureaucratic party, the Jesuits, and the friars, who prized him highly on account of the great favour in which he held them.[66]

The central problem relating to Baños's term is to explain how a colony which was so completely submissive under his predecessor became under him, tense, angry, and resentful. Part of the answer lies no doubt in the assertions of his detractors. According to them, the viceroy was the 'captive' of his wife and her physician Dr Pavino and the evil men who attended them. Creoles consequently were denied administrative offices, which went invariably to the conde's and condesa's relatives, friends, and sycophants or, in the case of the lesser positions, to those who offered most for them.[67] The favourites of the conde and condesa were permitted, indeed encouraged, to cut into such lucrative niches as the sale of pulque and mercury, displacing, or partially displacing, most previous operators including Antonio Urrutia de Vergara whom the viceroy banished from the capital.[68] Responsibility for collecting sales tax in Mexico City was withdrawn from the merchant guild against its will, and assigned to the city council, and several merchants who ventured to protest were arrested and fined.[69]

62 Ibid. ii. 133; see below, p. 262.

63 Rubio Mañé, *Introduccion al estudio de los virreyes*, i. 252–3.

64 AGI México 77: Gines Morote to council, 4 June 1663; ibid., Bishop Osorio de Escobar to council, 4 June 1663.

65 AGI México 77: *Audiencia* to council, 14 July 1664; Rivera Cambas, *Los Gobernantes de Mexico*, i. 205–11; Bancroft, *History of Mexico*, iii 165.

66 Father Alegre judged him 'one of the most exemplary and just viceroys that have governed in the Indies', *Historia de la Compañía* ii. 424–6, a view shared by Vetancurt and Cavo.

67 AGI México 77: Ginés Morote to council, 26 May and 4 June 1663.

68 AGI México 77: Ginés Morote to council, 26 May 1663; *Audiencia* to council, 8 June 1663; and *Audiencia* to council, 24 Mar. 1666.

69 Guijo, *Diario*, ii. 165; ADA a25ca–3: Mexico City *consulado* to Albuquerque, 21 July 1664.

And the *corregidores*, as one would expect, were given a free hand to operate as they pleased. 'The viceroys,' wrote Alonso de Cuevas y Dávalos, Evia y Valdés's, successor as bishop of Oaxaca.

'when they come to these provinces, bring an excessive number of retainers and dependents with them . . . and these they provide for by assigning them the principal administrative posts, which provide the means to reap profit, and even to extract all the wealth from districts or most of it, as is happening at the moment; and in some cases, such offices are allotted to members of the viceroy's family, as is happening at present with the *corregimiento* of Villa Alta, within the boundaries of this diocese, one of the most considerable at the disposal of the viceroys, from which huge sums stand to be taken, which the viceroy, conde de Baños, has assigned to his eldest son, Don Pedro de Leyva, who administers it through a deputy, a member of his household, who, on behalf of Don Pedro, trades and operates and reaps more profit from the position than did his predecessors, though they too were rapacious.'[70]

And as with the principal *corregimientos*, so too, according to Cuevas y Dávalos, with the lesser; the system was such that virtually all *corregidores* oppressed the wretched Indians and 'monopolized, preventing others from trading in their districts, even citizens'.

But the corruption of the viceroy, the oppressiveness of the *corregidores*, and the disruptive interloping in commerce are by no means the whole story. After all, these evils were the usual evils of seventeenth-century Mexico and usually they were put up with quietly enough. Doubtless Baños was among the worst of the seventeenth-century viceroys, but even so it seems at least likely that the crucial factor relating to the discontent of his time is that under him bureaucratic exploitation began to bite more deeply owing to a worsening of the economic depression. Undoubtedly the economic situation in the early 1660s deteriorated markedly, the 'poverty and exhaustion in which this colony finds itself now' being, as the *Audiencia* expressed it in the summer of 1664, 'the greatest that has ever been seen.'[71] The years 1661–3 were years of unmitigated disaster for central Mexican agriculture, severe drought and untimely frosts combining to create a fearful food shortage and impose great hardship on the poor.[72] And this calamity coincided with the trough of the depression in silver mining caused by Baños's tampering with the sale of mercury, the unprecedentedly low level of mercury distribution in the

---

70 Cuevas Dávalos to council, 26 Nov. 1663, printed in Cuevas, *Historia de la Iglesia en México*, iii. 459.
71 AGI México 77: *Audiencia* to council, 21 July 1664, fol. 5.
72 Guijo, *Diario*, ii. 150, 161, 169, 198–200. Gibson, *The Aztecs*, pp. 454–5.

early 1660s,[73] and the consequent bankruptcy of many miners;[74] silver output at Zacatecas in the quinquennium 1660–5 was the lowest of the century.[75] Moreover, the further collapse of silver, it may be presumed, caused a new shortage of specie and loss of confidence which in turn brought about a further recession of commerce.

The conde de Baños had commenced his rule in a confident manner surrounded by his numerous dependents and proud, impetuous sons who were accustomed to ride in carriages drawn by six mules, a privilege supposedly reserved for viceroys and archbishops. One of his first acts was to dispatch the magistrate Montemayor y Cuenca whom his predecessor Albuquerque had accounted overbearing, presumptuous, and corrupt,[76] but of whom he strongly approved,[77] to southern Oaxaca to investigate the so-called rebellion of Tehuantepec. This affair chiefly consisted in the overthrow and killing of a *corregidor* and his deputies, and was provoked not by bureaucratic oppression alone but by bureaucratic oppression combined with drought and crop failure.[78] The Indian governor and principals of the district were apparently not involved, and it does seem that the movement, which was certainly not aimed against Spanish Rule as such, ceased with the death of Avellano, that is to say some months before the commencement of Baños's rule.[79] Officially, the Indians were pacified and quietened by Bishop Cuevas Dávalos who travelled to Tehuantepec at the bidding of Viceroy Albuquerque and who received the thanks of the crown for what came to be regarded by the Creoles as a heroic exploit.[80] However, Baños and Juan Francisco Montemayor y Cuenca, partly in order to discredit and injure Albuquerque and Cuevas Dávalos, partly in order to be able to claim credit for having pacified Tehuantepec themselves, and partly to raise the level of tribute in the Tehuantepec district under the pretext of punishing rebellion, appear to have made strenuous efforts to build up the whole affair, maintaining that dangerous agitation persisted in Tehuantepec and adjoining

[73] Bakewell, *Silver Mining and Society*, p. 251.
[74] AGI México 77: Ginés Morote to council, 26 May 1663, fol. 2.
[75] Bakewell, *Silver Mining and Society*, p. 246.
[76] ADA a15c15–12, no. 16: Albuquerque to Méndez de Haro, 23 Sept. 1659.
[77] AGI México 38, r 5: Baños to council, undated but 1661.
[78] See the passage from Antonio de Robles quoted in Francisco Sosa, *El Episcopado Mexicano* (3rd edn., 1962), i. 297.
[79] AGI México 77: caciques of southern Oaxaca to council, 2 Dec. 1662.
[80] Crown to Cuevas Dávalos, 2 Oct. 1662 in Sosa, *El Episcopado Mexicano*,, i. 298–9; Antonio de Robles, *Resguardo contra el olvido en el breve compendio de la vida admirable y virtudes heroycas del Ilmo. sr. Dr. D. Alonso de Cuevas Dávalos* (Mexico 1757), pp. 150–60.

districts until the summer of 1661.[81] In this work they were helped by a number of southern *corregidores*, enemies of Cuevas Dávalos, including Cristobal Manso de Contreras,[82] and opposed by the Indian caciques of southern Oaxaca who protested strongly against the operations of Montemayor y Cuenca in a letter to Madrid of December 1662.[83]

The attitude of mind revealed by the viceroy in connection with the Tehuantepec affair was displayed further in 1661 and 1662 in various other contexts. A characteristic gesture was his response to the attempt of the *Audiencia*, with which he was on very bad terms, to interfere with the operations of certain of his officers, and particularly those of Don Austasio Coronel Salcedo Benavides, *corregidor* of Metepec, who was impeached by the Indians of his jurisdiction for forcing them to buy mules, chocolate, and other goods from him at inflated prices.[84] At the condesa's birthday party at the palace on 25 May 1662, an ostentatious affair, typical of the Baños régime, particular favour was shown to Don Austasio and a week later, though the *Audiencia* had suspended him from office, Baños nominated him, as a special sign of his favour, *corregidor* of Mexico City. Almost immediately changes were made in wheat and maize prices. A week later, on 8 June 1662, there was further cause for general murmuring when the conde broke precedent by re-routing the Corpus Christi day procession, against the wishes of the diocesan council, making it pass by the palace so that the condesa, who was unwell, should not miss it.[85]

Opposition to the conde de Baños began to crystallize in 1663 around the figure of Diego Osorio de Escobar, the Galician bishop of Puebla, who, though he refused the office of archbishop of Mexico, which was then vacant owing to the departure of Mateo Sagade Bugueiro in April 1661, had agreed to administer the archbishopric in the interim until a new metropolitan should be found. Osorio de Escobar, if not exactly a *Palafoxista*, on account of his ecclesiastical ideas, did sympathize strongly with the Creoles and their grievances[86] and was, it is evident, immensely popular.

Relations between bishop and viceroy were not good at any stage, but they became particularly strained after the funeral of the commander

81 AGI México 77: Montemayor y Cuenca to council, 23 Mar. 1662; AGI México 78: Montemayor y Cuenca to council, 14 Oct. 1665.

82 Christoval Manso de Contreras, *Relacion cierta y verdadera de lo qve svcedio y a svcedido en esta villa de Gvadalcacar provincia de Tehuantepeqve desde los 22 de Marco de 1660 hasta los quatro de Iulio de 1661* (Mexico 1661).

83 AGI México 77: caciques of southern Oaxaca to council, 2 Dec. 1662.

84 Guijo, *Diario*, ii. 170.

85 AGI México 39, r 1: Osorio de Escobar to council, 26 May 1663.

86 AGI México 39, r 2: Osorio de Escobar to council, 20 July 1664.

of the garrison of Veracruz, whom Baños had imprisoned in Mexico City. The bishop attended the funeral, along with a vast multitude of the laity, and it turned into a kind of controlled demonstration against the régime,[87] provoking the viceroy to banish from the capital several notables who attended it, among them Antonio Urrutia de Vergara. Then on 19 March 1664 began the dramatic climax to Baños's term, when Osorio de Escobar, having learned that *cédulas* had been dispatched by Madrid, in response to the jeremiads emanating from Mexico, removing the conde from office and appointing himself temporary viceroy, *cédulas* which the conde's agents had intercepted at Veracruz and suppressed, had a notice read in Mexico City cathedral proclaiming that such *cédulas* existed and threatening with excommunication those who had seized them.[88] This, an open challenge to the regime, led the conde and his sons to attempt to murder the functionary who had read the notice, which in turn induced the bishop, who feared for his life, to seek sanctuary in the Carmelite priory of Santa Ana, outside the capital. On 12 June, day of Corpus Christi, the secular clergy in the capital, having been instructed by the bishop to prevent the procession from passing the viceregal palace as it had done in 1662 and 1663, complied with the bishop's orders, thereby openly defying the conde and condesa.[89] At this the viceroy, receiving assurances from Franciscan and Augustinian theologians that he might lawfully expel the bishop from the capital, began to work out a pretext for his expulsion, with the assistance of Montemayor y Cuenca and others of his officers. Then, on 28 June, with the city very tense and the viceroy closeted with the *Audiencia* completing arrangements for the bishop's expulsion, news arrived that a royal *cédula* addressing Osorio de Escobar as viceroy had reached the bishop owing to a shipwreck on the coast near Veracruz in circumstances that had enabled the local secular clergy to prevent Baños's officers from seizing its documents.[90] On learning that the city was in uproar, the conde abandoned his plan for disposing of Osorio de Escobar and retreated to his palace in confusion. The people and secular clergy gave way to exultation and for the rest of that day and the following morning the village of San Angel where the priory of Santa Ana was situated was engulfed by a great multitude of rejoicing supporters of the bishop.[91] In Puebla also there were extraordinary scenes and a great anti-Baños demonstration in which grotesque effigies of the conde and condesa were carried round the streets and subjected to savage mockery and obscenities.[92]

[87]Guijo, *Diario*, ii. 204–5. [88]Ibid. ii. 207. [89]Ibid. ii. 208–9.
  [90]Ibid. ii. 211–12. [91]Ibid. ii. 212.
  [92]AGI México 77: *Audiencia* to council, 21 July 1664, fol. 3ᵛ; Antonio de Robles, *Diario de sucesos notables*, i. 29.

On the morning of the 29th, Osorio de Escobar re-entered the capital accompanied by a vast crowd, the ringing of cathedral and church bells, and deafening applause, and proceeded directly to a meeting with the *Audiencia* in the archiepiscopal residence where he presented his *cédula*. Then the magistrates and various other dignitaries repaired to the viceregal palace where the viceroy was confronted with the document and asked to yield his title and keys.[93] At first Baños refused, but when his papers were examined and more documents were found naming Osorio de Escobar as viceroy, again he grew confused and was forced to yield. The bishop was then proclaimed viceroy and various steps were taken to quieten the people. That afternoon the conde, accompanied by his sons and an escort of guards, crossed to the archbishop's residence to acknowledge the new viceroy, and as he returned without a guard stones were thrown and he was harassed and mocked and compelled to run to safety. A day or two later his son, Don Pedro de Leyva, had a similar experience, being stoned and yelled at in the street as he passed in a carriage. Meanwhile the bishop-viceroy was cheered wildly whenever he appeared and all kinds of celebrations took place. Baños himself and his family had to move out of the palace under pressure from Osorio de Escobar, who according to the conde proved spiteful and vindictive[94] and into a private residence. On Tuesday 1 July all the bells of the capital chimed for two hours

Politically, a considerable change now ensued.[95] In July those whom the conde had expelled from the capital to various outlying townships returned. A number of corrupt officials were suspended from office and arrested, and twenty-three officers whom Baños had appointed during the time that the bishop should have been viceroy were dismissed. Also dismissed were two *regidores* who had been revealing the secrets of the Mexico City council to the conde and joining in his tyranny. Illegal *pulque* taverns were closed and huge quantities of *pulque* destroyed, and it was decreed that from then on *pulque* might only be sold in a small number of specially licensed establishments. The feud between Don Pedro de Leyva and the conde de Santiago Calimaya was effectively interrupted. This had been in progress since the start of Baños's term when Don Pedro had had occasion to make certain offensive remarks concerning the Creoles in the conde's presence; the affair had culminated in the viceroy's son

93 AGI México 77: *Audiencia* to council, 21 July 1664, fol. 3; Guijo, *Diario*, ii. 213–14.

94 AGI México 39, r 2: Baños to council, 25 Aug. 1664; Robles, *Diario de sucesos notables*, i. 29.

95 AGI México 39, r 2: Osorio de Escobar to council, 20 July 1664; Guijo, *Diario*, ii. 216, 218–27.

shooting the conde's favourite servant dead at his side, and after Baños' deposition was threatening to end in a duel between the two principals. Both nobles were now placed under arrest at the bishop-viceroy's orders.[96] But the bishop's rule, despite the intense desire of the Creoles and also of the *Audiencia* that it should be prolonged,[97] was in fact very short, and in late September 1664, a mere three months after coming to power, the bishop moved back into the archiepiscopal residence to make way for the twenty-third viceroy, the marqués de Mancera, who was then already at Puebla.

The people were not at all pleased to see Mancera,[98] for apart from the fact that they were more than satisfied with Osorio de Escobar, it was known that Mancera was a second cousin of Baños. However, Mancera was an astute man and although Baños made strenuous efforts to enlist his aid against the bishop's party,[99] and, according to Guijo,[100] even offered his cousin a huge bribe, the marquis was very careful to dissociate himself from the conde's cause. On 8 October, at a bull-fight put on in Mancera's honour and attended by the nobility and notables of the colony, Baños together with his family appeared in public and was met with a tremendous hissing and booing.[101] A week later, Mancera was sworn in as viceroy and moved into the palace, appointing on the same day, as captain of his guard, the conde de Santiago Calimaya, the Leyvas' sworn enemy. On 10 November the new archbishop of Mexico, Alonso de Cuevas Dávalos, the first Creole ever to attain that honour, entered the capital and moved into his new residence. Finally, a month later, Bishop Osorio de Escobar left Mexico City for Puebla, being escorted as far as Guadalupe by Mancera, the *Audiencia*, and a vast multitude of the common people.

96 Guijo, *Diario*, ii. 226–7.
97 AGI México 77: *Audiencia* to council, 21 July 1664, fol. 5.
98 AGI México 77: Ginés Morote to council, 25 Aug. 1664.
99 AGI México 39, r 2: Mancera to council, 2 Sept. 1664.
100 Guijo, *Diario*, ii. 226.
101 Guijo, *Diario,* ii. 233.

CONCLUSION

The marquis of Cerralvo, at the end of the report that he had addressed to King Philip IV of Spain in 1636 on the state of the viceroyalty of Mexico, had referred to the tranquillity of the colony and accounted it as being 'en toda paz y quietud'. And although at that time Cerralvo was especially anxious to impress his monarch with the competence of his eleven-year rule, owing to the probing into the less exemplary aspects of his administration by the *visitador* Don Pedro de Quiroga who was then taking his *residencia*, there can be no disputing the ex-viceroy's claim when the relative quietness of seventeenth-century Mexico is considered against the background of contemporary European turbulence. A monarch who was then at war with France and the Protestant Netherlands, and perilously involved in the turmoil of Germany and Italy, was hardly likely to be much troubled by events in New Spain apart, that is, from the worrying state of its economy. Cerralvo was able to dismiss the rising of 1624 and overthrow of Gelves plausibly enough as an isolated incident, exclusively the work of the despised middle grouping in Mexican society, the Negroes, mulattoes, and mestizos, a grouping which he acknowledged to be capable of causing commotions but only when badly mismanaged and unwisely provoked. For the rest, according to his account, the minor disturbances of his own term had been the consequence of the arrogance and irresponsibility of Archbishop Manso y Zúñiga and of Pedro de Quiroga.

Cerralvo's reassuring tone was reminiscent of that of certain of his predecessors and was to be echoed after him by one or two of his mid-century successors. Albuquerque, for example, fresh from the battlefields of Flanders and Catalonia, referred in several of his letters, at any rate before he became embroiled in his feud with Archbishop Sagade Bugueiro, to the placidness of Mexico and the ease with which the Mexican Creoles could be governed. Alva de Liste and Mancera were also given to expressing such thoughts from time to time. But this vaunted calm of Mexico was in fact only relative, and when one considers that it was very much in the interest of a viceroy to persuade the King's ministers that his rule was marked by orderliness and efficient government, what is really remarkable is how few viceroys of the half-century 1620–70 were able to follow Cerralvo's example and represent their rule as instances of successful administration. In fact no fewer than six viceroys more or less lost control of the colony amid varying degrees of social and political turmoil–Guadalcázar, Gelves, Cadereita, Escalona, Salvatierra, and Baños. Most of these, and the others who experienced difficulties, including Cerralvo and Albuquerque, preferred to blame their failures and misfortunes on the irresponsibility of such individuals as Bishops Palafox and Osorio de Escobar, rather than admit that there were profounder and more general causes of disturbance. Only Gelves was prepared to admit that a great deal was wrong and that he had stirred up widespread opposition; but then he had no choice, for his authority had totally collapsed and he had been overthrown by popular insurrection.

To claim that only one viceroy acknowledged the truth whilst the rest sought pretexts and excuses would be presumptuous indeed were it not for the great weight of evidence suggesting that the viceroys were in fact concealing a good deal from the eyes of Madrid. No fewer than four visitors–general to New Spain of the period, Landeras de Velasco, Carrillo y Alderete, Quiroga, and Palafox, repeatedly asserted that the state of the viceroyalty was such as to cause grave concern and that Mexico was in the grip of widespread, if muted, social and political conflict. The claims of these four visitors-general moreover, were vigorously seconded by the indignant reports of at least six leading churchmen apart from Palafox–Archbishops Pérez de la Serna, Manso y Zúñiga, and Sagade Bugueiro, and Bishops Benavente, Cuevas Dávalos, and Osorio de Escobar–and by various Creole writers such as Hernán Carrillo Altamirano and Juan Fernández de Vivero.

The reasons for the glaring discrepancy between the views of the viceroys on the one hand, and those of the *visitadores*, bishops, and Creoles plus Gelves on the other, are not hard to detect. The viceroys stood at the head of an administrative system which weighted the scales of power in their favour both as against control from Madrid and as against the local power of the Spanish settlers.

This system provided them with every opportunity for their own private gain, and for making the fortunes of relatives and friends, and was, if the reasoning embodied in this study is correct, the principal source of dissension in Mexican society. The viceroys as a group, always excepting Gelves, were permanently disinclined to expose fundamental weaknesses in the *status quo*, for they benefited from it far more than they possibly could from either of the two alternatives–more royal power or more settler power. Furthermore, such material considerations were supplemented by certain other kinds of considerations. In particular there were the moral and intellectual implications of the question of the future of the Indian population. The seventeenth-century viceregal system was the heir to the policy of racial segregation developed in the sixteenth century, a policy which still had the blessing of the religious orders and which was said by its apologists to be less burdensome and disruptive to Indian society than the alternative—more Creole power and a more integrated Mexican society. And although its critics argued that this claim was false and gave reasons for their belief that the Indians would benefit if the system were dismantled, it is far from certain that they were right and it must be admitted that the viceroys could at least partly satisfy their consciences that they were doing what was best for the Indians in resisting the pressure of the Creoles and preserving the *status quo*. This fundamentally conservative bias in the outlook of the viceroys was further encouraged by the profoundly unaggressive disposition of the colonists. Indeed the Creoles are remarkable in colonial history for their apparent complete lack of frontier spirit, their utterly unwarlike inclinations, the startling contrast between themselves and the Conquistadores from whom they claimed descent, and their almost total lack of arms. Rarely in the seventeenth century was so unified an opposition so devoted to non-violence and to the use of indirect means in quest of its goal. Bishop Palafox, in his report to his successor Salvatierra in 1642, gave eloquent expression to these characteristics whilst in the same breath pointing to what he, like the Creoles, regarded as the fundamental defect in Mexican society:

'The Spaniards in these provinces are not only loyal but exemplary in the service of His Majesty, and, with good government, they support. . .with joy whatever is decided in the name of His Majesty. The Indians are a people so wretched that they can give your excellency no other worry than that of the need to protect them, for by their sweat and on their shoulders are performed the extortions of the Spanish officers, of the friars that minister to them, and of the Indian governors.'

With so peaccable an opposition as this one can be forgiven for wondering how it was that the viceroys, whatever the dislike of their methods of administration among the Creoles, ever came to find themselves in deep trouble. The answer is that there was one glaring gap in the viceregal armour which the viceroys themselves had no way of filling. Maintaining the ascendancy of their district officers, and of their allies the Indian officers and friars in the Mexican countryside compelled the viceroys to keep parishes in 'Indian' areas out of the hands of the secular clergy, which was largely Creole in composition, and in mendicant hands, thus intruding on the power of the bishops and severely limiting the number of livings available to the ordinary priesthood. The bishops, although generally not Creoles, were in no wise dependent for their posts on the viceroys, being appointed in Madrid, and had not only great influence and prestige in Creole society, but the means of promoting effective opposition to the viceroys. Thus it was that the Creoles closely supported the bishops in their disputes with the viceroys, and what was at root a fundamental social conflict as to what kind of system should prevail in Mexico became translated, to the bafflement of some later historians, into unruly and long-drawn-out Church—state battles in which the bishops, employing mainly ecclesiastical channels, were on several occasions able to undermine the position of their opponents. In the light of this it is not surprising that seventeenth-century viceroys of Mexico were often given to using the most violent language in reference to the upper secular clergy even in reports to Madrid.

Established Indian society, as a consequence of the power and conservatism of the viceregal administration and the religious orders, seems to have stood up to the pressures of declining population, and the expansion of Spanish agriculture and enterprise, better than has sometimes been supposed. Though the white settlers, and also many mestizos and mulattoes, would have liked to take advantage of Indian weakness more extensively than they did, though Creole entrepreneurs were short of labour and wanted more of the Indians' working-time, and although hacendados frequently cast covetous eyes over Indian lands, the disruption of Indian communities and land tenure was effectively checked by the determination of the *alcaldes mayores* and *corregidores* and their ubiquitous deputies. The *corregidores* wanted the profits of intercourse with, and of tribute-collecting from, the Indians for themselves and this inevitably led them to defend the integrity of the traditional Indian villages and towns. Here the Indians continued to speak their own languages rather than Spanish, the Indian governors and other officers managed to maintain themselves and their hold over a large part of the Indian population, and the Indians still practised the Catholic religion under the guidance of the friars in the distinctive Indian style that had evolved in the sixteenth century.

However, there is no question but that there was also another Indian society, an espanolized, less tightly-knit and disciplined Indian society, which was separated from the traditional Indian communities, which dressed differently and which was growing steadily where the *corregidores* had less power, on the plantations and estates of Creole landowners and in the inner sections of the big towns. Culturally and economically this was a society much more closely linked to the life of the Spanish settlements than the other, and being mixed with large numbers of mestizos, Negroes, and mulattoes, it was in a sense the embryo of the future Mexican nation. It was in this milieu that specifically Mexican cultural phenomena, whether the sordid *pulquerías*, as the low taverns were called, or the religious cult of the Virgin of

Guadalupe, made their most spectacular progress. These ladino Indians were the fruit of that alternative system with which the Creoles aspired to replace the one defended by the viceregal administration. They were employees in what Creole apologists and such sympathizers as Archbishop Manso optimistically referred to as a free wage–labour economy, though more often than not they were subjected to that pernicious method of labour exploitation known as debt-peonage. Often they became involved in vice and crime and were capable of an unruliness which according to mendicant critics was all but unknown in the traditional Indian communities.

The two white minorities, the bureaucracy and the settlers, contending for the privilege of exploiting the wretched Indians, corresponded largely, though by no means invariably, to the party of the *gachupines* and the party of the Creoles. From the earliest period after the Conquest, the Spanish settlers had resented the tendency of the centralizing power in Mexico City to recruit its officers from among newcomers from Spain. But the tendency had not diminished and nor was it likely to. It was natural that the viceroys should wish to draw their bureaucracy from among those who had no links with local Mexican interests and who were dependent for their power, authority, and fortunes on the viceroys themselves. The divisive effects ensuing from this arrangement were considerable, for differences of social background, modes of speech, and education provided fertile ground for the growth of prejudice and discrimination, and many Mexican-born Spaniards came to see themselves as a semi-degraded people denied the the best offices in their own land. But although there is ample evidence of the passion that could be stirred up between *gachupines* and Creoles, the political rift between bureaucracy and settlers remained pre-eminent. Thus one finds the predominantly non-*gachupín* religious orders firmly tied to the bureaucracy and the predominantly non-Creole bishops securely bound to the settlers. If, in the case of the friars, political orientation, though partly determined by interest, was also partly governed by the unfair advantage gained by the *gachupín* minority by means of the *alternativas* and the Franciscan *ternativa*, the bishops, or most of them, were constrained to side with the colonists by pressure of interest and pressure from the lower secular clergy.

Yet another major factor tending to deepen the split between bureaucracy and Mexican Spaniards was disagreement over economic policy. The contours of the Mexican economic crisis of the seventeenth century are by no means yet entirely clear, but it does seem that the Creoles had plausible reasons for blaming Madrid and the viceregal government for many of their economic woes. After 1621 Madrid's policy with respect to the Mexican economy was marked by an increasing determination to make New Spain contribute more to the needs of a world-empire caught in a long and exhausting struggle with its Dutch, German, Swedish, and French enemies. Gelves, Cadereita, and Albuquerque in particular were avid collectors of the King's taxes, and with at least some measure of success introduced a new tightness into the regulation of Mexican trade. Beginning with Gelves, and even more under Cadereita and his successors, the administration cut off Mexico's trade with Peru, in the interest of Seville and Spanish exporters, and regulated commerce with the Philippines ever more tightly. Cerralvo and Cadereita introduced new taxes, first for the Union of Arms and then for the Aramada of Barlovento, taxes which the overstrained Mexican economy could ill afford. Still more damaging in the long run, the crown ended the era of easy credit for mercury and other supplies in the silver-mining towns and by so doing hastened the collapse of many of the less profitable silver-mining concerns and the general onset of depression. Admittedly many Spanish officers, often including the viceroys themselves, collaborated in fraud and evasion of the King's regulations and imposts, but invariably they did so for their own profit, and in co-operation with their own associates, so that net effect was still one of loss to Creole enterprise and the intensification of friction between officers and colonists.

The three principal commotions of the period 1621–65 in Mexico were certainly the conflict between the parties of Gelves and Pérez de la Serna in the years 1621–8, that between the parties of Salvatierra and Palafox in the years 1642–9, and between those of Baños and Osorio de Escobar in the years 1660–5. Of these the first two were the most considerable, both being extremely complex and involving very large numbers of persons and different interest groups, though both have generally been much oversimplified in the past by partisans of one side or the other and those who have sought a quick explanation for so much turbulence in the supposed excessive zeal and tactlessness of Gelves in the one case and Palafox in the other. None of these commotions led to much violence or destruction of property—the bread-riots of 1692 in Mexico City caused more—and kept in proper perspective, the three Mexican disturbances were very small by comparison with the risings and revolutions of the 1630s, 1640s, and 1650s in the Iberian peninsula, southern Italy, France, and England. Nevertheless, by the standards of Spanish American colonial history, they stand out as major social and political events, and given the obscurity which still surrounds much of that history in the seventeenth century, they represent valuable openings for historical scholarship.

The ultimate conclusion that emerges from a study of the social tensions and political events of the period 1620–70 in Mexico is that the viceroyalty, after more than four decades of uninterrupted economic growth, expansion northwards, and stable government, entered a period of crisis and difficulty which seems to show some important points of kinship with the so-called 'general crisis' of the half-century 1620–70 that historians have discerned in the history of Europe. Just as the mounting difficulties of the western world's leading but sick power, Spain, contributed greatly to the commercial recession and monetary chaos in much of Europe, so they added immeasurably to the economic difficulties of New Spain. Just as the end of economic expansion in much of Europe seems, as least in the view of some historians, to have increased the tension between parasitic bureaucracies and entrepreneurial elements, so in Mexico it appears to have intensified the endemic struggle between the viceroy's party and the Creoles. And finally, just as in Europe there appeared at this time many reformers zealously devoted to the correction of defects in society and administration, so in Mexico resolute reformers appeared such as Gelves and Palafox, men who greatly enlivened the politics of their time and left an indelible stamp on the history of the viceroyalty.

BIBLIOGRAPHY

1. MANUSCRIPT SOURCES

Indubitably the most valuable body of manuscripts for most aspects of seventeenth-century Mexico is the Archivo General de Indias (AGI) in Seville, for this is the archive that has the bulk of the letters and reports of the viceroys and *Audiencia* magistrates to the Spanish government in Madrid. The principal items of the AGI consulted for this study were the twenty-one boxes of viceroys' letters covering the period 1603–75 and the six boxes of *Audiencia* reports covering the years 1609–70: AGI section v (gobierno), part i, Audiencia de México, legajos 26–46 and 73–9. Also valuable were the *consultas* of the council of the Indies regarding Mexico for the years 1611–79–AGI México legajos 2–7–and the collections of letters to the council from Mexican *cabildos*, *corregidores*, and *visitadores*: AGI México legajos 91–4, 148, and 274. In section i (Patronato real) of the Archivo much useful material was encountered relating to the tumult of 1624 and the investigations of the *visitador* Don Martín Carrillo: AGI Patronato real, legajos 221–5; also of some interest in this section is the book of Palafox papers, legajo 244. A final legajo of the AGI to which reference was made contained the papers relating to the investigations of the *visitador* Landeras de Velasco in the years 1607–8: AGI section v (gobierno), 'Indiferente de Nueva España', legajo 77.

The second archive for seventeenth-century Mexico is the Archivo General de la Nación (AGN) in Mexico City. Particularly useful here are the files of the Mexican Inquisition which provide not only a good deal of information on the Jews in seventeenth-century Mexico and on various Church matters, but important details relating to the incident at Coyoacán in 1629 (Inquisición 366, legajo 19), on the Portuguese scare of 1641–2 (Inquisición 407, legajo 12) and the disturbances of 1646–7 in Puebla and Mexico City (Inquisición 424, legajos 1–2). Also helpful were the four books containing the ordinances of Viceroys Guadalcázar, Gelves, and Cerralvo: AGN ordenanzas i–iv; the eight books of viceregal ordinances on Indian matters for the years 1616–51: AGN Indios ix–xvi; the seven books of royal *cédulas*: AGN 'Ramo de reales cédulas originales' 1–6 and 233; and volume 413 of the 'Ramo de historia relating to the tumult of 1692. The 'Ramo de reales cédulas duplicados' is an intriguing section; of those volumes consulted, vols. 1–9 contain *cédulas*, as one would expect; vols. 48–9 and 57–64, however, contain the ordinances of Viceroys Escalona, Palafox, Salvatierra, Torres de Rueda, and Alva de Liste, while volume 50 yields a register of Cerralvo's 'composition' of foreigners of 1625.

Third perhaps among the archives, for seventeenth-century Mexico, is the Mexican collection of the British Museum (BM). Here the main items of interest are certain relatively lengthy *discursos* and *relaciones*. First and foremost among these are the 'Discurso de Juan Fernández de Vivero, natural y vecino de la ciudad y provincia de Tlaxcala del reino de la Nueva España, de los puntos en las materias mas principales y necessarias que necessitan de remedio en el dicho reino; ofrecido a la sacra catolica magestad del rey nuestro señor Felipe IV' (1634) (Add. MS. 13, 974) and the anonymous 'Relacion sucinta de lo sucedido en la Nueva España entre los señores conde de Salvatierra virrey, y el obispo de la Puebla, visitador general sobre las diferencias que han tenido por sus puestos; hecha por persona despasionada y que ha visto lo que en ello ha pasado' (Add. MS. 13, 976, doc. 47). Also valuable in the BM are the 'Papeles varios de Indias' (Add. MS. 13, 977, docs. 9, 18, 78, and 115), all relating to the tumult of 1624, and concerning the same subject, the 'Relazion del pleito que el licenciado Pedro de Vergara Gabiria, oidor de la real audiencia de Mexico, trata con el señor fiscal del consejo de Indias acerca del tumulto de Mexico, año de 1624' (a review of this important case composed in 1637; Add. MS. 13, 975, fols. 276–96, a book which also contains two letters from Archbishop Manso to the council of the Indies (fols. 297–303)). The manuscript version of Juan Gutiérrez Flores and Juan de Lormendi, 'Relazion sumaria y puntual del tumulto y sedicion que hubo en los quince de henero de 1624' has certain passages which are omitted in the printed version. Finally, there are some relevant documents among the 'Consultas del consejo de Estado tocantes a Indias, 1625–7' (Egerton 320–2) and in Add. MS. 13, 974 (doc. 21) the 'Relacion del viaje del obispo de Puebla de los Angeles desde Veracruz a dicha ciudad' (1640) which provides some interesting details relating to Palafox's early reforms in Puebla.

After the BM, come the archives of Madrid. The department of manuscripts of the Biblioteca Nacional (BND) has various papers relating to the tumult of 1624, notably MSS. 2355, 18, 660–2, and 20, 066–13 ('Relacion de los subcedido en la ciudad de Mexico en el alboroto y tumulto que se lebanto nacido de ciertas competencias entre el marques de Gelves, virrey, y el arzobispo de ella'). Perhaps the most useful document, however, was the 'Relacion de la llegada y estancia en la Nueva España del virrey duque de Escalona y del visitador del reino y obispo de la Puebla de los Angeles, Don Juan de Palafox y Mendoza' (MS. 19, 286). Also noteworthy are the various miscellaneous papers relating to the government of New Spain (MSS. 2719, 2940, 3048, 3636, and 18, 684–8) and Jerónimo de Mercado, 'Relacion de la inundazion de la ciudad de Mexico y del gran daño que padecio' (1630) (MS. 2362, fols. 267–8). In the private Archivo de los duques de Albuquerque, Madrid (ADA), is preserved an important collection of letters from Viceroy Albuquerque to Philip IV's valido, Luis Méndez de Haro (a15ca9–legajo 3, a15c15, A15–c16, and A15c17), covering the period 1653–60, and certain miscellaneous documents relating to Viceroy Cadereita, mainly letters from *corregidores* and other

personages to him (7b–cn–3, 24–n–ii). The private Archivo de los
duques del Infantado, Madrid (ADI), has some ninety volumes of
Palafox papers, an extremely valuable collection. Of these, among the
most noteworthy are volume xiii on the Portuguese scare of 1641–2,
vols. xx and liii containing Palafox's records relating to the rule of
Viceroy Cerralvo, volume xxxv relating to the political quarrels of
1646, volume xxxiii comprising letters from Bishop Benavente, the
Palafoxista bishop of Oaxaca, to Palafox, volume xliii relating to the
rule of the marqués de Cadereita, volume liv relating to the government
of the conde de Salvatierra, and finally, volume lxiii dealing with
conflict between the secular and regular clergy in the diocese of Puebla.

After the archives of Madrid, come the archives of the United States.
A good deal of important material was encountered in the manuscripts
division of the Bancroft Library at Berkeley, California (BL), and the
Latin American department of the library of the University of Texas at
Austin (UTL). At Berkeley, the main prize is the group of documents
relating to the tumult of 1624 collected by H. H. Bancroft whilst he
was engaged on his *History of Mexico*. The most important of these are
M–M236, 'Tumultos de Mexico', and M–M149–50, 'Mexico y sus
disturbios: documentos para servir a la historia de los disturbios y
tumultos acaecidos en Mexico durante el siglo xvii, colegidos por José
Fernández Ramírez'. Also relevant are the Palafox papers M–M503,
i–2, and M–M84–5, 'Disturbios de Frailes', two books of papers
concerning dissension among the clergy. At Austin, Texas, there are
various interesting documents among the papers which formerly
belonged to the Mexican historian and biographer of Palafox, Don
Genaro García. Of these the most useful were the 'Relación verídica de
lo acaecido en la ciudad de la Puebla de los Angeles en el año 1647
entre el Ilmo. exmo. y venerable sr. Don Juan de Palafox y Mendoza y
los religiosos de la Compañía' (1647) (G105) and the 'Relación de lo
occurido en la Puebla de los Angeles por un testigo ocular' (1647)
(G106), but also of interest were the 'Manuscritos de asuntos de las
Americas, 1621–1780' (G88).

Finally, there are the secondary archives of Mexico City. Of these,
that most consulted was the manuscripts division of the Biblioteca
Nacional (BNX). The most useful of the documents encountered (it is,
or was, not an easy archive to use owing to the primitive state of its
indexing) were the Palafox papers, MSS. 1, 216, 868, and 890, and the
correspondence of the Mexican Inquisition with the supreme council of
the Spanish Inquisition in Madrid (MS. 1,259). Also of interest were the
papers relating to the position of the Franciscan friars in the diocese of
Puebla (MS. 1, 066) and the jurisdiction of Texcoco (MS. 1, 510).
Finally, also of some interest was MS. 783, Francisco Calderón's
'Cuestion moral en que se trata de si los negros son o estan
comprendidos en este nombre, neofitos, y si gozan los privilegios de los
indios', a Jesuit tract on the status of the races and racial mixtures. In
the microfilm division of the Instituto de Antropología e Historia,

Mexico City (IAH), the main source used was the microfilm copy of the 'Libros de cabildo', vols. xvi–xxii. (1620–50) from the Archivo del Ayuntamiento de la ciudad de Puebla; also consulted were copies of books iii–iv of the 'Reales cédulas y mandamientos de los virreyes', from the same archive, and the seventeenth-century items from the 'Papeles de la alcaldía mayor de Guanajuato'. In the Archivo Histórico of the Instituto de Antropología e Historia, a small number of documents of marginal interest were encountered.

2. PRIMARY PRINTED SOURCES

Acosta, Joseph de, *Historia natural y moral de las Indias* (1st edn., Seville, 1590).

Actas de Cabildo de la Ciudad de México (54 vols., Mexico, 1889–1916). Title varies.

Advertimientos generales que los virreyes dejaron a sus sucesores para el gobierno de Nueva España, 1590–1604, ed. F. V. Scholes and E. B. Adams in *Documentos para la Historia del México Colonial*, ii (Mexico, 1956).

Agia, Miguel, *Servidumbres personales de Indios* (Lima, 1604; Seville, 1946).

Alaves Pinelo, Alonso de, *Addiciones a la alegacion de derecho por la provincia de San Nicolas de Mechoacan de la orden de San Agustin* (not in Toribio de Medina or Andrade) (Mexico?, 1635?).

Alegaciones en favor del clero, estado eclesiastico, i secular, españoles e Indios del obispado de la Puebla de los Angeles en el pleito con los sagradas religiones de Santo Domingo, San Francisco, i San Agustin (Puebla?, 1650?) (BNX and BP).

Alemán, Mateo, *Sucesos del gobierno de Fray Garcia Guerra* (1612), in *Revue Hispanique*, xxv (Paris and New York, 1911).

Altamirano, Diego, *Por la real Audiencia de Mexico* (c. 1632) (defence of Pedro de Vergara Gabiria in the Bodl.).

Arlegui, José de, *Crónica de la provincia de N.S.P.S. Francisco de Zacatecas* (Mexico, 1737; Mexico, 1851).

Arregui, Domingo Lázaro de, *Descripción de la Nueva Galicia* (1621), ed. François Chevalier (Seville, 1946).

Avendaño Villela, Pedro de, short tract complaining of the damage done to Spanish interests in America by the Portuguese (Madrid, 1608) (BM).

Avila, Juan de, *Sermon de el glorioso martyr San Felipe de Jesus Patron y Criollo de Mexico* (Mexico, 1681) (Toribio de Medina 1220) (BNX).

Ayeta, Francisco de, *Crisol de la verdad, en defensa de su provincia . . . sobre el despojo de las treinta y un doctrinas de que la removio el obispo don Juan de Palafox* (Madrid?, 1693?) (BNX).

Balbuena, Bernardo de, *La Grandeza Mexicana* (1604; Mexico, 1963).

Barrio Lorenzot, Francisco del, *El Trabajo en México durante la época colonial: ordenanzas de gremios de la Nueva España*, ed. G. Estrada (Mexico, 1921).

Basalenque, Diego, *Historia de la provincia de San Nicolas de Tolentino de Mechoacan del orden de Nuestro Padre San Agustin* (Mexico, 1963).

Becerra Tanco, Luis, *Felicidad de Mexico en la admirable aparicion de la Virgen Maria Nuestra Señora de Guadalupe* (1695) in the *Coleccion de obras y opusculos pertenecientes a la milagrosa aparicion de la bellisima imagen de Nuestra Señora de Guadalupe de Mexico* (Madrid, 1785).

Betancurt i Figueroa, Luis de, *Derecho de las iglesias metropolitanas i cathedrales de las Indias, sobre que sus prelacias sean proveidas en los capitulares dellas, i naturales de sus provincias* (1st edn., Madrid, 1637) (BM).

Bocanegra, Mathias de, *Auto General de la Fee celebrado ... en la muy noble y muy leal ciudad de Mexico, 11 de Abril de 1649* (Mexico, 1649).

Boletín del Archivo General de la Nación (Mexico, 1930–).

Breve resumen qve se haze para la mejor inteligencia del pleyto qve litiga la religion de San Francisco de la provincia del Santo Evangelio de los reynos de Nueva Espana con el clero, curas, y beneficiados del obispado de la Puebla de los Angeles (Madrid? , 1660?).

Broken Spears, The, The Aztec Account of the Conquest, ed. Miguel Leon Portilla, trans. L. Kemp (Boston, Mass., 1962).

Bueno de Roxas, Juan, *Por la clerecia de la provincia de Yucatan en el pleyto con los religiosos de San Francisco de dicha provincia* (n.p., n.d.).

Burgoa, Francisco, *Geográfica descripción de la parte septentrional del polo Artico de la America ... sitio de esta provincia de predicadores de Oaxaca* (1671; Mexico, 1934).

Calderón Juan Alonso, *Memorial historico ivridico politico de la santa iglesia catedral de la Puebla de los Angeles en la Nueva España* (Madrid? , 1651?).

Cancionero histórico Guadalupano, ed J. G. Gutiérrez (Mexico, 1947).

Cárdenas, Rodrigo de, *Consulta que se hizo por parte de el convento de la Puebla de esta Nueva España de el orden de predicadores, en el punto de la ternativa* (Andrade gives different title—no. 358) (Mexico, 1650) (BNX).

Carrillo Altamirano, Hernán, *El Doctor Hernan Carrillo Altamirano, vezino y natural de la ciudad de Mexico, en la Nueva España, y abogada de la real Audiencia della, y protector general de los indios de aquel Reyno, dize ...* (Madrid? 1627).

Cartas de Indias (Madrid, 1877).

Cartas de Religiosos, 1539–94, ed. J. G. Icazbalceta (Mexico, 1941).

Cedulario de los siglos xvi y xvii. El obispo Don Juan de Palafox y Mendoza y el conflicto con la Compania de Jesus, ed. Alberto Maria Carreno (Mexico, 1947).

Cepeda, Fernando de, an account of the detention of the flota of 1638 (Toribio de Medina no. 501) (Mexico, 1638).

Cepeda, Fernando de, and Fernando Alonso Carrillo, *Relacion universal legitima y verdadera del sitio en que esta fundada la muy noble insigne y muy leal ciudad de Mexico* (Mexico, 1637).

Cespedes y Velasco, Juan Gallardo, Petition to the king by the procurator of the foreign merchants of Seville (Madrid?, 1620?) (BM).

Champlain, Samuel de, *Brief discovrs des choses plvs remarqvables qve Sammvel Champlain de Brovage a reconnuves aux Indes Occidentalles*, in *Oeuvres* (6 vols., Toronto, 1922–36) i. 1–80.

Cisneros, Diego de, *Sitio, naturaleza, y propriedades de la civdad de Mexico* (Toribio de Medina no. 307) (Mexico, 1618).

Cisneros, Luys de, *Historia de el principio y origen pregressos venidas a Mexico y milagros de la santa imagen de Nuestra Señora de los Remedios* (Toribio de Medina no. 329) (Mexico, 1621).

Cobo, Bernave, *Obras* (2 vols., Madrid, 1956).

Códice Franciscano, ed. J. G. Icazbalceta (Mexico, 1941).

Colección de bulas, breves, y otros documentos relativos a la iglesia de América y Filipinas, ed. F. J. Hernaez (2 vols., Brussels, 1879).

Colección de documentos inéditos para la historia de España, ed. M. F. Navarrete and others (112 vols., Madrid, 1842–95).

Colección de documentos inéditos para la historia de Ibero-América (14 vols., Madrid, 1927–32). Title varies.

Colección de documentos inéditos relativos al descubrimiento, conquista, y organización de las antiguas poseciones españolas de ultramar. (25 vols., Madrid, 1885–1932).

Colección de documentos para la historia de la formacion social de Hispanoamérica, ed. R. Konetzke (3 vols., Madrid, 1953–62).

Colección de documentos para la historia de San Luis Potosí, ed. P. F. Velázquez (4 vols., Mexico, 1899).

Colmenero de Ledesma, Antonio, *Cvrioso tratado de la natvraleza y calidad del chocolate, dividido en qvatro pvntos* (Madrid, 1631).

Conquistadors, The. First-person Accounts of the Conquest of Mexico, ed. and tr. Patricia de Fuentes (New York, 1963).

Consulta de la ciudad de Mexico al exmo. señor virey marques de Cadereyta sobre quatro puntos que miran a la conservacion deste reyno (Toribio de Medina–468) (Mexico, 1636) (BM).

Consulta de la ciudad de Mexico al exmo. señor virey marques de Cadereyta sobre que se abra la contratacion del Piru, se comersie libremente con este reyno por las causas expressas (Mexico, 1636).

Copia de las cartas qve las civdades de Mexico y la Pvebla de los Angeles escrivieron a la real persona, y a sus conseios de Estado y de las Indias informando la verdad de lo qve svcedio en la Nueva España (Mexico?, 1648) (BNX).

Corchero Carreño, Francisco, *Desagravios de Christo en el triumpho de su cruz contra el judaismo, poema heroico* (Toribio de Medina no. 683) (Mexico, 1649).

Cortés, Hernán, *Five Letters of Cortes to the Emperor*, tr. J. B. Morris (New York, 1962).

Cruz, Sor Juana Inés de la, *Poesia, teatro, y prosa*, ed. A. C. Leal (Mexico, 1965).

Descripción de la Nueva España en el siglo xvii por el padre Fray Antonio Vázquez de Espinosa y otros documentos del siglo xvii, ed. Mariano Cuevas (Mexico, 1944).

Descripción del virreinato del Peru. Crónica inédita de comienzos del siglo xvii, ed. B. Lewin (Rosario, Argentina, 1958).

Díaz del Castillo, Bernal, *Historia verdadera de la Conquista de la Nueva España* (Mexico, 1968).

Diez de la Calle, Juan, *Memorial informatorio al rey nuestro señor en su real y supremo conseio de las Indias* (Madrid, 1645) (BM).

     Memorial y noticias sacras y reales del imperio de las Indias occidentales (Madrid, 1646).

Documentos inéditos del siglo xvi para la historia de México, ed. Mariano Cuevas (Mexico, 1914).

Documentos inéditos o muy raros para la historia de México, ed. Genaro García and Carlos Pereyra (36 vols., Mexico, 1905–11).

Documentos para la historia de la ciudad de Valladolid, hoy Morelia (1541–1624) both separately and in *BAGN* 2nd series, iii (Mexico, 1962).

Documentos relativos al tumulto de 1624, ed. M. Fernández de Echeverría y Veitia (2 vols., Mexico, 1855) in Documentos para la Historia de México, ser. 2, vols. ii–iii.

'Documents pour l'histoire des Franciscains au Mexique', ed. Robert Ricard, *Revue d'Histoire Franciscaine* i (1924), 216–35.

Dorantes de Carranza, Baltasar, *Sumaria relacion de las cosas de la Nueva España con noticia individual de los descendientes legítimos de los conquistadores y primeros pobladores españoles* (1604; Mexico, 1902).

Durán, Fray Diego, *Historia de las Indias de Nueva España y islas de tierra firme* (2 vols., and atlas, Mexico, 1867–80).

Echave, Balthasar de, *Discursos de la Antiguedad de la lengua cantabra Bascongada* (Toribio de Medina no. 234) (Mexico, 1607). Microfilm copy used in Library of Congress, Washington D.C., surviving original in Biblioteca Nacional, Santiago, Chile.

El fvero privilegios franqvezas y libertads de los caballeros hijos dalgo del señorío de Vizcaya, confirmados por el rey don Felippe IIII (Bilbao, 1643).

En el pleyto que se trata entre el ordinario y sagrada religion de Sancto Domingo sobre el conocimiento del excesso que dicen cometieron ciertos religiosos de dicha orden en la villa de Cuyuacan (n.p. [Mexico], 1630?) (BM).

Epistolario de Nueva España, 1505–1818, ed. Francisco Paso y Troncoso (16 vols., Mexico, 1939–42).

Espinosa, Isidro Felix de, *Cronica de la provincia Franciscana de los*

Apostoles San Pedro y San Pablo de Michoacan (1731) (Mexico, 1945).

Ferriol, Joseph, *En nombre del prior y consules, consulado, y comercio de la ciudad de Mexico y de toda la Nueva España* (n.p., n.d. [1646?] (BM).

Florencia, Francisco de, *Estrella del norte de Mexico* (edn. used Mexico, 1741).

Flores, Juan Gutiérrez, and Juan de Lormendi, *Relacion sumaria y puntual del tumulto y sedicion que hubo en Mexico a los quince de enero de 1624 y de las cosas mas notables que los precedieron, y despues se han seguido asta los seis de Marzo del dicho ano* (Mexico, 1625) (Bodl.).

Franco y Ortega, Alonso, *Segunda parte de la historia de la provincia de Santiago de Mexico, orden de predicadores de la Nueva España* (Mexico, 1900).

Fuentes para la historia del trabajo en Nueva España, ed. S. A. Zavala and M. Castelo (8 vols., Mexico, 1939—46).

Gage, Thomas, *Thomas Gage's Travels in the New World*, ed. J. Eric S. Thompson (Norman, Oklahoma, 1958).

A Duel between a Jesuite and a Dominican begun at Paris, Gallantly Fought at Madrid, and Victoriously Ended at London, 16 May 1651 (London, 1651).

Garcés de Portillo, Pedro, *Cerca de lo que se ha dudado sobre si el ilmo. senor arcobispo de Mexico pueda descomulgar a los religiosos que tienen curas de almas* (Mexico, 1621) (BL M—M85).

García, Esteban, *Crónica de la provincia Augustiniana del santisimo nombre de Jesús de México, libro quinto* (Madrid, 1918).

Gemelli Carreri, Giovanni Francesco, *Voyage du tour du monde* (in Mexico in 1698) (6 vols., Paris, 1727).

Gómez de Cervantes, Gonzalo, *La Vida económica y social de la Nueva España al finalizar del siglo xvi* (1599), ed. Alberto María Carreño (Mexico, 1944).

González Dávila, Gil, *Teatro eclesiastico de la primitiva iglesia de las Indias Occidentales, vidas de sus arzobispos, obispos, y cosas memorables de sus sedes* (2 vols., Madrid, 1649—55).

González de Rosende, Antonio, *Vida del ilmo. y exmo. señor Don Juan de Palafox y Mendoza*, vol. xiii of the *Obras* of Palafox (Madrid, 1762).

Gonzalvo de Ribero, Blas, *Por las provincias de la Compania de Jesus de las Indias Occidentales, Nueva España, provincias de Mexico, y en especial la de la Puebla de los Angeles* (Madrid, c. 1649) (HSA).

Grav y Monfalcon, Juan de, *Memorial informativo al rey nuestro señor en ... por la insigne y siempre leal ciudad de Manila, cabeca de las islas Filipinas* (Madrid, 1637) (BM).

Grijalva, Juan de, *Cronica de la orden de nuestro padre San Agustin en las provincias de la Nueva España* (1624; Mexico, 1924).

Guerra, Diego, *El Dr Diego Guerra, tesorero de la santa iglesia cathedral de la ciudad de Mexico y su procurador general ... dice que los arzobispos y obispos de las Indias Occidentales pretenden que vuestra magestad les haga merced . . . para que los religiosos . . . que exercen officio de curas . . . esten subordinados immediatemente a los ordinarios* (Mexico, 1631) (BL M–M85).

Guijo, Gregorio Martin de, *Diario, 1648–64* (2 vols., Mexico, 1952).

Gutiérrez de Medina, Christobal, *Viaje del virrey marques de Villena* (1640; Mexico, 1947).

Hakluyt, Richard, *The Principall navigations, voiges, and discoveries of the English nation* (1589; 2 vols., Cambridge, 1965).

Historia de Nuevo León con noticias sobre Coahuila, Tamaulipas, Texas, y Nuevo México, escrita en el siglo xvii por el capitán Alonso de León, Juan Bautista de Chapa y el general Fernández Sánchez de Zamora, ed. Israel Cavazos Garza (Monterrey, Nuevo Leon, 1961).

Instrucciones que los virreyes de Nueva España dejaron a sus sucesores (Mexico, 1867).

Instrucciones que los virreyes de Nueva España dejaron a sus sucesores (2 vols., Mexico, 1873).

Ixtlilxochitl, Fernando de Alva, *Obras Historicas*, ed. A. Chavero (2 vols. Mexico, 1892).

Konetzke (ed.) *see Coleccion . . .*

La Puebla de los Angeles en el siglo xvii, crónica de la Puebla por don Miguel Zeron Zapata, cartas del venerable don Juan de Palafox y de don Manuel Fernández de Santa Cruz, ed. Mariano Cuevas (Mexico, 1945).

López de Solís, Francisco, *Compendio de lo mucho que esta escrito en defensa de los religiosos curas de los ordenes de Santo Domingo, San Francisco, y Santo Agustin destas provincias de la Nueva España* (Toribio de Medina no. 541) (Mexico, 1641).

Defensa del derecho que los rr. pp. provincial absoluto y diffinidores de esta provincia del santo nombre de Jesus del orden de San Agustin tienen para elegir rector provincial, por el tiempo que falta de su triennio al provincial que durante el muere (Mexico, 1642) (BM).

Informe en derecho en favor de las religiones que en esta Nueva España exercen ministerios de curas . . . (Mexico, 1637).

Por las religiones de Santo Domingo, San Francisco, y San Agustin de las provincias desta Nueva España (Mexico, 1638) BM.

Por la jurisdiccion de los superiores de las religiones y ordenes mendicantes y la de los jueces conservadores que en virtud de sus privilegios pueden nombrar los religiosos . . . (Mexico, 1647?).

López de Velasco Juan, *Geografia y descripcion universal de las Indias* (Madrid, 1894).

Luzuriaga, Fray Juan de, *Paranympho celeste. Historia de la mystica zarza, milagrosa imagen, y prodigioso santuario de Aranzazu* (Mexico, 1686).

Manso de Contreras, Christoval, *Relacion cierta y verdadera de lo que sucedio en esta villa de Guadalcacar, provincia de Tehuantepeque desde los 22 de 1660 hasta los cuatro de Iulio de 1661* (Toribio de Medina no. 885) (Mexico, 1661).

Medina, Balthasar de, *Chronica de la santa provincia de San Diego de Mexico de religiosos descalcos de nuestro santo padre San Francisco en la Nueva España* (Toribio de Medina no. 1250) (Mexico, 1682).

Memorial de lo sucedido en la ciudad de Mexico desde el dia primero de Noviembre de 1623 hasta quinze de enero de 1624 (Mexico, 1624, a rare and little-known work). (Bodl.).

Memorial y relacion qve el antiqvissimo reyno de Navarra y las nobilissimas prouincias de Gvipvzcoa, Vizcaya, y Alava, presentan a la reyna nvestra senora en sv real consejo de Indias satisfaciendo a los siniestros informes qve con titvlo de defensa de Gaspar de Salcedo, se han esparcido y presentado por sv parte, en graue perjvicio de los leales vassallos de sv magestad, y especialmente de los vascongados qve assistieron a los ivsticias en los reynos del Perv, con ocasion de los disturbios de Puno (Madrid? , 1669?).

Memorias de los virreyes que had gobernado el Peru (Lima, 1895),

Mendieta, Gerònimo de, *Historia eclesiástica Indiana* (Mexico, 1870).

Moderación de doctrinas de la real corona administradas por las ordenes mendicantes (1623), ed. F. V. Scholes and E. B. Adams, *Documentos para la historia del Mexico colonial*, vi (Mexico, 1959).

Molina, Christobal de, *Informe que presenta a Felipe IV Christobal de Molina regidor de la ciudad de Mexico sobre el sistema de repartimientos y servicio personal de los indios . . .* (Madrid? , 1625) (AHN MS. Indias, no. 307).

Montemayor y Cuenca, Juan Francisco de, *Recopilación de algunos mandamientos y ordenanzas del gobierno de esta Nueva España* (1677, Mexico, 1787).

Moscoso y Cordova, Christobal, *Discvrso ivridico y politico en la sedicion qve hvvo en Mexico el ano passado de 1624* (Madrid, 1635) (BND).

Mota y Escobar, Alonso de la, *Descripción geográfica de los reynos de Nueva Galicia, Nueva Vizcaya, y Nuevo León* (1604) (Guadalajara, Jalisco, 1966).

Motolinia (Toribio de Benavente), *Memoriales e Historia de los Indios de la Nueva España. Biblioteca de autores espanoles* ccxl (Madrid, 1970).

Carta al emperador, refutacion a las Casas sobre la colonizacion espanola (Mexico, 1949).

Muñoz Camargo, Diego, *Historia de Tlaxcala* (Mexico, 1947).

Navarrete, Fray Domingo de, *The Travels and Controversies of Friar Domingo de Navarrete, (1618–86)*, ed. J. S. Cummins (Cambridge, 1962).

Nueva Colección de documentos para la historia de México, ed. Joaquín García Icazbalceta (5 vols., Mexico, 1886–92).

Nulidades expressas y notorias que contiene la causa del alboroto sucedido en la ciudad de Mexico a 15 de enero de 1624 asi en general

como en lo particular que toca al lic. Pedro de Vergara Gaviria (n.p., *c.* 1625) (Bodl.).

Ortiz de Cervantes, Juan, *Informacion en favor del derecho que tienen los nacidos en las Indias a ser preferidos en las prelacias dignidades canongias y otros beneficios eclesiasticos y oficios seculares de ellas* (Madrid, 1619).

Palafox y Mendoza, Juan de, *Obras* (12 vols., Madrid, 1762).

Cartas del venerable siervo de Dios Don Juan de Palafox y Mendoza al reverendisimo Padre Andres de Rada, provincial de la Compania de Jesus en Mexico y de este a su excellencia ilustrisima y otros documentos, ed. D. T. Vasconcellos (Rome, 1700).

Informes sobre el pleyto que la catedral de la Puebla de los Angeles siguio con los Padres de la Compania de Jesus sobre los diezmos (Puebla, 1642–5) (BP).

Ideas políticas, a selection from his writings by J. Rojas Garciduenas (Mexico, 1946).

Senor. Razon qve da a vuestra magestad el obispo visitador Don Juan de Palafox y Mendoza, de los acaecimientos del ano 1647 y obrado por el conde de Salvatierra, vuestro virey, en favor de los religiosos de la Compania de Jesus, retiro del obispo, y graves escandalos que han sucedido en la Nueva España, y cuanto conviene que V.M. lo mande averiguar y remediar (Madrid?, 1648?).

Carta del venerable Don Juan de Palafox y Mendoza al inquisidor general, Don Diego de Arce y Reynoso, obispo de Plasencia, en que se queja de los atentados cometidos contra su dignidad y persona por el tribunal de inquisicion de Mexico (1st edn., Cadiz, 1813).

Al Rey nuestro senor. Satisfaccion al memorial de los religiosos de la Compania del nombre de Jesus de la Nueva España. Por la dignidad episcopal (Madrid, 1652) (BNX).

Carta del venerable siervo de Dios Don Juan de Palafox y Mendoza al sumo pontifice, Inocencio decimo (8 Jan. 1649; 3rd edn., Madrid, 1768).

Lettre de l'Illustrissime Jean de Palafox . . . evesque d'Angelopolis dans l'Amerique . . . au Pape Innocent X, contenant diverses plaintes de cet evesque contre les entreprises et les violences des Jesuites et leur maniere peu evangelique de prescher l'evangile dans les Indes (Paris, 1659).

El venerable señor Don Juan de Palafox y Mendoza justificado en el tribunal de la razón por haber remitido a España y separado del virreinato de México al exmo. señor Don Diego López Pacheco, duque de Escalona, title and ed. by Carlos María de Bustamante (Mexico, 1831).

A los fieles del obispado de la Puebla. Juan indigno obispo electo de Osma (Madrid, 1653).

History of the Tartars (London, 1679).

Carta pastoral a la venerable congregacion de San Pedro de la ciudad de los Angeles y a los reverendos sacerdotes de todo el obispado (Puebla, 1640) (BM).

Puntos que el senor Don Juan de Palafox dexa encargados a las almas de su cargo al tiempo de partirse de estas provincias a los reynos de España (Puebla, 1649) (BNX).

Palma y Freites, Luis de la, *Por las religiones de Santo Domingo, San Francisco y San Agustin de las provincias de la provincias de la Nueva España, en defensa de las doctrinas de que fueron removidos de hecho sus religiosos doctrineros por el ilustrisimo señor D. Juan de Palafox y Mendoza* (Madrid, 1644) (Newberry Library, Chicago).

Papeles de Nueva España, ed. Francisco del Paso y Troncoso (Madrid and Mexico City, 1905–48).

Pareja, Francisco de, *Crónica de la provincia de la visitación de nuestra señora de la Merced de la Nueva España* (1688; Mexico, 1882).

Parras, Joseph, *Gobierno de los regulares de América* (2 vols., Madrid, 1783).

Pérez de Ribas, Andrés, *Historia de los triumphos de nuestra santa fee entre gentes de las mas barbaras y fieras del nuevo orbe, conseguidos por los soldados de la milicia de la Compania de Jesus en las misiones de la provincia de Nueva España* (Madrid, 1645).

Plaza y Jaén, Cristobal Bernardo de la, *Crónica de la real y insigne universidad de México de la Nueva España* (2 vols., Mexico, 1931).

Razonamiento que el exmo. señor marques de Cerralvo virrey desta Nueva España hizo al cabildo de Mexico sobre la Union de Armas en la Nueva España (Mexico, 1628).

Rea, Alonso de la, *Cronica de la orden de nuestro santo padre San Francisco, Provincia de San Pedro y San Pablo de Mechoacan en la Nueva España* (1639) (ist edn., Mexico, 1643) (Bodl.).

Recopilacion de Leyes de Indias, ed. Joaquin Ibarra (3 vols., Madrid, 1791)

Relacion del alçamiento que los negros y mulatos . . . de la ciudad de Mexico . . . pretendieron hacer (1612) (by Antonio de Morga?), ed. L. Querol y Roso, in *Anales de la Universidad de Valencia*, xii (Valencia, 1935).

Relacion del estado en que el marques de Gelves hallo el reyno de la Nueva España (Madrid? 1628?) (BL).

Relacion de los fundamentos, informes, y pareceres que por una y otra parte se ha deduzido y visto en el consejo real de las Indias sobre si se ha de abrir el commercio que solia aver entre el Peru i la Nueva España o continuarse la suspension o prohibicion que del corre (Madrid, 1644) (BM).

Relacion de todo lo sucedido en estas provincias de la Nueva España desde la formacion de la Armada real de Barlovento . . . (Toribio de Medina no. 564) (Mexico, 1642) (HSA).

Ricard (ed.) *see Documents . . .*

Robles, Antonio de, *Diario de Sucesos notables, 1665–1703*, ed. A. Castro Leal (3 vols., Mexico, 1946).

Resguardo contra el olvido en el breve compendio de la vida admirable y virtudes heroycas del ilmo. sr. Dr D. Alonso de Cuevas Davalos (edn. used, Mexico, 1757).

Roxas, Alonso de, *Al Rey por la Compania de Jesus de la Nueva España en satisfaccion de un libro de el visitador obispo Don Juan de Palafox y Mendoza* (Madrid? , c. 1649) (BNX).

Ruiz de Cabrera, Christoval, *Algvnos Singvlares y extraordinarios svcesos del gobierno del exmo. señor Don Diego Pimentel, marques de Gelves* (Toribio de Medina no. 372) (Mexico, 1624) (BM).

Sahagún, Bernardino de, *General History of the Things of New Spain; Florentine Codex*, tr. and ed. A. J. O. Anderson and C. F. Dibble (13 vols., Santa Fe, New Mexico, 1950-.)

Salguero, Pedro, *Vida del venerable padre y exemplissimo varon el maestro Fray Basalenque* (edn. used, Rome, 1761).

Salmerón, Pedro, *Vida de la venerable madre Isabel de la Encarnacion, Carmelita descalca, natural de la ciudad de los Angeles* (Mexico, 1675) (BM).

San Miguel, Juan de, *Sermon qve predico . . . por los felices svcesos de las armas de España* (Mexico, 1646).

Sánchez, Miguel, *Imagen de la virgen Maria madre de Dios de Guadalupe milagrosamente aparecida en la ciudad de Mexico . . .* (1648).

Sánchez Baquero, Juan, *Fundación de la Compañia de Jesús en Nueva España* (c. 1612; Mexico, 1945).

Sánchez de Guevara, Cristobal, *Informacion en derecho de los fundamentos juridicos que tuvo la provincia de San Nicolas de Mechoacan de la orden de San Agustin para el capitulo que celebro en el convento de Santiago Cupandaro* (Mexico, c. 1632) (UTL).

Serna, Jacinto de la, *Sermon predicado en la santa iglesia cathedral de Mexico en la fiesta qve sv ilvstrissimo cavildo hizo a el insigne Mexicano prothomartyr ilvstre del Japon, San Felipe de Jesvs en su dia* (Mexico, 1652) (BNX)-Laf.

Serna, Juan de la, *Sermon qve predico el illvstrissimo senor Doctor Don Ivan de la Cerna, arcobispo de Mexico, del consejo de S.M., Domingo infra octavo de la celebridad y fiesta de la beatificacion del santo padre Francisco Xavier* (Mexico, 1621) (BNX-Laf).

Sigüenza y Góngora, Carlos de, *Obras historicas*, ed. J. Rojas Garcidueñas (Mexico, 1960).

Solórzano y Pereira, Juan de, *Política Indiana* (Madrid, 1647).

Soria, Martín de, *Relacion verdadera de la commocion popular que hubo en la ciudad de Mexico, el quinze de enero de 1624* (Mexico, 1624) (Bodl.).

Suárez de Peralta, Juan, *La conjuración de Martín Cortés*, selections from the *Tratado*, ed. Agustín Yañez (Mexico, 1945).

Tamariz de Carmona, Antonio, *Relacion y descripcion del templo real de la ciudad de la Puebla de los Angeles en la Nueva España* (Madrid? , 1650?).

Testimonio de una provision del rey en que se imparte plenamente el real auxilio a la legitima jurisdiccion apostolica de los muy rr. pp. jueces delegados conservadores de la Compania de Jesus en el pleyto con el ilustrisimo señor Don Juan de Palafox y Mendoza in Francisco González Cossio. *La Imprenta en México* (Mexico, 1952), pp. 66—77.

Testimonios de Zacatecas, selection of documents by Gabriel Salinas de la Torre (Mexico, 1946).

Torquemada, Fray Juan de, *Los veynte y un libros rituales y monarchia Yndiana con el origen y guerras de las Yndias Occidentales de sus poblaciones descubrimiento conquista conversion y otras cosas maravillosas de la mesma tierra distribuydos en tres tomos* (1st edn., Seville, 1615).

Torres, Nicolás de, *Festin hecho por las morenas criollas de la muy noble y muy leal ciudad de Mexico al recibimiento del exmo. senor marques de Villena* (Mexico, 1640) (HSA).

Un desconocido cedulario del siglo xvi perteneciente a la catedral metropolitana de Mexico, ed. Alberto Maria Carreno (Mexico, 1944).

Veitia Linage, Joseph de, *Norte de contratacion de las Indias* (Seville, 1672).

Ventancurt, Agustin de, *Teatro Mexicano. Descripcion breve de los svcessos exemplares, historicos, politicos, militares, y religiosos del nuevo mundo occidental de las Indias* (2 vols. in one, Mexico, 1697—8).

Victoria Baraona, Francisco de, a short discourse in six ff, on the economic state of the Indies (Madrid, 1639) (BM).

Zorita, Alonso de, *The Lords of New Spain*, tr. B. Keen (London, 1965).

3. SELECT LIST OF SECONDARY SOURCES

Aguirre Baltrán, Gonzalo, 'The Slave Trade in Mexico', *Hispanic American Historical Review*, xxiv (1944), 412—51.

    La Población negra de México, 1519—1810, estudio etnohistórico (Mexico, 1946).

Aiton, A. S. *Antonio de Mendoza, First Viceroy of New Spain* (Durham, N. Carolina, 1927).

Albi Romero, G., 'La Sociedad de Puebla de los Angeles en el Siglo XVI', *Jahrbuch für Geschichte von Staat, Wirtschaft und Gesellschaft Lateinamerikas*, vii (Cologne-Vienna, 1970), 76—145.

Alegre, Francisco Javier, *Historia de la Compañá de Jesús en Nueva España*, ed. Carlos María Bustamente (3 vols., Mexico 1841—2).

Arcila Farías, Eduardo, *Comercio entre Venezuela y México en siglos XVII y XVIII* (Mexico, 1950).

Astrain, Antonio, *Historia de la Compañá de Jesús en la Asistencia de España* (7 vols., Madrid, 1902—25).

Azevedo, João Lucio d', *Historia dos Cristãos Novos Portugueses* (Lisbon, 1921).

Bakewell, P. J., *Silver Mining and Society in Colonial Mexico, Zacatecas, 1546—1700* (Cambridge, England, 1971).

Bancroft, Hubert Howe, *History of Mexico* (6 vols., San Francisco, 1883—8); *Works*, ix—xiv.

Bayle, C., *Los Cabildos seculares en la América Española* (Madrid, 1952).

Bazant, J. 'Evolución de la industria textil poblana, 1544–1845', *Historia Mexicana*, xiii (1963–4), 473–516.

Berthe, Jean-Pierre, 'Xochimancas. Les travaux et les jours dans une hacienda sucrière de Nouvelle-Espagne au XVIIe Siècle', *Jahrbuch für Geschichte . . . Lateinamerikas*, iii (1966).

Borah, Woodrow, *New Spain's Century of Depression*, Ibero-Americana no. 35 (Berkeley and Los Angeles, 1951).

   Early Colonial Trade and Navigation between Mexico and Peru, Ibero-Americana no. 36 (Berkeley and Los Angeles, 1954).

   'The Portuguese of Tulancingo and the special *donativo* of 1642–3', *Jahrbuch für Geschichte . . . Lateinamerikas*, iv (1967), 386–98.

   'Latin America, 1610–60', in *The New Cambridge Modern History* iv (Cambridge, 1970).

   'Un gobierno provincial de frontera en San Luis Potosí, 1612–1620', *Historia Mexicana* xiii (1963–4), 532–50.

   and S. F. Cooke, 'The Indian Population of Central Mexico 1531–1610', Ibero-Americana no. 44 (Berkeley and Los Angeles, 1960).

Bowser, F. P., 'The African in Colonial Spanish America: Reflections on Research Achievements and Priorities', *Latin American Research Review*, vii (1972), 47–76.

Brading, D. A. *Miners and Merchants in Bourbon Mexico, 1763–1810* (Cambridge, 1971).

Brading, B. A. and Cross, H. E., 'Colonial Silver Mining in Mexico and Peru', *Hispanic American Historical Review*, lii (1972), 545–79.

Brodrick, J., *The Economic Morals of the Jesuits* (London, 1934).

Cabrera y Quintero, Cayetano de, *Escudo de armas: celestial proteccion de esta nobilissima ciudad de Mexico de la Nueva España y de casi todo el nuevo mundo* (Mexico, 1746).

Calderón Quijano, José Antonio, 'Población y Raza en Hispano-américa', *Anuario de Estudios Americanos* (Seville, 1970), 733–785.

Camara Barbachano, Fernando, 'El Mestizaje en Mexico', *Revista de Indias*, xxiv (1964), 27–85.

Carreón, Antonio, *Historia de la ciudad de la Puebla de los Angeles* (2 vols., Puebla 1896–7).

Cavo, Andrés, *Los Tres Siglos de México durante el gobierno español* (Mexico, 1852).

Chaunu, Pierre, 'Pour un tableau triste du Mexique au Milieu du XVIIe Siècle', *Annales: Economies, Sociétés, Civilisations,* x (1955), 79–85.

   'Veracruz en la segunda mitad del siglo XVI y primera del XVII', *Historia Mexicana*, ix (1960).

   Les Philippines et le Pacifique des Ibériques XVIe, XVIIe, XVIIIe siècles (Paris, 1960).

Chaunu, Pierre and Hugnette, *Séville et l'Atlantique, 1504–1650* (8 vols., Paris, 1955–60).

Chevalier, François, *La Formation des grands ʿdomaines au Mexique, Terre et Société au XVIe–XVIIe siècles* (Paris, 1952).

'Les Cargaisons des flotes de la Nouvelle Espagne vers 1600', *Revista de Indias*, iv (1943), 323–30.

'Les Municipalités indiennes en Nouvelle Espagne 1520–1620', *Anuario de Historia del Derecho Español*, xv (1944), 352–86.

Cline, H. F., 'Civil Congregations of Indians in New Spain 1598–1606', *Hisp. Am. Hist. Rev.* xxix (1949), 349–69.

Crisis in Europe, 1560–1660, essays from *Past and Present*, ed. T. Aston (London, 1965).

Cuevas, Mariano, *Historia de la Iglesia en México* (5 vols., Mexico, 1946).

Davidson, D. M., 'Negro Slave Control and Resistance in Colonial Mexico, 1519–1650', *Hisp. Am. Hist. Rev.* xlvi (1966), 235–53.

Décorme, G., *La Obra de los Jesuitas Mexicanos durante la época colonial, 1572–1767* (3 vols., Mexico, 1941).

Domínguez Ortiz, Antonio, 'Los Caudales de Indias y la Política exterior de Felipe IV', *Anuario de Estudios Americanos*, xiii (1956), 311–83.

'La Concesión de naturalezas para comerciar en Indias durante el siglo XVII', *Revista de Indias*, xix (1959).

Durand, José, *La Transformación Social del Conquistador* (2 vols., Mexico, 1953).

Ewald, Ursula, 'Versuche zur Änderung der Besitzverhältnisse in den letzten Jahrzehnten der Kolonialzeit. Bestrebungen im Hochbecken von Puebla-Tlaxcala und seiner Umgebung zur Rückführung von hacienda Land an Gutsarbeiter und indianische Dorfgemeinschaften', *Jahrbuch für Geschichte . . . Lateinamerikas*, vii (1972), 239–251.

Feijoo, R., 'El Tumulto de 1624', *Historia Mexicana*, xiv (1964), 42–70.

'El Tumulto de 1692', *Historia Mexicana*, xiv. 4 (1965), 656–79.

Fernández Echeverría y Veytia, M., *Historia de la fundación de la ciudad de la Puebla de los Angeles en la Nueva España* (2 vols., Puebla, 1931).

García, Genaro, *Don Juan de Palafox* (Mexico, 1918).

Gerhard, Peter, *A Guide To The Historical Geography of New Spain* (Cambridge, 1972).

Gibson, Charles, *Tlaxcala in the Sixteenth Century* (New Haven, Conn., 1952).

The Aztecs Under Spanish Rule. A History of the Indians of the Valley of Mexico 1519–1810 (Stanford, Calif., and Oxford, 1964).

'The Aztec Aristocracy in Colonial Mexico', *Comparative Studies in Society and History*, xi (1959–60), 169–96.

Spain in America (New York, 1967).

and M. Mörner, 'Diego Muñoz Camargo and the Segregation Policy of the Spanish Crown', *Hisp. Am. Hist. Rev.* xliii (1963), 558–68.

González de Casanova, Pablo, 'Aspectos políticos de Don Juan de Palafox y Mendoza', *Revista de Historia de América* xvii (1944), 27–67.

González Obregón, Luis, *México viejo, 1521–1821* (Paris and Mexico, 1900).

Greenleaf, R. E., 'The Obraje in the late Mexican Colony', *The Americas* xxiii (1966–7), 227–50.

Guthrie, Chester L., Riots in seventeenth-century Mexico: A Study in Soc:al History with Special Emphasis upon the Lower Classes' (Doctoral dissertation of the University of California) (Bancroft Library, Berkeley, Calif.).

    'Colonial Economy, Trade, Industry, and Labour in Seventeenth-Century Mexico City', *Revista de Historia de América*, vii (1939), 103–134.

    'Riots in Seventeenth-Century Mexico City: a Study of Social and Economic Conditions', in *Greater America, Essays in Honour of Herbert Eugene Bolton* (Berkeley and Los Angeles, 1945), pp. 243–258.

Humboldt, Alexander von, *Essai politique sur le royaume de la Nouvelle Espagne* (4 vols., Paris, 1811).

Ispizua, Segundo de, *Historia de los Vascos en el Descubrimiento, Conquista, y Civilización de Améri a* (6 vols., Bilbao, 1914).

Israel, J. I., 'Mexico and the "General Crisis" of the seventeenth century', *Past and Present* no. 63 (May 1974), pp. 33–57.

Israel, J. I., 'The Portuguese in seventeenth-century Mexico', *Jahrbuch für Geschichte . . . Lateinamerikas*, xi (1974).

Katz, F., 'The Evolution of Aztec Society', *Past and Present*, xiii (1958).

Keith, R. G., 'Encomienda, Hacienda, and Corregimiento in Spanish America: a structural analysis', *Hisp. Am. Hist. Rev.* li (1971), 431–446.

Konetzke, R. 'Die "Geographischen Beschreibungen" als Quellen zur hispanoamerikanischen Bevölkerungsgeschichte der Kolonialzeit', *Jahrbuch für Geschichte . . . Lateinamerikas* vii (1970), 1–75.

    'El Mestizaje y su importancia en el desarrollo de la población hispanoamericana durante la época colonial', *Revista de Indias*, xxiii (1946), 215–37.

    'La emigración de mujeres españolas a América durante la época colonial', *Revista internacional de Sociología* vol. 1 (1949) pp. 441–80.

    'Spanische Universitätsgründungen in Amerika und ihre Motive', *Jahrbuch für Geschichte . . . Lateinamerikas*, v (1968), 111–159.

Labayru y Goicoechea, Estanislao de, *Historia general del Señoría de Bizcaya* (6 vols., Bilbao and Madrid, 1895–1903).

Lang, M. F., 'New Spain's Mining Depression and the Supply of Quicksilver from Peru, 1600–1700', *Hisp. Am. Hist. Rev.* xlviii (1968), 632–641.

Lascurain, Vicente, 'Los primeros vascos pobladores de la Nueva España', *Boletín del Instituto Americano de Estudios Vascos*, v (1954).

Lea, H. C., *The Inquisition in the Spanish Dependencies* (New York, 1908).

Lea, R. L., 'American Cochineal in European Commerce, 1526–1625', *Journal of Modern History* xxiii (1951).

León, N., *Las Castas del México Colonial o Nueva España* (Mexico, 1924).

León Borja, D., and A. Szaszdi Nagy, 'El Comercio del cacao de Guayaquil', *Revista de Historia de América*, lvii (1964), 1–50.

Leonard, I. A., *Baroque Times in Old Mexico* (Ann Arbor, Michigan, 1966).

Leonard, I. A., *Don Carlos de Sigüenza y Góngora. A Mexican Savant of the Seventeenth Century* (Berkeley, 1929).

Alboroto y Motín de los Indios de México del 8 de Junio de 1692 (Mexico, 1932).

Liebman, S. B. *The Jews in New Spain* (Miami, 1970).

'The Great Conspiracy in New Spain', *The Americas*, xxx (1973).

Lockhart, J., 'Encomienda and Hacienda: The Evolution of the Great Estate in the Spanish Indies', *Hisp. Am. Hist. Rev.* xlix (1969), 411–29.

Lockhart, J., 'The Social History of Colonial Spanish America: Evolution and Potential', *Latin American Research Review*, vii (1972), 6–45.

Lynch, John, *Spain Under the Habsburgs* (2 vols., Oxford, 1965–9).

Marroquí, José María, *La Ciudad de Mexico* (3 vols., Mexico, 1909–1913).

Marshall, C. E., 'The Birth of the Mestizo in New Spain', *Hisp. Am. Hist. Rev.* xix (1939), 161–84.

Martin, N. F., *Los Vagabundos en la Nueva España, siglo XVI* (Mexico, 1957).

Martínez Cosío, L., *Los Caballeros de las órdenes militares en México, catálogo biográfico y genealógico* (Mexico, 1946).

Mauro, F., *Le Portugal et l'Atlantique au XVIIe Siécle 1570–1670, étude economique* (Paris, 1960).

McAlister, L. N., 'Social Structure and Social Change in New Spain', *Hisp. Am. Hist. Rev.*, xliii (1963), pp. 349–70.

Medina, José Toribio, *Historia del Tribunal del Santo Oficio de la Inquisición en México* (Santiago, Chile, 1905).

Miranda, José de, 'La Población Indígena de México en el Siglo XVII', *Historia Mexicana*, xii (1962–3), 182–9.

Morales Rodríguez, Sergio, 'Costumbres y creencias en la Nueva España', in *Homenaje a Silvio Zavala. Estudios Históricos Americanos* (Colegio de México, Mexico, 1953), pp. 425–475.

Moreno Toscano, A., 'Tres problemas de la geografía del Maiz 1600–1624' *Historia Mexicana*, xiv (1965), 631–55.

Mörner, Magnus, 'Das Verbot für die Encomenderos unter ihren eigenen Indianern zu wohnen', *Jahrbuch für Geschichte . . . Lateinamerikas*, i (1964), 187–206.

Navarro García, Luis, *Sonora y Sinaloa en el Siglo XVII* (Seville, 1967).

Novinsky, A., *Os Cristãos Novos na Bahia* (São Paulo, 1972).

Osborn, W. S., 'Indian Land Retention in Colonial Mestitlán', *Hisp. Am. Hist. Rev.* liii (1973), 217–38.

Parry, J. H., *The Sale of Public Offices in the Spanish Indies Under the Habsburgs*, Ibero-Americana XXVII, (Berkeley and Los Angeles, 1953).

Parry, J. H., *The Spanish Seaborne Empire* (London, 1967).

Pietschmann, Horst, 'Alcaldes Mayores, Corregidores und Subdelegados. Zum Problem der Distriktbeamtenschaft im Vizekönigreich Neuspanien' *Jahrbuch für Geschichte* ... *Lateinamerikas*, ix (1972), 173–270.

Phelan, J. L., *The Millennial Kingdom of the Franciscans in the New World. A Study of the Writing of Gerónimo de Mendieta (1525–1604)* (Berkeley and Los Angeles, 1956).

Phelan, J. L., *The Kingdom of Quito in the Seventeenth Century, Bureaucratic Politics in the Spanish Empire* (Madison, Wisc., and London, 1967).

Pohl, H., 'Zur Geschichte des adligen Unternehmers im spanischen Amerika (17/18 Jahrhundert)', *Jahrbuch für Geschichte* ... *Lateinamerikas*, ii (Cologne-Graz, 1965), 218–44.

Pompa y Pompa, Antonio, *El Gran Acontecimiento Guadelupano* (Mexico, 1967).

Porras Muñoz, Guillermo, 'Don Marcos de Torres y Rueda y el Gobierno de la Nueva España', *Anuario de Estudios Americanos*, xxiii (Seville, 1966), 669–80.

Powell, P. W., *Soldiers, Indians and Silver. The Northward Advance of New Spain, 1550–1600* (Berkeley and Los Angeles, 1952).

Querol y Roso, Luis, 'Negros y Mulatos de Nueva España', *Anales de la Universidad de Valencia* xii (1935).

Raynal, the Abbé, *A Philosophical and Political History of the Settlement and Trade of the Europeans in the East and West Indies* (tr. from French, 5 vols., 2nd edn., London, 1776).

Ricard, R., *La Conquête Spirituelle du Mexique. Essai sur l'Apostolat et les méthodes missionaires des ordres mendicants en Nouvelle Espagne*, Université de Paris, Travaux et memoires de l'Institut d'ethnologie no. 20 (Paris, 1933).

'Los Portugueses en las Indias Españolas', *Revista de Historia de América*, xxxiv (1952).

Ríos, Eduardo Enrique, *Felipe de Jesús, el santo criollo* (3rd edn., Mexico, 1958).

Riva Palacio, Vicente, *México Atraves de los Siglos* (5 vols., Barcelona, 1888–9).

Rivera Cambas, Manuel, *Los Governantes de México* (2 vols., Mexico, 1872–3).

Robertson, William, *The History of America* (1788) (4 vols., London, 1817).

Rojas, Basilio, *La Rebelión de Tehuantepec* (Mexico, 1962).
Romero de Terreros, Manuel, *Ex Antiquis, Bocetos de la vida social en la Nueva España* (Guadalajara, Jalisco, 1919).
Rosenblat, Angel, *La Población indígena y el mestizaje en América* (2 vols., Buenos Aires, 1954).
Rubio Mañé, J. Ignacio, *Introducción al estudio de los virreyes de Nueva España, 1535–1746* (4 vols., Mexico, 1955).
Saco, José Antonio, *Historia de la esclavitud de la raza africana en el Nuevo Mundo y en especial en los paises Americo-hispanos* (4 vols., Havana, 1938).
Sánchez Pedrote, Enrique, 'Los Prelados Virreyes', *Anuario de Estudios Americanos* vii (1950), 211–53.
Sandoval, F. B., *La Industria del Azúcar en Nueva España* (Mexico, 1952).
Santiago Cruz, Francisco, *Las Artes y los Gremios en la Nueva España* (Mexico, 1960).
Saraiva, Antonio José, *Inquisicão e Cristãos Novos* (Oporto, 1969).
Scelle, Georges, *Histoire politique de la traite negrière aux Indes de Castille* (2 vols., Paris, 1906).
Schaffer, Ernst, *El Consejo real y supremo de las Indias* (2 vols., Seville, 1935–47).
Schmitt, K. M., 'The Clergy and the Independence of New Spain', *Hisp. Am. Hist. Rev.* xxiv (1954), 289–312.
Scholes, F. V., *Church and State in New Mexico, 1610–70*, Publications of the Historical Society of New Mexico nos. 7 and 11 (Albuquerque, New Mexico, 1937 and 1942).
Schons, D., *Book Censorship in New Spain* (Austin, Texas, 1949).
Schurz, W. L., 'Mexico, Peru, and the Manila Galleon', *Hisp. Am. Hist. Rev.* i (1918), 389–402.
Schurz, W. L., *The Manila Galleon* (New York, 1939).
Simmons, C. E. P., 'Palafox and his critics: re-appraising a controversy', *Hisp. Am. Hist. Rev.* xlvi (1966).
Simpson, L. B., *Studies in the Administration of the Indians of New Spain no. 2: The Civil Congregation*, Ibero-Americana no. 7 (Berkeley and Los Angeles, 1934).
　The Encomienda in New Spain. The Beginning of Spanish Mexico (Berkeley and Los Angeles, 1950).
　Studies in the Administration of the Indians of New Spain no. III: The Repartimiento system of Indian Labour in New Spain and Guatemala (Berkeley, 1938).
　'Mexico's Forgotten Century', *The Pacific Historical Review*, xxix (1953), 113–21.
Sluiter, Engel, 'The Fortification of Acapulco, 1615–16', *Hisp. Am. Hist. Rev.* xxix (1949).
Smith, R. S., 'The Institution of the Consulado in New Spain', *Hisp. Am. Hist. Rev.* xxiv (1944), 61–83.
　'Sales Taxes in New Spain, 1575–1770', *Hisp. Am. Hist. Rev.* xxviii (1948), 2–37.

Spalding, K., 'The Colonial Indian: Past and Future Research Perspectives', *Latin American Research Review*, vii (1972), 47–76.

Sosa, Francisco, *El Episcopado Mexicano* (2 vols., Mexico, 1939).

Soustelle, Jacques, *La Vie quotidienne des Aztèques a la veille de la conquête Espagnole* (Paris, 1955).

Stevenson, R., 'The "Distinguished Maestro" of New Spain: Juan Gutiérrez de Padilla'. *Hisp. Am. Hist. Rev.* xxv (1955), 363–73.

Sticker, Georg, 'Die Einschleppung Europäischer Krankheiten in Amerika während der Entdeckungszeit; ihr Einfluss auf den Rückgang der Bevölkerung', *Ibero-Amerikanisches Archiv*, vi (1932–3), 62–83, 194–224.

Taylor, W. B., *Landlord and Peasant in Colonial Oaxaca* (Stanford, California, 1972).

Toro, Alfonso, 'La Influencia de la Raza Negra en la Formación del Pueblo Mexicano', *Ethnos* i (1920–2), 215–18.

Tudela, José, *Los Manuscritos de América en las Bibliotecas de España* (Madrid, 1954).

Valle, Rafael, 'Judíos en México', *Revista Chilena de Historia y Geografía* lxxxi (1936).

Velázquez, Primo Feliciano, *Historia de San Luis Potosí* (2 vols., Mexico, 1947).

Vicens Vives, J. (ed.), *Historia social y económica de España y América* (5 vols., Barcelona, 1957–9).

Vigneras, D. A., 'El Viaje de Samuel de Champlain a las Indias Occidentales', *Anuario de Estudios Americanos*, x (1953).

Villasanchez, Fray Juan de, *Puebla sagrada y profana* (1746; 2nd edn. Puebla, 1835).

Villaseñor y Sanchez, Joseph Antonio, *Theatre Americano, Descripcion general de los reynos y provincias de la Nueva España y sus jurisdicciones* (2 vols., Mexico, 1746–8).

Vollmer, G., 'Mexikanische Regionalbezeichnungen im 16. Jahrhundert', *Jahrbuch für Geschichte . . . Lateinamerikas*, ix (1972), 40–101.

West, R. C., *The Mining Community in Northern New Spain: The Parral Mining District*, Ibero-Americana no. 30 (Berkeley and Los Angeles, 1949).

Wiznitzer, A., 'Crypto-Jews in Mexico during the Seventeenth Century', *The American Jewish Historical Quarterly* li (1961).

Wolf, E. R., *Sons of the Shaking Earth* (Chicago, 1959).

Wolff, I., 'Negersklaverei und Negerhandel in Hochperu, 1545–1640', *Jahrbuch für Geschichte . . . Lateinamerikas*, (1964), 157–186.

Yalí Román, Alberto, 'Sobre alcaldías mayores y corregimientos en Indias. Un Ensayo de Interpretación, *Jahrbuch für Geschichte . . . Lateinamerikas* ix (1972), 1–39.

Zavala, Silvio, *La Encomienda Indiana* (Madrid, 1935).

Zavala, Silvio, *Ensayos sobre la colonización española en América* (Buenos Aires, 1944).

Zavala, Silvio, *Estudios Indianos* (Mexico, 1948).

INDEX

Acapulco, 25, 36, 68, 71, 120, 167, 184, 193.
  fraud at: 121, 138, 175, 184, 191, 193.
  mercantile restrictions at: 100, 184, 191, 193.
  see also San Diego de Acapulco (fortress).
Albuquerque, duque de (viceroy, 1653–60), 252–9, 262, 275.
  antipathy to Palafox, 252 n, 256.
  completes Mexico City cathedral, see Mexico City, cathedral.
  puritanism of, 253–5, 259.
  view of Creoles, 254, 255.
alcabala (sales tax), 28, 122–3, 138, 193, 197–8, 254, 260, 272.
alcoholism (of Indians), see pulque.
alcaldes mayores, see *corregidores*.
alcaldes ordinarios, 95–6, 181, 227.
alternativa; see Augustinian friars and Dominican friars.
Alva de Liste, conde de (viceroy, 1650–3), 249–52, 267.
Alva Ixtlilxochitl, Fernando de (mestizo historian), 43, 62, 64.
Alvarado, Juan de (*oidor*), 144, 159, 176.
Andalusians, 110, 111 n, 115, 116.
Antequera (Oaxaca), 3, 122, 180, 257; Jews in, 246; Scots in, 122.
Aragon, 110, 136, 179, 248.
Aranzazu, Nuestra Señora de, 115 n.
Armada of Barlovento, 193–4, 195, 198, 205, 216, 272; see also taxation.
Aróstegui, Matheo de (Basque *contador de tributos*), 139, 157, 165, 166, 173, 177.
Atlixco, 1, 32, 45, 56, 120, 180, 207.
Audiencia (of Mexico).
  second *Audiencia* (1530–5), 6–7, 10, 11, 12.
  fourth ruling *Audiencia* (Feb.–Oct. 1612), 70, 71.
  fifth ruling *Audiencia* (Mar.–Sep. 1621), 137–8.

opposition of *Audiencia* to Gelves (1621–4), 139, 143, 144, 145, 148–9, 153, 154, 156, 164, 171.
  sixth ruling *Audiencia* (Jan.–Sep. 1624), 161–8.
  Madrid's distrust of as an executive organ after 1624, 170–1, 171 n, 247.
  under Cerralvo, 181, 183, 187–8.
  under Cadereita, 194, 195, 198, 199.
  and Palafox, 222, 224, 225, 226, 232, 239, 242, 247, 251 n.
  seventh ruling *Audiencia* (Apr. 1649–May 1650), 247–9.
  under Albuquerque, 255, 262.
  under Baños, 263, 264, 266.
Augustinian friars.
  alternativa among, 104–7, 254, 271.
  Creole ascendancy among, 103, 254.
  numbers of in New Spain, 48 n.
  opposition to Palafox, 207, 228, 233, 234, 240, 249.
autos de fe, 130, see also Inquisition.
Auto General de la Fe (11th April 1649), 243, 246.
  role in of Jesuits, 245–6, 246 n.
Aztecs, 6, 8–9, 12, 18, 57.
  transformation of dress and cutting short of hair of in 16th century, 9, 18–19, 56–7.

Bajío, 1, 3, 18, 20, 21, 30, 31, 58, 80.
Baños, conde de (viceroy, 1660–4), 260–6, 268, 272.
  high reputation of among Jesuits and mendicant orders, 260, 264.
  popular demonstration against in Puebla, 264.
Baños, condesa de (vicereine), 260, 263, 264.
barbers, 76, 120.
Barroso, Fray Luis (Dominican), 147, 155.
Basques and Navarrese, 18, 110–117.
  antipathy to Creoles, 116–7, 228.
  Basque language in Mexico, 115.
  and insurrection of 1624, 165–6.

Benavente y Benavides, Bartolomé de (Castilian bishop of Oaxaca, 1638–52), 226, 232, 242, 247, 256, 268, 276.
bishops, attitude to ordaining mestizos, 65.
conflict of with friars, 19–20, 47–9, 54, 55, 65, 86–8, *see also* archbishops Pérez de la Serna, Manso y Zúñiga and bishops Palafox, Benavente y Benavides, and Evia y Valdés.
mostly *gachupines*, 87–8, 269.
political alliance or with Creoles, 19, 47–9, 86–7, 171, 224, 269–70.
viceroys' complaints concerning, 224, 257, 258, 270.
Brámbila y Arriaga, Antonio de (Basque maestrescuela of Antequera), 85, 116, 176.
Bueras, Juan de (Jesuit Provincial), 228, 229.
bureaucracy, *see corregidores, alcaldes ordinarios, Audiencia, repartimiento, residencia,* taxation, corruption, *gobernadoryotl, cabildos,* and the names of individual viceroys.
Burguillos, Fray Bartolomé de (Gelves' confessor), 145, 158, 176.

cabildos (Indian), 11, 43, 46, 141, 208, *see also gobernadoryotl.*
cabildos (Negro), 75, 75 n.
cabildos (Spanish), 29, 34, 94–99, 179–80, 189, 194, 198; support of for secular clergy, 97, 207; Attitude of to *corregidores,* 195, 215, 226; *see also* Mexico City, *cabildo* and Puebla de los Angeles, *cabildo.*
cacao, 28, 127, 191, 195.
Cadereita, marqués de (viceroy, 1635–40), 82, 188, 190–99, 250, 255, 268, 275; discontent of Mexico under rule of, 190–1, 193; seizure of French capital in Mexico by, 193; *see also* taxation.
Calderón, Francisco (Jesuit), 66 n, 222, 229.
Cano Moctezuma, Diego de (Creole noble), 81, 157.
Carmelite friars (*descalzos*), 48 n; opposition of to Viceroy Gelves, 145; alliance of with Bishop Palafox,

212, 217 n, 225, 238, 239; alliance with Bishop Osorio de Escobar, 264.
Carrillo, Fernando (*escribano mayor* of Mexico City under Cerralvo), 33 n, 178, 180, 182, 199.
Carrillo Altamirano, Hernán (Creole nobleman and lawyer), 33, 157, 158, 163, 173, 177, 268.
Carrillo y Alderete, Martín de (*visitador*) 122, 152, 164, 169, 170–6, 268, 274; attitude of to Gelves, 168–9, 171–2; attitude of to Cerralvo, *see* Cerralvo; attitude of to Archbishop Pérez de la Serna, *see* Pérez de la Serna.
castizos, 65; *see also mestizos.*
Catalans and Catalonia, 83 n, 88, 110–111, 111 n, 179.
Celaya (Michoacán) 18, 20, 30, 41, 120.
Cerralvo, marqués de (viceroy, 1624–35), 41, 46, 118, 119, 122–3, 163–4, 167–89; relations of with Gelves, *see* Gelves; relations of with Martín de Carrillo y Alderete, 171, 175–6; conflict of with Archbishop Manso y Zúñiga, 175, 178, 180, 181, 183, 184, 186–9, 267; and Mexico City *cabildo, see* Mexico City; prejudice against Creoles, 182; corruption of, *see* corruption (viceregal); and military garrison of Mexico City, *see* garrison; and inundation of Mexico City (1629–34), *see* Lake Texcoco; and Dutch blockade of Acapulco, *see* Dutch; and Jesuits, *see* Jesuits; and Union of Arms in Mexico, *see* Union of Arms; alliance of with mendicant orders, 183, 187–8; recall of to Spain, 183–8; *residencia* of, 191; feud of with Cadereita, 191.
Cervantes Casaus, Juan de (Creole noble), 81, 154 n, 157, 164, 199.
Chichimec Indians, 18–19, 20, 41, 111.
China, as magnet for Mexican silver, 20, 100–2; Jesuit-Dominican rivalry in, 232; Chinese rites controversy, 232, 243.
Chinos and *Indios Chinos,* 75 n; *see also* Filipinos.
chocolate, *see* cacao.

Cholula (Province of Puebla de los Angeles), 40, 46, 180, 208, 224.
Cisneros, Diego (Creole physician), 91.
cloth, see Puebla de los Angeles, grograms, trade (Atlantic) and silk.
cocoliztli, 6, 12, 17, 27, 39, 185, 191, 251; see also depopulation.
cochineal, 20.
cofradías, Negro, 70; Basque, 115 n, Indian, 243.
commerce, see trade.
complicidad grande, the, see Jews.
Conquistadores, 3–5, 6, 9, 13, 15, 60, 67, 79–80.
consulado (Mexico City), 97, 99, 101, 140, 171, 184, 194, 195, 198, 254, 260; for consulado of Seville, see Seville.
conversos (New Christians), see Jews.
Cortés, Hernán (1st marqués del Valle), 3, 4–5, 18, 61, 94.
Cortés, Martín (2nd marqués del Valle) 15, 16, 62.
Cortés, Pedro de (4th marqués del Valle) 80, 154, 159, 163, 175.
corregidores, in sixteenth century, 11, 12, 14, 16, 18, 20; political role of in seventeenth century, 36, 95, 98, 140 n, 165, 171, 180, 186, 188, 209, 223, 226, 251, 259, 271; gachupín character of, 36–7, 84, 271, Creole hostility to, 33–4, 38, 53, 82, 97, 177, 195, 226, 261, 271; relation to viceroys, 35–7, 98, 225–6, 227, 271; exploitation of Indian market by, 34–5, 37, 143–4, 261, 263, 269, 270; alliance with Indian cabildos, 45, 270; alliance with friars, 49–50; and Negroes, 73; salaries of, 35, 181; residencias of, 34 n, 137, 195.
corregimientos, see corregidores.
Coyoacán (Province of Mexico), 181, 182–3.
corruption, bureaucratic, 19, 35–6, 161, 176, 181, 215, 230, 251, 253, 254, 255, 273, 274; viceregal, 175, 184. 192, 242, 245–6, 251, 260–1, 268, 272.
Council of the Indies (Consejo de Indias), 174, 183–4, 185, 188, 191, 193, 226, 271–2; reaction of to friction between Viceroy Albuquerque and Archbishop Sagade

Bugueiro, 258–9.
Council of State (Consejo de Estado, Madrid), 170–1, 174, 271–2.
crafts, see guilds.
Creoles, political attitudes of, 67, 79, 84–94, 108–9, 131, 181, 195, 261, 270–1, 272; see also segregation policy, Creole hostility to; loyalty to Spanish Monarchy, 91–2, 269; military weakness of, 80, 92, 139, 269; aspirations regarding Audiencia, 83, 195; and insurrection of 1624, 151, 170–1, 172, 175; antipathy to Basques, see Basques and Navarrese; Albuquerque's view of, see Albuquerque; dislike of Cerralvo, 182, 188; support of for Palafox, 215–216, 238, 247.
crypto-Judaism, see Jews.
Cuernavaca (Province of Mexico), 7, 44, 120, 186.
Cuevas y Dávalos, Alonso de (Creole ecclesiastic), 34, 83, 239, 261, 262, 268.

debt-labour, 39, 45, 216, 271; see also labour supply.
depopulation, 12–13, 17, 21, 27–8, 39, 40, 44, 177, 185, 191; see also cocoliztli.
diocesan clergy, see secular clergy.
doctrinas see Indian parishes.
Dominicans, 48–9, 207; numbers of in Mexico, 48 n; in Oaxaca, 7, 48 n, 182, 209, 226, 232, 247, 257; alternativa among, 104, 232, 271; Creoles among, 103; and incident at Coyoacan (1629), see Coyoacan; support for Viceroy Gelves, 144, 147, 154–5; opposition to Palafox, 207, 230, 231–2, 241, 249.
Dorantes de Carranza, Baltasar (Creole noble and author), 79–80, 82.
Durango (Nueva Vizcaya), 3, 18, 29, 30, 192, 226, 257.
Dutch, 71, 129, 167, 168, 176, 178, 184, 190–1, 194, 198; seizure of Mexican silver fleet at Matanzas (1628) by, 30, 185.

Echave, Balthasar de (Basque artist and writer), 115.
encomenderos, see encomiendas.

encomiendas, 4, 10–11, 12, 14, 15–16, 79, 195.

Enríquez de Almansa, Martín de (viceroy, 1568–80), 16–17, 62; criticisms of friars, 17.

Escalona, duque de (viceroy, 1640–2), 199–200, 204–14, 244, 268; quarrel of with Cadereita, 205; conflict of with Palafox, see Palafox; relationship of with King Joao IV (duke of Braganza) of Portugal, 210; alliance with the friars, 209; and Portuguese crisis (1641–2), 210–12; and Portuguese New Christians, 205, 211, 214; see also Armada of Barlovento.

Estrada y Escovedo, Pedro de (inquisitor) and hatred of Jews, 125.

Evia y Valdés, Diego de (bishop of Nueva Vizcaya, 1639–54), 209, 226, 257.

Fernández de Vivero, Juan (Creole propagandist), 37, 50, 52–3, 177, 268, 275.

fiesta (of Saint Ignatius Loyola in Puebla, 1647), 239–240.

Filipinos, 75–77.

Flanders and Flemish immigrants in Mexico, 118, 119, 121, 122, 191.

food-prices (and political conjuncture), 138, 159, 159 n, 166, 192, 259, 259 n; and opposition to Baños, 261, 263; and opposition to Gelves, 138, 159.

Franciscan friars, numbers of in New Spain, 48 n, 106; commissary-general of, 107; hostility of to Virgin of Guadalupe, 54; and insurrection of 1624, 154, 158; *ternativa* among, 105–7, 271; alliance with Salvatierra, 223; conflict with secular clergy, see secular clergy, bishops, Manso y Zúñiga, Pérez de la Serna, Palafox *and* Evia y Valdés; see also Mendieta *and* Torquemada *and* friars.

Frenchmen, 117, 118, 119, 193.

friars, 7–10, 13–14, 17, 47–50, 239, 269, 271; antipathy to nomadic Indians, 18–19, political alliance of with *corregidores*, 49–50, 53, 96, 223; low reputation of Creole friars in Spain, 107–8, 254; Creole-*gachupín* dissension among, 89, 102–8, 116, 195, 254; friction of

with Spaniards in 'Indian' areas, 50, 269; support of for Gelves, 143, 145, 164, 168; see also Augustinians, Dominicans, Franciscans, Carmelites, *and* Mercenarians.

gachupines (peninsular Spaniards), 36–7, 58, 83, 84, 86–7, 89 n, 93, 103, 108, 117, 271; prejudice of against Creoles, 84–5, 116, 265, 271; see also Basques, *corregidores*, bishops, Jesuits, Franciscans (ternativa), Dominicans (*alternativa*), *and* Augustinians (*alternativa*).

Gage, Thomas (English Dominican), 73, 92, 103 n, 107 n, 108, 108 n, 118, 139, 151, 184 n, 185.

Galdós de Valencia (*oidor*) 137, 139, 143, 153, 154, 170, 173, 176.

Galicians (gallegos), 110, 240, 263.

Gálvez, Pedro de (*visitador*), 249–50, 251, 256.

Garcés de Portillo, Pedro, 142, 142 n, 173.

garrisons, The Mexico City palace guard under Gelves, 144, 149, 151, 155–6, 158; infantry mobilized by the sixth *Audiencia*, 161–2, 165; Mexico City infantry under Cerralvo, 168, 170, 171, 177–8; see also San Juan de Ulúa *and* San Diego de Acapulco.

Gelves, marqués de (viceroy, 1621–4) rule of, 135–56; previous career of, 135, 136; tax reforms of, 138, 272; drive against fraud, 122, 138, 272; puritanism of, 122, 123, 136–7, 138, 202, 268, 273; repression of crime by, 57, 139, 268; reduces food prices, 138, 140, 143–4, 166; sympathy for the poor, 138, 142, 166; antagonizes Portuguese, 123, 151; repression of Negroes, 74, 151, 155; ecclesiastical policy of, 142–3, 145; drive against vagabondage, 78, 159; Basque attitude to, 117; conflict with Pérez de la Serna, see Pérez de la Serna; confinement to Franciscan priory of, 162, 163; after September 1624, 166, 167, 169, 172; departure from New Spain, 176;

see also Audiencia, Cerralvo and Jesuits.
Genoese, see Italians.
Germans, 118, 119.
gobernadoryotl, 43–4, 45–6, 53, 164, 208.
Gómez incident (1618), 84–86, 91.
Gómez de Cervantes, Gonzalo (Creole noble and author), 33, 68, 80, 81, 82.
Gómez de Mora, Andrés (oidor), 198, 199, 205, 248, 251.
González, Antonio (secular priest), 152, 173.
González de Avila, Gil and Alonso (Creole conspirators), 16, 79.
Grijalva, Fray Juan de (Cadereita's confessor), 16, 16 n, 194, 197.
grograms (coarse cloth), 20, 196.
Guadalajara, (New Galicia), 12, 32 n, 48, 126, 192, 254; as commercial centre, 2, 121, 192, 254; as centre of crypto-Judaism, 126; bishops of, 87.
Guadalcázar, marqués de (viceroy, 1612–21), 84, 104 n, 119, 122, 137, 184, 268.
Guadalcázar, marquesa de (Anna von Rieder), 118.
Guadalupe (Villa, Province of Mexico), 53, 54 n, 148.
Guadalupe, Nuestra Senora de, 53–5, 181, 270–1; favoured by Archbishop Pérez de la Serna, 54, 148; opposition of friars to, see Franciscans.
guilds, 66, 74, 76–7.

haciendas, 14–15, 25–6, 30, 31–2, 39, 41, 45, 46, 96, 177, 186 n, 216, 223, 224, 270, 271; acquisition of by religious orders, 50, 196, 218, 220, 243; secular clergy send Indians to, 52–3, 223, 224; Bishop Palafox favours, 216; friars remove Indians from, 50; Indian cabildos in conflict with, 45–6; see also labour-supply and Bajio.
Huejotzingo (Province of Puebla de los Angeles), 40, 45, 223–4.

Iguala, corregimiento of (Province of Mexico), 165.

illegitimacy, see marriage; of Palafox, see Palafox.
Indian parishes, 7, 18, 47–50, 52, 53, 141–2, 143, 147, 164, 182–3, 187, 207–9, 220–1, 250.
Indians, alcoholism of, see pulque; caciques, principals and minor officials of (mandones), 7, 10, 11, 12, 39, 42–7, 53, 55, 64, 164, 181, 262, 263, 269, 270; labour repartimiento of, see repartimiento; delinquency among, 57–9, 253, 271; and friars, 7, 10, 19, 13–14, 47–53, 55, 183, 269, see also Indian parishes, Mendieta and Torquemada; and insurrection of 1624, 148, 151, 152, 154, 157, 159; ladino Indians, 56–9, 253, 270–1; land tenure of, 15, 270; mestizo element among, 62–3; migration of, 17–18, 20, 39–41, 44, 181, 182; marriage of womenfolk of with Spaniards, 60–1, 120; intimidation of by Negroes and mulattoes, 57–8, 74, 253; declining religious piety of, 10, 13–14, 51–2, 55, 56–7; submissiveness and discipline of, 8, 9, 13, 14, 15, 44, 57, 269, and secular clergy, 52–3, 152, 154, 182–3, 187–8, 223, 224, see also Guadalupe, Nuestra Señora de; sexual life of, 8–9, 18; tribute of, 4, 14, 34–5, 43, 46, 177; for numbers of in New Spain see depopulation and cocoliztli; see also haciendas, labour-supply and segregation policy.
Innocent X (Pope, 1644–55), 242, 243 n, 244.
Inquisition, 72, 130, 146 n, 147, 153, 171, 195, 214–5, 228, 230–1, 233–4, 235, 240, 242, 245, 246–7, 274; and insurrection of 1624, 147, 153, 154, 162, 162 n, 164, 171; sporadic persecution of Jews by, 130, 214–15, 228, 245, 246; opposition to Palafox, 215, 215 n, 228, 229, 230, 231, 233–235, 240; forbids possession of portraits of Palafox, 252; and sexual scandals among clergy, 125, 125 n, 146–7.
insurrection of 15 January 1624, 78, 92, 123, 150–158, 172, 229, 267, 274; see also, Gelves, Pérez de la Serna, Vergara Gabiria, militia,

garrisons, Indians, mestizos, Negroes, Portuguese, Franciscans, Jesuits, Inquisition, Creoles and secular clergy.
Italy and Italians, 110, 117, 119–120, 120 n, 121, 126, 127, 129.

Jesuits, numbers of in New Spain, 48n; attitude to mestizos, Negroes and mulattoes, 66, 70, 276; *gachupín* character of, 84–6; Creole-*gachupín* dissension among, 103; in education, 48, 86 n, 89, 219, 221, 233, 243; wealth of, 146, 196, 218–20, 243; sexual scandals among, 125, 125 n, 146–147, 146 n, 239; dishonesty of, 146, 182, 182 n, 225, 238, 239, 242, 243; conflict with Gelves, 145–147, 156, 159, 163, 171, 173, 218; and Archbishop Pérez de la Serna, 85–6, 86 n, 145–6, 159; alliance with Cerralvo, 182, 182 n, 183; conflict with Palafox, *see* Palafox; relationship with Dominicans, 231–2, 237, 241, 251; compromise with Merlo, 250; good relations with Bishop Osorio de Escobar, 258; *see also* Auto General de la Fe.
Jews, 124–30, 214–5, 228, 230, 234, 245, 274; distribution of in seventeenth-century Mexico, 126; Portuguese character of, 125–6; knowledge of Hebrew and Jewish religious practices among, 129.
Juárez, Melchor (Palafox's *converso* political secretary), 205, 215 n, 237.
jueces conservadores (Agustín de Godines and Juan de Paredes), 231–3, 236, 237, 239; *see also* Paredes, Juan de.

labour-supply, 22, 27–8, 31, 33, 41, 45, 177, 270–1; of silver mines, 25–6, 30; of public works, 26, 185–6; of *haciendas*, 26, 41 n, 45, 177, 180, 216, 223, 224, 270–1; of Mexican textile industry, 20, 31, 31 n, 39, 41, 45; of the friaries, 47, 49–50, 186, 209, 223; *see also* *repartimiento*.
Lake Texcoco, overflowing of (1629–34), 36, 180–1.

Landeras de Velasco, Diego (*visitador-general*), 35–6, 122, 123, 268.
Ledesma, Juan de (Creole Jesuit), 146, 147, 173.
Legorreta, Pedro de (Basque commander of fortress of San Diego), 164, 166, 167, 168.
Leyva, Pedro de (eldest son of conde de Baños), 261, 264, 265–6.
limpiez de sangre, 93–4, 115, 125.
López de Azcona, Marcelo (Archbishop of Mexico, 1653), 252, 255.
Lormendi, Fray Juan de (Franciscan prior), 154, 173.

Mancera, marqués de (viceroy), 38, 64, 65, 93, 117, 266, 267.
Manila, gun foundries of, 198, 205; silk trade of with Mexico, 20, 29, 99–100, 101, 102, 196, 272.
Mañozca, Juan de (Basque, Archbishop of Mexico, 1644–50), 116, 228, 230–1, 232, 233, 237, 239, 241, 242, 245, 249; as *visitador* of Mexican Inquisition, 228, 230–1, 233, 242; rebuked by Council of State in Madrid for role in Palafox affair, 241; imbroglio with Bishop Benavente of Oaxaca, 242; prejudice of against Creoles, 116.
Manso y Zúñiga, Francisco de (Archbishop of Mexico, 1628–35), special commissions of, 174, 178, 268; Creole sympathies of, 86, 177, 189, 268, 271; conflict with Martín de Carrillo y Alderete, 175–6; popularity of, 175–6, 178; conflict with Cerralvo, *see* Cerralvo; hostility to *corregidores*, 177, 181, 181 n, 271; financial corruption of, 188; recall of to Spain, 184–8; subsequent career of, 188.
marriage (as social and political institution), 9, 12, 60, 63, 65, 258.
Matanzas, seizure of the Mexican silver fleet at (1628), *see* Dutch.
Méndez de Haro, Luis, 253, 258.
Mendieta, Fray Gerónimo de (Basque Franciscan historian and propagandist), 15, 49, 102–3, 112, 116.
Mendoza, Antonio de (viceroy, 1535–40), 7, 10, 11, 12.

Mercenarian friars, 48 n, 70, 108, 164, 254.
Merlo, Juan de (ecclesiastic), 220, 221, 231, 239, 247, 249, 250.
mestizos, 60–66, 151, 152, 154, 155, 178, 235, 267, 270; debate concerning eligibility of for public office, 65–6; illegitimacy of, 61, 62, 65; entry of into secular clergy, 65; mestizo nobility, 61, 62–3, 64.
Mexico City, corregimiento of, 36, 187, 246, 256, 259; consulado of, see consulado; cabildo of, 83, 95, 97, 98, 100–2, 124, 139–40, 163, 175, 177, 245, 259, 260; opposition of Mexico City cabildo to Gelves, 137, 138, 139–40, 142, 154, 156–7, 171–2, 173; opposition of cabildo to Cerralvo, 177, 178, 179, 181, 184; opposition of cabildo to Cadereita, 194–7, 199; support of cabildo for Palafox, 215, 225–6; clergy of, 47, 48, 48 n, 150, 187; Indian population of, 40, 46, 51, 56, 181; black population of, 68–71, 74; white population of, 30, 181; Portuguese in 120, 126, 211; Asiatic population of, 76; as commercial and manufacturing centre, 30, 181; disturbances in apart from insurrection of 1624, 98, 149, 171, 234, 242, 264, 265; cathedral of, 149, 150, 152, 156, 256–7, 259, 265; support for Palafox among population of, 230–1, 234, 242, 247; inundation of (1629–34), see Lake Texcoco; see also insurrection of 1624.
Michoacán, Augustinians in, 48 n, 104 n; Franciscans in, 48 n, 106, 107; secular clergy of, 47, 48, 48 n, 150, 187; see also Valladolid, Celaya and San Luis.
militia, in Mexico City, 70, 151, 156, 157, 158, 159; in Puebla de los Angeles, 70, 112, 112 n, 235.
Mixtec Indians, 8, 40–1, 182.
Mohammedanism, 125.
Molina, Cristóbal de (regidor of Mexico City), 33, 163, 173, 177.
Montemayor y Cuenca, Juan Francisco de (oidor), 74, 262, 263, 264, 283.
Montesclaros, marqués de (viceroy, 1603–7), 21, 49–50, 84, 119.

Morga, Antonio de, 69 n, 70–1.
Motolinía (Fray Toribio de Benavente), 8.
mulattoes, see Negroes and mulattoes, mulatta girls as mistresses and concubines, 73, 73 n, 74, 214; employed to lure passers-by into pulquerías and taverns, 214; as dancing girls, 204, 204 n, 214, 237; as serving maids in nunneries, 73.
Muñoz Camargo, Diego (mestizo noble and historian), 61, 62, 62 n, 63 n.

Navarrese, see Basques and Navarrese.
Neapolitans, see Italy and Italians.
Negroes, 13, 25, 63–4, 67–74, 235, 238, 253, 267; black women, 70, 72, 73, 237, see also mulattoes; Negro slavery, 68, 72–3, 127, and insurrection of 1624, 92, 151, 155, 178; Christianity of, 69, 74; intimidation of Indians by, see Indians; April laws relating to (1612), 70, 71, 74; see also Gelves and San Lorenzo de los Negros.
New Galicia, 2, 18, 21, 64, 91, 107, 120, 120 n, 121, 126, 192; see also Guadalajara and Zacatecas.
nuns and nunneries, in Mexico City, 48, 73, 214, 233–4; in Puebla de los Angeles, 48, 73, 196, 220, 233–4, 238; sympathy of Carmelite nuns for Palafox, 234.
Nuño de Guzmán, Beltrán, 5–6, 95.

Oaxaca, province of, decline of silver mines in, 29 n; Indian land–tenure in, 15 n, corregidores in, 226, 257, 259, 261, 262, 263; bishops of mainly Creole, 87; see also Antequera, Tehuantepec, Villa Alta, Dominicans, Benavente y Benavides and Montemayor y Cuenca.
Olivares, conde–duque de (valido of King Philip IV of Spain), 135–6, 163, 178–9, 185, 198, 200, 244.
Orejón, Diego de (corregidor), 225, 236, 238, 241, 248, 256.
Oroz, Pedro de, 254.
Osorio, Critóbal de (Gelves' political secretary), 144, 150, 159, 176.
Osorio de Escobar y Llamas, Diego

(Galician bishop of Puebla, 1656–73), 255, 258, 263, 268, 272; Creole sympathies of, 263, 266; appointed temporary viceroy (1664), 264–6.
Otomi, Indians, 8, 18, 41.

Pachuca (Province of Mexico), 120, 181.
Palafox y Mendoza, Juan de (Aragonese bishop of Puebla, 1640–9), illegitimacy of, 200, 202; career in Spain and Austria, 200–1; special commissions of, 197, 200–1, 258; political and social ideas of, 200–204; Creole sympathies of, 86, 202, 215–6, 269; puritanism of, 202, 220, 228, 230, 237, 238, 273; hostility to theatre, 237–8; views on episcopacy of, 203–4; sympathy of for Pérez de la Serna and Manso y Zúñiga, 204, 227; involvement of in Vergara Gabiria case, 200; as *visitador general* of New Spain, 205–6, 224–6, 238, 244, 249, 251, 268; viceregal term (1642), 213–216; ecclesiastical reforms of in Puebla, 206, 220, 221 n; *and Audiencia, see Audiencia*; and Indians, 57, 243, 269; and Jews, 128–9, 215 n, 245, 247; and white vagabonds, 77; antipathy to *corregidores*, 205–6, 223–7, 269; conflict of with Viceroy Escalona, 206–13, 244; conflict of with Viceroy Salvatierra, 223–241; conflict of with Franciscans, 55, 206–9, 214, 223, 224, 227–8; conflict of with Mexican Inquisition, 214–5, 230–1, 235, 240, 252; conflict of with Augustinians, *see* Augustinians; conflict of with Dominicans, *see* Dominicans; conflict of with Jesuits, 217–223, 225, 228, 229–233, 237, 239–40, 241, 242–4, 246, 249, 250, 251; educational reforms of, 221, 233, 243; love for Puebla of, 204, 221, 224, 247, 256; completion of Puebla cathedral by, *see* Puebla de los Angeles; interest of French Jansenists in, 217 n; development of church music in Puebla by, 221, 247, 247 n;

flight of (1647), 236–240; recall of to Spain, 244, 252, 256.
Paredes, Fray Juan de (Dominican), 231, 249, 251.
peninsular Spaniards, *see gachupines*.
Peralta, Mathias de (*oidor*), 199, 248, 251.
Pérez de la Serna, Juan (Archbishop of Mexico, 1613–24), previous career of, 140; imbroglio with Guadalcázar, 141; condemnation by of Mexican administration, 142; political role of, 138, 140, 268; conflict of with mendicant orders, 141–2, 143; conflict of with Gelves, 142, 144–5, 147, 156, 272; Creole sympathies of, 54, 84–5, 141, 189; and cult of Virgin of Guadalupe, 54, 141; declaration of *cesatio a divinis* by in Mexico City, 147, 148, 150; excommunicates Viceroy Gelves, 145; expulsion of from Mexico by Gelves, 148–50; returns to Spain, 163, 170, 170 n, 176; Carrillo y Alderete's findings relating to, 173.
Peru, trade of with Mexico, *see* trade.
Philippines, 18, 74, 77, 195, 196; for Mexican trade with Philippines, *see* Manila.
Piedmontese, *see* Italy and Italians.
Pimentel, Francisco (Gelves' son), 149, 167.
Pisa (Livorno), *see* Italy and Italians.
population, Indian, 21, 27, 31, 40–1, *see also* depopulation; Negro and mulatto, 21, 63, 67–8; mestizo, 22, 63; white, 21, 63; Asiatic, 76; ecclesiastical, 48, 48 n.
Portuguese, 67, 70, 73, 99, 117–123, 161, 257; occupation–structure of, 120–1; and insurrection of 1624, 123, 151; crisis after secession of Portugal from Spanish Monarchy (1640–2), 209–12, 274; and slave trade, 67, 69, 70, 124, 127, 211.
prostitutes and prostitution, 77, 139, 161, 214, 238.
Puebla de los Angeles (city of), early development of, 11, 60; agricultural wealth of surrounding area, 21, 181, 219; as textile centre, 20, 29–30, 30 n, 39, 196–7; Indian population of, 40, 40 n, 56, 186; Negro and

mulatto population of, 70, 74, 235, 236, 238, 264; Basque population of, 112, 165; Portuguese in, 120; fewness of judaizers in, 126; clergy of, 47, 48 n, 87, 207, 247; unrest in (1647) 234–41, 256, 276; *cabildo* of, 80, 81–2, 95, 96, 97, 193, 194, 197, 248, 256, 277; *cabildo*'s opposition to Cerralvo, 180; *cabildo*'s dispute with Cadereita over tax on cloth, 193; *cabildo*'s support for Palafox, 207, 226, 238–9, 245; Puebla cathedral, 221, 244–5, 247, 248–9, 250; college of San Juan Evangelista, 221, 233, 238, 242, 250; Puebla alameda, 237; rivalry of Puebla with Mexico City, 245, 249.

pulque and *pulquerías*, 14, 51, 56, 253, 260, 265.

purity of blood, *see* limpieza de sangre.

Querétaro (Province of Mexico), 18, 32, 41, 46, 120.

Quiroga, Pedro de (*visitador*), 191, 192, 193, 205, 267, 268.

Rada, Andrés de (Jesuit Provincial), 242–3.

Ramírez del Prado, Fray Marcos (Castilian bishop of Michoacán), 1639–66; Archbishop of Mexico, 1666–7), 209, 229; sexual licentiousness of, 209 n.

Rea, Fray Alonso de la (Franciscan Provincial of Michoacán), 106, 285.

Realejo (Nicaragua), 29.

regidores, 96; *see also cabildos* (Spanish).

religious orders, *see* friars, Jesuits, Augustinians, Dominicans, Franciscans, Carmelites and Mercenarians.

repartimiento (of Indians), 16–17, 33–34, 46, 47, 177, 180, 186; ecclesiastical *repartimiento* 47, 49–50, 186, 209; Manso y Zúñiga's condemnation of, 177; abolition of agricultural *repartimiento* by Cerralvo, 185–6.

representative institutions, 179, 188, 189; *see also cabildos*.

residencias, viceregal, 19, 188, 191, 205, 212, 213, 267; of *alcaldes*

mayores and *corregidores, see corregidores.*

Riofrio, Esteban de (secular priest), 182–3.

Ríos, Guillermo de los (Jesuit), 173.

Ruiz de Cabrera, Cristóbal (Creole secular priest and propagandist), 164, 173, 286.

Sáenz de Mañozca, Juan (Basque inquisitor), 229.

Sagade Bugueiro, Mateo (Galician Archbishop of Mexico, 1656–62), 255, 257, 263, 267, 268; wealth of, 258; marriage of 'nephew' of to daughter of conde de Santiago Calimaya, 258.

salaries, *see corregidores and* wealth.

Salinas y Córdoba, Fray Bonaventura de (Franciscan commissary-general), co-operation with Palafox of, 227–8.

Salvatierra, conde de (viceroy, 1642–8), 217, 223–7, 232–3, 236–7, 240, 241, 246, 268, 272; alliance of with friars, 223, 225, 228 n; alliance of with Jesuits, 231–2, 233, 236, 239; delays in surrendering the government of New Spain to Torres y Rueda, 240–1; intimidation of *cabildos* of Mexico City and Puebla by, 225–6; influence of wife with, 227, 230, 233; conflict of with Palafox, 223–41.

Salcedo Benavides, Austasio (*corregidor*), 263.

Sánchez, Miguel (Creole propagandist for the cult of Nuestra Señora de Guadalupe), 54–5.

San Diego (fortress of, at Acapulco), 118, 162, 164, 167.

San Juan de Ulúa (fortress of, at Veracruz), 162, 184, 213.

San Lorenzo de los Negros (Province of Puebla), 71.

San Luis Potosí, as silver-mining centre, 2, 20, 21 n, 29, 122, 181, 196; Portuguese in, 118, 120, 123; Scots in, 122.

San Miguel, Juan de (Jesuit preacher), 229, 230, 286.

San Miguel el Grande (Michoacán), 18.

Santa María (salt-pan), exploitation of salt deposits of, 184, 184 n.

Santiago Calimaya, conde de (Fernando de Altamirano y Velasco, 1597–1657), as a leading Creole noble, 80; as latifundist of the Bajío, 80; and insurrection of 1624, 151, 163; opposition to agricultural *repartimiento*, 177; marriage of daughter of to Benito Fosino Bugueiro, 258.

Santiago Calimaya, conde de (second) (Juan de Altamirano y Velasco), *corregidor* of Puebla in 1661, 80; feud with Don Pedro de Leyva, 265–6.

Scots, 110, 122.

secular, clergy, 47–8, 52–3, 55, 65, 148, 187, 189, 207, 220, 223–4, 235, 269–70; numbers of in New Spain, 48 n, 187, 206–7; Creole character of, 52–3, 189, 235; conflict with religious orders, 19, 22, 55, 154, 183, 223–4, 243, 250, 259; and insurrection of 1624, 150, 152, 173; sending of Indian labourers to haciendas by, 52–3, 223, 224; and Palafox's ecclesiastical reforms, *see* Palafox.

segregation policy, 14–15, 19, 32, 37–8, 41, 76 n, 103, 268–9, 270, 271; Creole hostility to, 38–9, 131, 270, 271.

Seville, *consulado* of, hostility of to Mexican Peru trade, 100–2, 196–7, 272; *see also* trade (Atlantic).

silk, Chinese, 20, 29, 99–100, 101, 193, 196; Spanish, 100, 196.

silver-mining, 12, 13, 17–18, 25–7, 29, 29 n, 30, 31, 120, 192, 196, 254, 261–2; *see also* labour-supply (for silver mines).

slavery and slave trade, Negro, *see* Negroes *and* Portuguese, Filipino, 75.

Society of Jesus, *see* Jesuits.

Solórzano, Juan de (legal and political writer), 65, 90.

Sotomayor, Juan Manuel de (*alcalde del crimen* and *corregidor*), 241, 248, 256.

Tarascan Indians, 18, 41.

Tacuba, 169, 181, 195, 241.

Tacubaya, 181.

taxation, *see alcabala*, Gelves (tax reforms of), Union of Arms; Cadereita's tax drive, 193–4, 272; Albuquerque's tax drive, 254, 256, 259, 272.

Tecamachalco, 1, 32, 45, 81, 207.

Tehuantepec (Province of Oaxaca), 260, 262, 263.

Tenochtitlán, *see* Mexico City.

Teotihuacán, San Juan de (Province of Mexico), 149–50, 153, 185.

Tepeaca (Province of Puebla), 20, 32, 45, 180, 237, 248; *corregimiento* of, 205.

Texcoco (Province of Mexico), 7, 20, 32, 40, 41, 44, 45, 141, 185, 205.

Texoso, Francisco de (Portuguese-Jewish merchant), 122, 126, 127 n, 215.

textile manufacture, 20, 29–30; *see also* Puebla de los Angeles (as textile manufacturing centre *and Tlaxcala*, as textile centre.

Tixtla, *corregimiento* of (Province of Puebla), 165.

Tlatelolco, Santiago de (Mexico City), 32, 40, 157, 181.

Tlaxcala, in sixteenth century, 1, 6, 7, 19, 21; Indian population of, 40, 61, 186, 208; as textile centre, 20, 30; *corregimiento* of, 162, 180, 223; parishes of taken from Franciscan hands (1641), 207–8, 220; insurrection at (1692), 59.

Torquemada, Fray Juan de, 19, 51–2, 56.

Torres y Rueda, Marcos de (bishop-governor of New Spain, 1648–9), 98, 171, 240, 241, 242, 246, 247, 248, 249; purge of *corregidores* and other officers associated with Salvatierra by, 241–2; corruption of, 242, 245–6; break of with Palafox, 246.

trade, Atlantic, 27–8, 99–102, 185, 192, 196; Caribbean, 185, 190–1, 193, 194, 198; Peru trade, 20, 29, 100–2, 123, 191, 192, 196–7, 205, 272; Venezuela-Mexico, 28, 191; Phillippines, *see* Manila.

Treviño de Sobremente, Tomás, 246.

Union of Arms, 178–180, 194, 272.
Urrutia de Vergara, Antonio (Basque merchant and political intriguer), 178, 191, 198–9, 205, 255, 260, 264.

Váez de Acevedo, Sebastián (*purveedor general* of Armada of Barlovento), 205, 211, 213, 214, 246.
Váez de Sevilla, Simón (Jewish merchant), 126, 128, 215, 246.
vagabonds and vagabondage, 11–12, 13, 21, 77–8, 96, 120, 126, 151, 159, 161, 196, 255.
Valdéz y Portugal, Agustín de (*corregidor*), 235, 236, 238, 240, 242, 248, 256.
Valladolid (Michoacán), Indian population of, 41; as manufacturing centre, 20; clergy in, 48 n, 229 n.
Valle de Orizaba, conde de (Rodrigo de Vivero), 80–1.
Valmaseda, Andrés de (*regidor* of Mexico City), 156, 173, 180.
Varaez, Melchor de (*corregidor* of Metepec), 137, 139, 143–4, 155, 161, 174.
Vázquez de Cisneros, Alonso, 137, 144, 153, 161, 173.
Vázquez de Espinosa, Fray Antonio, 39, 63, 90.
Vega, Juan de (Castilian ecclesiastic), 239, 240, 241, 249.
Velasco I, Luis de (viceroy, 1550–64), 14–15, 17, 49, 62, 67.
Velasco II, Luis de (viceroy, 1590–95 and 1607–11), 20, 21, 68, 69, 82.
Velasco, Pedro de (Jesuit Provincial), 229, 231, 239.
Venetians, *see* Italy and Italians.
Veracruz, 2, 25 n, 36, 72, 94, 120, 126, 136, 162, 220, 247, 264; illegal immigration through, 77, 94, 119, 123; fraud at, 121–2, 188; confiscation of French capital at (1635–6), 193.
Vergara Gabiria, Pedro de (Basque *oidor*), 122, 137, 139, 141, 153, 154, 156, 157, 161, 165, 167, 168, 169; arrest and trial of, 172, 173, 174, 175, 176, 200.

Villa Alta (Province of Oaxaca), 261.
Villalba, Alonso de (*oidor*), 214, 224, 230, 248.
Villamanrique, marqués de (viceroy, 1585–90), 19–20, 49, 62.
Villamayor de las Ibiernas, marqués de (Creole noble), 80, 252.
Villegas, Diego de (*corregidor*), 223 n, 241, 249.
Villena, marqués de (Castilian grandee, viceroy, 1640–2), *see* Escalona, duque de.
Villenas, Gaspar de (Jesuit), sexual scandal surrounding, 125, 146.
visitadores, 268; *see also* Landeras de Velasco, Carrillo y Alderete, Quiroga, Palafox y Mendoza, Gálvez and Oroz; for *visitador* to the Mexican Inquisition, *see* Mañozca, Juan de.
Vitoria Baraona, Francisco de (converso merchant and writer on trade), 101, 287.

wealth, merchant fortunes, 93 n, 126, 127 n, 193, 215; salaries, 35, 96, 249, 251, *see also corregidores*; spoils of office, 96, 184–5, 188, 246, 251; bequests and legacies, 188, 193, 220, 259.
wine, Spanish, 14, 90, 101, 122, 196, 253; Peruvian, 101.
women, Spanish, 60–161 n, *see also* nunneries; Negresses and mulattas, *see* Negros, mulattoes; Indian women, *see* Indians.

Xuarez Maldonado, Antonio (secular priest), 234.
Xochimilco (Province of Mexico), 20.

Yanga, (Negro insurgent leader), 68–9.
Yuririapúndaro (Michoacán), 104 n.

Zacatecas, as silver-mining centre, 2, 13, 17, 29, 192, 196, 254, 262; Indians of, 31, 32, 41, 46; black population of, 68; Spaniards of, 90, 112; Portuguese in, 120 n, 123, 126; *cabildo* of, 95, 138, 1197–8.
Zapotec Indians, *see* Mixtecs.